Internet and Intranet
Engineering

Internet and Intranet Engineering

Daniel Minoli
Teleport Communications Group (TCG)
Stevens Institute of Technology

McGraw-Hill

New York   San Francisco   Washington, D.C.   Auckland   Bogotá
Caracas   Lisbon   London   Madrid   Mexico City   Milan
Montreal   New Delhi   San Juan   Singapore
Sydney   Tokyo   Toronto

Library of Congress Cataloging-in-Publication Data

Minoli, Daniel, date.
    Internet and intranet engineering / Daniel Minoli.
        p.   cm.
    Includes index.
    ISBN 0-07-042977-4 (hc)
    1. Internet (Computer network)   2. Intranets (Computer networks)
I. Title.
TK5105.875.I57M557   1997
004.6'7—dc20   96-42361
                                                                            CIP

McGraw-Hill

A Division of The McGraw-Hill Companies

1 2 3 4 5 6 7 8 9 0   BKP BKP   9 0 1 0 9 8 7 6

ISBN 0-07-042977-4

The sponsoring editor for this book was Steven Elliot and the production supervisor was Donald F. Schmidt. It was set in Century Schoolbook by North Market Street Graphics.

Printed and bound by Quebecor/Book Press.

This time, for Gabrielle

Contents

Chapter 4. HTML Technology, Applications, and Examples   169

Preface

From the vantage point of the late 1990s, the opportunities afforded by evolving Internet technologies appear palatable, productivity-enhancing, and profitable for all. The importance of on-line access, research, collaboration, communication, and commerce is simply going to increase in the coming years.

Many kinds of information are now available on World Wide Web (WWW) servers. WWW offers hypertext technology that links together a "web" of documents so that these can be navigated in any number of ways using sophisticated Network Graphical User Interfaces (NGUIs) (e.g., Mosaic, Netscape). Some of the information on WWW consists of hypermedia. (*Hypermedia* is hypertext where the content includes some or all of the following: text, graphics, video, voice, and/or music.) WWW uses Internet-based architectures employing public and open specifications, along with free sample implementations on the client and server end, so that anyone can build a client or a server. Corporations are not only contemplating taking advantage of Internet access, but are building intranets, deploying Internet-based technologies in their enterprise networks.

As examples, some magazines are now available *only* on Web servers, having migrated there from a paper format. Advertisements and technical information are now being delivered via Web servers. As time goes by, increasingly more magazines, technical specifications, documents, etc., having business interest, will be available on these servers, generating considerable inter-enterprise corporate traffic as knowledge workers access them via the enterprise network. Corporations are now also deploying intranets, which use the same Web technology but at the corporate level, for internal use.

Corporate users may elect to access the Internet over a dial-up line (for example, using PPP) or, better yet, through the corporate LAN and a dedicated connection. Access through the enterprise network raises concerns about the ability to access volumes of information over the corporate communication infrastructure. Issues as to the best kind of technology required to support effective Internet access need to be addressed by corporations as they prepare for the next wave of information-based industries and economics. In addition, special considerations must be given to the deployment of intranets.

Observers see the WWW market as still being in its infancy. Issues center on networking, performance, security, and presentation richness. There are already extensions to the basic Web browsers under way. Today's Web browsers are limited to HTML specifications, which are reasonable for two-dimensional page layout, but not necessarily for truly interactive browsing. Newly emerging languages such as Virtual Reality Modeling Language (VRML) and Java are designed to enhance the Web-browsing experience. Sun's VRML offers a method of describing three-dimensional space so that users can navigate in 3-D. Java is an object-oriented software tool that adds animation and real-time interaction through in-line applications.

The emergence of new features, including new versions of HTML or de facto industry extensions, could introduce some lack of interoperability in the short term, but users are now looking for more flashy, colorful, and attractive Web places to explore. This is temporarily forcing designers to choose between (1) lowest-common-denominator design tools, ending up with a bland but universally accessible Web site, or (2) leading-edge HTML tags (e.g., to support tables) or vendor-based extensions. Nonetheless, the user and corporate requirement is in the direction of increased sophistication, complexity, speed, and bandwidth. Activities on the Web that are CPU- and communications-intensive include applications generating real-time graphics using charts and colors to show trends in the stock market, voter returns, Geographic Information Systems (GISs), weather maps, database statistics, and analysis related to economic commerce.

Some of the Web server software is based on the concept of streaming media, which delivers audio and video on demand, rather than requiring a user to download a file from the Web and play it back from the local server or hard drive. Using this technology, some say that more than 100 stations could be broadcasting live, FM-quality or better programming on the Internet in the near future. Web-TV services are also appearing, which make use of unutilized spectrum of TV and cable channels. Related services have been developed for NBC Desktop video and Reuters Financial Television, which are accessed over the corporate enterprise network. The major commercial on-line services (e.g., Prodigy, America Online, and CompuServe) have also added WWW access and the ability for users to create their own home pages.

This book takes a fundamental look at the set of technologies described thus far, with an eye to educating the corporate planner as to the course of action that will best benefit his or her company in terms of Internet and intranet services and applications. Chapter 1 describes the Internet structure, protocols, and access. Chapter 2 provides a primer on router technology. For large institutions and companies that opt to access the Internet by direct router connection, this coverage should prove useful.

Chapter 3 examines Web server technology, access, and protocols. Web servers are examples of distributed multidatabase systems. Such distributed systems are the building blocks of evolving telematic architectures, which place information close to where the user has the most need for data. The three key components of WWW are Uniform Resource Locator (URL), HyperText Transfer Protocol (HTTP), and HyperText Markup Language (HTML). These are introduced and discussed in this chapter.

HTML technology, applications, and examples are covered in Chapter 4. Chapter 5 covers browsing systems for the Web and Internet. Chapter 6 provides useful information on establishing a Web site. Chapter 7 examines the commercial environment, namely, on-line services. Technology, applications, and vendors are discussed. Chapter 8 covers broadband communications in a Web/Internet context. Finally, Chapter 9 covers the topic of virtual reality applications, which are currently deployed in a number of venues, including on the Internet.

Acknowledgments

This book is based on a course given at Stevens Institute of Technology over a two-semester period (1995 to 1996). Portions of the material are based on class projects and activities. The following individuals have participated and/or contributed:

Chapter 1	D. Derkacs, R. De Sa', S. D. Desai, S. Desai, and J. S. Ghaly
Chapter 3	M. Forzani, P. Means, and H. Smith
Chapter 4	D. J. Holicki, M. Walls, and A. Carmel
Chapter 5	S. Y. Muhammad, S. Y. Wong, and A. Pane
Chapter 6	D. J. Holicki, A. Carmel, and S. Y. Muhammad
Chapter 7	A. Krishnamurthy
Chapter 8	M. Burns, P. Hennigan, and B. Bowling

In addition, the author would like to thank Shaw-Kunk Jong, AT&T Bell Laboratories, for providing the insightful treatment of router technology documented in Chapter 2.

R. Taluy, Teleport Communications Group, is warmly thanked for his input on Chapters 3 through 9. L. Sookchand is thanked for his input on Chapters 1 and 2.

Thanks to Jo-Anne Dressendofer for the support on Chapter 9 on Virtual Reality applications.

The author also acknowledges the support of R. D. Rosner, Vice President and General Manager, Teleport Communications Group, Internet and Data Services, for the insight, guidance, and assistance provided.

The author also thanks Ben Occhiogrosso, President, DVI Communications, for his suggestions and assistance based on DVI's extensive corporate practice in this field.

Finally, I would like to thank Robert O'Brian for the excellent, complete, and insightful review of this manuscript. I'd gladly settle for this kind of review as being the standard by which all other book reviews should be conducted. Naturally, I alone take full responsibility for any lack of clarity, occasional typo, or inexactness that may occur.

Internet Structure, Protocols, and Access with an Eye to Intranets

1.1 Overview

1.1.1 The Internet/intranet landscape

Data communication has clearly become a fundamental part of how institutions, corporations, and individuals now do business. Worldwide networks gather data and technical information about subjects ranging from atmospheric conditions to airline traffic to crop production. Groups establish electronic mailing so they can share information. Hobbyists exchange programs for their home computers. Corporations keep service orders, customer records, inventory, and customer service information in large-scale client/server systems. Vast databases of credit and other marketing information are kept by credit bureaus. The list goes on and on. We have evolved to a stage where the *corporation is the network.*

A few years ago, most networks were independent entities, established to serve the needs of a single group, whether in an intraenterprise or interenterprise environment. Users choose hardware technology appropriate to their communication problems. In the past couple of decades, technology has evolved that makes it possible to interconnect many disparate physical networks and make them function as a coordinated system. The technology, called *internetworking technology,* accommodates diverse underlying hardware by providing a set of communication mechanisms based on common conventions. The internetworking technology hides the details of network hardware and permits computers to communicate independently of their physical network connections.

An *internet* consists of a set of connected networks that act as an integrated whole. The chief advantage of an internet is that it provides universal interconnections while allowing individual groups to use whichever network hardware is best suited to their needs. The trend, as we enter the first decade of the new century, is toward ubiquitous connectivity.

There is a large internet par excellence. This is *the* Internet. The *Internet* with a capital *I* is a massive, worldwide collection of networks connecting a plethora of subnetworks and computing/information resources located on these subnetworks, including devices such as computers, servers, and directories. As a "network of networks," it provides a capability for communication to take place between research institutions, government agencies, businesses, educational institutions, individuals, and among all "Internet citizens." It is estimated that over 20 million users a day in 90 countries access the Internet.

As a complex system of interlinked networks, the Internet supports millions of "server" computers housing large volumes of all sorts of information. The Internet is where millions of friends and strangers can chat. It lets people browse through thousands of on-line libraries, play new games, and trade software. Another feature of the Internet is that it has no geographic bounds. Users (called *internauts* by some) are logging on from Brooklyn to Bangkok, Singapore to Siberia. From 13 million host computers around the world at press time, the Internet is expected to grow to more than 100 million systems in five years. But because there is no central control over the Internet, there is also no master index. In the past, that has kept the Internet largely a playground for the techno-intelligentsia who used nonfriendly programs such as Gopher, Archie, and FTP. Recently, however, with the introduction of World Wide Web (WWW) browsers, it has become much easier to bring out what is stored in all those databases.

The latest breakthrough began in 1993 with the creation of an Internet environment called the WWW—really just a software scheme for imposing order over the mass of free-form information on the Internet by organizing it into easily understood "pages." What makes the Web* such a powerful cyberhelper is a software technique known as *hyperlinking*. When composing a Web page, an author can create hyperlinks—words that appear in bold type and indicate a path to some other information. Using a program known as a *Web browser* on a personal computer (PC) or workstation, you can read pages stored on any Web computer. Say you are reading a page that describes recent discoveries about allergies. You see the word *antigen* in bold type. Using the mouse, you click on the word, and without any effort you are transferred to another Web page that tells you what an antigen is. That page

---

* We use *WWW* and *Web* interchangeably.

could be in the same system as the first page or in another computer thousands of miles away.

This type of intuitive access did not occur overnight. Internet development and deployment began in the late 1960s and early 1970s under the auspices of the U.S. Department of Defense (DOD) as a means to connect government agencies with research companies, contractors, and academic institutions. In the recent past, the Internet was used mainly by nonprofit entities for research and development. More recently, the Internet has experienced significant growth as corporations, home users, and nongovernment academic and research entities have gained access. At press time, some 68 million Americans had direct access to the Internet, and 4 million others use commercial on-line services, according to O'Reilly & Associates; there are predictions that more than six million more users will go on-line in 1997.[1]

There are a variety of ways for individuals, companies, or institutions to connect to the Internet. Large organizations usually connect by means of direct, dedicated, high-speed links to give their users high-bandwidth networking capabilities. Home users typically connect by means of a telephone line and a modem. Users search the Internet for all types of information, including images, graphics, and sound and movie clips, in an ever growing number of remote host computers. When users retrieve and distribute this information to others, network activity becomes highly intensive in terms of file transfer times and traffic volume—especially considering the large size of multimedia files, even when they have been compressed. This is now fueling the upgrade of the Internet to wideband and broadband access and backbone facilities.

Interestingly, nobody *owns* the Internet (collection of backbone and access networks and homed servers), or centrally controls what happens there. The networks within different countries are funded and managed according to local policies. The Internet allows any end system that is equipped with a minimal set of communication capabilities to connect to a large pool of information. The specifications of the Internet technology are publicly available, allowing anyone to develop the software needed to communicate over the Internet. Many details of the network hardware are hidden from the user. The physical connection to the network mostly controls only the speed of access.

Internet-based technology has now migrated to what are called *intranets*. These networks are corporate networks, basically portions of or overlays to traditional enterprise networks, which use the same lower-layer and application-level protocols as the Internet, specifically WWW-related technology. Companies are deploying intranet technology in increasing numbers. For example, Federal Express already has 60 internal Web sites, mostly created for and by employees. The company is equipping its 30,000 office employees around the world with

Web browsers so they will have access to a plethora of new sites being set up inside the company headquarters.[2] Corporations are seizing the Web as a swift way to streamline and transform their organizations. It is expected that intranets will have as significant an impact on corporations as the reengineering effects of the 1980s and early 1990s had. These private intranets use the structure and standards of the Internet and the WWW, but are separated from the public Internet by *firewalls*. These firewalls allow employees to access the Internet while preventing unauthorized users from entering the corporate intranet.

The intranet is an inexpensive yet very effective alternative to other forms of internal communications in that it provides the mechanism to eliminate paper while increasing accessibility to information. Examples of applications of intranet-based information include internal telephone books, procedure manuals, training materials, and requisition forms. All of this information can be converted to electronic form on the Web and updated in a low-cost manner. To prepare for a meeting, an executive could tap into the finance department's home page, which has hyperlinks to information such as revenues and forecasts. Employees can order supplies from an electronic catalog maintained by the purchasing department.

Most companies already have the foundation for an intranet—a network that uses the Internet set of networking and transport protocols. Computers using Web server software store and manage documents built on the Web's HyperText Markup Language (HTML) format. With a Web browser on the user's PC, the user can call up any Web document, no matter what kind of computer it is on. Firewalls are other elements that may already be in place. Intranets allow the presentation of information in the same format to every computer. It is a single system with universal reach.[2] Intranets will fuel the migration to the "corporation is the network" paradigm in the next few years.

1.1.2   The scope of this text

1.1.2.1   The environment studied and corporate opportunities. More extensive use of the Internet is expected in the future, along with deployment of analogous technology in intranets. Electronic commerce is also expected to become increasingly more important. This book examines issues related to Internet-based communications, protocols, applications, and access. Many of these concepts also apply to intranets, as implied earlier. The book also covers corporate opportunities, strategies, and approaches to deployment of Internet-access resources and Internet-based work paradigms. As noted in the Preface, from the vantage point of the late 1990s, the opportunities afforded by evolving Internet technologies appear palatable, productivity-enhancing, and

TABLE 1.1   Glossary of Key Internet/Intranet-Related Terms

client   An application program that establishes connections for the purpose of sending requests.

connection   A transport layer (virtual) circuit established between two application programs for the purpose of communication.

FTP   File Transfer Protocol. A service to move computer files from one computer to another over a network. Requires userid and password.

Gopher   An older method of displaying information on the Internet.

HTML   HyperText Markup Language. Specialized commands and tags for WWW documents that allow you to specify hyperlinks, lists, paragraphs, and typographic attributes.

HTTP   HyperText Transport Protocol. A communications protocol for documents that contain hypertext links.

Internet   An international fabric of interconnected government, education, and business computer networks—in effect, a network of networks. A person at a computer terminal or personal computer with the proper software communicates across the Internet by placing data in an IP packet and "addressing" the packet to a particular destination on the Internet. TCP guarantees end-to-end integrity. Communications software on the intervening networks between the source and destination networks "read" the addresses on packets moving through the Internet and forward the packets toward their destinations. From a thousand or so networks in the mid-1980s, the Internet has grown to an estimated 1 million connected networks with about 100 million people having access to it (by 1997). The majority of these Internet users live in the United States or Europe, but the Internet expands as telecommunication lines are improved in other countries.[4,5]

intranets   Corporate networks that use the same networking/transport protocols and locally based Web servers to provide access to vast amounts of corporate information in a cohesive fashion. Documents must be stored in HTML, and clients need Web browser software.

server   An application program that accepts connections in order to service requests by sending back responses.

SLIP/PPP   Serial Line Internet Protocol and Point-to-Point Protocol. Allows computers to communicate over a serial link, such as a telephone line. PPP also provides error detection and compression.

TCP/IP   Transmission Control Protocol and Internet Protocol. A key set of networking protocols.

TELNET   A service that allows a user to log on to a remote computer.

WAIS   Wide Area Information System. A system that searches for a subject located on several databases over the world.

WWW   World Wide Web. A standard format used to easily access and display documents on the Internet. The format supports pictures and hypertext links to other documents, thus forming a web.

profitable. The importance of on-line access, research, collaboration, communication, and commerce will increase in the coming years. Corporations should start planning how best to deploy this technology in their environments. This book will help. Table 1.1 provides both a glossary and, by implication, a list of key topics covered in the text.[3] The glossary at the end of the book includes additional concepts.

Many kinds of information are now available on World Wide Web servers. WWW offers *hypertext* technology that links together a "web" of documents so that these can be navigated in any number of ways with the use of sophisticated Internet-specific graphical user interface (GUI*) software (e.g., Mosaic, Netscape, Explorer). Some of the information on WWW also consists of *hypermedia*. (Hypermedia is hypertext in which the content includes some or all of the following: text, graphics, video, voice, and/or music.) Web server software now also allows the delivery of live, real-time audio and video.

As examples, some magazines now are available *only* on Web servers, having migrated there from a paper format. Advertisements and technical information are now being delivered via Web servers. Perhaps in the not-too-distant future, many magazine, specs, documents, etc., of interest to businesspeople will be available on these servers, generating considerable corporate traffic as knowledge workers access them via the enterprise network. In addition, there are virtual reality (VR) applications now available at Web sites.

Specifically, the WWW is a set of public specifications and a library of code for building information servers and clients. WWW is ideal to support cooperative work in complex research fields. WWW uses Internet-based architectures employing public and open specifications along with free sample implementations on the client and server end, so that anyone can build a client or a server.

The three key components of WWW are URL (Uniform Resource Locator), HTTP (HyperText Transfer Protocol), and HTML. A URL is the address of the document which is to be retrieved from a network server. It contains the identification of the protocol, the server, and the filename of the document. When the user clicks on a link in a document, the link icon in the document contains the URL which the client employs to initiate the session with the intended server. HTTP is the protocol used in support of the information transfer. It is a fixed set of messages and replies that both the server and the client understand. The document itself, which is returned using HTTP upon the issuance of a URL, is coded in HTML. The browser interprets the HTML to identify the various elements of the document and render it on the screen of the client.

Corporate users may elect to access the Internet over a dial-up line or, better yet, through the corporate local area network (LAN), which is connected in a more resilient way to the Internet. Access through the enterprise network raises concerns about the ability to access volumes of information over the corporate communication infrastructure. Hence,

---

* GUIs are interfaces based on a windowing-screen management and icons that represent specific functions, programs, or groupings.

issues as to the best kind of technology required to support effective Internet access need to be addressed by corporations as they prepare for the next wave of information-based industries and economics. Other issues center on performance, security, and presentation richness.

There are already extensions to the basic Web browsers under way. Today's Web browsers are limited to HTML specifications, which are reasonable for two-dimensional page layout, but not necessarily for truly interactive browsing. Newly emerging languages such as Virtual Reality Modeling Language (VRML) and Java are designed to enhance the Web browsing experience. For example, VRML offers a method of describing three-dimensional space so that users can navigate in 3-D. Java is an object-oriented program that adds animation and real-time interaction through in-line applications. The delivery of VR applications is one of the more recent goals.

The emergence of new features, including new versions of HTML or de facto industry extensions, will introduce some lack of interoperability in the short term, but users are now looking for more flashy, colorful, and attractive places to hang out. This is temporarily forcing designers to choose between (1) lowest-common-denominator design tools, ending up with a bland but universally accessible Web site, or (2) leading-edge HTML tags (e.g., to support tables) or vendor-based extensions. Nonetheless, user and corporate requirements are in the direction of increased sophistication, complexity, speed, and bandwidth. Activities running on Web servers that are CPU- and communications-intensive include applications generating real-time graphics using charts and colors to show trends in the stock market, voter returns, Geographic Information Systems (GISs), weather maps, database statistics, and analysis related to economic commerce.

Some of the Web server software is based on the concept of streaming media, which delivers audio and video on demand, rather than requiring a user to download a file from the Web and play it back from the local server or hard drive. Using this technology, some say that more than 100 stations could be broadcasting live, FM-quality or better programming on the Internet within a year. TV-like Web service also may follow. This last technology, developed for NBC Desktop video and Reuters Financial Television, would be accessed over the corporate enterprise network. The major commercial on-line services (e.g., Prodigy, America Online, and CompuServe) have added WWW access and the ability for users to create their own home pages.

1.1.2.2 The course of investigation. This book takes a fundamental look at this set of technologies with an eye to educating the corporate planner as to the course of action that will best benefit his or her company. A number of books are available to help the lone professional learn something about the Internet and how to gain access as an individual. This book is aimed at the corporate professional who must assess *how to deploy this technology in his or her company for more than entertainment value.*

Chapter 1 describes the Internet structure, protocols, and access. Chapter 2 provides a primer on router technology. For large institutions and companies that opt to access the Internet by direct router connection, this coverage should prove useful.

Chapter 3 examines Web server technology, access, and protocols. Web servers are examples of distributed multidatabase systems. Such distributed systems are the building blocks of evolving telematic architectures, which place information close to where the user has the most need for data.

HTML technology, applications, and examples are covered in Chapter 4. Chapter 5 covers browsing systems for the Web and Internet. Chapter 6 provides useful information on establishing a Web site. Chapter 7 examines the commercial environment, namely, on-line services. Technology, applications, and vendors are discussed. Chapter 8 covers broadband communications in a Web/Internet context.

Chapter 9 is a stand-alone chapter describing the possibilities afforded by virtual reality (VR), which some call the "killer application" for the next wave of software. VR can be accessed locally, over intranets, or over the Internet.

1.1.3   The Internet: a short retrospective

1.1.3.1   The beginning. It all began in the late 1960s when the Pentagon asked computer scientists to find the best way for a large number of computers to communicate without relying on any single computer as a centralized controller. So, betting on a newly conceived communication technology called *packet switching,* the Pentagon in 1969 funded the Advanced Research Projects Agency (ARPA)* for the task. At that time, the U.S. Department of Defense created an experimental network using telephone lines. Out of this initial collection of networks, the ARPANet network was created. ARPANet eventually connected research institutions, universities, and corporate and government labs at diverse sites via electronic mail (e-mail) and real-time conversations.[6]

Packet switching implies that a message may be segmented into *packets.*[†] When sent from one user to another individual packets *may*

---

* At some point the name was changed to Defense ARPA, or DARPA, but the name then reverted to the original.

[†] Packets are Network Layer Protocol Data Units; the term *datagram* is also employed.

go by different routes,* and technology in the network puts them together again when delivering the original message to the intended recipient. This contrasts with *circuit switching* in which the two users are actually connected by an *end-to-end circuit* (e.g., this is how telephone calls are supported). Packet switching[†] affords a number of advantages for the user; namely, it makes more effective use of telecommunication resources, so that user costs can be lower, and it makes it possible to build in fail-safe mechanisms. If a route between the two users should fail or become congested, the network can reroute the packets.

At first, this new research network linked just a few research labs, letting scientists and engineers test networking technology. Other sites that were not connected to ARPANet quickly began to see the advantages of electronic communications. Many of these sites found ways to connect their private networks to the ARPANet. This led to the need for connecting computer systems that were fundamentally different from each other. (For example, IBM computers had to be able to communicate with non-IBM machines.) Throughout the 1970s, facilities worldwide began connecting to the network. The 1980s saw the addition of other networks. The Internet as we know it today was born from the consolidation of these networks. As more and more colleges and research companies joined the Internet, ARPA's role diminished and commercial applications became prevalent.

1.1.3.2 More recent history. Starting in 1973, ARPA initiated a research program to investigate techniques and technologies for interlinking packet networks of various kinds. The objective was to develop communication protocols that would allow networked computers to communicate transparently across multiple-packet networks.

The project became very successful, and there was increasing demand to use the network, so the government separated military (and defense research) traffic from civilian research traffic, bridging the two by using common protocols to form an internetwork, or internet. The term *internet* is defined as "a mechanism for connecting or bridging different networks so that two communities can mutually interconnect." (The Internet proper is a well-known, specific, set of global networks.) Specifically, ARPA became interested in establishing a packet-switched

---

* This happens when *connectionless* methods are used—most packet networks have in fact used a connection-oriented approach, where all packets associated with a connection take the same path through the network.

† In effect, nearly all data communication systems now use some form of packet switching, where the (original) bit stream is put in distinct frames at one level or another, and addressed/routed to the destination at some level or another.

network to provide communications between research institutions in the United States. With the goal of heterogeneous connectivity in mind, ARPA funded research by Stanford University and Bolt, Beranek, and Newman (BBN) to create an explicit series of communication protocols. The ARPA-developed technology included a set of network standards that specified the details of the computers that would be able to communicate, as well as a set of conventions for interconnecting networks and routing traffic. The result of this development effort, completed in the late 1970s was the *Internet suite of protocols,* of which the *Transmission Control Protocol* (TCP) and the *Internet Protocol* (IP) are the two best known. The set of protocols is also known as the *TCP/IP protocol suite.* Soon thereafter, there was a large number of computers and thousands of networks using TCP/IP, and it is from their interconnections that the modern Internet has emerged.

While the ARPANet was growing into a national network, researchers at Xerox Corporation's Palo Alto Research Center (PARC) were developing one of the technologies that would be used in local area networking: Ethernet. In the meantime, ARPA funded the integration of TCP/IP support into the version of the UNIX operating system that the University of California at Berkeley was developing. It follows that when companies began marketing powerful non-host-dependent workstations that ran UNIX, TCP/IP was already built into the operating system software, and vendors such as Sun Microsystems included an Ethernet port on the device. Consequently, TCP/IP over Ethernet became a common way for workstations to connect to one another.[7]

The same technology that made PCs and workstations possible made it possible for vendors to offer relatively inexpensive add-on cards to allow a variety of PCs to connect to Ethernet LANs. Software vendors took the TCP/IP software from Berkeley UNIX and ported it to the PC, making it possible for PCs and UNIX machines to use the same protocol on the same network.

In 1986, the U.S. National Science Foundation (NSF) initiated the development of the NSFNet. NSFNet has provided a major backbone communication service for the Internet. The National Aeronautics and Space Administration (NASA) and the U.S. Department of Energy (DOE) contributed additional backbone facilities in the form of the NSINET and ESNET, respectively. In Europe, major international backbones such as NORDUNET and others provide connectivity to over 100,000 computers on a large number of networks.

It should be noted that the NSFNet operated utilizing a Service Acceptable Use Policy (AUP). The policy stated that the NSFNet was to support open research and education in and among U.S. research and intellectual institutions, plus research arms of for-profit firms when engaged in open scholarly communication and research. Other uses are not acceptable. Unacceptable uses include for-profit activities (e.g., consulting at universities), sales of books and tickets, and/or extensive private or personal use. The recent commercialization of the Internet is not based on the AUP.

During the course of its evolution, particularly after 1989, the Internet began to integrate support for other protocol suites into its basic networking fabric. The present emphasis is on multiprotocol internetworking and, in particular, on the integration of the Open Systems Interconnection (OSI) protocols into the architecture. Integration of broadband technology is also under way. Both public domain and commercial implementations of the roughly 100 protocols of TCP/IP protocol suite became available in the 1980s. During the early 1990s, OSI protocol implementations also became available, and by the end of 1991 the Internet had grown to include some 5000 networks in over three dozen countries, serving over 700,000 host computers.[8] These numbers have continued to grow at geometric rates throughout the 1990s. There are now over 1900 Internet access providers (ISPs), which use various commercial Internet backbones, although the number is expected to decrease greatly in the next five years.

One of TCP/IP's most significant features, for instance, is that it is not tied to any single computer or communications technology. Internet traffic can move over almost any physical channel—telephone lines, cable-TV setups, satellite links, wireless links, or high-speed optical facilities. While the first computing systems connected to the Internet were mainframes and minicomputers, the Internet now connects every advanced microprocessor technology.[6]

Table 1.2 depicts highlights of the history of the Internet over a 30-year span.[9]

1.1.3.3 Where we are. As of January 1995 the Internet had almost 13 million hosts connecting millions of people in over 90 countries worldwide. The Internet is now used by many people: educators,[10] telecommuters,[11] librarians, hobbyists, researchers, government officials, and business personnel. It is used for a variety of purposes, from communicating with each other to accessing valuable information and resources. The Internet provides connectivity for a wide range of application processes called *network services*. One can exchange electronic mail, access and participate in discussion forums, search databases, browse indexes, transfer files, and so forth.

TCP and IP were developed for basic control of information delivery across the Internet. Application layer protocols, such as TELNET (Net-

TABLE 1.2   A Snapshot of Internet-Related Activities over the Years

- Late 1960s: ARPA (think tank of DOD) introduces ARPANet.
- During 1970s ARPANet expands geographically and functionally (allows nonmilitary traffic, e.g., universities and defense contractors).
- By late 1970s realization takes hold that ARPAnet cannot scale.
- TCP/IP is developed for heterogeneous, interenterprise connectivity. Protocols to support global addressing and scalability.
- Early 1980s (1983) TCP/IP is a standard operating environment for all attached systems.
- Network splits into a military component (MILNet) and a civilian component (ARPANet).
- 1986: Six supercomputer centers established by NSF.
- Interagency dynamics and funding considerations lead to creation of NSFNet by the NSF. IP protocol and newer equipment utilized in NSFNet. NSFNet and ARPANet intersected at Carnegie Mellon University.
- Late 1980s: ARPANet absorbed into NSFNet.
- *Phase 1:* Three-tiered architecture developed.
  1. NSF to undertake overall management; fund the Internet backbone operationally and in terms of technology upgrades.
  2. Regional and state network providers; supply Internet services between universities and the backbone; to become self-supportive on service fees.
  3. Campus networks, organizations, colleges, and universities; use TCP/IP-based system to provide widespread access to researchers and students.
- Six supercomputer sites interconnected in 1987 using DEC routers and 56-Kbps links.
- Traffic congestion begins to develop in 1987–1988.
- *Phase 2:* Merit partnership formed between IBM and MCI to upgrade network.
- By mid-1988 a DS-1 line (1.544-Mbps) network connects over a dozen sites. IBM-based switches were used.
- Reengineering in 1989 due to fast growth (15 percent per month); new routers and additional T1 links (MCI) installed.
- *Phase 3:* Third redesign of NSFNet uses outsourcing approach, whereby NSFNet is "overlaid" on a public Internet (NSF relieved from responsibility of upgrading the network on an ongoing basis). Lines upgraded to DS-3 rates (45 Mbps).
- Merit, IBM, and MCI form Advanced Network Services (ANS), a not-for-profit organization to build/manage a commercial Internet.
- DS-3 lines provided by MCI; routers by IBM (RS/6000-based). Network also called ANSNet. NSFNet is now a virtual network in the ANSNet (migration accomplished in two years).
- 1992: Original NSFNet dismantled.
- ANS launches for-profit subsidiary (ANS CORE) to face costs.
- Debates sparked by commercial Internet providers.
  1. PSINet, CERFNet, and AlterNet formed Commercial Internet Exchange (CIX) as an Internet backbone and bypass to the NSFNet. Joined by 155 other members, including NEARNet, JvNCNet, SprintLink, and InfoLAN.
  2. (Based on CIX approach) CICNet, NEARNet, BARRNet, North WestNet, NYSER-Net WestNet, and MIDNet form the Corporation for Regional & Enterprise Networking (CoREN).
  3. Regional commercial providers (not in CoREN) compete against CoREN.

TABLE 1.2   A Snapshot of Internet-Related Activities over the Years (*Continued*)

- *Phase 4:* Rapid increase requires NSF to redesign the backbone.

- Two years of bidding and planning leads to two awards to replace current NSFNet: (1) MCI to deploy very high speed Backbone Network Service (vBNS), based on 155-Mbps SONET/ATM, to connect NFS supercomputing centers; (2) Merit and USC Information Sciences Institute to do routing coordination.

- Network Access Providers (NAPs) to provide access to the vBNS; NAP functions went to Ameritech, Sprint, MFS, and PacTel.

- NFS instituted the Routing Arbitrer for: fair treatment among various Internet service providers with regard to routing administration; database of route information, network topology, routing path preferences, interconnection information; deployment of routing that supports type of service, precedence routing, bandwidth on demand, and multicasting (accomplished by route servers using Border Gateway Protocol and Inter-domain Routing Protocol).

- Fund established to support Network Information Center (NIC).
  1. Registration Services (by Network Solutions): IP and Domain Names; whois and whitepages.
  2. Directory Services (by AT&T): Directory of directories, white pages, yellow pages.
  3. Information Services (by General Atomics): Coordination services, clearinghouse for information, training, workshops, reference desk, education (General Atomics operates CERFNet and San Diego Supercomputer Center).

- Key backbones: AGIS (200 access points); ANS (103); BBN Planet (350); DIGEX (30); MCI (450); NetCom (240); PSINet (350); Sprint (400); UUNET/MFS (750).

- Backbone speeds (as of press time): 45 Mbps for most providers; 155 Mbps for AGIS; 622 Mbps for MCI.

- Backbone technologies: ATM, AGIS, BBN, MCI, NetCom, PSINet; Frame Relay (Sprint); dedicated lines (others).

- Shakeout of ISP is predicted by 1999: of 1900+ ISPs in 1996, about 100 are expected to survive by the turn of the century.

work Terminal), FTP (File Transfer Protocol), SMTP (Simple Mail Transfer Protocol), and HTTP (HyperText Transfer Protocol), have been added to the TCP/IP suite of protocols to provide specific network services.

Speeds have increased from 56 Kbps to 1.5 Mbps (most common now) to 45 Mbps and beyond for most of the backbones. A very high speed Backbone Network Service (vBNS) is being developed now to link NSF-supported high-performance computing centers.[12] Figure 1.1 depicts the current view of the Internet model.

1.1.3.4   Who runs the Internet.   The Internet is a society of thousands of organizations and networks that work together without government or centralized management. No single office or group has authority over the whole Internet. The Internet Society (ISOC) is a private, nonprofit organization composed of member organizations and individuals who are connected to the Internet. Membership is voluntary, and it is sup-

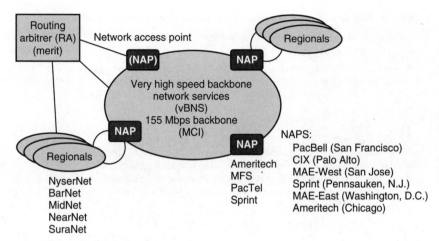

Figure 1.1   NSFNet Internet re-bid model.

ported by membership dues. The Internet Society does not run the Internet, but it does support the Internet Activities Board (IAB). The IAB consists of the Internet Engineering Task Force (IETF), which is concerned with the ongoing evolution of the TCP/IP protocols, and the Internet Research Task Force, which works on advancing network technology. The IAB operates the Internet Assigned Numbers Authority (IANA), which oversees the assigning of network IP addresses. The IAB also operates the Internet Registry, which keeps track of the root database of the Domain Name Service and is responsible for associating Domain Names with IP addresses. See Table 1.3.

Hence, the Internet Architecture Board is a body of the Internet Society responsible for overall architectural considerations in the Internet. It also serves to adjudicate disputes in the standards process. The IETF is the protocol engineering and development arm of the Internet. The IETF is a large, open, international community of network designers,

TABLE 1.3   Internet Governance

- Internet Society (ISOC)

    Quasi-governing body

    Guardian of TCP/IP and common IP addressing

    Composed of research and commercial elements

    Oversees IETF, InterNIC

- The Internet Activities Board (IAB)

    Internet Engineering Task Force (IETF)

        Administrator of Request for Comments (RFCs) for standards and policies

    IANA/InterNIC

        Administers the IP address

operators, vendors, and researchers concerned with the evolution of the Internet architecture and the smooth operation of the Internet. It is open to any interested individual. The actual technical work of the IETF is done in its working groups, which are organized by topic into several areas (e.g., routing, network management, security). Much of the work is handled via mailing lists; however, the IETF also holds meetings three times per year.

There are two types of Internet documents: Internet Drafts and Request for Comments (RFCs). Internet-Drafts have absolutely no formal status and can be changed or deleted at any time. The secretariat maintains an Internet-Drafts index. RFCs are the official document series of the IAB and are archived permanently (i.e., they are never deleted, and once an RFC is published, it will never change); however, it is important to note that not all RFCs are standards. The Database and Directory Services part of the InterNIC, provided by AT&T, has an RFC index.

IANA is the central coordinator for the assignment of unique parameter values for Internet protocols. The IANA is chartered by the ISOC and the Federal Network Council (FNC) to act as the clearinghouse to assign and coordinate the use of numerous Internet protocol parameters.

Although the Internet originally started with government funds, it is not run with government money today. The Internet is paid for by those who use it. The company or user who establishes a network connection is responsible for paying for it. While this approach works well for large colleges, universities, government facilities, and corporations, smaller companies and individuals may find it expensive to connect directly to the Internet (by establishing a backbone). To make it economically possible for these users to have access, Internet service providers began to appear. These providers pay the linking costs and then rent time on their systems to others who want access, or sublet their connections via dial-up protocols (such as SLIP/PPP, discussed later).

By agreement, all of the Internet's subnetworks move each other's traffic at no charge to the others. As a result, its users essentially pay a flat fee based on the length of the time they are connected to a local subnetwork and the potential capacity, or bandwidth, of that connection. In contrast, other networks charge customers according to the number of messages they actually generate or receive. In fact, the Internet's unique technology and pricing scheme ensure that it will be around in one form or another for many years to come. Table 1.4 depicts a summarized characterization of the state of the Internet as of press time.

Hardware components of the Internet include routers (by companies such as Cisco, Bay Networks, and 3Com), PCs, workstations, and servers (by companies such as Sun Microsystems, SGI, HP, and Compaq). Software vendors include NetScape, SpyGlass, Spry, NetManage, Microsoft, and PC-NFS. Carriers include providers of dial-up access

TABLE 1.4   Summarized Characterization of the State of the Internet, circa 1997[6]

- NSF involvement completely out since April 1995
- Broadband backbones being deployed
- InterNIC manages addresses
- MCI, ANS, Sprint, PSInet, UUnet/MFS, and NetCom are major players
- Merit is routing arbitrer, though bilateral agreements are important
- ANS and Sprint developed first major bilateral agreement
- CIX is large collection of members (150+)
- Phenomenal growth (e.g., traffic went up from 200 to 2900 percent for ISPs from June 1995 to June 1996)
- WWW access
- Internet outages seen by some in future

(e.g., alternate access providers, regional Bell operating companies) and providers of dedicated access (e.g., interexchange carriers, alternate access providers, regional Bell operating companies). Major Internet backbone providers include MCI, Sprint, AT&T, ANS, PSI, UUNet (MFS), and Netcom. Secondary providers include small companies (e.g., Pipeline, IDT, and Visicom). Other players include the following:

- Publishing, training, and conference companies (e.g., McGraw-Hill, O'Reilly & Associates)
- Integration and consulting companies (major companies, such as EDS, and small consulting establishments)
- Web home page designers
- Service providers such as America Online, CompuServe, and Prodigy
- A large number of content providers, including government, companies, educational institutions, publishers, and recreational outfits; information includes references, databases, directories, on-line commerce, advertisements, market research, broadcasting-related information, and so on.

1.1.3.5 Routing across the Internet. At the time the NSF Network backbone was decommissioned in early 1995, it was replaced by a number of network access points, which are exchanges where commercial Internet service providers (that is, ISPs) pass traffic to one another. Today, network operators are responsible for their own infrastructure, but no agency or organization has overall responsibility. What we have is an overlay of separate networks, both in the backbone and in the access. In the United States, there are about a dozen backbone providers, called Network Service Providers, or NSPs, (e.g., AGIS, MCI, Sprint, UUNET/MFS, PSINet, and BBN Planet).

The NSPs share commercial (and research) traffic at exchange points, utilizing routers. The exchange points are as follows: Pacific Bell NAP (San Francisco), Commercial Internet Exchange NAP (Palo Alto), Metropolitan Area Exchange–West (MAE-West) NAP (San Jose), Sprint NAP (Pennsauken, New Jersey), MAE-East (Washington, D.C.), Ameritech NAP (Chicago), and DIX (Digital Internet Exchange). In addition to handing off traffic destined for another provider's network at these exchanges, some NSPs have private exchanges, established bilaterally between two NSPs (e.g., ANS and MCI, BBN Planet and UUNET). To be an Internet backbone, a network needs to support most (if not all) of the exchange points and have national/international interconnection network of significant capacity (e.g., carry 300 tera-bytes per month and/or switch at a combined 400 Mbps).

Local and regional ISPs contract with backbone providers to carry their traffic over the long haul. Today, the traffic routing rules are as follows:

- If a user tries to reach a resource located on the same ISP network to which the user is connected, the traffic is examined by the ISP router which in turn forwards it to the destination (this applies to both backbone providers and regionals).

- If a user tries to reach a resource not located on the same ISP net-work to which the user is connected, the traffic is examined by the ISP/NSP router, which in turn finds the nearest point at which it can hand off data to the exchange point (e.g., MAE-East). The traffic is then transferred to the appropriate target network. The issue of interest to the user is that the exchange point can become congested and thus becomes a choke point. To counter these problems, faster routers are being installed at these locations, and entirely new router technologies are under development.

- Backbone ISPs/NSPs do not want to incur the cost of carrying traffic destined for another provider's network. So they hand off the traffic to the nearest exchange point, destination network, or inter-mediate transit provider (a practice known as *hot-potato routing*). NSPs and larger ISPs do not want a local or regional provider to dump traffic to their backbone, when that local provider has no pres-ence elsewhere in the country to handle a comparable load of return traffic. In this case, the local or regional provider must pay the back-bone carrier for transit carrying charges.

Consider for example, a client in Boston (on NSP A) wanting to reach a server in Seattle (on NSP Z). In general, an intermediate NSP may be used via the exchange point, or the two NSPs can trans-fer traffic directly at the exchange point. In this example, we assume that the two NSPs had a special peering agreement, so that they have dedicated circuits to transmit information, at some (commonly) unspecified geographic location. NSP A looks for the nearest exchange point, which here turns out to be a private interconnection in Boston with NSP Z. When the server answers, NSP Z searches for the closest place to hand off data to NSP A. The private interconnection in not an option because the destination NSP is expected to bear the (bulk) of the transport cost. Hence, NSP Z sends the data to MAE-West in San Jose, where it is handed to NSP A for deliver over its network.

There is an exception to this: some service providers offer enhanced IP service or so-called private Internet services. These services give users a connection to the Internet, but the users' data rides over the provider's backbone until it reaches the point of exit nearest to the destination.

Since the Internet is based on router technology, described at length in this book, there are routing updates that have to be exchanged among users, ISPs, and NSPs. There currently are in the vicinity of 35,000 routes over the Internet. The network, as a core, can exchange 5-10 million routing updates a day. These updates are a contributing factor to the bottlenecks alluded to and which could affect service in the future.

1.1.3.6   The emergence of the World Wide Web.   As noted, Internet access usually means access to several services: electronic mail, interactive discussions/conferences, access to information resources, network news, and the ability to transfer files. Most people now access these services through a WWW browser. The WWW uses the Internet to transmit hypertext/hypermedia documents between computer systems nationally or internationally. The World Wide Web refers to the body of information—the abstract space of knowledge. The Internet refers to the physical side—the conglomerate of computers and transmission facilities connected to this global set of networks.

The WWW is a worldwide, Internet-based, multimedia presentation system. It is gaining in popularity as more users demand more intuitive access to the Internet. The WWW is a system of cooperating Internet host computers that offer multimedia presentations, indexes, cross-references, and text-search capabilities so that users can find text documents across the globe. The main vehicle for users to traverse the WWW are *directories,* which organize WWW sites by topic and evaluate them, and *search engines* ("automated crawlers"), which scan WWW pages for keywords or phrases.

Just as nobody owns the Internet, nobody owns the World Wide Web. People are responsible for the documents they create and make available to the public. Via the Internet, hundreds of thousands of people generate information that is accessible from homes, schools, and workplaces around the world. The WWW software can be used without using the Internet, but Internet access is necessary to make full use of the worldwide capabilities for sharing this data with others who may find your information useful.

To realize the importance of this new approach to sharing data, take the Canadian Medical Association (CMA) as an example. The CMA publishes the *CMA Journal,* which keeps physicians up-to-date with new techniques and practices. It also contains original papers on research and clinical practices, topical review articles, editorials, political processes, association news, and book reviews. The CMA created an on-line *Journal,* which provides physicians with rapid access to new health care news, up-to-date clinical alerts and information, and provides a mechanism for electronic discussion among health care providers worldwide. Now physicians around the globe have rapid access to information that normally would take months or even years to circulate. The increase in technology and the increase in user knowledge allows the World Wide Web to be a comprehensive "virtual" medical library for physicians, patients, and other interested Internet browsers.[13]

World Wide Web activity began in March 1989. Tim Berners-Lee of CERN (The European Particle Physics Laboratory) proposed the project to be used as a means of transporting research and ideas effectively throughout the organization. CERN had a long-standing goal to create an effective method for communicating, since its members were located in different countries.[14–21] The initial project proposal outlined a simple system of using networked hypertext mechanisms to transmit documents and communicate among members in the high-energy-physics community. There was no intention of adding sound, video, or image transmission.

By the end of 1990, the first piece of WWW software was introduced on a NEXT computer. It had the capability to view and transmit hypertext documents to other people on the Internet, and came with the on-screen capability of editing hypertext documents. Demonstrations were given at CERN committees and seminars, and a demonstration was given at the Hypertext '91 conference. Things progressed rapidly from there. In May of 1994, the First International World Wide Web Conference was held at CERN in Geneva.

Since the beginning of the WWW project, hundreds of people throughout the world have contributed their time writing Web software and documents and promulgating the concept of the WWW. The project has reached global proportions. In the first four months of 1994 alone, for example, the World Wide Web was mentioned by CNN, *The Wall Street Journal, The Economist, Fortune* magazine, *The New York*

Times, and dozens of computer publications. All of this "popular" press has fueled the growing interest in the technology by corporations and individuals.

1.1.3.7 Using the World Wide Web. The World Wide Web exists virtually. There is no standard way of viewing it or navigating around it. However, many software interfaces to the Web have similar functions and generally work the same way. The type of computer or type of display is insignificant when the appropriate software is used. In fact, many users navigate the WWW using text-only interfaces and are able to see all of the textual information that a user with a graphic display would.[14–21]

The WWW interface may be black and white or in color. The interface, called a *Web browser,* works in a window and may be a software program on any computer with a graphic interface, such as a Macintosh or an IBM-compatible computer running Microsoft Windows. (See Fig. 1.2.)

The browser has a menu bar on top, where the user can quit, get help on using the program, and change certain display characteristics (font size, background color, etc.). Some local configuration may be required under one of the menu options. The browser may be purchased separately or may be provided by the Internet access provider.

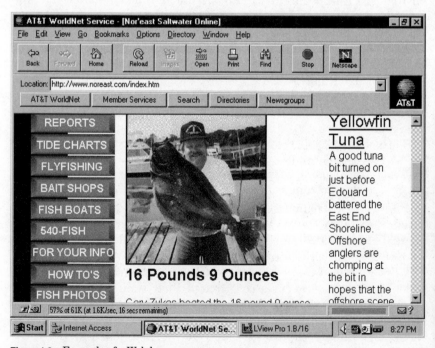

Figure 1.2 Example of a Web home page.

A scroll bar allows the user to scroll through the document, forward or backward. Because there is no limit to how wide or small a hypertext/hypermedia document can be, scroll bars are often needed when the document is larger than the viewing window.

Usually, the first document on the screen is a home page. This is a special document that is intended to be viewed first. It contains an introduction of the information displayed and/or a master menu of the documents contained within this collected set of topics. Home pages are generally associated with a particular site, person, or named collection. Other interrelated documents are hyperlinked to other Web pages.

Typically, clicking on the word (or link) with a mouse will cause another document to appear on the screen, which may hold more images and/or hyperlinks to other places. Some browsers represent text that is linked to other things by underlining or by using special colors. Images, also known as *inline images,* can be displayed within a page.

Users often create their own personal documents with collections of their favorite links or biographical information and make them publicly available. Usually called *home pages* (they are a virtual "home" for the user), they may also be called *personal pages* or *hyplans* (hypermedia plans).

In the display screen, there is also a set of navigation buttons. A user might go to many different screens by selecting multiple hyperlinks; these buttons provide a method for retracing the user's steps and reviewing the documents that were previously explored. The Back button brings the user to previously viewed documents. The Forward button will bring the user to the page most recently viewed prior to taking the backward steps.

An Open button allows the user to connect to other documents and networked resources by specifying the address of the desired document or resource. The user might be able to connect to a document stored locally on the machine currently being used or to one stored in another country. Such a document is normally transferred over the Internet in its entirety. Most browsers have a cache setting to allow faster access to these documents once they have been visited.[14-21]

The Print button allows the user to print out the document that is on the screen. The user may be given the choice of printing the document with images and formatting as seen on the screen or as a text-only document.

Typically, a person who is in charge of administrating a World Wide Web site is listed at the bottom of a home page. Any problems with the hyperlinks, images, documents, or questions about the site can be mailed to this Webmaster's address.

1.1.3.8 Extension to intranets. As discussed earlier, intranets use the same WWW/HTML/HTTP and TCP/IP technology used for the Internet. When the Internet caught on in the early to mid-1990s, planners were not looking at it as a way to run their businesses. But just as the action of putting millions of computers around the world on the same protocol suite fomented the Internet revolution, so connecting islands of information in a corporation via intranets is sparking what has been characterized as "unprecedented collaboration."[2] Hundreds of corporations had intranets by press time.

Across the business world, employees from engineers to office workers are creating their own home pages and sharing details of their projects with the rest of the company. For example, at Silicon Graphics, employees have access to 144,000 Web pages stored on 800 internal Web sites. A press-time survey of 50 major corporations found that 16 percent already have an intranet in place, and 50 percent either plan to build one or are considering it.[2]

At first, software makers focused on Web browsers, but more recently, with Internet commerce taking off, software makers are focusing on the intranet opportunity. Software related to intranets is expected to have an $8 billion market by 1998; for comparison Internet-based Web revenues for the same year are expected to be $2 billion.[2] Companies such as Netscape, Microsoft, IBM, and Sun Microsystems, to list a few, have intranet-related Web products.

1.1.3.9 Future growth and technology. Both the TCP/IP technology and the Internet continue to evolve. New protocols are being proposed. The National Science Foundation added considerable flexibility to the system by introducing a backbone network, regional networks, and hundreds of campus networks. Other groups around the world continue to connect to the Internet as well. And as the Internet became popular and users began to browse information using services such as Gopher and the WWW, traffic increased. To accommodate growth in traffic, the capacity of the NSFNet backbone has been increased three times, and an additional increase by another factor of 3 was scheduled for 1996 for the vBNS. Figure 1.3 summarizes expansion of the Internet and illus-

	Number of networks	Number of computers	Number of managers
1980	10	100	1
1990	1000	100,000	10
1997	1,000,000	100,000,000	100

Figure 1.3 Internet expansion and growth.

trates the growth. The initial design for many subsystems depended on centralized management. Much effort is needed to extend those designs to accommodate decentralized management.

For all its capabilities, however, the Internet does have limitations. While creating a system to survive a nuclear attack ARPANet designers were not thinking about electronic commerce, so the Internet lacks network-based security features. This makes businesses wary of trusting it with data such as credit card numbers needed for on-line shopping. Closing these gaps is the focus of much Internet activity today. Companies such as DigiCash and CyberCash are now introducing solutions for secure cash transactions over the Internet (see Sec. 1.9 for more information).[6]

1.1.4   The TCP/IP standardization approach for Internet and intranets

As summarized in the previous sections, U.S. government agencies realized the importance and the potential of Internet technology and funded the research that has made possible a global Internet. The technology developed by ARPA includes a set of network standards that specify the details of how computers communicate, as well as a set of conventions for interconnecting networks and routing traffic. The original ARPANet was a collection of custom-built packet-switching nodes connected by very expensive long-distance leased telephone lines; hosts on the network were classical mainframes. Hosts were connected (again, by custom hardware and software) directly to the nearest packet switch. The development of industrywide standards was, therefore, highly desirable.[22]

The Transmission Control Protocol and Internet Protocol (TCP/IP) is now commonly used to communicate across any set of interconnected networks. It can be used both in the Internet context and in any (corporate) internet context. For example, many corporations use the TCP/IP to interconnect networks within their corporation, even though the corporation has no connection to outside networks. The TCP/IP forms the base technology for a global internet that connects homes, university campuses and other schools, corporations, and government labs in dozens of countries.

This section describes some preliminary protocol-related issues.

1.1.4.1   Internet protocols services.

Protocols like TCP and IP provide the rules for communications between computers. They contain the details of message formats, describe how a computer responds when a message arrives, and specify how a computer handles errors or other abnormal conditions. Most important, they handle communications independently of any particular network hardware.[22]

1.1.4.2 Application-level Internet services. From the user's point of view, a TCP/IP internet appears to be a set of application programs that use the network to carry out useful communication tasks. In a corporate internet these relate to interconnecting the organization's enterprise. The most popular and widespread Internet and application services include[22-27]:

- *Electronic mail.* Electronic mail allows a user to compose memos and send them to individuals or groups. Although many electronic mail systems exist, TCP/IP makes mail delivery reliable because it operates by having the sender's machine contact the receiver's machine directly. Thus, the sender knows that once the message leaves the local machine, it has been successfully received at the destination site.

- *File transfer.* The TCP/IP protocols include a file transfer application program that allows users to send or receive arbitrarily large files of programs or data.

- *Remote login.* Remote login allows a user sitting at one computer to connect to a remote machine and establish an interactive login session.

1.1.4.3 Network-level Internet services. At the network level, an internet provides two broad types of service that all application programs use[23-27]:

- *Connectionless packet delivery service.** This means that a TCP/IP internet routes small messages from one end system to another, based on address information carried in the message. Because it usually maps directly onto the underlying hardware, the connectionless service is relatively efficient,† and, more important, it makes the TCP/IP protocols adaptable to a wide range of network hardware.

- *Reliable stream transport service.* The reliable transport service in TCP/IP protocols (specifically, in TCP) handles problems such as transmission errors and lost packets. It allows an application on one computer to establish a "connection" with another application as if it were a permanent, direct hardware or hardwire connection.

Many networks provide basic services similar to those mentioned, but the primary features that distinguish TCP/IP are as follows[22]:

---

* More exactly, connectionless at the network layer.

† The great increases in available network bandwidth because of advances in fiber-optic technology may well (or should) decrease the importance of the issue of bandwidth efficiency as a key driver of protocol design in the future, just as the efficient utilization of memory in PC programs at the expense of ease of use has been abandoned in the past decade. The introduction of Asynchronous Transfer Mode (ATM) based protocols with 15 to 25 percent overhead attests to this trend.

- *Network technology independence.*   While TCP/IP is based on conventional packet-switching technology, it is independent of any particular vendor's hardware.

- *Universal interconnection.* TCP/IP allows any pair of computers with appropriate drivers to communicate. Each computer is assigned an *address* that is universally recognized throughout the internet/Internet.

- *End-to-end acknowledgments.* The TCP/IP internet protocols (specifically, TCP) provide acknowledgments between the source and the destination, even when they do not connect to a common physical network.

- *Application-level protocol standards.*   The TCP/IP protocols include standards for many common applications, including electronic mail, file transfer, and remote login.

1.1.5   Related networks

This section describes some networks related to the Internet, but not identical.

1.1.5.1   BITNET/CREN.   In the early 1980s, two networking projects, BITNET and CSNET, were initiated. BITNET adopted the IBM protocol suite and utilized direct leased-line connections between participating sites. Most of the original BITNET connections linked IBM mainframes in university data centers. This rapidly changed as protocol implementations became available for other systems. From the beginning, BITNET has been multidisciplinary in nature, with users in all academic areas. BITNET and its parallel networks in other parts of the world (e.g., EARN in Europe) have several thousand participating sites. In recent years, BITNET has established a backbone that uses the TCP/IP protocols with IBM-based applications running above TCP.

CSNET was initially funded by the National Science Foundation to provide networking for university, industry, and government computer science research groups. CSNET used the Phonenet MMDF protocol for telephone-based electronic mail relaying. CSNET pioneered the first use of TCP/IP over X.25 using commercial public data networks. The CSNET name server provided an early example of a white pages directory service and this software is still in use at numerous sites. At its peak, CSNET had approximately 200 participating sites and international connections to approximately 15 countries.

In 1987, BITNET and CSNET merged to form the Corporation for Research and Educational Networking (CREN). In the fall of 1991, CSNET service was discontinued, having fulfilled its important early role as an academic networking service. A key feature of CREN is that its operational costs are fully met through dues paid by its member organizations.[28]

1.1.5.2 Mass-market information services. Mass-market information services include CompuServe, America Online, Prodigy, Genie, Delphi, and others. These firms sell access to on-line discussion groups, up-to-the-minute news summaries, airline reservations and travel information, and so forth. These vendors try to present their customers with seamless access to their various services, even though, in fact, services may be spread across multiple computers.

1.1.5.3 Specialized commercial data vendors. Vendors such as Mead Data Central with its Nexis/Lexis service, Lockheed's Dialog Service, and the Dow Jones Information Service offer specialized data services. Subscribers include research libraries, information centers, and libraries in professional firms such as law offices and hospitals, and in some cases, individuals. In general, access to commercial data vendors entails higher fees than the mass-market services.

1.1.5.4 Commercial public data networks. These services allowed companies to send and receive data nationwide or worldwide without having to pay for expensive, end-to-end, leased telephone lines of their own. During the late 1970s and 1980s, one standard for this type of network, X.25, was widely deployed in North America and Europe. Frame-relay-based and Asynchronous Transfer Mode (ATM)–based networks are now appearing.

1.1.5.5 Private corporate networks. Many large corporations have built their own private data networks to support data communications nationally or internationally. Corporations run their own networks in order to meet their demands for security, reliability, and performance. Different elements of these corporate networks are connected together to form a (corporate) internet. Often these private networks have gateways and/or fire walls to the Internet.

1.1.5.6 Fidonet. Fidonet endows dial-up bulletin board systems (BSSs)* with a special capability: to exchange electronic mail from one BBS site to another. Typically, a Fidonet host calls one or more peers via modem and exchanges "echo mail" during hours when long-distance telephone rates are lowest. Fidonet is not entirely distinct from the Internet: some of its traffic is carried over Internet paths, and electronic mail gateways allow Fidonet and Internet users to exchange mail with one another.

---

* Bulletin board systems flourished in the mid-1980s. BBSs have many features; the simplest among these is the ability for people to carry on a discussion electronically. Participants need not be located in the same place, and they need not log in at the same time.

1.1.5.7 The UUCP network. The UUCP network has its roots in the UNIX operating system, which gives it its name: the command copy file under UNIX is CP, and this protocol supports UNIX-to-UNIX CP functions (hence the name). The main use of this network is electronic mail and as a medium of distributed discussion called Usenet News.[29]

1.1.6 Network technologies for intranets

This section discusses key network technologies that come into play either in the Internet backbone, for Internet access, or for intranets.

Network communications can be divided into two basic types: *circuit-switched* (sometimes called *connection-oriented*) and *packet/ fastpacket-switched* (these can be connectionless or connection-oriented). Circuit-switched networks operate by forming a dedicated connection (circuit) between two points. In packet-switched networks, data to be transferred across a network is segmented into small pieces called *packets* that are multiplexed onto high-capacity intermachine connections. A packet, which usually contains a few hundred bytes of data, carries identification that enables the network hardware to know how to send it to the specified destination. In frame relay, the basic transfer unit is the (data link layer) *frame;* in cell relay, this basic unit is the (data link layer) *cell.* It should be noted that although the "bearer" service of packet/fastpacket services is "packet," the WAN implementations that are commercially available use circuit-switching principles; namely, they use the call setup mechanism similar to that of a circuit-switched (ISDN) call.[22]

1.1.6.1 Wide area and local area networks. Packet-switched technologies are often divided into two broad categories: wide area network technologies in which networks span large geographical distances (e.g., a metropolitan area, the continental United States) and local area network technologies in which networks span short distances (e.g., a single building).

WAN technologies support communications over large distances. The network can span a continent or can connect computers across oceans. Usually, but not always, WANs operate at lower speeds than LANs and have higher end-to-end delay. Typical WAN speeds range from 56 Kbps to 155 Mbps. Delay across a WAN can vary from a few milliseconds to several tenths of a second.

LAN technologies provide high-speed connections among computers. Typically, a LAN, which spans a small distance such as a single building or small campus, operates between 10 and 100 Mbps (token ring LANs support 4 or 16 Mbps). Newer ATM-based technologies can support higher speeds (e.g., 622 Mbps). The delay across a LAN can vary from a few tenths of a millisecond to few milliseconds.

1.1.6.2   Ethernet technology. *Ethernet* is the name given to a popular packet-switched LAN technology developed at Xerox PARC in the early 1970s. Xerox, Intel, and Digital Equipment standardized Ethernet in 1978. Soon thereafter, IEEE released a compatible version using the siglum IEEE 802.3.

The Ethernet is a 10-Mbps broadcast bus technology.* It is a *bus* because all stations share a single communication medium (channel); it is *broadcast* because all transceivers receive every transmission. The Ethernet access scheme is called *carrier sense multiple access with collision detect* (CSMA/CD). It is a multiple-access technology because multiple stations can access the Ethernet simultaneously, and each station determines whether the channel is idle by sensing whether a carrier wave is present. Namely, all stations wanting to transmit monitor the medium. The Ethernet handles collisions in a characteristic fashion: each transceiver monitors the cable while it is transmitting to see if a foreign signal interferes with the transmission. Technically, the monitoring is called *collision detect* (CD). When a collision is detected, the host interface aborts transmission, waits for activity to subside, and tries again at a randomly selected (short) time later.

Ethernet uses a 48-bit addressing scheme. Each computer attached to an Ethernet network is assigned a unique 48-bit number known as its *Ethernet (MAC) address*. Ethernet hardware manufacturers assign Ethernet addresses in sequence as they manufacture the hardware; thus, no two hardware interfaces have the same Ethernet address.[23–27]

The data transmission on the Ethernet is viewed as occurring in frames. Ethernet frames are of variable length, with no frame smaller than 64 bytes or larger than 1518 bytes. Figure 1.4 shows that the Ethernet frame format contains the physical source address as well as the destination address.

In addition to identifying the source and destination, each frame transmitted across the Ethernet contains preamble, frame type, data field, and cyclic redundancy check (CRC, or frame check sequence) field. The preamble consists of alternating 0s and 1s to help receiving nodes synchronize. The CRC helps the interface detect transmission errors.

---

* 100 Mbps technology (IEEE 802.30) has now been defined, and there is work under way on "gigabit" technology.

Preamble	Destination address	Source address	Frame type	Frame data	CRC (also known as *flag check sequence*)
8 bytes	6 bytes	6 bytes	2 bytes	64–1500 bytes	4 bytes

Figure 1.4   The format of an IEEE 802.3 frame (packet) as it travels across an Ethernet.

The frame type contains a 16-bit integer that identifies the type of data being carried in the frame.* The station's operating system uses the frame type to determine which protocol software module should process the frame. This means that the Ethernet frames are *self-identifying*. The main advantages of self-identifying frames are that they allow multiple protocols to be used together on a single system and multiple protocols to be intermixed on the same physical network without interference.

1.1.6.3 Fiber distributed data interface (FDDI). FDDI is a popular campus networking technology of the late 1980s and early 1990s that provides 100 Mbps. FDDI uses optical fiber for transmission media instead of copper wire.† The FDDI network is a 100-Mbps token-passing technology with a self-healing capability (see Fig. 1.5). Network devices are connected in a logical ring. FDDI is a *token-passing* technology because it uses a token to control transmission. When the network is idle, a special frame called a *token* passes from one station to another. When a station is ready to send a packet, it waits for the token to arrive, sends its packet, and then passes the token to the next station. FDDI is now increasingly being replaced with ATM-based campus networks.[22]

1.1.6.4 Asynchronous Transfer Mode. Newer LAN/WAN connection technologies offer the prospect of carrying a mixture of traditional data with real-time information such as voice telephone calls, image,

---

* This is for the original Ethernet. In IEEE 802.3 this field represents the length; the protocol type is identified by the Subnetwork Access Protocol (SNAP) bytes in the Logical Link Control (LLC) layer.

† Now 100 Mbps can also be obtained on twisted-pair media.

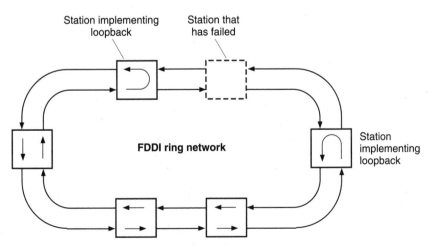

Figure 1.5 An FDDI ring after failure.

and data, all over standard digital telephone services. One important technology in this area is ATM. ATM is the name given to a high-speed connection-oriented networking technology that has been used in both local area and wide area networks. ATM transmits data in short, fixed-length "cells" containing 48 bytes of data and 5 bytes of header information. ATM is designed to transmit time-critical data, such as real-time voice, intermingled with other kinds of information for which delivery times are less critical.

ATM is an important technology because it is manifesting itself in corporate local area networks, corporate wide area networks, in access networks to the Internet, and within the Internet itself.

ATM can provide a flexible and (ultimately) cost-effective network for handling a wide variety of communications. ATM technology uses a protocol data unit format that is independent of the user application. The data could be sent through a high-speed virtual connection from the client to the Internet. ATM is recognized as a platform that provides a high-speed data-link-layer service with multiple *quality of service* (QOS) features. Because each cell is exactly the same size, ATM switch hardware can process cells quickly. Networks can be interconnected through private ATM switches and/or routers. ATM LANs interconnected with existing network platforms (i.e., high-speed Ethernet), will still need to be segmented by routers and/or utilize LAN emulation capabilities.[30,31] This topic is revisited in Sec. 1.9.2 of this chapter as well as in Chap. 5.

1.2   Internet Protocol Model Overview

As discussed, TCP and IP are protocols originally developed by the Department of Defense to connect numerous networks designed by different vendors into a network of networks—the Internet. TCP/IP is the standard protocol that nearly all systems are able to use to "talk" to another machine as if it were its peer, whether the system is IBM-compatible, Macintosh, UNIX, or mainframe. It was necessary that TCP/IP be robust enough to automatically recover from any node or communications-line failure. This protocol was to be used in battlefield communications. In battlefield conditions, the loss of a node or line is a common occurrence. This design allows very large networks to operate with less central management (however, because of the automatic recovery, network problems can go undiagnosed and uncorrected for long periods of time).

These protocols have succeeded in delivering a number of basic services: file transfer, electronic mail, and remote logon across a very large number of client and server systems. TCP/IP can be used for communication between any set of interconnected networks. TCP/IP can be used, for example, along with other network protocols, by several computers in a small department or LAN. The IP component provides routing from one LAN to another LAN, or maybe a WAN, and finally to the Internet, if so desired.[14–21] This internetworking provides a method in which LANs and WANs are connected together to form a seamless network. Information that travels across the internet/Internet must be broken down into smaller units called *packets*. Breaking data into packets improves network performance. These packets contain the data being sent, as well as the destination's address and the packet order (this allows the packets to be rejoined in proper sequence).

Creation and documentation of the Internet Protocol suite closely resembles an academic research project. As mentioned earlier, the protocols are specified in documents called *Requests for Comments*. RFCs are published, reviewed, and analyzed by the Internet community. Protocol refinements are also published in RFCs. Taken together, the RFCs provide a history of the people, companies, and trends that shaped the development of what is today the most popular open-system protocol suite. There were over 1900 RFCs at press time. Draft RFCs eventually become RFCs, which, once stabilized, are in turn implemented by vendors. Newer RFCs supersede older RFCs.

1.2.1 The need for multiple protocols

Complex data communication systems no longer utilize a single protocol to handle all transmission tasks. Instead, they require a set of protocols, called a *protocol suite*. The reason for using multiple protocols is to make them less complicated; this simplifies dealing with problems that arise when machines communicate over a network. Such problems include the following[22–27]:

- *Hardware failure.* When a router or a host hardware fails, the protocol software needs to detect the failure and recover from it.

- *Network congestion.* The protocol software needs to detect when the network capacity has been exceeded and arrange a way to handle the congestion.

- *Packet delay or loss.* The protocol software needs to adapt to long delays in order not to lose packets that were significantly delayed.

- *Data corruption.* The protocol software needs to detect and recover from transmission errors and corruption due to transmission impairments or hardware failures.

- *Data duplication or sequence error.* Networks that offer multiple routes may deliver data out of sequence or deliver duplicates of packets. The protocol software needs to reorder packets and remove duplicates.

It is difficult or undesirable to write a single protocol that will handle everything in the network, particularly since many networks are heterogeneous. So the decision has been made to partition the communication problem into subproblems and organize the software into modules that handle one subproblem. The partitioning was based on the fact that the design of the network (or internet) and the organization of the protocol software are interrelated: one cannot be designed without the other.

Two main models of protocol layering are available today. The first is based on the International Organization for Standardization (ISO). The second is based on research that led to the TCP/IP protocol suite. Layered protocols are designed so that layer n at the destination receives exactly the same object sent by layer n at the source. In other words, they operate in a peer-to-peer mode.

1.2.2   ISO seven-layer reference model

This model is known as the ISO's Open System Interconnection Reference Model (OSIRM), referred to as the ISO Reference Model. The ISORM layering scheme has been the basis for international protocol development and implementations. (See Fig. 1.6.)

The OSIRM layers are as follows:

- *Physical layer.*   Layer 1 specifies the physical-link interconnection, including electrical/photonic characteristics.

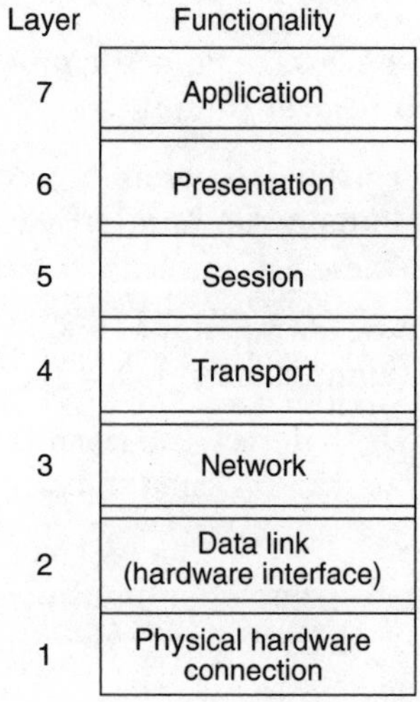

Layer	Functionality
7	Application
6	Presentation
5	Session
4	Transport
3	Network
2	Data link (hardware interface)
1	Physical hardware connection

Figure 1.6 The ISO seven-layer reference model for protocol software.

■ *Data link layer.*   Layer 2 specifies how data travels between two endpoints of a communication link (e.g., a host and a packet switch). At this level, data is delivered in a *frame,* which consists of a stream of binary data 0s and 1s in which checksum techniques are applied to detect errors. It is important to know that a successful transfer at this level means a frame has been passed across a link (e.g., to the network packet switch), but it does not mean that the packet switch was able to route it correctly end to end. The Ethernet protocol is one example of this.

■ *Network layer.*   Layer 3 defines the basic unit of transfer across the network and includes the concept of multiplexing and routing. At this level, the software assembles a packet in the form the network expects and uses layer 2 to transfer it over single links.

■ *Transport layer.*   Layer 4 provides end-to-end reliability by having the destination host communicate with the source host to compensate for the fact that (perhaps) multiple networks with different qualities of service may have been utilized.

■ *Session layer.*   Layer 5 describes how protocol software can be organized to handle all the functionality needed by the application programs, particularly to maintain transfer-level synchronization.

■ *Presentation layer.*   Layer 6 includes functions required for the basic encoding rules used in transferring information, be it text, voice, video, or multimedia.

■ *Application layer.*   Layer 7 includes application programs such as electronic mail or file transfer programs.

As of yet, OSI-based protocols have not played a significant role in the Internet, where the focus is an TCP/IP.

1.2.3   The TCP/IP Internet layering model

TCP/IP is the de facto name for a family of over 100 data communications protocols used to organize computers and data communications equipment into practical computer networks. The most accurate name for the set of protocols is the *Internet protocol suite;* TCP and IP are two of the protocols in this suite. Because TCP and IP are the best known of the protocols, it has become common to use the term TCP/IP or IP/TCP to refer to the whole family. Some of the protocols in the TCP/IP suite of protocols provide low-level functions needed for many applications. These include IP, TCP, User Datagram Protocol (UDP), and Internet Control Message Protocol (ICMP). Other protocols undertake specific tasks (e.g., transferring files between computers, sending mail, or finding out who is logged in on another computer).

As with the OSIRM, TCP/IP protocols are normally deployed in layers, with each layer responsible for a different facet of the communications.[32] A protocol suite such as TCP/IP is the combination of different protocols at various layers. TCP/IP is normally considered to be a four-layer system, as shown in Fig. 1.7.*

Each layer has a different responsibility.[33-38]

1. The *link layer* (sometimes called the *network interface layer*) normally includes the device driver in the operating system and the corresponding network interface card in the computer.† Together they handle all the hardware details of physically interfacing with the cable.

2. The *network layer* (sometimes called the *internet layer*) handles the movement of packets in the network. Routing of packets, for example, takes place here. IP and ICMP provide the network layer in the TCP/IP protocol suite.

3. The *transport layer* provides a flow of data between two end-system hosts for the application layer above. In the Internet protocol suite there are two different transport protocols: TCP and UDP. TCP provides a reliable flow of data between two hosts. It is concerned with things such as partitioning the data passed to it from the application into appropriately sized frames for the network layer below, acknowledging received packets, and setting time-outs to make certain the other end acknowledges packets that are sent. Because this reliable flow of data is provided by the transport layer, the application layer

---

* These layers are not identical to the OSIRM layers, although TCP does equate with the transport layer (layer 4), and IP equates with the network layer (layer 3).

† In effect, this is the OSIRM physical and data link layer.

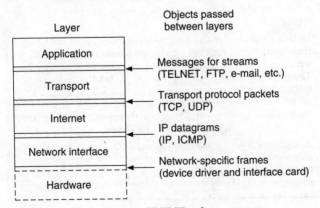

Figure 1.7 The four layers of TCP/IP software.

can ignore all those details. UDP, on the other hand, provides a much simpler service to the application layer. It sends packets of data called *datagrams* from one host to the other, but there is no guarantee that the datagrams will be delivered to the other end. Any desired reliability must be added by the application layer.

4. The *application layer* handles the details of the particular application. There are many common TCP/IP applications that almost every implementation provides. Among them are the following:

- TELNET, for remote login
- FTP, the File Transfer Protocol
- SMTP, the Simple Mail Transfer Protocol for electronic mail
- SNMP, the Simple Network Management Protocol

See Fig. 1.8.[23–27] Table 1.5 provides added insight on the key Internet applications.[8]

Figure 1.9 shows some of the more important Internet protocols and their relationship to the OSI reference model. In this architecture, IP is

Network interface layer	This layer is responsible for accepting and transmitting IP datagrams. This layer may consist of a device driver (e.g., when the network is a local network to which the machine attaches directly) or a complex subsystem that uses its own data link protocol.
Network layer (internet layer)	This layer handles communication from one machine to the other. It accepts a request to send data from the transport layer along with the identification of the destination. It encapsulates the transport layer data unit in an IP datagram and uses the datagram routing algorithm to determine whether to send the datagram directly onto a router. The internet layer also handles the incoming datagrams and uses the routing algorithm to determine whether the datagram is to be processed locally or forwarded.
Transport layer	In this layer the software segments the stream of data being transmitted into small data units and passes each packet along with a destination address to the next layer for transmission. The software adds information to the packets, including codes (called *sockets*) that identify which application program sent it as well as a checksum. This layer also regulates the flow of information and provides reliable transport, ensuring that data arrives in sequence and with no errors.
Application layer	At this level, users invoke application programs to access available services across the TCP/IP internet. The application program chooses the kind of transport needed, which can be either messages or stream of bytes, and passes it to the transport level.

Figure 1.8 Functionality of the TCP/IP suite layers.

TABLE 1.5   Internet Applications

- E-Mail
    - —The most popular Internet application
    - —user@organization.domain
        - —com, edu, gov, net, org, mil
            - —Foreign networks (e.g., .uk, .fr, .jp)
    - —Most LAN packages support SMTP
- File Transfer Protocol (FTP)
    - —Over 8000 servers
    - —Files (compressed or not) and executables
    - —Login with password or as "anonymous"
- Archie
    - —The FTP search tool
    - —Archie derived from the word *archive*
    - —Updated by monthly polls
    - —Minimal commands and overwhelmed with evolving information
- TELNET
    - —Basic terminal emulation
    - —Gain control of a server or workstation on the Internet
    - —For example, "telnet archie.rutgers.edu"
- Gopher
    - —Developed by University of Minnesota
    - —Client/server menu-driven interface
    - —"All the Gophers Servers in the World" list (approx. 1800)
    - —Most are run by universities
- Network News (USENET)
    - —Collection of special-interest bulletin boards
    - —On the order of 5500
    - —Divided into general categories (e.g., comp, biz, sci, etc.)
    - —Many are serious while many are pure leisure
    - —Very specific and sometimes amazing (e.g., sci.biology.redbees.reproduction)
- World Wide Web (WWW)
    - —The Web "home page" is at top of a hierarchy
    - —Popular among businesses
    - —Based on hypertext, graphics, and images
    - —Most popular browser is Netscape Navigator (also Mosaic and Microsoft's Internet Explorer)
    - —Mosaic developed at National Center for Supercomputing (NCSA) at the University of Illinois Urbana-Champaign
- Other protocols are Ping, WAIS, whois, SNMP, NFS, DNS, TCP, UDP, etc.

responsible for relaying packets of data (protocol data units) from node to node. IP provides the basis for connectionless best-effort packet delivery service. IP can work in conjunction with the ICMP control and error message protocol. ICMP is used by gateways (that is, routers) and hosts to send reports of problems back to the original source that sent the

	OSI reference model		Internet protocol suite	
7	Application		FTP, TELNET	NFS
6	Presentation		SMTP, SNMP	XDR
5	Session			RPC
4	Transport		TCP	UDP
3	Network		Routing protocols	IP, IPX
2	Link		LLC/MAC	
1	Physical		Not specified	

Figure 1.9   Internet protocol suite and the OSI Reference Model.

packet. TCP is responsible for verifying the correct delivery of data from the sender to the receiver. TCP allows a process on one end system to send a stream of data to a process on another end system. It is connection-oriented: before transmitting data, participants must establish a connection. Since data can be lost in the intermediate network(s), TCP adds support to detect lost data and to trigger retransmission until the data is correctly and completely received.

TCP and IP are separate protocols with separate jobs. TCP's job is to provide a reliable mechanism for computers to transmit data over one or more interconnected networks. Data must be delivered reliably, in sequence, completely, and with no duplication, in spite of the fact that there may be multiple networks along the way. IP's job is to move (specifically, to route) frames of data over each of the networks that sit between the computers that want to communicate. IP provides for the carriage of datagrams from a source host to destination hosts, possibly passing through one or more gateways (routers) and networks in the process. An IP protocol data unit (datagram) is a finite-length sequence of bits containing a header and a payload. The header information identifies the source, destination, length, handling advice, and characteristics of the payload contents. The payload is the actual data transported. Both end-system hosts and routers in an Internet are involved in the processing of the IP headers. The hosts must create and transmit them, and process them on receipt; the routers must examine them for the purpose of making routing decisions, and modify them, if needed, as the IP packets make their way from the source to the destination. See Fig. 1.10 for an illustration of encapsulation and decapsulation of IP packets across routers in an Internet.

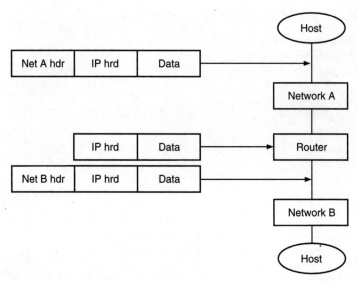

Figure 1.10   Encapsulation and decapsulation of IP packets across routers in an Internet.

1.2.4   Interconnection approach

The Internet is not a single circumscribable network but rather a "network of networks," all of which conform to a common set of protocols for connection and traffic-handling purposes. Similarly, a corporate internet is by definition a group of two or more interconnected subsystems. In computing and communications, the word *protocol* is used the same way as in diplomacy—it is just a recognized way of establishing who does what and in which order things happen. The TCP/IP protocol suite allows computers of all sizes, from many different computer vendors, running totally different operating systems, to communicate with each other. The "transmission control" aspect handles the partition of messages into packages and its reassembly for delivery to the user, while the "internet protocol" aspect takes care of addressing and routing, ensuring that the right packets get to the right places. It is an open system in that the definition of the protocol suite and many of its implementations are publicly available at little or no charge.[33–38]

How are TCP/IP networks interconnected to form an internetwork? The answer has two parts. Physically, two networks can be connected only by a communication nth-layer relay device that attaches to both of them. A physical attachment does not provide the interconnection needed for the internet, because such a connection does not guarantee that the computer will cooperate with end systems that wish to communicate. To have a viable internet, the computers should be able to process,

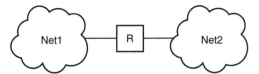

Figure 1.11 Two physical networks interconnected by R, a router (IP gateway).

filter, forward, route, and pass packets from one network to another;
these computers are called *internet gateways,* or *internet routers.*[23-27]

Figure 1.11 shows router R connected to both physical networks
1 and 2. For R to act as a router, it must capture packets on network
1 that are bound for machines on network 2 and transfer them and vice
versa.

When internet connections become more complex, routers need to
know about the topology of the internet beyond the networks to which
they connect. Figure 1.12 shows three networks interconnected by two
routers. In this example, router R1 must transfer from network 1 to
network 2 all packets destined for host computers on either network 2
or 3. For a large internet composed of many networks, the router's task
of making decisions about where to send the packets becomes more
complex. The idea of a router seems simple, but it is very important
because it provides a way to interconnect networks. It must know how
to route packets to their destination. Routers used with TCP/IP are
often powerful processors with large main memories and sometimes
limited disk storage. These topics are revisited later in more detail. The
reader may wish to refer to Ref. 30 for a complete discussion of routing
protocols.

1.3 Internet Addresses: Foundations
for Internet and Intranets

An IP address is used to uniquely identify host computer connections
to the IP-based network. A computer can have more than one network
connection; each network connection is assigned a *unique* IP address.
Uniqueness is a requirement for reliable communications. It is impor-

Figure 1.12   Three networks interconnected by two routers.

tant to note, however, that an IP address uniquely identifies a network connection, not necessarily a computer. Multiple IP addresses are used when there is more than one port on a system requiring connectivity (e.g., multiple clients on an internet service who want their own address, larger systems, virtual private networks, and value-added networks).

In traditional networks IP addresses tend to be associated with specific devices. However, this is not always the case (e.g., when using SLIP/PPP); this allows such companies as America Online to provide numerous Internet connections with a specified set of IP addresses. Each computer connects to the same set of IP addresses. Each time a computer connects to the Internet, a different IP may be used. Here, different computers may use the same IP address, but their connection to the Internet takes place at different hours of the day. This allows Internet access providers to buy access lines to connect to the Internet and then rent out time on their connection line.[14-21]

IP addresses are contained within a 32-bit binary number. The address is normally divided into 4 bytes and is expressed in dotted-decimal notation—for example, 34.10.2.1. The leftmost part of the IP address determines the address class. The absolute maximum decimal value for any of the fields is 255. Rules are given for the first byte of the address and are based on the class of the IP address.

The assignment of these unique Internet IP numbers for public communication is controlled by the InterNIC service. The InterNIC will assign a Class A, B, or C network ID (discussed in the next section) for a (customer) network. It is up to the receiver of this network ID to assign subnet addresses and host IDs on their network.

1.3.1 Addressing scheme

Each host (end system) on a TCP/IP internet,* particularly when connected to the Internet, is assigned a unique, registered, 32-bit *internet address* or *IP address* that is used in all communication with that host. The Internet address scheme is designed to make routing efficient. Specifically, an IP address encodes the identification of the network to which a host attaches, as well as the identification of a unique host on that network.

An IP address is 32 bits in length, traditionally divided into either two or three parts. The first part designates the network address (*netid*); the second part (if present) designates the subnet address; and the final part designates the host address (*hostid*). Subnet addresses are present only if the network administrator has decided that the net-

---

* That is to say, each end system that incorporates a TCP/IP protocol entity.

work should be divided into subnetworks. The lengths of the network, subnet, and host fields are all variable.

Class A addresses are used with networks that have more than 65,536 hosts and devote 7 bits to *netid* and 24 bits to *hostid.* Class A network can theoretically have 16,777,216 host computers. Class B addresses are used with intermediate-size networks that have between 256 and 65,536 hosts and allocate 14 bits to *netid* and 16 bits to *hostid;* these networks can theoretically have 65,536 hosts. Class C addresses are used with networks that have less than 256 hosts and allocate 21 bits to *netid* and only 8 bits to *hostid;* there can be up to 256 hosts each in each network. Given an IP address, its class can be determined from the 3 high-order bits. (See Fig. 1.13).

The IP address has been defined in such a way that it is possible to extract the *hostid* or *netid* portions quickly. Routers use the *netid* portion of an address when deciding where to send a packet. Thus a router connecting *n* networks has *n* distinct IP addresses, one for each network connection. Internet addresses can be used to refer to networks as well as individual hosts. By convention, an address that has all bits of the *hostid* equal to 0 is reserved to the network. Figure 1.14 shows three

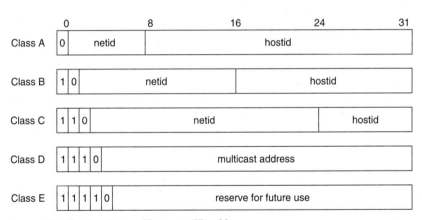

Figure 1.13   The five forms of Internet (IP) addresses.

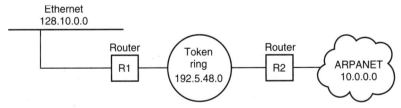

Figure 1.14   The logical connection of two networks to the Internet backbone. Each network has been assigned an IP address.

networks and the network numbers they have been assigned: the ARPANet (10.0.0.0), an Ethernet (128.10.0.0), and a token ring network (192.5.48.0). The assigned addresses are Class A, Class B, and Class C, respectively. IP addresses are assigned according to a scheme intended to allow large networks to manage large numbers of addresses and small networks to manage small parts of the IP address space.

Encoding network information in an internet address does have some disadvantages. The most obvious disadvantage is that addresses refer to network connections, not to the host computer. If a host computer moves from one network to another, its IP address must change. Another weakness of the internet addressing scheme is that when any Class C network grows to more than 256 hosts, it must have its address changed to Class B (or get multiple Class C addresses).

1.3.1.1   Class A address.   Class A addresses utilize 7 bits in the first byte to define the network ID (*netid*) of the address. *The value of the first byte for Class A addresses ranges from 0 to 127*. The remaining 3 bytes define the host ID (*hostid*) or local portion of the address. A value of 127 should never be used to define a network ID. The IP address of 127.0.0.0 is reserved by the IP standards as a loopback address to use for diagnostics and interprocess communication purposes. An example of a Class A address:

Internal net ID	Local host ID
74.	103. 14.138

1.3.1.2   Class B address.   Class B addresses utilize 14 bits in the first and second bytes to define the network ID portion of the address. *The value of the first byte for Class B addresses ranges from 128 to 191*. The host ID is defined within the last two bytes. An example of a Class B address:

Internal net ID	Local host ID
134.64.	143.24

1.3.1.3   Class C Address.   Class C addresses utilize 21 bits in the first three bytes to define the network ID portion of the address. *The value of the first byte for Class C addresses ranges from 192 to 223*. The last byte defines the host ID. An example of a class C address:

Internal net ID	Local host ID
199.31.78.	132

Figure 1.15 illustrates examples of the address classes.

1.3.1.4   Other classes.   There are also Class D addresses, used for multicasting, and experimental Class E addresses. Specifically, Class D

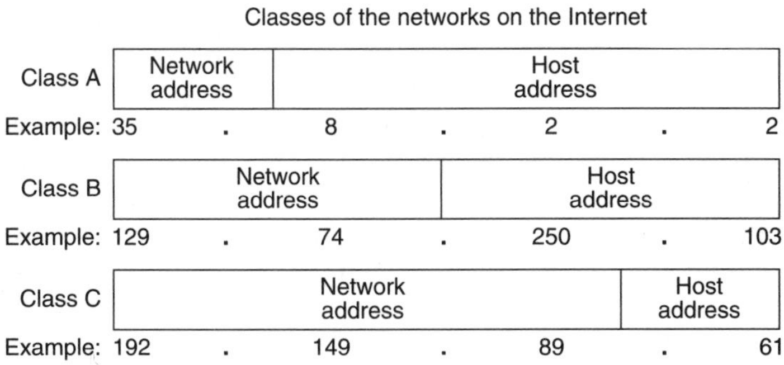

Classes of the networks on the Internet

Class A	Network address	Host address		

Example: 35   .   8   .   2   .   2

Class B	Network address	Host address	

Example: 129   .   74   .   250   .   103

Class C	Network address	Host address

Example: 192   .   149   .   89   .   61

Figure 1.15   Classes of networks.

addresses are reserved for multicast groups, as described formally in RFC 1112. In general use of the Internet, you will not encounter these addresses.[39]

As noted, to ensure that the network portion of an Internet address is unique, all Internet addresses are assigned by a central authority. The Internet Assigned Number Authority (IANA) has ultimate control over numbers assigned. Internet addresses can be obtained from the Internet Network Information Center (InterNIC).[23–27] Private networks not connected to the Internet can create, assign, and track their own IP addresses, including the *netid*. Once the company decides to access the Internet, however, addressing conflicts will likely occur. For this reason, it has been recommended that even private networks apply to the InterNIC for IP addresses.* The InterNIC Registration Services gives more control over IP addresses to certain large organizations, such as regional networks.

One can assume that the *netid* portion of the IP address corresponds to a physical site, which may contain more than one physical network. The physical site can be spread over a wide geographic area, but it tends to represent one private network entity. IP networks can also be divided into smaller units, called *subnets*. The local portion of the address is divided into two parts, identifying a physical network (or subnet) and a host. In the Class A example, 74.103.14.138, the unique subnet is identified as 103.14.

Subnets provide extra flexibility for network administrators. For example, assume that a network has been assigned a Class B address and all the nodes on the network currently conform to a class B address format. Then assume that the dotted-decimal representation of this network's address is 128.10.0.0 (all zeros in the host field of an address

---

* Now the approach of Network Address Translation (NAT) has been advanced to conserve numbers, among other reasons.

specifies the entire network). Rather than change all the addresses to some other basic network number, the administrator can subdivide the network using subnetting. This is done by borrowing bits from the host portion of the address and using them as a subnet field, as shown in Fig. 1.16.

If a network administrator has chosen to use 8 bits of subnetting, the third octet of a Class B IP address provides the subnet number. For example, address 128.10.1.0 refers to network 128.10, subnet 1; address 128.10.2.0 refers to network 128.10, subnet 2; and so on.

The number of bits borrowed for the subnet address is variable. To specify how many bits are used, IP provides the subnet mask. Subnet masks use the same format and representation technique as IP addresses. Subnet masks have 1s in all bits except those bits that specify the host field. For example, the subnet mask that specifies 8 bits of subnetting for Class A address 34.0.0.0 is 255.255.0.0. The subnet mask that specifies 16 bits of subnetting for Class A address 34.0.0.0 is 255.255.255.0.

1.3.2 Network byte order

When software on one computer sends a 32-bit binary integer to another computer, the sequence of the bits should not change. However, not all machines store 32-bit integers in the same way. On some (called *little endian*), the lowest memory address contains the low-order byte of the integer. On the others (called *big endian*), the lowest memory address contains the high-order byte of the integer. Thus, direct copying of bytes from one machine to another may change the value of the number. The TCP/IP protocols solve the byte-order problem by defining a *network standard byte order* that all machines must use for binary fields in an Internet packet. The Internet standard for byte order specifies that the big-endian approach be used, namely, integers are sent with the most significant byte first.

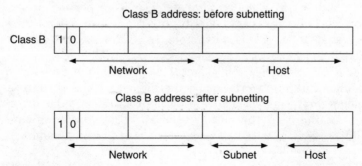

Figure 1.16 Subnet address.

1.3.3 Domain name server and IP addresses

The domain name service (DNS) is a hierarchical, distributed method of organizing the name space of the Internet. The DNS administratively groups hosts into a hierarchy of authority that allows addressing and other information to be widely distributed and maintained. A key advantage to the DNS is that using it eliminates dependence on a centrally maintained file that maps host names to addresses. DNS is supported via a set of network-resident servers, also called domain name servers.

The IP address is a numeric address that serves a role analogous to a telephone number. In representation, IP addresses always consist of four numbers: four decimal values separated by periods. Figure 1.17 illustrates the IP addresses. The computer named mugwump.cl.msu. edu, for instance, is assigned a number of 35.8.1.212. The reason a computer would have two names is that IP addresses are numeric; they can be easily understood and manipulated by the hardware and software that must move information over the Internet. So IP addresses are better-suited to computers, and domain addresses are better-suited to humans. DNS allows a translation between the domain name and the IP address. Domain names do not necessarily have four parts. They might have only two parts—a top-level domain such as "edu" or "com," preceded by a subdomain—or three, four, or many (see Fig. 1.18). The only limitations are (1) a domain-style name cannot exceed 255 characters and (2) each part of the name cannot exceed 63 characters.[40]

1.3.4 Mapping Internet addresses to physical addresses

As discussed in the previous section, in the TCP/IP address scheme, each device is assigned a 32-bit address that is used when sending and receiving packets. We can see that two machines can easily communicate on a physical network *only if they know each other's physical network address.*

IP addresses read from general to specific:

35.8.1.212

Network address   Host address

The middle parts of the IP address can belong to the network address or to host address depending on the "class" of the network

Figure 1.17   IP addresses.

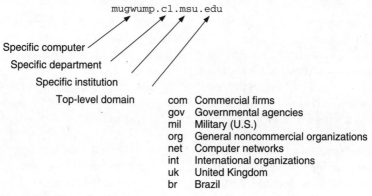

Figure 1.18   Domain names.

1.3.4.1 Address Resolution Protocol (ARP).

Consider two machines, A and B, that share a physical network. Each has assigned IP address IA and IB and a physical address PA and PB. The goal is to devise low-level software that hides physical addresses and allows higher-level programs to work with internet addresses. Suppose machine A wants to send a packet to machine B across a physical network. A has only B's internet address IB. The question arises: How does A map that address to B's physical address PB? The problem of high-level addresses to physical address is known as the *address resolution problem.*[23–27]

We stated earlier that each Ethernet interface is assigned a 48-bit physical address when the device is manufactured. As a consequence, when hardware fails and requires that an Ethernet interface be replaced, the machine's physical address changes. Furthermore, the 48-bit Ethernet address cannot be encoded in a 32-bit IP address.

On these and other networks (e.g., ATM) physical addresses and IP addresses are dynamically discovered through the use of two other members of the Internet protocol suite: the Address Resolution Protocol (ARP) and the Reserve Address Resolution Protocol (RARP). The TCP/IP protocols have a solution to the address resolution problem for networks like the Ethernet that have broadcast capabilities. ARP uses broadcast messages to determine the hardware media access control (MAC)–layer address corresponding to a particular internetwork address. ARP is sufficiently generic to allow use of IP with any type of underlying media-access mechanism. RARP uses broadcast messages to determine the IP address associated with a particular hardware address. RARP is particularly important to disk-

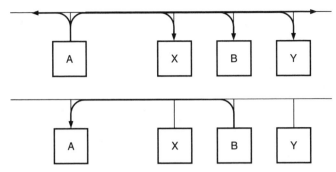

Figure 1.19   The Address Resolution Protocol.

less nodes, which may not know their internetwork address when they boot.[33-38]

The ARP is a low-level protocol that provides an easy and efficient mechanism to bind addresses dynamically. Figure 1.19 shows the idea behind dynamic resolution with ARP. When host A wants to resolve IP address IB, it broadcasts a special packet that asks the host with IP address IB to respond with its physical address PB. All hosts receive the packet, but only host B recognizes its IP address and sends a reply that contains its physical address. Host A will use the physical address to send internet packets directly to B. To make ARP efficient, each machine caches IP-to-physical-address bindings (*bindings* are associations or mappings). Because internet traffic tends to consist of a sequence of interactions between pairs of machines, the cache eliminates most ARP broadcast requests. Information stays in the cache for a specified amount of time (e.g., 15 minutes); this interval is hardware/vendor-dependent.

1.4   Internet Protocol: Basis for Internet and Intranets

1.4.1   Connectionless datagram delivery

As discussed in the previous sections, Internet software is designed based on three conceptual networking services:

- Application services
- Reliable transport service
- Connectionless packet delivery service

Much of the Internet success has resulted because this architecture is surprisingly robust and adaptable. One of the advantages of the conceptual separation is that it becomes possible to replace one service without disturbing others. These same concepts and techniques apply directly to a private internet.

The most fundamental Internet/internet service consists of a packet delivery system. The service is defined as a best-effort, unreliable, connectionless packet delivery system. The service is called *unreliable* because delivery is not guaranteed. The packet may be lost, duplicated, delayed, or delivered out of order, but the system will not detect such conditions, nor will it inform the sender or receiver. "Somebody else" besides IP has to worry about this. The service is connectionless at the network layer because each packet is treated independently from all others. A sequence of IP packets sent from one computer to another could travel over different paths (e.g., if a router table has been updated since transmission of the last packet).

The protocol that defines this networking service is IP. IP provides three important definitions. First, the IP defines the basic unit of data transfer; it specifies the exact format of all data as it passes across the TCP/IP network. Second, IP software performs the routing function, choosing a path over which data will be sent. Third, IP includes a set of rules that characterize how hosts and routers should process packets and how and when error messages should be generated.

1.4.2   The Internet datagram

The *IP datagram* (that is, the network layer protocol data unit) consists of a datagram header and datagram data, where the datagram header includes the source and destination IP addresses. (See Fig. 1.20.)

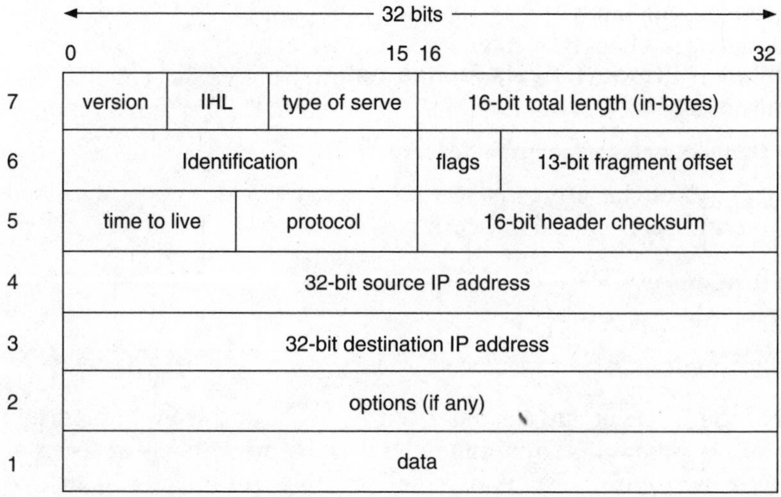

	version	IHL	type of serve	16-bit total length (in-bytes)		
	Identification			flags	13-bit fragment offset	
	time to live		protocol	16-bit header checksum		
	32-bit source IP address					
	32-bit destination IP address					
	options (if any)					
	data					

Figure 1.20   IP packet format (IPv4).

Because the datagram is processed by the software, the contents and the format of the datagram are not constrained by any hardware. The first 4-bit field (*VERS*) contains the version of the IP that was used when the datagram was created. Receivers will reject datagrams with protocol versions that differ from theirs, preventing them from being misinterpreted. Currently, the IP version is 4.

The 4-bit IP HEADER LENGTH (*IHL*), gives the datagram header length measured in 32-bit words. That means if the header length field is equal to 5, then the header measures $5 \times 32 = 160$ bits, or 20 bytes.

The *TOTAL LENGTH* field gives the length of the IP datagram measured in bytes, including bytes in the header and data. The *TOTAL LENGTH* field is 16 bits long; the maximum possible size of an IP datagram is 2^{16} or 65,535 bytes.

The *SERVICE TYPE* or TYPE OF SERVICE (TOS), specifies how the datagram should be handled; it contains *precedence* bits ranging from 0 to 7. Although most of the host's and the router's software ignores type of service, it is important to have precedence over data. For example, if all hosts and routers honor precedence, it is possible to implement congestion algorithms that are not affected by the congestion they are trying to control.

FRAGMENTATION takes place as follows. In the ideal case, the entire datagram fits into one physical frame, making transmission across the physical network efficient. Each packet-switching technology has a different physical frame size. For example, the Ethernet limits transfers to 1500 bytes (the actual frame is 1518 bytes), while FDDI permits a maximum of 4500 bytes per frame. This is referred to as a *maximum transfer unit* (MTU). Problems will arise when trying to transfer data from large MTU networks to smaller MTU networks. The TCP/IP software chooses a convenient datagram size and arranges a way to fragment a large datagram into smaller pieces when the datagram needs to be sent to a smaller MTU network; this process is called *fragmentation*. Fragmentation usually occurs at a router. Figure 1.21

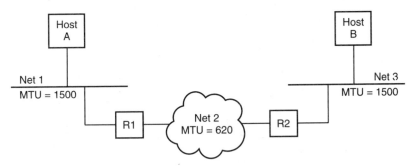

Figure 1.21   An internet with different MTU networks.

shows the router receiving a datagram from a network with a large MTU and sending over a network for which the MTU is smaller. Router R1 fragments a large datagram sent from host A to host B; router R2 fragments a large datagram sent from B to A.

Time to live (TTL) specifies how long, in seconds, the datagram is allowed to remain in the internet system. Routers and hosts that process a datagram must decrement the *time to live* as time passes and must remove the datagram from the internet when its time expires.

Protocol field is analogous to the type field in a network frame. The value is that the *Protocol* field specifies which high-level protocol was used to create the message being carried in the data area of a datagram.

1.4.3   IP routing concepts

In a packet-switching network *routing* refers to the process of choosing a path over which to send packets, and a *router* refers to a device making such choice. Within a wide area network that has multiple physical connections, the network itself is responsible for routing packets from the time they enter until the time they leave. In a corporate internet where the user employs a set of dedicated lines provided by a carrier (with the carrier adding no additional intelligence), the router will (often) be required to appropriately route and move packets to the destination. Routing can be divided into two forms: *direct delivery* and *indirect delivery*.[23–27]

Two systems can engage in *direct delivery* only if they both attach directly to the same physical network (e.g., a single Ethernet). The sender system encapsulates the datagram in a physical frame, which binds the destination IP address to a physical hardware address and sends the resulting frame directly to the destination. For the sender to know whether the destination is on the same physical network, it extracts the network-specific prefix from the IP address and compares it to its own IP address. This works because the internet address of all machines on a single network include a common network prefix.

Indirect delivery occurs when the destination is not on a directly attached network, forcing the sender machine to pass the datagram to a router for delivery. When one host wants to send data to the other, it encapsulates the datagram and sends it to the default gateway router. Once the frame reaches the router, software extracts the encapsulated datagram, and the IP selects the next router along the path toward the destination. The datagram is again placed in a frame and sent over the next physical network to a second router, and so on, until it can reach the destination network.

Routing devices in the Internet have traditionally been called *gateways* (elsewhere in the industry, the term applies to a device with a somewhat different function; hence, from this point forward we call gateways by their more accurate name: *routers.*) Routers within the Internet are organized hierarchically. Some routers are used to move information through one particular group of networks under the same administrative authority and control (such an entity is called an *autonomous system*). Routers used for information exchange *within* autonomous systems are called *interior routers,* and they use a variety of *interior gateway protocols* (IGPs) to accumulate topology information to accomplish this purpose. Routers that move information *between* autonomous systems are called *exterior routers,* and they use an *exterior gateway protocol* for this purpose. The internet architecture is shown in Fig. 1.22.

IP routing protocols are dynamic. Dynamic routing calls for routes to be calculated at regular intervals by software in the routing devices. This contrasts with static routing, where routes are established by the network administrator and do not change until the network administrator changes them. An IP routing table consists of destination-address/next-hop pairs. A sample entry, shown in Fig. 1.23, is interpreted to mean "to get to network 34.1.0.0 (subnet 1 on network 34), the next stop is the node at address 54.34.23.12."

IP routing specifies that IP datagrams travel through internetworks one hop at a time. The entire route is not known at the outset of the journey. Instead, at each stop, the next destination is determined by matching the destination address within the datagram with an entry

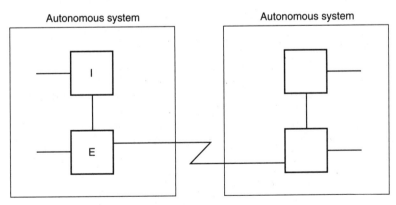

E = Exterior gateway
I = Interior gateway

Figure 1.22   Architecture of an internet (with a small *i*).

	Next hop
34.1.0.0	54.34.23.12
78.2.0.0	54.34.23.12
147.8.5.0	54.32.12.10
17.12.0.0	54.32.12.10

Figure 1.23   IP routing table.

in the current node's routing table. Each node's involvement in the routing process consists only of forwarding packets based on internal information, regardless of whether the packets get to their final destination. In other words, IP does not provide for error reporting back to the source when routing anomalies occur. This task is left to the ICMP.

A physical network can be built using commercially available IP (or more generally, multiprotocol) router devices. Each router has tables with entries to translate the subnets into a selected destination on that subnet or another subnet on that router. If the *netid* of the destination IP address does not match the *netid* of the sender of the message, the outgoing IP datagram will be sent by the router to an external gateway for delivery to the target host on the foreign network. Networks must be updated as new subnets and departments are added, but it is not affected by changes outside that physical network or the movement of machines within that subnet.

When an IP packet arrives at a router, the decision about where to send it next is made by the router. Consider a company with facilities in Massachusetts, California, Texas, and Washington. It could build a network from four communication lines forming a loop (Massachusetts to Texas to California to Washington). A message arriving at the Massachusetts router could go to the California router via either the Texas router or the Washington router. The reply could come back the other way. There is no single correct answer as to how the router makes each decision for routing traffic. However, they generally use the shortest available path or the path with greater bandwidth. Traffic could be routed by the clockwise algorithm (go Massachusetts to Texas, California to Washington). The routers could alternate, sending one message to Texas and the next to Washington. More sophisticated routing measures traffic patterns and sends data through the least-busy link.[14–21]

If a communication line in this network breaks down, traffic can still reach its destination through a roundabout path. After losing the Massachusetts to Texas line, for example, data can be sent from Massachusetts to Washington to California to Texas. This provides continued service, although the performance is degraded. This kind of recovery is the primary design feature of IP. The loss of the line is immediately detected by the routers in Massachusetts and Washington, but somehow this information must be sent to the other nodes. Otherwise, California could continue to send Massachusetts messages through Texas, where they arrive at a dead end. Each network utilizes some router protocol that periodically updates the routing tables throughout the network with information about changes in route status.[30]

The complexity and cost of transmitting the routing updates will increase as a function of the size of the network. As the network grows larger, updates become more complicated. Building a single network that covers the entire United States would be complicated. Fortunately, the Internet is designed to be the network of networks (large corporate internets should be similarly partitioned). This means that loops and redundancy are built into each regional carrier. The regional network handles its own problems and reroutes messages internally. Its routing protocol updates the tables in its own routers, but no routing updates need to propagate from a regional carrier to the Internet backbone or to the other regions (unless, of course, a subscriber switches permanently from one region to another).[14-21]

Sometimes the router finds itself having to handle an excessive amount of data transmission. When data arrives at a congested router there is no place to hold the overflow. Excess packets must then be discarded. It becomes the responsibility of the sender to retry the data a few seconds later and to persist until it finally gets through.

This built-in recovery is provided by the TCP component of the TCP/IP protocol. TCP was designed to automatically recover from node or line failures where the network propagates routing table changes to router nodes. Since the updates take time, TCP may be slow to initiate recovery. The TCP algorithms are not optimally tuned to handle packet loss due to traffic congestion. Instead, the traditional Internet response to traffic problems has been to increase the speed of lines and equipment in order to stay ahead of the demand for growth. TCP handles the data as a stream of bytes. It logically assigns a sequence number to each byte. The TCP packet has a header that reads, in effect, "This packet starts with byte 546982 and contains 300 bytes of data." The receiver detects missing or incorrectly sequenced packets. TCP acknowledges data received and retransmits data that is lost. The TCP design recovers data automatically.[14-21]

1.4.4 Table-driven IP routing and next-hop routing

As implied by the discussion in the previous section, for the hosts and routers to know to which route they should send the data until it reaches the destination, a *table-driven IP routing algorithm* must be employed by the IP software. The *IP routing table* stores information on both hosts and routers, about all possible destinations and how to reach them. It is more efficient to have the router make decisions with minimal information. The IP address scheme helps achieve this goal, because the IP routing software keeps information only about destination network address prefixes, not the individual host addresses. More important, the host's addresses will be handled by the local environment in which those hosts operate.[23-27]

A routing table contains pairs (N, R), where N is the IP address of a destination network, and R is the IP address of the "next" router along the path to network N. All routers listed in any machine routing table must lie on the physical network to which that machine is connected. When a datagram has been received by the router, the IP software locates the IP address and extracts the network portion. The router then makes the routing decision with the help of the routing table and selects the router that can be reached directly.

Figure 1.24 shows an internet that consists of four networks and three routers. The routing table gives the routing information that R uses. Because R connects directly to networks 20.0.0.0 and 30.0.0.0, it can use direct delivery to hosts on either of those networks. Given a datagram destined for a host on network 40.0.0.0, R routes it to address 30.0.0.7, which is the address of router S, which is connected to the same physical network 30.0.0.0. S will then deliver the datagram directly in the 40.0.0.0 network.

1.4.5   Routing-related protocols

1.4.5.1   ICMP.   Another protocol in the TCP/IP suite is ICMP. ICMP is used for error messages such as occur when something is detectably

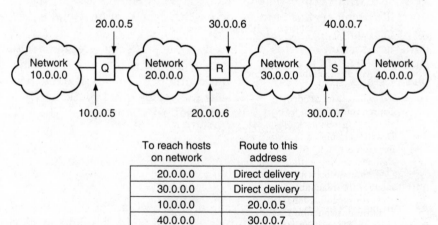

To reach hosts on network	Route to this address
20.0.0.0	Direct delivery
30.0.0.0	Direct delivery
10.0.0.0	20.0.0.5
40.0.0.0	30.0.0.7

Routing table in router *R*

Figure 1.24   Internet with four networks and three routers.

wrong with the packet format, with the selection of a router, or with the condition of some intermediate node in the internet. Such abnormal conditions are reported to the source of the datagram for possible remedial action. For example, if you attempt to connect to a host, the user's system may get back an ICMP message saying "host unreachable" (Table 1.6 shows examples of ICMP codes). ICMP can also be used to find out some information about the network. ICMP is similar to UDP in that it handles messages that fit in one datagram. However, it is even simpler than UDP (discussed later). It does not even have port numbers (sockets) in its header. Since all ICMP messages are interpreted by the network software itself, no port numbers are needed to say where an ICMP message is supposed to go.[40]

Although the principal reason ICMP was created was to report routing failures back to the source, ICMP provides helpful messages, such as the following:

- Echo and echo reply (PING) messages to test node reachability across an internetwork

- Redirect messages to stimulate more efficient routing

- Time exceeded messages to inform sources that a datagram has exceeded its allocated time to exist within the internetwork

- Router advertisement and router solicitation messages to determine the addresses of routers on directly attached subnetworks

ICMP also provides a way for new nodes to discover the subnet mask currently used in an internetwork. Hence, ICMP is an integral part of any IP implementation, particularly those that run in routers.[33-38]

TABLE 1.6   ICMP Destination Unreachable Codes

0	Net unreachable
1	Host unreachable
2	Protocol unreachable
3	Port unreachable
4	Fragmentation needed; do-not-fragment flag set
5	Source route failed
6	Destination network unknown
7	Destination host unknown
8	Source host isolated
9	Communication with destination network administratively prohibited
10	Communication with destination host administratively prohibited
11	Network unreachable for selected type of service
12	Host unreachable for selected type of service
13	Communication administratively prohibited due to filtering
14	Host precedence violation; requested precedence for two packets is not permitted
15	Precedence cutoff in effect; network operators have imposed a minimum level of precedence required for acceptance of any packets

1.4.5.2 IRDP. The ICMP Router Discovery Protocol (IRDP) uses router advertisement and router solicitation messages to discover addresses of routers on directly attached subnets. The way IP works is that each router periodically multicasts router advertisement messages from each of its interfaces. Hosts discover the addresses of routers on the directly attached subnet by listening for these messages. Hosts can use router solicitation messages to request immediate advertisements, rather than waiting for unsolicited messages.

IRDP offers several advantages over other methods of discovering addresses of neighboring routers. Primarily, it does not require hosts to recognize routing protocols, nor does it require manual configuration by an administrator. Router advertisement messages allow hosts to discover the existence of neighboring routers, but not which router is best to reach a particular destination. If a host uses a poor first-hop router to reach a particular destination, it receives a redirect message identifying a better choice.

1.4.5.3 IP multicast. The Internet protocol suite was designed for communication between two computers using unicast addresses (that is, an address specifying a single network device). To send a message to all devices connected to the network, a network device uses a broadcast address. These two forms of addressing have been sufficient for transferring traditional data (such as files and virtual terminal connections).

Now that application developers are trying to deliver the same data (such as the audio and video required for conferencing) to some, but not all, devices connected to the network, another form of addressing is required. This form of addressing is called *multicast addressing,* and it involves the transmission of a single IP datagram to multiple hosts. This section describes the following techniques for supporting IP multicast addresses:

- UDP flooding
- Subnet broadcast
- Internet Group Membership Protocol

Because IP networks tend to have complex topologies with alternate paths built in for redundancy, each technique is evaluated for its ability to deliver data without burdening the network with duplicate packets.

1.4.5.4 UDP flooding. UDP* flooding depends on the Spanning Tree Algorithm (STA) capabilities to place interfaces in the forwarding

---

* UDP itself is covered in a later section.

and blocking states (see Ref. 32 for a discussion of STA). By placing certain interfaces in the blocking state, the STA prevents the propagation of duplicate packets. The forwarding device sends specific packets (typically, UDP packets) out the interfaces that are in the forwarding state. This technique saves bandwidth by controlling packet flow in topologies that feature redundant routers and alternate paths to the same destination. Figure 1.25 illustrates packet flow.[33–38]

1.4.5.5   Subnet broadcast.   Subnet broadcast (defined in RFC 922) supports broadcasting to all the subnets of a particular network number. Packet duplication occurs when there are alternative paths in a network. Whenever there is a duplicate path in the network, a duplicate packet is delivered. Because many multicast applications are data-intensive, packet duplication is a significant disadvantage of subnet broadcast.

1.4.5.6   Internet Group Membership Protocol.   Internet Group Membership Protocol (IGMP), defined in RFC 1112, relies on Class D IP

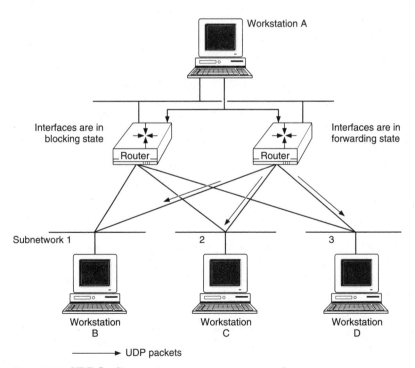

Figure 1.25   UDP flooding.

addresses for the creation of multicast groups. By using a specific Class D address, an individual host dynamically registers itself in a multicast group. Hosts identify their group memberships by sending IGMP messages. Traffic is then sent to all members of that multicast group. Routers listen to IGMP messages and periodically send out queries to discover which groups are active on which LANs. To build multicast routes for each group, routers communicate with each other using one or more of the following routing protocols[33–38]:

- Distance Vector Multicast Routing Protocol
- Multicast Open Shortest Path First
- Protocol-Independent Multicast

These routing protocols are discussed in the following sections.

1.4.5.7   Distance Vector Multicast Routing Protocol.   Distance Vector Multicast Routing Protocol (DVMRP), defined in RFC 1075, uses a technique called *reverse path flooding*. With reverse path flooding, on receipt of a packet, the router floods the packet out all paths except the path that leads back to the source of the packet, which ensures that a data stream reaches all LANs. If the router is attached to a LAN that does not want to receive a particular multicast group, the router sends a "prune" message back to the source to stop the data stream. When running DVMRP, routers periodically reflood the network to reach new hosts, using an algorithm that takes into account the frequency of flooding and the time required for a new multicast group member to receive the data stream.

To determine which interface leads back to the source of a data stream, DVMRP implements its own unicast routing protocol. The DVMRP unicast routing protocol is similar to Routing Information Protocol (RIP) and is based on hop counts only. The path that multicast traffic follows may not be the same as the path that unicast traffic follows.[33–38]

The need to reflood prevents DVMRP (especially early versions that do not implement pruning) from scaling well. In spite of its limitations, DVMRP is widely deployed in the IP research community. It has been utilized to build the multicast backbone (MBONE) across the Internet. The MBONE is used to transmit conferences and deliver desktop videoconferencing. Networks that wish to participate in the MBONE dedicate special hosts to the MBONE. The hosts establish tunnels* to

---

* *Tunneling* refers to the use of a high-level transport network service to carry packets or messages from another service. For example, routers can tunnel through an X.25 service and send IP datagrams to one another. The difference between tunneling and encapsulation lies in whether IP transmits the datagram in hardware packets or uses a high-level transport service to deliver them. IP encapsulates each datagram in a packet when it uses the hardware directly. It creates a tunnel when it uses a high-level transport delivery service to send datagrams from one point to another.[41]

each other over the IP Internet and run DVMRP over the tunnels. The MBONE is a high consumer of bandwidth because of the nature of the traffic (audio and video) and because it is implemented with host-based tunnels. Host-based tunnels tend to result in packet duplication, which the backbone networks transmit unnecessarily. Because of this, the MBONE has caused problems to the Internet when popular events or multiple events are active.

1.4.5.8 Multicast Open Shortest Path First.

Multicast Open Shortest Path First (MOSPF) is an extension to OSPF. OSPF is a unicast routing protocol that requires each router in a network to be aware of all available links in the network. Each OSPF router calculates routes from itself to all possible destinations. MOSPF works by including multicast information in OSPF link states. MOSPF calculates the routes for each source/multicast group pair when the router receives traffic for that pair. These routes are cached until a topology change occurs, which requires MOSPF to recalculate the topology.[33-38]

MOSPF works only in internetworks that are using OSPF, and it is best suited for environments in which relatively few source/group pairs are active at any one time. MOSPF performance degrades in environments that have many active source/group pairs and in environments in which links are unstable.

1.4.5.9 Protocol-Independent Multicast.

Multicast traffic tends to fall into one of two categories: (1) traffic that is intended for almost all LANs (known as *dense*) and (2) traffic that is intended for relatively few LANs (known as *sparse*). Protocol-Independent Multicast (PIM) is an Internet protocol (under discussion by the IETF Multicast Routing Working Group) that has two modes of behavior for the two traffic types: *dense mode* and *sparse mode*. A router that is running PIM can use dense mode from some multicast groups and sparse mode for other multicast groups.[33-36]

Dense mode. In dense mode (DM), PIM uses reverse path flooding and is similar to DVMRP. One significant difference between PIM and DVMRP is that PIM does not require a particular unicast protocol to determine which interface leads back to the source of a data stream. Instead, PIM uses whichever unicast protocol the internetwork is using.

Sparse mode. In sparse mode (SM), PIM is optimized for environments in which there are many data streams but each data stream goes to a relatively small number of the LANs in the internetwork. For this type of traffic, reverse path flooding wastes bandwidth. PIM-SM works by defining a rendezvous point. When a sender wants to send data, it first sends to the rendezvous point. When a host wants to receive data, it registers with the rendezvous point. Once the data stream begins to flow from the sender to the rendezvous point and to the receiver, the routers in the path optimize the path automatically to remove any unnecessary hops, including the rendezvous point.

1.4.5.10 Comparison of multicast routing protocols. Table 1.7 compares the characteristics of each routing protocol when handling multicast traffic.

1.4.5.11 The Internet over phone lines: SLIP or PPP dial-up access. SLIP (Serial Line Internet Protocol) and PPP (Point-to-Point Protocol) are schemes that make it possible for IP to communicate over dial-up lines rather than over traditional dedicated lines into the Internet.

With SLIP or PPP, you can undertake TCP/IP communications as if you were directly attached to the Internet. In order to use the options, you would install SLIP or PPP drivers that work with TCP/IP software installed on your computer. The software allows the calling computer to be assigned a temporary IP address, lasting for the duration of the telephone connection. (In some cases, the service provider may offer a permanent IP address, which will always be used when the user dials into a dedicated port.) There is some overhead to setting up such configurations, but the benefit is that you can run the same client software at home or on the road as you could over a corporate or campus network that is directly attached to the Internet.[42]

SLIP and PPP connections use a high-speed modem (e.g., 28.8 Kbps) to connect a computer to the Internet over phone lines. The user dials in, connects, and the user's computer becomes part of the Internet. The user has full access, up to the power and storage capacity of the user's computer. PPP is the newer of the two. It is a more sophisticated protocol and is able to monitor the stream of data moving over the line (it can also be used for protocols other than IP). PPP can automatically have packets retransmitted if they get garbled, something that could happen on dial-up telephone lines. Because SLIP does not check the packets being sent, it is faster than PPP, but not as reliable.[43]

TABLE 1.7 Comparison of Multicast Routing Protocols

Unicast protocol algorithm	Routing requirements	Environment
DVMRP	RIP	Small
MOSPF	OSPF	Few senders, stable links
PIM-dense mode	Any	Dense distribution pattern
PIM-sparse mode	Any	Sparse distribution pattern

SLIP is currently more widely available from commercial Internet service providers (ISP), although PPP is considered to be the eventual replacement to SLIP. This topic is treated in more detail in Sec. 1.7.1.

1.5 Transport Layer

The Internet transport layer is implemented by TCP and by the UDP. TCP provides connection-oriented data transport, while UDP operation is connectionless.* We treat UDP first.

1.5.1   User Datagram Protocol (UDP)

In many applications, there are messages that will always fit in a single datagram. An example is a name lookup. When a user attempts to make a connection to another system, he or she will generally specify the system by the name rather than by Internet address. So the user's system needs to send a query to one of the systems that uses the database to translate names to addresses. This query will be very short; it fits in one datagram. For applications like this, the most common approach is to use the User Datagram Protocol (UDP). For short transactions it is not necessary to use TCP to do this because TCP will segment information into datagrams and will also make sure that the data arrives, resending datagrams when necessary.

UDP is designed for applications where you do not need to put sequences of datagrams together. UDP is a much simpler protocol than TCP and is useful in situations where the reliability mechanisms of TCP are not necessary. The network software puts the UDP header in front of the data, just as it would a TCP header. Then the UDP process gives the data to the IP process, which adds the IP header, putting UDP's protocol number in the protocol field instead of TCP's protocol number. However, UDP does not do as much as TCP does. It does not segment data into multiple datagrams. It does not keep track of what it has sent so it can resend if necessary. The UDP header has only four fields: source port, destination port, length, and UDP checksum. The source and destination port fields serve the same functions as they do in the TCP header. The length field specifies the length of the UDP header and data, and the checksum field allows packet integrity checking. The UDP checksum is optional. UDP provides mostly just port numbers, so that several programs can use UDP at once. UDP port numbers are used just like TCP port numbers. There are well-known port numbers for servers that use UDP. Note that the UDP header is shorter than a TCP header. It still has

---

* Connectionless at the transport layer.

source and destination port numbers and a checksum, but that is about it. There are no sequence numbers, since they are not needed. UDP is used by the protocols that handle name lookup and by a number of similar protocols.[43]

1.5.2 Transmission Control Protocol (TCP)

TCP allows two computer programs to exchange information over a network or a group of networks in a reliable manner. When a computer wants to establish a dialog with another system over the Internet, it opens a TCP connection to the other computer. More precisely, when an application program, such as a TELNET or Gopher client, wants to communicate with a corresponding process on a remote computer, such as a TELNET or Gopher server, it opens a TCP connection. The connection that TCP provides between two cooperating computers allows data to move in both directions simultaneously.

TCP relies upon the services of IP to actually move the data across a series of networks hops. Each message to be sent is broken up into one or more network layer *datagrams* (network layer *protocol data units*). Each datagram may have to traverse multiple networks before reaching the destination (see Fig. 1.26). On each network along the way, a *router* determines if the destination address of each datagram it sees resides on a remote network; the router forwards datagrams

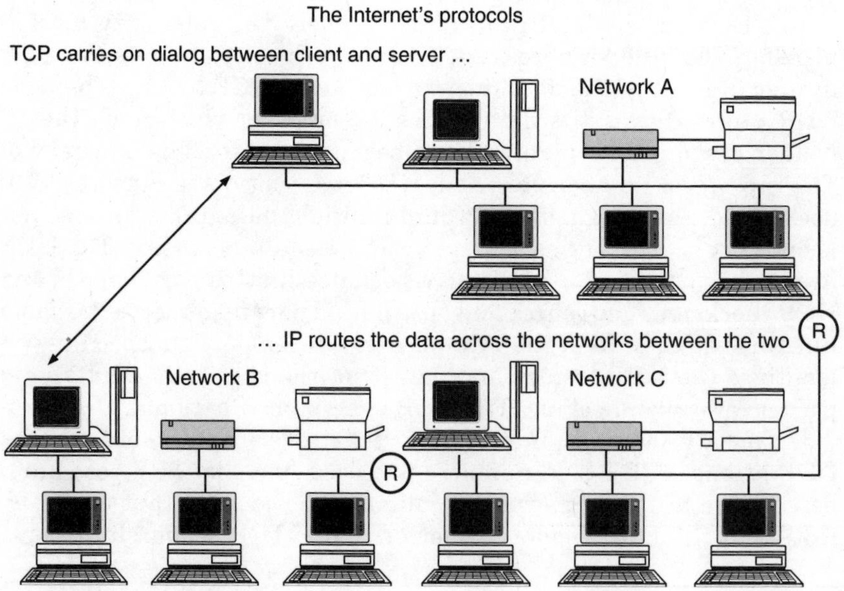

Figure 1.26 Internet's protocols.

accordingly. The data actually undergoes a series of transformations in order to be delivered. In fact, IP may have to break the datagram up into smaller fragments for efficient delivery, and the various fragments may follow different paths along the way. IP does not guarantee that it will deliver datagrams in order. As discussed, IP does not even guarantee that the datagrams will get there at all. It is the TCP's job to figure out when one does not and ask for a retransmission.

TCP provides full-duplex, acknowledged, and flow-controlled service to upper-layer protocols. It moves data in a continuous byte stream where bytes are identified by sequence numbers. TCP can also support numerous simultaneous upper-layer conversations. The TCP packet format is shown in Fig. 1.27.

The fields of the TCP packet are as follows:

- *Source port and destination port.* Identify the points at which upper-layer source and destination processes receive TCP services.

- *Sequence number.* Usually specifies the number assigned to the first byte of data in the current message. Under certain circumstances, it can also be used to identify an initial sequence number to be used in the upcoming transmission.

- *Acknowledgment number.* Contains the sequence number of the next byte of data the sender of the packet expects to receive.

- *Data offset.* Indicates the number of 32-bit words in the TCP header.

- *Reserved.* Reserved for future use.

- *Flags.* Carries a variety of control information.

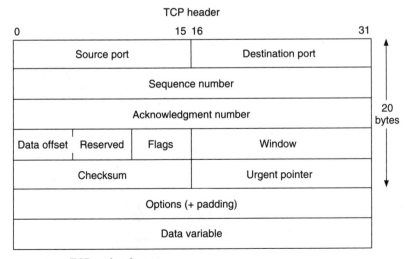

Figure 1.27 TCP packet format.

- *Window.*   Specifies the size of the sender's receive window (that is, buffer space available for incoming data).

- *Checksum.*   Indicates whether the header was damaged in transit.

- *Urgent pointer.*   Points to the first urgent data byte in the packet.

- *Options.*   Specifies various TCP options.

- *Data.*   Contains upper-layer information.

1.6   Upper-Layer Protocols

The Internet Protocol suite includes many upper-layer protocols representing a wide variety of applications, including file transfer, terminal emulation, and electronic mail. Table 1.8 maps the best-known Internet upper-layer protocols to the applications they support.

The File Transfer Protocol (FTP) provides a way to move files between computer systems. TELNET allows virtual terminal emulation. The Simple Network Management Protocol (SNMP) is a network management protocol used for reporting network conditions and setting network threshold values. X Windows is a popular protocol that permits intelligent terminals to communicate with remote computers as if they were directly attached. *Network file system* (NFS), *external data representation* (XDR), and *remote procedure call* (RPC) combine to allow transparent access to remote network resources. The Simple Mail Transfer Protocol (SMTP) provides an electronic transport mechanism. These and other network applications use the services of TCP/IP and other lower-layer Internet protocols to provide users with basic network services.[33–38]

1.6.1   SMTP

E-mail is the baseline application of the Internet and is responsible for much of its early growth. It is possible to build e-mail connections into WWW sites to provide an easy response mechanism. But e-mail, as a distinct tool in its own right, is arguably still the most powerful as well as the simplest to use.

TABLE 1.8   Internet Protocol/Application Mapping

Application	Protocols
File transfer	FTP, TFTP
Terminal emulation	TELNET
Electronic mail	SMTP
Network management	SNMP
Distributed file services	NFS, XDR, RPC, X Windows

The basic protocol for transmitting messages between computers in the Internet is the Simple Mail Transfer Protocol (SMTP). SMTP describes the allowed sequences of control messages passed between two computers to transfer a computer mail message. There are provisions for verifying that the two computers know that they are correctly connected, for identifying the message sender, for negotiating a set of recipients, and for delivering the message itself.

Users read and compose mail with a user interface application program. Most of these application programs provide extensive mail-management functions to the users. These functions are not required, or even defined, in the protocol specifications. Nonetheless, most users have available a mailbox that collects incoming messages, along with functions that aid in reviewing the contents of the mail-box.[44]

The interaction between the application program and the SMTP modules is generally through the file system. When the user has prepared a message to send, the user program leaves it in the file system, where it will be found by the sender SMTP module (sometimes called the *mailer program*). When messages arrive, the receiver SMTP program places them in the file system, where they will be found by the user program. The place in the file system where received messages are left is often called *mailbox*. Usually, the mailbox is a file or directory private to the user, and the receiver SMTP must execute as a privileged or *root* process to access it. See Fig. 1.28 for illustration of the model for SMTP use.

Originally, people tended to use only one or two specific computers. They would maintain mail files on those machines. The computer mail system is simply a way for a user to add a message to another user's mail file. There are some problems with this in an environment where PCs are used. The most serious is that a PC is not well suited to receive computer mail. When a user sends mail, the mail software

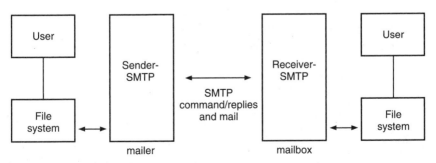

Figure 1.28   Model for SMTP use.

expects to be able to open a connection to the addressee's computer in order to send the mail. If this is a microcomputer, it may be turned off, or it may be running an application other than the mail system. For this reason, mail is normally handled by a larger system, where it is practical to have a mail server running all the time. Microcomputer mail software then becomes a user interface that retrieves mail from the mail server.

1.6.2   File Transfer Protocol

FTP is a traditional Internet application for receiving or downloading files from the Internet to a computer or sending or uploading files from a computer to another computer. FTP allows a user to connect to a remote computer and download vast quantities of documents and software for all types of computer systems. The name, IP address, or URL* must be known for the connection to be established.

Users may come across the term *anonymous FTP*. Some FTP sites allow users to use an "anonymous" user ID, with their personal e-mail ID as the password.[†] This does not mean that the person obtaining a file remains anonymous; it just means "use the ID *anonymous* when you are asked for a user ID." In fact the computer with the document library also asks for your e-mail address—not much anonymity about that. Once the connection to the host computer has been established, files can be downloaded to the desktop. Text-based FTP programs use commands such as "cd" for change directory, "get" followed by a file name for retrieving files, and "dir" for listing directories. New GUI applications allow all of this to happen with a couple clicks of the mouse.[14–21]

FTP provides mechanisms for authenticating users for the access control, setting file transmission parameters, identifying the files to be transferred, and some file and directory maintenance functions. There are three relatively independent aspects to the FTP: access control, filename, file translation.

1.6.2.1   Access control.   FTP uses the same access control procedures that the hosts normally use for access control on files. In time-sharing systems, this generally means that users must log in by giving a name

---

* Uniform Resource Locator—a standard for specifying an object on the Internet, such as a file or newsgroup, typically used with World Wide Web applications to specify a location on the Internet.

† In other words, the user submits the ID as ANONYMOUS and then puts the user's ID as password. This lets the site manager know what types of domains are reaching their site.

and a password (and in some systems an account number). FTP provides a means for communicating this identification information.

1.6.2.2   Filename. There are two approaches to the question of which filenames to use in a File Transfer Protocol: the native filenames or a new set of universal filenames. Establishing a universal naming convention requires providing a mapping between it and all the possible native naming conventions. The FTP uses the native filenames.

1.6.2.3   File translation. There are two choices for file format: use the local types, or create a new universal file type. Using a universal type requires all files to be translated from the local type to the universal type on transmission and from the universal type to a local type for storage. The FTP uses the local types, with the provision of describing properties of the type such that a host can translate the transmitted file into an appropriate local type.

1.6.2.4   The FTP model. FTP follows the user-server model of operation, with the additional feature that there are two functional units in each host and two connections between the hosts. At each host there is a protocol interpreter (PI) module and a data transfer (DT) module. The two modules are linked internally to the host by some communication mechanism and shared state information. The user protocol interpreter sends commands to the server protocol interpreter over a control connection. The server protocol interpreter sends back replies over the same connection. The result of the command-and-reply exchange may be for the two data transfer modules to open a data connection between themselves and to actually transmit a data file. Figure 1.29 shows the FTP model. The FTP PIs exchange information via the request-and-reply paradigm.[45]

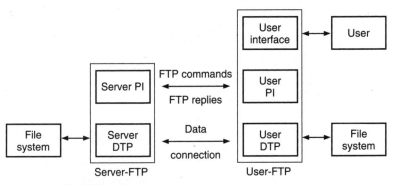

Figure 1.29   The FTP model.

FTP has been the Internet's main mechanism for providing access to information files and documents (documents and libraries) prior to the advent of WWW. FTP still has an important role to play, for the following reasons[33-38]:

1. Not everyone has access to WWW.

2. FTP is arguably a better mechanism for transferring large files once you know you want them, while WWW is a better mechanism for finding out what information is available by browsing shorter, specially formatted pages.

3. FTP preserves whatever structure the file had originally, while WWW is best for information that has been specially structured for Web presentation.

Against all this, FTP has some limitations in the hands of the nontechnical user, though some of these can be overcome by integrating FTP into a Mosaic-style application set.

File transfer is among the most frequently used TCP/IP applications, and it accounts for much network traffic. Standard file transfer protocols existed for the ARPANet before the TCP/IP became operational. These early versions of file transfer software evolved into a current standard known as the FTP. FTP offers many facilities beyond the transfer function itself:

- *Interactive access.* Although FTP is designed to be used by programs, most applications provide an interactive interface that allows humans to easily interact with remote servers.

- *Format (representation) specification.* FTP allows the user to specify the type and format of stored data. For example, the user can specify whether a file contains ASCII or EBCDIC character sets.

- *Authorization control.* FTP requires users to authorize themselves by sending a login name and password to the server before requesting file transfers. The server refuses the access to a user who cannot supply a valid login name and password.

Like other servers, most FTP server implementations allow access by multiple clients. Clients use TCP to connect to a server. A single master process awaits connections and creates a slave process to handle each connection. The slave process does not perform all the necessary computations; instead, it accepts and handles the *control connection* from the client, but uses an additional process or processes to handle a separate *data transfer connection.* The control connection carries commands that tell the server which file to transfer. The data transfer connection, which also uses TCP as the transport protocol, carries all data transfers. *Data transfer connection* and *data transfer process* can be created dynamically when needed, but the control connection persists throughout a session. Once the control connection disappears, the session is terminated and the software at both ends terminates all data transfer processes.[23-27]

1.6.3 Trivial File Transfer Protocol (TFTP)

The TCP/IP suite contains a second file transfer protocol that provides inexpensive, unsophisticated service known as the Trivial File Transfer Protocol (TFTP). TFTP restricts operations to simple file transfers, and it is a smaller program than the FTP. The rules of TFTP are simple. The first packet sent requests a file transfer and establishes the interaction between the client and server. The packet specifies a filename and whether the file will be read (transferred to the client) or written (transferred to the server). Blocks of the file are numbered consecutively starting at 1. Each data packet contains a header that specifies the number of blocks it carries. A block of less than 512 bytes signals the end of the file. It is possible to send an error message in place of data, and that will terminate the transfer.

1.6.4 TELNET

High-level protocols are implemented with application programs to allow users to interact with automated services on remote systems. The network terminal protocol (TELNET) allows a user to log in on any other computer on the network. You start a remote session by specifying a computer to connect to. From that time until you finish the session, anything you type is sent to the other computer. Generally, the connection to the remote computer behaves much like a dial-up connection. That is, the remote system will ask the user to log in and give a password, in whatever manner it would normally ask a user who had just dialed it up. TELNET allows a user to establish a TCP connection to a login server. It then passes keystrokes from the user's keyboard attached to the remote server. TELNET also carries output from the remote machine back to the user's screen. When you log off the other computer, the TELNET program exits, and you will find yourself talking to your own computer. Microcomputer implementations of TELNET generally include a terminal emulator for some common type of terminal.

TELNET offers three basic services. First, it defines a *network virtual terminal* that provides a standard interface to remote systems. Second, it includes a mechanism that allows the client and server to negotiate options (e.g., whether data uses the standard 7-bit or an 8-bit ASCII character set). Finally, TELNET utilizes a mechanism that

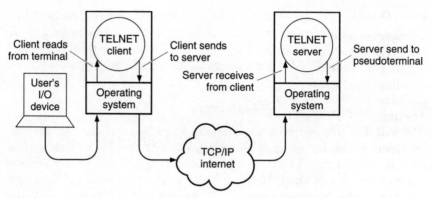

Figure 1.30   The path of data in a TELNET remote terminal session.

allows both ends of the connection to be treated symmetrically. As Fig. 1.30 shows, when a user invokes TELNET, an application on the user's program becomes the client. The client establishes a TCP connection to the server. The client accepts keystrokes from the user and sends them to the server, which sends them back to the user's screen. The operating system on the server receives characters as if they came from the keyboard.[23–27]

Prior to WWW, TELNET was the main Internet mechanism for reaching out and using a distant computer. TELNET enables a user to inspect the contents of any computer that agrees to open itself up to such use and to "control" the distant computer to whatever extent its owner may permit. This is one way that users search for and find useful files of information if those files are available for FTP rather than in World Wide Web format. Generally, TELNET is a tool for people with computer skills.

The TELNET command itself is almost trivial. You need only a host name or an IP address to identify the computer to which you want to connect. Once the TELNET connection is established, you should be prepared to enter a login name and password that are valid for the computer you have reached. A minimal TELNET session is as follows:

```
NYUModem>> TELNET 128.122.156.10
Trying...
Connected to 128.122.156.10. Escape character is'^]'.
SunOS UNIX (nucmed10)
login: subhas
Password:
Last login: Tue Oct 31 00:29:39 from ANNEX-2.NET.NYU.E
SunOS Release 4. 1.3 (NYU_TP_TV) #15: Thu Apr 7 17:41:29 EDT
  1994
nucmed10:441>
```

1.6.5   Other browsing/access applications

(Intelligent) agents. This is a term in increasingly wide use. It derives from real-world parlance, where an *agent* is someone who acts on your behalf. For example, a real estate agent is supposed to act on your behalf in selling your house. In Internet parlance the agent has the same role. It undertakes some kind of work on behalf of the user. The industry is working hard to develop capable and usable agents—for example, ones that will continuously scan the networks for breaking news and report the items it "thinks" are likely to be of interest to you. The term *intelligent* is used somewhat loosely. No software yet exists that really behaves like human intelligence, though systems can be programmed using the tools derived from artificial intelligence research to *appear* as if they are intelligent. The most useful feature of intelligent programs is usually the way they use pattern matching and pattern building to "learn" about the user's interests by monitoring how you use your computer and how you respond to existing news items.

USENET and its newsgroups. USENET is a kind of computer-conferencing overlay on the open Internet. Its main application is to support newsgroup discussion centers for particular topics. There are many thousands of different newsgroups on almost every subject imaginable.

E-mail lists and Listserv. E-mail lists are a kind of kid sister for newsgroups. Each item I send to the list is duplicated to everyone who subscribes to that list (including me). This provides a primitive kind of computer discussion mechanism which can be effective if some sensible rules of engagement are followed. It is also a useful mechanism for distributing news items to large groups of people who have interests in common. Listserv is the particular software that supports e-mail lists on one of the Internet's family of networks, BITNET.

Lists, and to some extent newsgroups, tend to be constrained in their usefulness more by user behavior and lack of guidance and skills than by the simplicity of their technology. An effective list or newsgroup is one where the majority of subscribers have mutually agreed upon the range of topics and the style of discussion, and where one or more alert facilitators intervenes quickly to keep discussion "on topic" and to gently assist new users who have not yet understood the behavior norms of the group.

1.7   Internet Access

1.7.1   Accessing the Internet

There are several ways to access the Internet backbone and servers connected to it. As discussed, the Internet can be accessed directly using high-level Internet services and protocols (e.g., *rlogin, TELNET*).

These services form an integral part of TCP/IP. In order to make such connections, the machine should be directly connected to the network or to a server that is connected to the network and provides a remote service. In that case, the client would establish a TCP connection from the local machine to the servers, and would begin sending keystrokes to the server and reading output that the server sent back.[23-26]

Another way to access the Internet remotely is with serial link communications. These types of communications are useful in laptop and portable PCs, because it is not always possible to find a physical connection to the network when a person travels with the machine. It affords a kind of lower-level, yet more ubiquitous kind of connectivity. Generally when residential (noncommercial) users access the Internet, this is the way they do it. In these types of connections, the computer uses a serial line for sending and receiving data. To make the connection via a modem and the normal telephone circuit, the computer dials a special server that is connected to the network. After the connection is made, there is a handshake dialog between the server and the computer for identification and password verification. There are standard protocols for the serial line connections, among which the most commonly used are async, the *Point-to-Point Protocol,* and the *Serial Line Internet Protocol* previously introduced.

Further examining access options, there are three main paths to connect to the Internet, as shown in Fig. 1.31.[37]

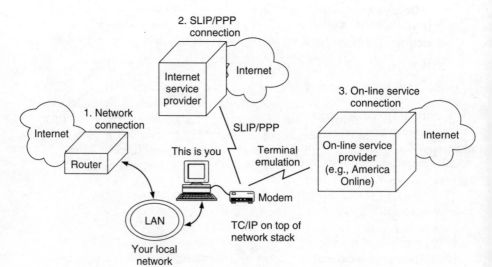

Figure 1.31 Making the Internet connection.

- Connect the computer to a (corporate) LAN whose server is an Internet host.

- Dial in to an Internet host using SLIP or PPP.

- Dial in to an on-line service that provides Internet services in async mode.

1.7.1.1 Network connections

What you need. You must be connected to a network that is connected to the Internet. This requires a network adapter card and ODI or NDIS packet drivers. You also need to run TCP/IP on your computer. If you're running Windows, you will need Winsock support.

What you get. Access to everything the Internet has to offer: mail, news, Gopher servers, Web servers, and more.[37]

1.7.1.2 SLIP/PPP connections

What you need. A modem and TCP/IP plus SLIP or PPP software. If you are running Windows you will need Winsock software. You must also have a service provider that lets you dial into a SLIP/PPP server.

What you get. Access to everything the Internet has to offer, although at speeds slower than a direct network connection would allow.[37]

1.7.1.3 On-Line connection

What you need. A modem, a PC running Windows, standard communication software, and an on-line service account.

What you get. Access to the Internet services your on-line service offers.[37]

Figure 1.32 shows some of the commercial Internet packages, commercial software suites, and some Internet service providers available at press time. It is important to note when choosing one of the services what your requirements are and also what the service provider has to offer.

SLIP and PPP make connections to the Internet possible via a type of interconnection known as *dial-up IP.* This allows PCs in the field or at home to connect to some central computer that is IP-connected. The calling computer is assigned a unique IP number by the central computer. The central computer acts as an intermediary agent for the calling computer. It sends and receives Internet packets to and from the

Figure 1.32 Commercial On-Line Services, Internet Service Providers, and Internet Suite Software

	America Online	CompuServe Information Serv	Delphi Internet	Genie Online Services	The Microsoft Network	Prodigy
			Commercial On-Line Services			
Company	America Online Inc.	CompuServe Inc.	Delphi Internet Services Inc.	GE Information Services Inc.	Microsoft Corp.	Prodigy Services Co.
Phone no.	800-827-6364	800-848-8199	508-323-1000	800-638-9636	206-882-8080	914-443-8000
E-mail address	info@aol.com	70006,101@compuserve.com	askdelphi@delphi.com	feedback@genie.com	info@msn.com	freetrial@prodigy.com
World Wide Web address	www.aol.com	www.compuserve.com	www.delphi.com	www.genie.com	www.msn.com	www.prodigy.com
Maximum connection speed	28.8 Kbps	28.8 Kbps	14.4 Kbps	14.4 Kbps	28.8 Kbps	14.4 Kbps
Points of presence (estimated)	166	420	Use Sprintnet	More than 600	Info n/a	325
ISDN	None	None	None	None	All	4
28.8 Kbps	166	16 cities	None	None	All	10
14.4 Kbps	All	300 cities	All	All	All	All
9.6 Kbps	All	All	All	All	All	All
Dial-up access	Yes	Yes	Yes	Yes	Yes	Yes
Direct TCP/IP connections	No	Yes	Yes (Boston area only)	Yes	Yes	No
Leased-line connections	No	Yes	No	Yes	No	Yes
Search Tools and Web Services						
Archie/FTP	Yes/yes	Yes/yes	Yes/yes	Yes/yes	Yes/yes	Yes/yes
Finger/Ping	No/no	Yes/yes	Yes/yes	No/no	No/no	No/no
Gopher/Veronica	Yes/yes	Yes/yes	Yes/yes	Yes/no	Yes/yes	Yes/yes
TELNET/rlogin	No/no	Yes/yes	Yes/yes	Yes/no	No/no	No/no
Web	Yes	Yes	Yes (text only)	Yes (text only)	Yes	Yes
Web-page const./hosting	Yes/yes	Yes/yes	Yes/yes	No/no	No/no	Yes/yes
Server storage included with Web account	Yes	Yes	No	N/A	N/A	Yes
Mail robots	No	Yes	Yes	N/A	N/A	No

Figure 1.32 (Continued)

Internet Service Providers

	IBM Internet connection service	internet MCI	NetCom Internet services	Interramp	Pipeline USA	AlterDial
Company	IBM Global network	MCI telecommunications	NetCom On-line Communications Services Inc.	Performance System Intl. Inc.	Performance System Intl. Inc.	UUNet Technologies Inc.
Phone no.	800-455-5056	800-353-3545	800-353-5600	800-774-0852	703-904-4100	800-488-6384
E-mail address	notify@ibm.net	moreinfo@networkmci.com	info@netcom.com	interramp.info@psi.com	info@psi.com	info@uu.net
World Wide Web address	www.ibm.com/.globalnetwork	www.internetmci.com	www.netcom.com	www.psi.net	www.psi.net/.internet	www.uu.net
Maximum connection speed	28.8 Kbps	28.8 Kbps	28.8 Kbps	28.8 Kbps	28.8 Kbps	28.8 Kbps
Points of presence (estimated)	300	200	175	150	140	100
ISDN	None	None	None	150	All	All
28.8 Kbps	60	All	All	75	70	All
14.4 Kbps	267	All	All	150	All	All
9.6 Kbps	All	All	All	150	All	All
Dial-up access	Yes	Yes	Yes	Yes	Yes	Yes
Direct TCP/IP connections	Yes	Yes	Yes	Yes	Yes	Yes
Monthly fee	$29.95	$9.95	$19.95	$29.00	$19.95	430.00
Hrs. included	30	5	40 (prime time)	29 (prime time)	Unlimited	25
Search Tools and Web Services						
Archie	Yes	Yes	Yes	Yes	Yes	Yes
Finger	Yes	Yes	Yes	Yes	Yes	Yes
FTP	Yes	Yes	Yes	Yes	Yes	Yes
Gopher/Veronica	Yes/yes	Yes/yes	Yes/yes	Yes/yes	Yes/yes	No/no
Ping	Yes	Yes	Yes	Yes	Yes	Yes
TELNET/rlogin	Yes/yes	No/yes	Yes/yes	Yes/yes	Yes/yes	Yes/no
Web	Yes	Yes	Yes	Yes	Yes	Yes/yes
Web-page construction/hosting	Yes/yes	Yes/no	No/no	No/yes	Yes/yes	Yes/yes
Server storage included with Web account	Yes	Yes	N/A	Yes	Yes	Yes
Mail robots	Yes	No	N/A	No	Yes	No

(Continued)

Figure 1.32 (Continued)

Internet Suite Software

	Explore 2.0	IBM Internet Connection for Windows 3.0	OS/2 wrap connect 3.0	Internet Chameleon 4.5	Internet Office Professional Edition 4.0	Netscape Navigator Personal ed.	Quaterdeck InternetSuite for Windows	Softerm Plus+4.0
List price	Single user $99	Single user $129	Single user $299	Single user $125	Single user $499	Single user $44.95	Single user $79.95	Single user $49.95
Interface	Windows	Windows	OS/2	Windows	Windows	Windows	Windows	Windows
TCP/IP Implementation	VxD	TSR	N/A	DLL	DLL/VxD	DLL	DLL	DLL/VxD
Connections support	CSLIP, PPP, SLIP	Direct, SLIP	Direct, PPP, SLIP	CSLIP, ISDN, PPP, SLIP	Direct, CSLIP, PPP, SLIP	Direct, PPP, SLIP	Direct, PPP, SLIP	CSLIP, PPP, SLIP
TCP/IP appl. included	FTP, TELNET	FTP, TELNET	FTP, TELNET	FTP, TELNET	FTP, TELNET	FTP, TELNET	FTP, TELNET	FTP, TELNET
TCP/IP utilities included	Query, statistics	Ping (SLIP only)	Ping	Autointernet connection, Finger, Ping	None	None	Ping	Ping
Internet appl. included								
Web browser	Yes	Yes	Yes	Yes	Yes	Yes	Yes	Yes
HTML 2.0/3.0	Yes/no	Yes/no	Yes/no	Yes/yes	Yes/no	Yes/yes	Yes/no	Yes/no
Multiple windows	Yes	No	No	No	No	Yes	Yes	Yes
Multithreading	No	No	No	Yes	No	No	No	No
Tables	No	No	Yes	Yes	No	Yes	No	Yes
Gopher	Yes	Yes	Yes	Yes	Yes	No	No	No
HTML editor	No	No	No	Yes	No	No	No	No
Mail	Yes	Yes	Yes	Yes	Yes	Yes	Yes	Yes
News	Yes	Yes	Yes	Yes	Yes	Yes	Yes	Yes
Server appl. included	FTP	FTP	None	None	FTP, lpr, rcp	None	None	FTP
Server supported by vendor	Gopher, Web	Archie, FTP, new Gopher, Web	Archie, news, IRC, Veronica	FTP, Web	FTP, Web	Web	Archie, Gopher, Web	FTP, Web
Terminal emulated	SCO ANSI, vt52, vt100, vt220, vt320	ANSI, hft, vt100 vt200, tn3270, tn5250	ANSI, vt100, vt220, tn3270, tn5720	ANSI, at386, tv1950/1955 vt55/220/320 wyse50/60	vt120/220/320	None	vt52/100/220 WAIS	ANSI, IBM 3101-310110/20, ripterm, tn3270, tty, vt52...340
Scripting languages	Connection Wizard, TELNET	None	None	PPP, SLIP, TELNET	PPP, SLIP	None	PPP, SLIP, TELNET	PPP, SLIP, TELNET

host computer. SLIP and PPP allow computers not directly connected to the Internet to exchange information in a user-friendly environment. SLIP is a communications protocol that supports an Internet connection (i.e., using TCP/IP) over a dial-up line. There is also a variant of SLIP called Compressed SLIP (CSLIP) which is somewhat faster than standard SLIP.

1.7.2 PPP

PPP is a feature-rich Internet Standard protocol for transmission of IP packets over serial lines. It supports synchronous and asynchronous lines. Although PPP has many functionality features, not all features are needed or even desired in every product to support basic communication. These are some of the features:

Demand dial.   Brings up a PPP interface and dials the phone when packets are queued for delivery; and brings the interface down after some period of inactivity.

Redial.   Brings up a PPP interface whenever it goes down, to keep a line up.

Scripting.   Negotiates through a series of prompts or intermediate connections to bring up a PPP link.

Paralleling.   Configures several PPP lines to the same destination and do load sharing between them.

Filtering.   Selects which packets to send down a link or whether to bring up a demand-dial link based on IP or TCP packet type.

Header compression.   TCP header compression. Useful on high-speed lines, essential for low-speed lines.

Tunneling.   Builds a virtual network over a PPP link across a TCP stream through an existing IP network.

The PPP mechanism specifies ways that other protocol families such as OSI, DECnet, Novell, and XNS can share the link equally with IP, without requiring that they be encapsulated within IP packets. A PPP link can even be used as a protocol-independent bridge.

PPP specifies a link control protocol used for negotiating such things as maximum frame size and HDLC-specific compression techniques. It also allows for control characters (such as the frame flag bytes) to be escaped. The control-character escaping scheme is negotiable, too, and can accommodate different special characters in each direction on the link. The link control protocol provides link loop detection and link quality monitoring that can be run in the midst of other traffic on the link.

As a PPP link comes up, all the variables that may make it unsuccessful are subject to negotiation. The PPP specification has a finite-state machine that formalizes many of these link management tasks. This eases the human administrative burden of establishing and running the link, and empowers less-skilled users to solve the most common problems.[23-27]

PPP overcomes a number of the limitations of SLIP. PPP has been designed to operate over both asynchronous (start/stop) connections and bit-oriented synchronous systems. The protocol also defines several management and testing functions to deal with line quality, option negotiation, and the setup of IP addresses. The standards suggest how data compression can be used to improve performance.

1.7.2.1 The service provided by PPP. PPP provides a point-to-point connection between two TCP/IP systems for the transfer of IP datagrams. These datagrams can carry any of the higher-layer protocols (discussed later). PPP can operate over any serial link interface; the only limitation is that it requires a full-duplex connection. It does not need serial interface control signals, but the standard recommends that they can be used to help improve performance. There is no restriction on the line speed used with PPP. RFC 1171 states that PPP is capable of operating over any data terminal equipment (DTE) and data communications equipment (DCE) interface, either asynchronous (character-based) or bit-oriented synchronous.* PPP is based on the HDLC standards of ISO, as originally adopted by the ITU-T for X.25 systems.

1.7.2.2 The PPP frame. The frame format of PPP is shown in Fig. 1.33. The address field is all 1s, and the control octet contains the value

---

* In fact there are four valid combinations: bit-oriented synchronous (e.g., HDLC), character-oriented synchronous (e.g., IBM's BSC), bit-oriented asynchronous (e.g., Kermit), and character-oriented asynchronous (e.g., Kermit).

Flag	Address	Control	Protocol	Data	FCS	Flag
0x7E	0xFF	0x03	0xXXXX	0-MTU bytes	16 or 32 bits	0x7E
01111110	11111111	00000011	(2 bytes)			01111110

Figure 1.33 Full PPP packet format.

0x03, the UI control field indicating a connectionless protocol. The protocol field defines protocol carried by this frame, which for TCP/IP systems is:

Link Control Protocol	0xC021
Network Control Protocol	0x8021
Internet Protocol	0x0021

For IP, the NCP is called the Internet Protocol Control Protocol (IPCP) with a protocol field of 0x8021. Other values assigned for the protocol field allowed other protocols, including XNS, Novell's IPX, Apple Talk, and DECnet, to share one PPP link.

Synchronous HDLC data link protocols detect the end of a frame by recognizing the flag sequence 0x7E. Special techniques, often known as *zero-bit insertion* or *bit stuffing,* must be employed to prevent a data pattern that has the same bit pattern as the flag from being misinterpreted as the end of the frame. It would be difficult to use the same techniques on asynchronous lines, so an octet insertion principle is used instead.

The octet insertion principle is based on use of an escape character 0x7D. If a data octet has the same value as the flag 0x7E, or if an octet containing a value of less than 0x20 is seen, 0x7D is placed in front of it, and the original octet has its sixth bit complemented. At the receiver the 0x7D is removed and the sixth bit returned to normal. Figure 1.34 shows some examples.[33–38]

Values of less than 0x20 represent ASCII control characters, so they are modified to prevent any misinterpretation by the communications

---

Example 1 (data same as escape character)
Data   0x7D (01111101)
Complement   bit 6 (01011101)
Add escape   0x7D (01111101–01011101)
Data transmitted   0x7D-0x9D

Example 2 (data is less than 0x20)
Data   0x01 (00000001)
Complement   bit 6 (00100001)
Add escape   0x7D (01111101–00100001)
Data transmitted   0x7D-0x21

Example 3 (data same as flag)
Data   0x7E (01111110)
Complement   bit 6 (01011110)
Add escape   0x7D (01111101–01011110)
Data transmitted   0x7D-0x5E

Figure 1.34 Octet insertion with PPP on asynchronous lines.

link. Examples include the flow-control characters XON and XOFF (0x11 and 0x12). If these octets are transmitted into an asynchronous communications link, they can disable or enable transmission at the wrong times, possibly causing loss of data and, at worst, total and irrevocable lockup of the link.

1.7.2.3 Operation. To initiate a connection, the Link Control Protocol (LCP) is used. It can test the quality of serial lines and then negotiate options for link establishment. The basic services provided by LCP will test its suitability for operation. However, a mechanism for performing this test is only hinted at and not explicitly defined. It is suggested that the LCP echo-request, echo-reply protocol is a method of testing a link.

One of PPP's strengths is its ability to configure a connection to a remote network dynamically. The LCP within PPP is responsible for selecting an appropriate IP address and testing whether the link is usable. After LCP establishes a connection through the use of the configure-request frame, IPCP comes into operation. It is responsible for handling the IP modules at each end of the serial link and will deal with negotiation of the IP addresses and the compression technique to be used. Once the connection is finished, LCP is used again to close the link with the terminate-link frame.

PPP can multiplex data from many sources, which makes it practical for high-speed connections between bridges or routers. RFC 1220 describes how PPP can be used for remote bridging. Because of the protocol field, it can be used to carry other protocols simultaneously with IP on the same point-to-point circuit. For the connection of a host to a remote network over a switched service, the major issue may be preventing unauthorized access.

Where PPP is used to interconnect bridges or routers from different manufacturers it is important to check the level of capability and interoperability. Testing is advised when mixing different vendors' equipment.

1.7.3 SLIP

SLIP is a simple framing scheme for putting IP packets on a serial line. It uses a special flag byte (0xC0) at the beginning and another at the end, as shown in Fig. 1.35.

Flag	Data	Flag
0xC0	MTU bytes	0xC0

Figure 1.35 SLIP packet format.

More specifically, SLIP defines two special characters referred to as SLIP END and SLIP ESC (escape). SLIP END is the character 0xC0 (octal 300, decimal 192), and SLIP ESC is 0xDB (octal 333, decimal 219). Datagrams sent using SLIP are framed by SLIP END characters as shown in Fig. 1.36. If a data octet within a frame has the same value as SLIP END (0xC0), a two-octet sequence of SLIP ESC (0xDB) and 0xDC (octal 334, decimal 220) is sent instead. The remote end then translates those two-octet codes back to the original octet. If a data octet within a frame has the same value as SLIP ESC (0xDB), a two-octet sequence of SLIP ESC (0xDB) and 0xDD (octal 335, decimal 221) is sent instead.

The initial flag is usually omitted, so that the ending flag signifies the boundary between two frames full of data. If one of the data bytes happens to be the same value as the flag byte, it is translated into a pair of characters (0xDB 0xDC) before transmission and then translated back upon reception, so that the data bytes are not mistaken for the end of a packet. SLIP's main advantage is simplicity and therefore ease of implementation.

SLIP contains no provision for error detection, assuming that the upper-level services will worry about that sort of problem. It does not provide for link management tasks, nor for any protocol family besides IP. It contains no mechanism for negotiating values for any of the many things that can be different between hosts, such as network-level addresses, or packet size, or various sorts of protocols used at the network layer, or data compression techniques. It contains no link-level authentication or loop-detection mechanism. These issues must be agreed upon in advance by the endpoint systems, and often the decisions are embedded in code that is not accessible to the user. For example, SLIP implementations that incorporate header compression typically must be identified in advance.

Figure 1.37 shows possible SLIP connections to a host using V.24 (RS-232C). In this diagram, PCs have been connected to the central host, but these could be any computer able to operate TCP/IP and SLIP. The host is also shown connected to a LAN, as it could be used as a router to allow

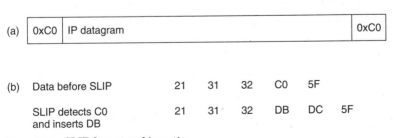

Figure 1.36 SLIP format and insertion.

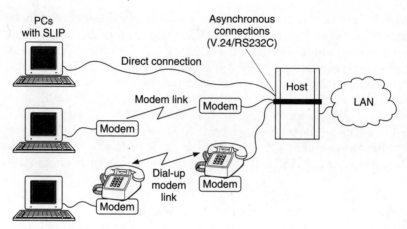

Figure 1.37   SLIP functionality.

the PCs to connect to other services on that LAN. As asynchronous lines normally operate only up to 28,800 bps,* SLIP will likely be slow, particularly for graphics-intensive applications. Data compression can improve throughput.

As the data in the IP header could be of any octet value 0x00 to 0xFF, it would not be practical to use SLIP through buffered communications systems that use special characters for control purposes. A typical example would be the use of XON/XOFF for the flow control. XON/XOFF is frequently enabled on terminal servers and multiplexer systems to control the flow of data bits, so that all 8 bits are available for the transmission of any octet value.

As noted, SLIP is a very simple protocol that does not provide any protection against line errors and frame corruption; it relies on the higher-layer protocols for this. Hence, some higher-layer protocols that operate over UDP (such as NFS) normally rely on the data link layer to detect errors, so the performance of those can be affected badly by corrupted frames. On error-prone communications lines, SLIP would not be satisfactory.

1.7.3.1   Configuration and management issues.   SLIP connections need two IP addresses with the same network number at both ends of the link. A SLIP connection is treated as a network that has only two nodes. There are no significant differences between configuring a SLIP connection, apart from loading the appropriate SLIP software drivers. SLIP is unable to determine its IP addresses dynamically; they must

---

* Theoretically, rates of 115,000 bps are possible.

be loaded manually when the system is configured. This is seen as a limitation, particularly where a user is dialing in to different routers. As each router would have a different IP network address, the computer must be configured with a different IP address each time. The higher-layer protocols will not recognize the difference between SLIP and another interface (e.g., PPP), apart from performance.

1.7.4   PPP versus SLIP

What follows is a brief comparison between PPP and SLIP.[23-27]

- Header compression can be implemented over both. (When SLIP is run with header compression, it is often called CSLIP.)

- Both PPP and SLIP have mechanisms for escaping characters in the data part of the frame that might be interpreted as part of the framing itself.

- Unlike SLIP, PPP can operate even in the presence of in-band XON/XOFF flow control. Therefore, PPP may need to escape those characters in the data, thus requiring more octets to be transmitted. This is an issue of the underlying transport, not of the protocol itself. In fact, this is an advantage in flexibility for PPP: the capability to escape almost any character is available.

- Since it has no option-negotiation phase during link start-up, SLIP can get under way more quickly, and therefore makes better use of connectivity time.

- SLIP has a simpler framing scheme compared to PPP's approach, so its per-packet overhead is lower, which means that the percentage of the link bandwidth devoted to paying transmission is much higher. Also, the typical MTU in SLIP implementations is smaller (256, 576, or 1006, nonnegotiable) than the typical MTU of a PPP link (1500, negotiable). If a fast link were to be used only for bulk data transfer, PPP could be instructed to negotiate an MTU and transmit the data.

- Since SLIP's framing scheme is simple, and since it specifies no finite-state machine to implement and no error checking, it absorbs fewer system resources than PPP.

- Since SLIP is so minimalist in its approach to the problem, it is much quicker to implement and verify than PPP. But the current engineering effort invested in PPP for IP will pay off in the future, when it will be much easier to plug in support for other protocol families.

1.7.5 PPP and SLIP applications: home access

With dial-up IP, TCP/IP software is run from the host computer and works together with the GUI application (e.g., Mosaic, Netscape, Eudora) so the user can easily access the World Wide Web. As a result of these applications running locally, the user benefits by (1) the user-friendly design of the GUI applications, making Internet searches less tedious from the Windows, Macintosh, or UNIX platforms, and (2) the fact that all data retrieved from the network is stored on the local hard drive, thereby eliminating the downloading and uploading of files from a mainframe account.

SLIP provides a point-to-point connection between two devices for the transmission of IP datagrams. The devices can be two computers or a computer and a router. It can be used for remote access to the TCP/IP network or for a simple connection between two machines. The IP layer remains the same as for any other medium; SLIP defines a method of framing used to carry IP over asynchronous lines. With CSLIP, performance is improved through the use of header compression. CSLIP recognizes small packets created by some applications (i.e., TELNET) and encodes them in an efficient manner before sending them across the serial line.[14–21] As discussed, PPP is superior to SLIP in that it uses a standardized method for autoconfiguring the host/client machine. During dial-up IP, information is exchanged when a connection is established (i.e., IP number); thus, SLIP can be inefficient compared to PPP's negotiated exchange. PPP repetitions provide error detection, authentication, compression, and may be used to set up dynamic addresses for dial-in connections. (See Fig. 1.38.)

In order to access the Internet, a home user would need the following: a modem (at least 14.4 Kbps is recommended; 28.8 Kbps is better);

Phases of PPP connectors

Link
   Parameters of the low-layer data link are exchanged; peers choose an authentication protocol.

Authentication
   Peers exchange authentication messages.

Network
   Peers agree on the network layer protocols, as well as operating parameters for each of the network protocols.

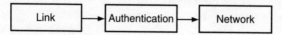

Figure 1.38 Phases of PPP connections.

TCP software; an account with an Internet service provider (ISP); a dialer (which is software for connecting to an ISP); and client software, which will allow you to browse the World Wide Web. Once a user has an account with an ISP, he or she should be provided an IP address. These accounts can use either PPP or SLIP to connect the user remotely to the provider's Internet connections. (See Fig. 1.39.)

Internet service providers should be chosen based on a number of criteria, including the following service criteria: (1) When calling potential ISPs with a problem or query, how long does it take for someone to answer the telephone? (2) Does the ISP provide all the necessary software for the initial setup of the TCP/IP software and PPP or SLIP dialer? (3) Is there a charge for technical support? Is there a limit to the number of technical calls? (4) How much is the monthly access charge? Is this comparable to the competition? (5) What is the speed of the modem that the ISP is running and what is the maximum connection speed? (6) Is ISDN supported? (7) Is the dial-up number a local call? (8) What is the percentage of blocked calls? (9) How quickly are dial-in calls serviced?

1.8   Internet Applications

1.8.1   Navigation tools

1.8.1.1   Archie.   Archie is a process that allows use of the File Transfer Protocol without an account at the host offering the files. Archie is a

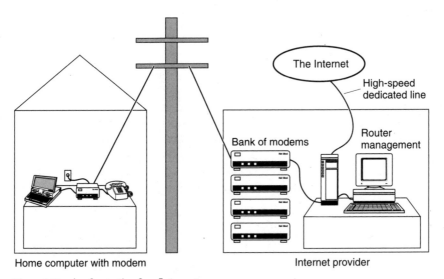

Figure 1.39   A schematic of an Internet access arrangement.

database that serves as an index to the holdings of some of the major anonymous FTP sites. Thousands of computers offer more than 2 million files for this kind of access. This is an important avenue for obtaining public domain or sharing software on the Internet.

The Archie service allows a user to locate files without knowing the file attribute. Archie servers index information based on filename. There are two database indexes: FILENAMES and WHATIS. The FILENAMES database indexes the names of files available from hundreds of Internet FTP sites. Archie allows queries based on specified patterns, archive sites, or filename match. The WHATIS database contains the names and descriptions of software packages and documents. Entries include text strings consisting of keywords and associated descriptions. Archie automatically updates entries in the FILENAMES, but the WHATIS database is manually maintained by a systems administrator.

1.8.1.2   Gopher.   Gopher is one of a whole range of information search and retrieval tools that preceded the widespread use of WWW. Its use is now commonly integrated with the more sophisticated Mosaic/Netscape-style user interfaces. Gopher was created in the "Gopher State" (Minnesota) at the University of Minnesota, but of course the term also suggests its role: "Go fer this, go fer that." In Internet parlance, the Gopher goes around the network on behalf of its user, sniffing out and reporting on interesting or useful finds.

Gopher is a simple tool, relatively easily implemented. It is described as a document delivery tool; in fact, Gopher can deliver documents, lists of documents, and indexes. Gopher servers offer not only textual information, but also organized browsing lists of resources on the Internet.

Gopher transparently links together groups of file servers, each with their own accumulation of files and folders. One folder on a computer may access other folders located on another computer. Gopher handles details that the user does not want to bother about. Text files, sound, and graphic images (including photographs and drawings) can be accessed and retrieved using Gopher. Gopher also gives the user tools to locate information on specific topics from computer systems around the world. Now there are GUI Gopher tools. Users can now access these Gopher sights with the point and click of a mouse. No password or login is required.[14-21]

1.8.1.3   World Wide Web (WWW).   Rather than offering simple folders with one-line descriptions of documents, the Web offers hypertext. This means that a document can have embedded links to other documents.

A user clicks on such an embedded link and the document appears on the screen.

Since 1993, new WWW clients have become available, greatly enhancing its usability and power. One tool, called Mosaic, is a multi-platform, multipurpose tool whose introduction has helped drive WWW from the hypertext mode into the hypermedia mode. Commercial clients have also appeared (e.g., Netscape, Explorer). A plethora of providers, vendors, organizations, magazines, stores, and other entities are delivering services no one dreamed of providing over the Internet until recently. WWW and Gopher are similar in some ways, and each tool has its adherents and detractors.

HTML, discussed in more detail in Chap. 4, is the standard language the World Wide Web uses for creating and recognizing hypermedia documents. It is related to, but technically not a subset of, the Standard Generalized Markup Language (SGML), a method of representing document-formatting languages. Languages such as HTML, which follow the SGML format, allow document authors to separate information from presentation. Documents containing the same information can be presented in a number of different ways. Users have the option of controlling visual elements such as fonts, font size, and paragraph spacing without changing the original information.

HTML is recognized for its ease of use. Web documents are typically written in HTML and are usually named with the suffix *.html*. HTML documents are nothing more than standard, 7-bit ASCII files with formatting codes that contain information about layout (text styles, document titles, paragraphs, lists) and hyperlinks.[14-21] Free conversion software is available on the Internet for translating documents from many other formats into HTML. Filters exist that can convert files in Rich Text Format (RTF) and Microsoft Word, as well as mail archives and text-only documents into HTML.

The World Wide Web uses Uniform Resource Locators (URLs) to represent hypermedia links and links to network services within HTML documents. It is possible to represent nearly any file or service on the Internet with a URL. The first part of the URL (before the two slashes) specifies the method of access. The second is typically the address of the computer where the data or service is located. Further parts may specify the names of files, the port to connect to, or the text to search for in a database. A URL is always a single unbroken line with no spaces. Sites that run World Wide Web servers are typically named with a *www* at the beginning of the network address.

Here are some examples of URLs:

```
file://www.hcc.hawaii.edu/sound.au
```

This file retrieves a sound file and plays it.

```
file://www.eit.com/picture.gif
```

This file retrieves a picture and displays it, either in a separate program or within a hypermedia document.

To access information on the Web you will use a browser application, such as Mosaic, Netscape, or Explorer. The browser interprets the information on the Internet and makes it more user-friendly. The browsers supply special tools, such as bookmarks and preference settings, to make the user feel more comfortable. The Internet is no longer for computer scientists; anyone who can use a mouse on a computer can access just about anything on the Internet.

1.8.1.4   Wide Area Information Servers (WAIS). WAIS is a tool that allows an information provider to prepare indexes of unstructured documents, and it is a tool that lets users search these indexes with natural-language questions. WAIS presents the user with a list of documents ranked in order of how closely they match the query. Some versions of WAIS "clients" can also index local information, such as a basket of electronic mail, on the user's workstation.[46]

1.8.2   Other Internet applications

1.8.2.1   Network file systems. A network file system allows a system to access files on another computer in a somewhat more closely integrated fashion than FTP. A network file system provides the illusion that disks or other devices from one system are directly connected to other systems. There is no need to use a special network utility to access a file on another system. The user's computer simply thinks it has some extra disk drives. These extra "virtual" drives refer to the other system's disks. This capability is useful for several different purposes. It lets the user place large disks on a few computers while allowing others access to the disk space. Aside from the obvious economic benefits, this allows people working on several computers to share common files. It makes system maintenance and backup easier, because you do not have to worry about updating and backing up copies on lots of different machines. A number of vendors now offer high-performance, diskless computers. These computers have no disk drives at all; hence, they are entirely dependent upon disks attached to common file servers.

1.8.2.2   Remote printing. This allows the user to access printers on other computers as if they were directly attached to the user. (The most commonly used protocol is the Remote Line-Printer Protocol from Berkeley UNIX.)

1.8.2.3 Remote execution. This allows the user to request that a particular program be run on a different computer. This is useful when the user can do most of the work on a small computer, but a few tasks require the resources of a larger system. There are a number of different kinds of remote execution. Some operate on a command-by-command basis. That is, you request that a specific command or set of commands should run on some specific computer. (More sophisticated versions can choose a system that happens to be free.) However, there are also *remote procedure call* (RPC) systems that allow a program to call a subroutine that will run on another computer. There are many protocols of this sort. Berkeley UNIX contains two servers to execute commands remotely: *rsh* and *rexec*. The user-contributed software with Berkeley 4.3 contains a *distributed shell* that will distribute tasks among a set of systems, depending upon load. Remote procedure call mechanisms have been a topic for research for a number of years, so many organizations have implementations of such facilities. The most widespread, commercially supported remote procedure call protocols are Xerox's Courier and Sun Microsystems' RPC. Protocol documents are available from Xerox and Sun. There is a public implementation of Courier over TCP as part of the user-contributed software with Berkeley 4.3. An implementation of RPC was posted to USENET by Sun, and also appears as part of the user-contributed software with Berkeley 4.3.

1.8.2.4 Name servers. In large installations, there are a number of different collections of names that have to be managed. These include users and their passwords, names and network addresses for computers, and accounts. It becomes very challenging to keep this data up-to-date on all of the computers. Thus, the databases are kept on a small number of systems. Other systems access the data over the network. Internet Experiment Note (IEN) 116 describes an older name-server protocol that is used by a few terminal servers and other products to look up host names. Sun's Yellow Pages system is designed as a general mechanism to handle user names, file-sharing groups, and other databases commonly used by UNIX systems.

1.8.2.5 Terminal servers. A terminal server is a communication device that facilitates data transfer between an async protocol and a LAN protocol for TELNET access and similar functions. If the user's terminal is connected to one of these, you simply type the name of a computer and you are connected to it. Generally, it is possible to have active connections to more than one computer at the same time. The terminal server will have the capability to switch between connections rapidly, and to notify the user when output is waiting for another connection. (Terminal servers use the TELNET protocol already mentioned.)

1.8.2.6   Network-oriented window systems. Until recently, high-performance graphics programs had to execute on a computer that had a bit-mapped graphics screen directly attached to it. Network window systems allow a program to use a display on a different computer. Full-scale network window systems provide an interface that lets the user distribute jobs to the systems that are best suited to handle them, but that still give the user a single, graphically based user interface. (The most widely implemented window system is X. A protocol description is available from MIT's Project Athena, and a reference implementation is publicly available from MIT.) A number of vendors also support NEWS, a window system defined by Sun. Both of these systems are designed to use TCP/IP.[47]

Many other applications and services are used in limited communities or on an experimental basis within the Internet community. In addition, there are a number of limited-use or experimental protocols at the service level; some of these may be considered specialized applications. Over 40 application-level protocols and over 20 service-level protocols are identified as Internet Standards.

Note that some of the protocols described previously were designed by Berkeley, Sun, or other organizations. Thus they are not officially part of the Internet protocol suite. However, they are implemented using TCP/IP, just as normal TCP/IP application protocols are. Since the protocol definitions are not considered proprietary, and since commercially supported implementations are widely available, it is reasonable to think of these protocols as being effectively part of the Internet suite.[48] Following is a list of some of these protocols:

Active Users Protocol

Character Generator Protocol

Cross Net Debugger Protocol

Daytime Protocol

Echo Protocol

Finger Protocol

Graphics Protocol

Host Monitoring Protocol

Loader Debugger Protocol

Logical Address Maintenance Protocol

Login Host Protocol

Mailbox Name Service

Packet Radio Measurement Protocol

Post Office Protocol

Quote of the Day Protocol

Reliable Data Protocol

Remote Job Entry Protocol

Remote Job Service

Remote TELNET Service

Remote Location Protocol

Remote Virtual Disk Protocol

1.9   Future of the Internet and Internet-Related Applications

The Internet faces a number of challenges on an ongoing basis, including the following:

- Increasing demand for backbone bandwidth
- Increasing demand for access bandwidth
- IP-related enhancements; for example,

    —IP-related issues, such as address limitations and type-of-service distinctions, and the need for newer versions of the protocol.

    —Support of multicasting over IP.

    —Support of multimedia traffic, using existing protocols such as IP and TCP. The issues are that multimedia is real time, requiring a lot of bandwidth, and the applications expect a well-defined quality of service. On the other hand, IP is a connectionless protocol, and TCP uses window-based flow control.

    —Routing issues, relating to the growth of routing tables, routing storms, and the need to use link-state protocols such as OSPF.

- The development of secure e-cash mechanisms

1.9.1   New backbone connection schemes

The creation of the NSFNet backbone was one of the most important events in the recent history of the Internet. It enabled the growth of the Internet that continues to this day. Having succeeded so well, the NFS has recently gotten out of the business of providing the backbone for the U.S. information infrastructure.

NFS has devised a new scheme, under which a multiplicity of national Internet backbones would be deployed. In a sense, the NSFNet itself would retreat to its original purpose of serving the needs of scientists using supercomputer applications. The new supercomputer backbone, to be called vBNS (very high speed Backbone Network Service), would operate at a significantly higher speed than the current backbone (155 megabits per second, replacing the current 45-megabits-per-second links).* Parallel to this network would be a variety of commercial and government backbones, operating in an environment of competition as well as cooperation. The NSF plan calls for NSF to provide funding for regional networks, leaving it up to them to connect to national backbone services. Over a five-year period since the project award, NSF has planned to reduce those subsidies to zero. NSF called for the creation of Network Access Points (NAPs), which allow interconnection of regional networks, the vBNS, and foreign networks.[49]

Options for connection LANs to Internet service providers will also change over the next few years. Alternatives to traditional leased lines are finally coming into their own. ISDN, talked about for many years, is finally being deployed in the United States as an access technology. Asymmetric Digital Subscriber Line (ADSL) is talked about, as is Internet over cable TV. Other alternatives to leased lines, such as frame relay, SMDS, and ATM, are also being deployed, as discussed next.

1.9.1.1 The use of Asynchronous Transfer Mode. As discussed earlier in the chapter, ATM will become an increasingly important technology, not only in corporate environments, but also within the realm of the Internet. Graphics- and video-intensive applications necessitate higher speeds. By current standards, *high-speed* refers to networks that operate at 155 Mbps; ATM hardware can switch data at gigabit speeds; protocols for standardized access to these speeds are expected in the next few years. An ATM network consists of one or more high-speed switches that each connect to host computers and other ATM switches. A typical ATM switch can connect between 16 and 64 ATM-ready devices. ATM uses optical fibers for connections, including connections from a host computer to an ATM switch. Optical fibers provide a higher transfer rate than a copper wire. Typically, the connection between a host and an ATM switch operates at 100 or 155 Mbps.[31]

Although a single ATM switch has finite capacity, switches can be interconnected to form a larger network. The connection between two switches differs slightly from the connection between a host computer and a switch, from a protocol point of view. Interswitch connection can operate at higher speeds and can use slightly modified protocols. Fig-

---

* Recently the speed has been raised to 622 megabits per second.

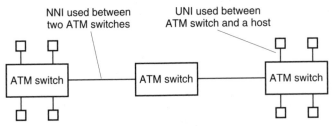

Figure 1.40   Three ATM switches combined to form a large network.

ure 1.40 shows the topology and shows the difference between *network node interface* (NNI) and a *user-to-network interface* (UNI). ATM is being contemplated for access as well as for backbone networks.

1.9.1.2   Connection-oriented networking.   ATM offers *connection-oriented service*. Before a host computer connected to an ATM can send cells, the host must first interact with the switch to specify a destination. The interaction is analogous to placing a telephone call. The host specifies the remote computer's ITU-T E.164 address and waits for the ATM switch to contact the remote system and establish a path. When a connection succeeds, the local ATM switch chooses a virtual identifier for the connection and passes the connection identifier to the host along with a message that informs the host of success. The host uses the connection identifier when sending or receiving cells. When it finishes using a connection, the host again communicates with the ATM switch to request that the connection be broken. The switch disconnects the two computers. LAN emulation[30] provides a mechanism for interworking connection-oriented ATM with connectionless LAN protocols.

1.9.1.3   ATM adaptation layers.   Although ATM switches small cells at the lowest level, application programs that transfer data over an ATM do not read or write cells. Instead, a computer interacts with ATM through an ATM *adaptation layer,* which is part of the ATM standard. The adaptation layer performs several functions, including PDU segmentation and reassembly, clock information transfer, and detection of errors such as lost or corrupted frames. Firmware that implements an ATM adaptation layer is located on a host interface along with the hardware and firmware that provide cell transmitting and receiving. Layers provide data transfer services for computers that use ATM. When a virtual circuit is created, both ends of the circuit must agree on which adaptation protocol will be used.

ATM adaptation layer 5 (AAL5) is used to send conventional data packets across an ATM network. Although ATM uses cells at the lowest level, AAL5 presents an interface that accepts and delivers large, variable-length packets. In particular, AAL5 allows each packet to contain between 1 and 65,535 bytes of data (AAL1 and AAL3/4 are also available for other applications).

1.9.1.4 Datagram encapsulation and IP MTU size. A computer can use ATM adaptation AAL5 to transfer an IP datagram over an ATM connection. On the sending host, AAL5 generates a trailer, segments the datagram into cells, and sends each cell over the circuit. On the receiving host, AAL5 reassembles the cells to reproduce the original datagram, strips off the trailer, and delivers the datagram to the receiving host or the IP. AAL5 uses a bit in the header of the *cell itself* to mark the *final* cell of a given datagram.

AAL5 uses a 16-bit length field, making it possible to send 65 KB in a single AAL PDU. Despite the capabilities of AAL5, TCP/IP restricts the size of datagrams that can be sent over ATM. The standards impose a limit of 9180 bytes per datagram. As with any network interface, when an outgoing datagram is larger than the network MTU, IP fragments the datagram and passes each fragment to AAL5. Thus, for these applications, AAL5 accepts, transfers, and delivers datagrams of 9180 bytes or less.

1.9.1.5 IP address binding in an ATM network. As in other network technologies, ATM assigns to each attached computer a physical address that must be used when establishing a virtual circuit. On one hand, because an ATM physical address is larger than an IP address, an ATM physical address cannot be encoded within an IP address.* Thus, IP cannot use static address binding for ATM networks. On the other hand, ATM hardware does not yet generally support broadcast. Thus, IP cannot use conventional ARP to bind addresses on ATM networks. Software on the host may not know the IP address or the ATM hardware address on the remote endpoint. Thus, an IP address-binding mechanism must provide for the identification of a remote computer connected over a virtual circuit.

TCP/IP allows a subset of computers attached to an ATM network to operate as an independent LAN using the Classical IP Over ATM model. Such a group is called a *logical IP subnet* (LIS) in RFC 1577. Computers in an LIS belong to a single IP subnetwork. A computer in an LIS can communicate directly with any other computer in the same LIS, but is required to use a router when communicating with a computer in another LIS. When a host creates a virtual circuit to a computer in its

---

* Additionally, ATM is a data link layer protocol while IP is a network layer protocol. The IP address is encapsulated within the Service Data Unit passed by IP to the AAL/ATM sublayer. Hence, it is difficult to use this address mechanism by the ATM route-selection process.

LIS, the host must specify an ATM hardware address for the destination. How can a host map a next-hop address in an appropriate ATM hardware address? The host cannot broadcast a request to all computers in the LIS because ATM does not offer hardware broadcast. Instead, it contacts a server to obtain the mapping. Communication between the host and the server uses ATM Address Resolution Protocol (ATMARP).

ATM is treated in more detail in Chap. 5.

1.9.2 Improved access approaches

As implied at various points in this chapter, higher access speeds are required if many of the promises of graphics-, multimedia-, and VR-based Web sites are to become realities.

On the dial-up side, ISDN promises a two- to threefold improvement in speed, but that will soon be swamped by requirements. A technology called *asymmetrical digital subscriber line*, which can be viewed as a mix between a private line and primary rate ISDN and supports up to 6 Mbps, has been advanced, as discussed in Chap. 8.

For corporate-headquarters applications, dedicated access using ISP-provided routers connected over dedicated DS1 (1.544 Mbps) or DS3 (45 Mbps) lines can be utilized. However, the issue of how to handle telecommuting employees remains.

The general use of broadband technology as related to the Internet and intranets is discussed in Chap. 8, including accessing the Internet over cable-TV systems.

1.9.3 A replacement for IP

The number of networks on the Internet doubles approximately every year. With this explosion of growth, there is an increased concern about the availability of IP addresses. The Internet Engineering Steering Group has been working on a new version of IP, called IPng (also called IPv6). The next-generation Internet Protocol will increase the address size from 32 bits to 128 bits, support authentication and security capabilities, and feature quality-of-service labeling of packets to distinguish real-time data from e-mail.

The "IP" part of TCP/IP was designed under the assumption that perhaps a few thousand hosts would be attached to the network. With over several million hosts now IP-accessible, IP is approaching its design limit. One problem IP faces is the consumption of address space. Due to the way IP addresses are segmented into classes of networks, much of the address space is "wasted." In particular, addresses for Class B networks are largely used up. The Internet community has adopted a scheme called Classless Internet Domain Routing (CIRD) that will preserve addresses by abandoning the old class rules. The specifications for CIDR can be found in RFC 1518–1520. CIDR works on the underlying fact that contiguous blocks of IP addresses share the same most significant bits. CIDR uses these summarized contiguous blocks, called *supernets,* to enable route table aggregation. CIRD is expected to provide relief until the late 1990s, when a new scheme is required.[49,50]

The IETF is working on the next-generation IP suite of protocols. In its current draft state, the next generation of IP is known as IP version 6 (IPv6). The version of IP now in use is known as IPv4. At press time, the IPv6 specifications were in draft form only. While the overall architecture is unlikely to change significantly, this can theoretically occur until the specification is released. (IPv6 in an earlier draft was known as Simple IP Plus (SIPP).)

The IETF chose IPv6 from several competing proposals that were discussed and debated during the early 1990s. The overall goal of IPv6 is to create an architectural framework that enables the Internet to grow into a system with millions of interconnected networks. Another equally important goal is to allow a gradual migration to IPv6 from IPv4 with minimal disruption to existing systems. Subgoals within this framework are portable computing and dynamic IP address discovery and assignment. The major competitor was called TCP and UDP with Bigger Addresses (TUBA), which embraces an OSI standard called CLNP. Some engineers believe that a successor to IP needs to be designed to handle the ultimate load imaginable—let's say, 10 devices for every person on the planet, with room for growth in population as well as devices.[49,51]

1.9.4 Support of electronic commerce

Many now claim that the "future belongs to electronic commerce." Effective methods of payment over the Internet have to be developed for this activity to take off. The issues of concern here have been *security* and *privacy.* A number of technologies are becoming available to improve both. Two examples are covered here. Refer to Ref. 52 for a more inclusive treatment.

One example of an approach that can be used is based on Cyber-Cash Incorporated's technology for cost-effective, convenient, and rapid payments over the Internet. Its system is designed to facilitate Internet commerce by enabling financial transactions between individuals, businesses, and financial institutions. The solution is based on establishing a trusted link between the Internet and the traditional banking world. Three services are available: credit card, electronic check, and electronic coin services, which are the Internet counterparts to credit cards, checks, and low-denomination cash payments. The CyberCash Wallet software is distributed to individuals free of charge through private-label arrangements with on-line service providers and financial institutions. It may be directly downloaded from Web sites of the company (www.cybercash.com) and participating merchants. CyberCash provides merchants with free server software and leverages a financial institution's existing infrastructure through its gateway server software. Recently an Internet-based entertainment service based on pay-as-you-play has come on-line. The DigiCash electronic coin service is employed to enable secure payments of as little as $0.95.[53]

Another example is provided by DigiCash (www.digicash.com). The company addresses the issue of privacy. Most e-cash systems have an audit trail in their system for reasons of security, to allow a transaction, or e-cash value of money, to be tracked back to the source, no matter how many times the "unit" of currency is traded between e-cash users. DigiCash is different from other e-cash systems, since it offers privacy in only one direction. As a DigiCash user requests a supply of e-cash tokens from the DigiCash server, those tokens are encrypted using a proprietary encryption system and e-mailed back to the holder. From there, when the holder buys something from a company or another e-cash account holder, he or she mails those tokens to the other person, who then banks them with DigiCash. While the recipient knows where the tokens have come from, and the sender knows where the e-cash was sent, DigiCash itself knows only that the e-cash has been banked by the person or organization who deposited the e-cash. So DigiCash knows where the e-cash has come from directly, but it does not know where the e-cash originated. This system is called one-way privacy, because no one, not even the police or legal authority can backtrack the chain to find out who has the e-cash and where it originated.[54,55] Currently, DigiCash's e-cash system is provided by Mark Twain Bank in the United States. Recently, EUnet, the largest European ISP, also started issuing e-cash in cooperation with Merita Bank, Finland's largest commercial bank.

1.10   Conclusion

With each day, more and more people are becoming computer literate. The increase in technology and the easy GUI applications allow everyone to browse the Internet. In the past, users needed to be concerned with the platform on which they were running. Now, nearly every PC in use has the potential to access the Internet. The decision to learn how to implement these new Internet tools is up to the individual user. The Internet is open to everyone, to explore any subject they ever wondered about.

New markets are expected to increase the load on the Internet. Remote personal computing devices, expanded cellular phone use, and digitally assisted services, may all be users of Internet services. These devices may use a wide range of network connections—radio frequencies, infrared, and wired docks. The evolving version of IP is designed to work with all these networking services. The entertainment industry will also put a large amount of stress on the current network. High bandwidth will be required in the multimedia environment. Some home-use remote-control devices for such things as security, heating, lighting, and watering may also require networking.

References

1. Clark, Tim, *Inter@ctive Week*, Ziff-Davis, October 9, 1995, p. 62.
2. "The Intranet," *Business Week*, February 1996, pp. 76 ff.
3. Means, Paula, "World Wide Web: Servers, Protocols, and Access," Stevens Institute of Technology, class project, fall 1995.
4. Walls, Matthew, "HTML Technology, Applications, and Examples," Stevens Institute of Technology, class project, fall 1995.
5. Krol, Ed, *The Whole Internet User's Guide & Catalog*, 2d ed., O'Reilly & Associates, 1994.
6. Subhas Desai, "An Overview of the Internet," Stevens Institute of Technology, class project, fall 1995.
7. Wiggins, Richard W., *The Internet for Everyone*, McGraw-Hill, New York, 1995, pp. 7–8.
8. Internet file, *A Brief History of the Internet and Related Network*, pp. 1–6.
9. Farzami, B., personal communication, May 1996.
10. Minoli, D., *Distance Learning Technologies*, Artech House, Norwood, Mass., 1996.
11. Eldib, O., and D. Minoli, *Telecommuting*, Artech House, Norwood, Mass., 1995.
12. *Internet History*, Internet file, mcbride@cc.bellcore.com.
13. Bolster, Ann, and Steven McCullough, "Medical Publishing on the Internet: the CMA Goes On-Line," *Canadian Medical Association Journal*, April 1, 1995, pp. 1103–1107.
14. Cromer, Douglas, *Internetworking with TCP/IP*, vol. 1, *Principles, Protocols and Architecture*, Prentice Hall, Englewood Cliffs, New Jersey, 1991.
15. Crotty, Cameron, and Joanna Pearlstein, "Make the Right Connection," *MacWorld*, October 1995, pp. 104–109.
16. Danzig, Peter, Shih-Hao Li, and Katia Obraczka, "Internet Resource Discovery Services," *Computer*, September 1993, pp. 8–22.
17. Esaki, Hiroshi, Masatake Ohta, and Ken-ichi Nagami, "High-Speed Datagram Delivery over Internet Using ATM Technology," *IEICE Transactions on Communications*, August 1995, pp. 1208–1218.
18. Glowniak, Jerry, "Medical Resources on the Internet," *Annals of Internal Medicine*, July 15, 1995, pp. 123–131.
19. Miller, Robert, and Bernard Robin, "Setting Up a SLIP (Serial Line Internet Protocol) Server and Gopher Site," *Computers and Geosciences*, July 1995, pp. 759–769.
20. Simms, David, "Next-Generation Internet Protocol," *IEEE Software*, Januay 1995, p. 113.
21. Demarks, Denise, "New Technologies for Internet Communications," Stevens Institute of Technology, class project, fall 1995.
22. Jean S. Ghaly, "Internet Overview," Stevens Institute of Technology, class project, fall 1995.
23. de Sa, Rosmena, "The Internet Structure, Protocols, and Access," Stevens Institute of Technology, class project, fall 1995.
24. Comer, Douglas E., *Internetworking with TCP/IP*, vol. I, Prentice Hall, Englewood Cliffs, N.J., 1995.
25. Stallings, William, *The Business Guide to Local Area Network*, Howard W. Sams & Company, Indianapolis, Ind., 1990.

26. McNamara, John, *Local Area Networks, An Introduction to the Technology,* DEC, Burlington, Mass., 1987.
27. From the World Wide Web, http://WWW.Morning Star.com.
28. Internet file, *A Brief History of the Internet and Related Network,* pp. 7–8.
29. Wiggins, Richard W., *The Internet for Everyone,* McGraw-Hill, New York, 1995, pp. 15–20.
30. Minoli, D., and A. Alles, *Understanding LAN Emulation and Other Related Technologies,* Artech House, Norwood, Mass., 1997.
31. Jean S. Ghaly, "ATM Communications," Stevens Institute of Technology, class project, fall 1995.
32. Minoli, D., *First, Second, and Next-Generation LANs,* McGraw-Hill, New York, 1994.
33. Falk, Bennet, *The Internet Roadmap,* SYBEX, 1994.
34. Washburn, K., J. T. Evans, *TCP/IP: Running a Successful Network,* Addison-Wesley, 1995.
35. Stevens, W. Richard, *TCP/IP Illustrated,* vol. 1, *The Protocols,* Addison-Wesley, 1995.
36. Various RFCs.
37. Trade press articles in *PC Computing* and *PC Magazine* (e.g., October 11, 1994).
38. Cisco and 3Com technical publications.
39. Wiggins, Richard W., *The Internet for Everyone,* McGraw-Hill, New York, 1995, pp. 73–87.
40. Hendrick, Charles L., *Introduction to Internet Protocols,* Rutgers University, New Jersey, 1987, pp. 1–17.
41. Comer, D. E., and D. L. Stevens, *Internetworking with TCP/IP,* vol. III, 2d ed., Prentice-Hall, Englewood Cliffs, N.J., 1996.
42. Lynch, Daniel C., and Marshall T. Rose, *Internet System Handbook,* Addison-Wesley Publishing Company, New York, 1993, pp. 104–106.
43. Eddings, Joshua, *How Internet Works,* Ziff-Davis Press, Emeryville, Ohio.
44. Lynch, Daniel C., and Marshall T. Rose, *Internet System Handbook,* Addison-Wesley Publishing Company, New York, 1993, pp. 186–188.
45. Lynch, Daniel C., and Marshall T. Rose, *Internet System Handbook,* Addison-Wesley Publishing Company, New York, 1993, pp. 216–217.
46. Wiggins, Richard W., *The Internet for Everyone,* McGraw-Hill, New York, 1995, pp. 14–15.
47. Hendrick, Charles L., *Introduction to Internet Protocols,* Rutgers University, New Jersey, 1987, pp. 1–17.
48. Lynch, Daniel C., and Marshall T. Rose, *Internet System Handbook,* Addison-Wesley Publishing Company, New York, 1993, pp. 270–271.
49. Laquey, Tracy, with Jeanne C. Ryer, *The Internet Companion: A Beginner's Guide to Global Networking,* Addison-Wesley Publishing Company, Reading, Mass., 1993.
50. Wiggins, Richard W., *The Internet for Everyone,* McGraw-Hill, New York, 1995, pp. 573–575.
51. Carl-Mitchell, Smoot, "The New Internet Protocol (IETF's IPv6) Will Replace 32-Bit Addresses with 128-Bit Addresses," Miller Freeman Inc., *UNIX Review,* vol. 13, no. 7, June 1995, p. 31(6).
52. Minoli, D., *Electronic Commerce over the Internet,* McGraw-Hill, New York, to appear early 1997.
53. "CyberCash & Rocket Science Pay-As-You-Play Online Arcade," *Newsbytes,* Feb. 13, 1996.
54. "Netherlands's DigiCash Opens for Business in Australia," *Newsbytes,* April 1, 1996.
55. "DigiCash Revealed at Smart Card '96 Show," *Newsbytes,* February 16, 1996.

2

Router Technology

Over the past decade, there has been growing demand for interconnected communication networks.* The need to have the end-to-end
connection, whether it be to support an e-mail application, a database
query, or Internet access, fuels the need to have a seamless internetwork (internet) environment. The 1980s-style LAN applications no
longer satisfy all of the customer's needs. Routers and bridges have
been playing a critical link to enable the metropolitan area network
(MAN) and wide area network (WAN) frame- and cell-switching technologies.

Full-fledged Internet access (for large institutions) is accomplished
using directly connected routers. This chapter provides an overview
of router technology for high-speed Internet access. Some of the concepts introduced in Chap. 1 are treated in greater depth, as needed.
However, it is not this chapter's goal to provide an exhaustive treatment of this topic, and a number of issues (such as the utilization of
level 2 switches—be these Ethernet switches or ATM switches—as a
way to relieve the need for MAC-level or network-level segmentation
in support of higher per-user bandwidth) are mentioned briefly or not
at all.†

Figure 2.1 depicts the environment to which router technology
applies, with an identification of pertinent "routed protocols" and "routing protocols." Routed protocols of particular interest include IP, previously discussed. Commonly implemented router protocols can be

---

* This chapter was contributed by Shaw-Kung Jong, AT&T Bell Laboratories, Business Broadband Networks.

† For a discussion of these topics as well as a discussion of virtual LANs, the reader
may wish to consult Ref. 1.

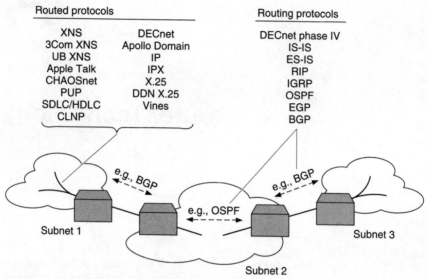

Figure 2.1 The router environment.

classified into two categories: *interior routing* and *exterior routing* protocols. Interior routing protocols, such as Routing Information Protocol (RIP), Open Shortest Path First (OSPF), and Interior Gateway Routing Protocol (IGRP), and exterior routing protocols, such as Exterior Gateway Protocol (EGP) and Border Gateway Protocol (BGP), will be studied.

2.1 Introduction

Prior to the late 1970s, centralized data processing prevailed, where a mainframe was connected via clusters of dumb terminals. The need for interhost communication was scarce, and the capability was very limited. In the IBM 360/370 world, data communication typically means an SNA network using multidrop lines, with X.25 as the remote communication network protocol.

The introduction of personal computers during the late 1970s created the need for sharing peripheral devices such as printers and disk space. The LAN enables PC users connected to the shared resources. Furthermore, the emergence of minicomputers drove the need for the distributed data processing.*

During the 1980s, corporations across the world were beginning to invest in their own infrastructures. Information was regarded as

---

* The minicomputer vendors during the 1970s and 1980s were Wang, DEC, Harris, Data General, Sperry, NCR, 3M, and Burroughs, to name a few.

an important asset. In order to enhance the corporate competitive edge, information must move freely among users within a company; to some extent this information infrastructure has been extended to customers and vendors. The Internet is the premier example of an interenterprise network. WAN and MAN tie the computers and their peripheral devices together.

Data processing applications have become more sophisticated. The client/server model often means that a network of machines are connected to run communication protocols such as TCP/IP. In this age of multimedia, data objects (data records, video/audio files, graphics and images, and large files) must be delivered to remote machines regardless of the host computers' operating systems, hardware platform, and physical network connection. There has been an explosion in the use of the World Wide Web. In short, today's challenge for communications professionals is to *mesh* the global internetwork into a seamless information repository for users so that they can *"get it, move it, use it!"**

2.2   Network Fundamentals (OSI Layers)

In order to simplify data movement among various end systems, it is pragmatic to modularize the communication mechanisms, so that each module behaves as a predefined communication standard. The OSIRM discussed in Chap. 1 is the standard for identifying the layers and the services provided in a communication system. There are seven layers of hierarchical communication levels. Each layer provides a service to the layer above it. For example, the network layer provides a service to the transport layer, and the transport layer presents "data" to the internetwork system.

The network layer *encapsulates* the data, passed down from the transport layer, within a *network header.* The header contains information such as source and destination *logical* addresses.

The data link layer adds *frame header* and *trailer* to the encapsulated packet passed down from the network layer. The frame header contains the *physical* addresses.

The physical layer provides the physical transmission medium (such as DS1, DS3, SONET) connections. Multiplexers, repeaters, and hubs are typical internetworking devices at the physical layer.

Repeaters and hubs are physical layer relays in the OSI terminology; bridges are data link layer relays; and routers are network layer relays. These are illustrated in Fig. 2.2.

---

* AT&T's official slogan.

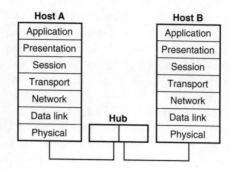

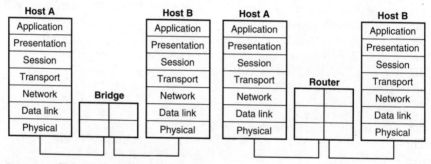

Figure 2.2   Hubs/bridges/routers internetwork protocol levels.

2.2.1   Hubs

Physical connections among hosts are limited by the length of the interconnecting cable. The distance between any two nodes must be within a cable-specific range or the signal will be diminished. A *hub* (or a *multi-port repeater*) is a physical layer device that receives, amplifies, and retransmits the signals to the other end. Hubs generally are inexpensive devices. Because the hub amplifies the signals, it also copies the signal disturbance of errors. In a LAN environment, the number of repeaters placed between segments should be limited to three. Another alternative is to use *bridges*.

2.2.2   Bridges

As networking technology proliferated, users required solutions that would allow them to add more users to the network, extend network distances, and translate data between different LAN technologies. These requirements essentially created demand for the local bridge. A bridge is an internetwork component designed to interconnect LANs to perform the function of a single large network. Bridge technology supports layer 2 (data link layer) protocols, namely, logical link control (LLC) and medium access control (MAC).[2] A bridge interconnects multiple networks, providing communications between networks. It examines the destination address of each frame received. If the source and destination are on the same network segment, the bridge filters the frame. If the destination is on a different network segment, the bridge forwards the frame. The protocols that support the bridge technology dictate the flow control, error handling, addressing, and media access algorithms. Examples of popular data link layer protocols include Ethernet, Token Ring, and FDDI (fiber distributed data interface). Figure 2.3 illustrates a typical LAN setup.[3]

The decision to keep traffic local or to forward the frame is made without regard to upper-layer protocols. Bridges can therefore be a cost-effective solution for physical-homogeneous, but protocol-heterogeneous, network environments. Bridges can also interconnect different physical layer media types such as coaxial cable, fiber-optic, or twisted-pair networks within the same data link layer.

2.2.3 Routers

The next technological challenge in the LAN arena involved connecting LANs to other geographically separate LANs over a wide area service. Routers provide connectivity by appropriately filtering and forwarding (routing) packets of information. Routers are more intelligent than bridges in that routers operate at the OSI model layer 3 (network layer). They are used to interconnect IP subnetworks or other subnetworks. Routers can also serve as the functions of hub (physical layer) and bridge (data link layer). Router technology is more sophisticated than bridge technology because routers can operate in bridging mode to handle LAN traffic and in routing mode to connect LANs to WANs.

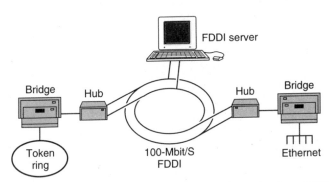

Figure 2.3 Dual-fiber-optic-rings FDDI configuration in a LAN environment.

Besides routing packets from source to destination, routers also can provide value-added features. The routing intelligence makes the value-added features feasible. These features include:

- Traffic sequencing
- Security filtering
- Network management
- Resource maintenance

Modern routers can parse the entire network layer header, thereby supporting sophisticated filtering (this was not always the case, since only a few fields could be examined until recently). Routers now forward an aggregate of 100,000 to 500,000 64-byte PDUs per second (fewer if the PDUs are of maximum data link layer level). Just the forwarding effort can place a burden on the router, but the addition of complex filtering further taxes the processor. The deep reading of the header and its storage translates into large amounts of RAM and flash memory on the router (e.g., 16 MB).

Typically, routers are required to support multiple protocol stacks, each with its own routing protocols, and to allow these different environments to operate in parallel. (See Fig. 2.4.)

As shown in Fig. 2.4, the router supports different data communication access media: FDDI, Token Ring, Ethernet, private and public networks, and switched LANs.

Routing algorithms are used to propagate connectivity information. While the particulars of each routing algorithm differ, there are several goals each routing algorithm attempts to achieve. These include:

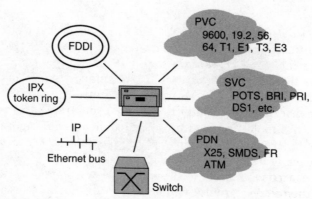

Figure 2.4 Router support multiple-access media.

- *Optimality.* A routing algorithm should always choose the best routes, based on the route selection criteria.

- *Rapid convergence.* A routing algorithm must behave not only with robustness in the event of topology changes, it must also allow other routers to know the situation quickly so that a decision can be made.

- *Robustness.* If the network topology changes, it produces the new best paths.

- *Simplicity.* It should minimize network bandwidth and router processing overhead.

Router algorithms can be classified by type, as in the following examples.

Static versus dynamic routing. The decision process of routing packets from one router to another can be either static or dynamic. For the static routing, the path between source and destination is fixed. The static routing algorithm is typically adopted where network traffic is relatively predictable and network design is relatively simple. Static routing tables do not adjust to the network changes, so they should be used only when routes do not change or the destination host can be reached only through one route.

Static routing, by definition, is not much of a "routing algorithm" because of the fixed nature of the routing. Dynamic, on the other hand, adjusts to the changing network traffic or topology and makes the hopping decision in real time. Dynamic routing algorithms must be capable of adjusting their routing tables quickly when adverse circumstances (interrupted circuits, congestion, etc.) occur. A router's dynamic routing table is built from the information exchanged by routing protocols. Routing protocols handle complex routing topology more quickly and accurately than the system administrators can.

Distance vector routing versus link state routing. Distance vector algorithm was the original form of dynamic routing. This algorithm requires that a router maintain a table of topology information that allows the algorithm to determine the direction (vector) and the distance to any link in the internetworks. The topology information indicates the numeric measurement (a metric) from any router to any other routers. The measurements can be a simple bandwidth, a hop count, or number of routers that must be traversed to arrive at the destination. Once a router calculates each of its distance vectors, it sends the information to its neighbors on a regular basis (e.g., once a minute). If network topology changes, the receiving router will modify its routing table and transmit it to each of its neighbors.

The distance vector routing algorithm does not allow a router to know the exact topology of an internetwork. Because the node realizes only the cost of its adjacent routers, the cost of reaching remote routers is derived. Therefore the distance vector routing encounters the slow convergence problem. This implies that information about route failures has a propagation delay (e.g., 30 seconds). The consequence of this is that there may be a period of vulnerability.

Link-state routing is a newer form of dynamic routing. Each router maintains a database of the entire network topology. The information is somewhat analogous to a road map with a *you-are-here* pointer showing a map reader's current location.

Each router sends out a link-state packet (LSP) that describes the current state of all its links. Sending the LSP is commonly referred to as *route advertisement*. An LSP is broadcast to all routers at a much longer interval than its counterpart in the distance vector routing algorithm.

Link-state routing eliminates many of the problems inherent in distance vector routing. Because each router knows the complete network topology, routing loops will not be formed. Link-state routing converges much faster than distance vector routing. Link-state routing sends routing updates only every half hour or when there is a change in network topology, whereas distance vector routing updates every minute or so. Link-state routing thus consumes much less bandwidth at the cost of increased route calculation processing.

2.2.4 Router/bridge/hub application example

This section provides an example of routers used in an internet. This will show you some of the key issues involved in building these kinds of corporate networks.

WorldPlus was an AT&T International calling-card application, allowing international subscribers to make phone calls from anywhere to anywhere in several languages. The service also provides voice recognition, language interpretation, international directory assistance, voice messaging, and travel assistance. This feature-rich service was merged with *USADirect* in 1995. (See Fig. 2.5.) The Cisco router used has three ports: one port each connected to the platform clusters' SynOptics (now Bay Networks) LattisSwitch System 3000 (there are two identical clusters in the WorldPlus platform for fault-tolerant and load-balancing reasons); another port is connected to the Ovation Manager messaging platform. Cisco router is the gateway to AT&T's Star-WAN service, which allows data connection to other WorldPlus nodes.

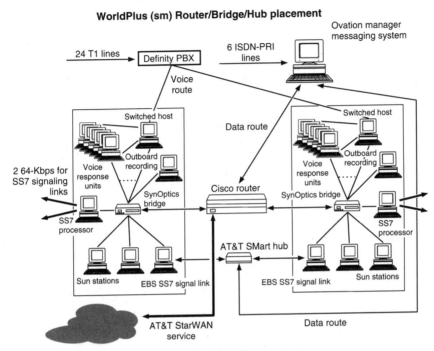

Figure 2.5   An internetworking example: WorldPlus service.

The SynOptics (now Bay Networks) bridges two separate subnets. It also provides connection points to other Sun Sparc 10 workstations, Voice Response Units, and Out-Board Recording machines (for Automatic Speech Modeling purposes). Voice and Fax Messaging accounts are provisioned through the Ovation Manager. Messaging account authentication was initiated through the SS7 protocol which is connected via an AT&T Smart Hub to the Ovation Manager. For the network topology management, WorldPlus uses Bay Networks' Optivity software, which is managed through SNMP over IP.

2.3   Internet routing

The internet technology* is the result of research funded by the Advanced Projects Research Agency. As discussed in Chap. 1, the technology includes a set of network standards that specify the details of

---

* We will capitalize the word *Internet* when referring specifically to the protocol supported by the Internet Advisory Board. Lowercase *internet* or *internetworking* describes the technology in generic terms.

how computers communicate, as well as a set of conventions for interconnecting networks and routing traffic. Commonly referred to as *TCP/IP*, it can be used to communicate across any set of interconnected networks.[4] Later, TCP/IP was included with the Berkeley Software Distribution (BSD) of UNIX.

The Internet protocol suite includes not only TCP (transport layer, layer 4) and IP (network layer, layer 3) protocols, but also specifications for such common applications as mail, terminal emulation, and file transfer. (See Fig. 2.6.)

2.3.1 Routing protocols

In order to route the packets from host A to host B, a set of rules must be established to coordinate the network topology and make intelligent routing decisions. Routing protocols are designed not only to switch to a backup route when the primary routes become severed, they are also designed to decide which route to a destination is "best." On any network where there are multiple paths to the same destination, a routing protocol should be used.

2.3.1.1 Autonomous system.

An *autonomous system* (AS) is one particular group of networks under the *same* administrative authority and control. An autonomous system, sometimes referred to as a *routing domain,* is not merely an independent network. It is a collection of networks and gateways with its own internal mechanism for collecting routing information and passing it to other independent network systems. Within an autonomous system, a protocol must be used for

OSI Model		The Internet Protocol Suite	
Application	7	Telnet FTP	NFS
Presentation	6	SMTP	XDR
Session	5	SNMP DNS	RPC
Transport	4	TCP, UDP	
Network	3	IP, ICMP, ARP, RARP, X.25 PLP, Routing protocols*	
Data link	2	LLC, MAC, X.25, Frame relay, ATM	
Physical	1	Sonet, X.21, RS-232, V.35, HSSI, HPPI	

* Routing protocols: RIP, OSPF, IGRP, EGP, BGP

Figure 2.6 A schematic diagram of OSI and corresponding Internet layers.

route discovery, propagating, and validating routes. Those that operate within the same routing domain use called Interior Gateway* Protocols (IGPs). The major IGPs include RIP, HELLO, and OSPF. A routing domain exchanges routing information with other domains using Exterior Gateway Protocol or Border Gateway Protocol. Cisco's proprietary interior routing protocol, Interior Gateway Routing Protocol (IGRP), has been in the marketplace the longest, has proved the most popular among router users, and can be used both within a domain and between domains. (See Fig. 2.7.[5])

The network topology illustrated in Fig. 2.7 has three autonomous systems (or domains): A, B, C. The interior protocols for them are RIP, IGRP, and OSPF, respectively. Their exterior protocols are BGP (domain A–B) and EGP (domain A–C).

2.3.1.2 Routing loops (bouncing effect). If all routers in an internetwork do not have up-to-date, accurate information about the actual state of the network topology, incorrect routing information may be used to make a routing decision. Using incorrect information may

---

* The word *Gateway* is misleading. The formal definition of *gateway* encompass the top four layers of the OSI reference model, whereas the *gateway* described here really means the OSI IP routing level (layer 3) only.

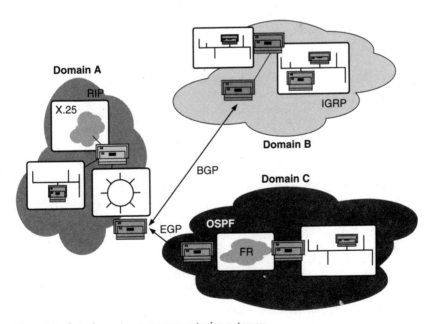

Figure 2.7 Interior gateway versus exterior gateway.

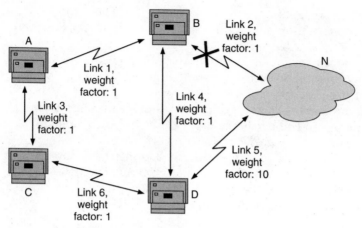

Figure 2.8 A sample network topology.

cause packets to take less-than-optimum paths or paths that return the packets they have already visited.

The network topology illustrated in Fig. 2.8 has four nodes (A, B, C, and D) and the network N. There are six links. All links, except link 5, have a weight-cost factor of 1. Link 5 has a cost factor of 10. Here is the scenario depicting the *routing loops*.

Time T1. The following routes are recorded in the routing table when all links are up. No route disconnects at time T1:

From	Link	Cost
A to N	1	2
B to N	2	1
C to N	3	3
D to N	4	2

This table says that from one node (for example, node A) to the network N, the packet has to traverse through link 1. The cost of reaching N is 2, because link 1 followed by link 2 has to be utilized. Note that although D is adjacent to N, because the weight-cost factor of link 5 is 10, D is taking Link 4, then Link 2 to N.

Time T2. Link 2 breaks; N is not reachable. Node B notices the problem within 30 seconds. (The *distance vector algorithm* requires the node to send out its own status to the neighboring nodes. This is how B detects something went wrong with N.) B updates the cost to N to "infinity." The table will appear as follows:

From	Link	Cost
A to N	1	2
B to N	2	Infinity
C to N	3	3
D to N	4	2

Time T3. Right after the table has been updated, and *before* B gets a chance to send out this new information to nodes A and C, A sends its own distance vector to B and C. B sees the just-arrived information and realizes that from A to N is still reachable and costs 2 units. It also knows that from B to A costs 1 unit. B "thought" the path to N would be by way of A. The B-to-N entry in the table, therefore, is updated as follows:

From	Link	Cost
A to N	1	2
B to N	1	3
C to N	3	3
D to N	4	2

Time T4. Within 30 seconds, B advertises the new status to A and D nodes as follows:

From	Link	Cost
A to N	1	4
B to N	1	3
C to N	3	3
D to N	4	4

Both A-to-N and D-to-N costs have been upgraded. Note that the routing table now includes a loop: packets from A bound to N will reach B until their *time to live* value (in the IP header) expires.

The routing loop (called the *bouncing effect,* as packets are bounced between two adjacent routers without passing directly to the end network) is a severe problem. A great deal of research has been invested in solving this problem. One of the solutions, called *hold-down* technique, has been adopted by most router vendors.

2.3.1.3 Hold-down technique. *Distance vector* routing algorithms are self-correcting, but it takes a long time before the loop is detected. This problem can be avoided by using a technique called *hold-down*. Hold-down works as follows: When B realizes that N is not reachable, a *hold-down timer* is activated. If N becomes reachable again before the timer expires, B removes the timer and a notable update occurs. If an update arrives from either A or D (its neighbors) with a better cost than originally recorded, B removes the timer and updates the table—N is accessible! If A or D sends B a worse cost (in this case, the cost is 3) than B's original cost (it was 1 before the break), the update is ignored. When 30 seconds expires, B will inform A and D of the new disruption status. The loop, therefore, is avoided.

2.3.1.4 Interior routing protocols. As indicated in the previous section, there are two different ways of making decisions to route packets from source to destination for the routing protocols: (1) *distance vector algorithm* and (2) *link-state algorithm.* In this section, we will be looking into three interior routing protocols: Routing Information Protocol, the Interior Gateway Routing Protocol, and the Open Shortest Path First. RIP (based on the distance vector algorithm) is much simpler but less powerful than OSPF and IGRP. IGRP is the Cisco proprietary protocol, but given the fact that the IGRP has been in the marketplace the longest and Cisco has a significant router market share, IGRP is very well known within the routing industry (an enhanced version, EIGRP is now also becoming available).

Routing Information Protocol (RIP). RIP was originally developed from research at the Xerox Palo Alto Research Center for the Xerox Network Systems (XNS). The major features of RIP include the following:

- A *hop count* is used as the RIP's cost metric. The hop count is the number of routers that each packet must traverse through. The maximum number of hops allowed is 15. The network is considered unreachable if the hop count is greater than 15.

- Updates of routing tables are sent by routers every 60 seconds.

- Routes are timed out in 3 minutes unless an update for that path has arrived.

The network topology indicated in Fig. 2.6 will produce the following:

From/to	Link	Cost
A	Local	0
B	1	1
D	3	1
C	1	2
E	1	2

Interior Gateway Routing Protocol (IGRP). During the mid 1980s, the protocol of the IP routing was RIP. People realized that the RIP has many shortcomings. For example, RIP uses hop count as the only metric. In reality, there should be more than one criteria to make the routing decision. The IAB is responsible for coming up with the solution for this problem. While waiting for IAB to come up with the standard, Cisco came up with a solution and implemented the IGRP proprietary protocol that cures some of RIP's defects and could be marketed before the IETF finishes its work on the new solution. IGRP incorporates the hold-down algorithm to avoid the loop situation. The improvements over RIP are as follows:

- Composite metrics (hop count, bandwidth, etc.)
- Multipath routing
- Loop avoidance (split horizon, path hold-down, and poison reverse updates)
- Default routing handling

Open Shortest Path First (OSPF). OSPF is a link-state routing protocol.[6] OSPF is based on the "distributed map" concept: all nodes have a copy of the network map, which is regularly updated. Each node (router) contains a routing directory database. This database contains information about the router's interfaces that are operable, as well as status information about adjacent routers. This information is periodically *advertised* (broadcast) to all routers in the same domain. The OSPF computes the shortest path to the other routers. OSPF has the following characteristics:

- It supports multiple circuit load balancing, because OSPF can store multiple routes to a destination.
- It authenticates routing update information to ensure it is valid. (See Sec. 2.3.2, "Routing Security.")
- It can converge very quickly to network topology changes.
- It supports multiple metrics.
- It is not susceptible to routing loops.

For the OSPF, the same network topology in the RIP section will have the following:

From	To	Link	Distance
A	B	1	1
A	D	3	1
B	A	1	1
B	C	2	1
B	E	4	1
C	B	2	1
C	E	5	1
D	A	3	1
D	E	6	1
E	B	4	1
E	C	5	1
E	D	6	1

2.3.1.5 Exterior routing protocols

Exterior Gateway Protocol (EGP). The EGP is an interdomain reachability protocol used in connecting internet backbone routers. EGP does not use routing metrics and therefore cannot make true routing decisions; it only exchanges reachability information. It reports which network is available through which routers.

EGP is the first exterior routing protocol. Internet has come a long way since the early years and EGP is the legacy of old ARPANet days. The new exterior protocol is Border Gateway Protocol (BGP).

Border Gateway Protocol (BGP). BGP represents an attempt to address the most serious of EGP's problems. BGP is an interdomain routing protocol created for use in the Internet. Unlike EGP, BGP was designed to detect routing loops and exchange routing updates. BGP and other exterior protocols are replacing EGP in the Internet. BGP uses TCP as its transport mechanism.

BGP routing updates consist of a combination of network number and autonomous systems (AS) path pairings. The AS path is simply a list of all autonomous systems that must be traversed to reach a specific network. Because BGP lists the complete route to the destination, routing loops and slow convergence issues are avoided.

2.3.2 Routing Security

In the age of the information superhighway, hosts that are connected to the highway are exposed to a wider range of security threats than unconnected hosts. The Internet provides equal access for all: welcome visitors as well as unwelcome intruders. Currently, when it comes to the highway security, the router industry really does not have very many preventive safeguards. Rather, emphasis has been placed more on the *computer host's* security. This is analogous to home security, where people lock their doors to prevent unwanted intruders (host machines) rather than blocking the streets. Some may argue that we could still put more security patrols and checkpoints on the streets.

The following are security measures that can be done by the router industry to prevent highway robbery:

Padlock the routers. Owners of routers may put their routers in a secured area and lock them up. As noted earlier, to implement AT&T's *WorldPlus* project, Cisco routers were used to allow data communication among WorldPlus global sites. (See Fig. 2.5 for WorldPlus technical diagram.) AT&T provided the StarWAN service, which includes routers. Service providers usually place a complicated lock on their routers, and only site managers have access to the key.

Encrypt data files. When application files depart from the host machines, they can be encrypted at the source router level and decrypted at the destination router.

Build firewalls. Firewalls are generally computer systems, not routers. A firewall system replaces an IP router with a host computer that does not forward packets. By not forwarding IP packets between networks, firewalls effectively sever the connection between the networks. Figure 2.9 shows a router and a firewall.[7] The firewall acts as a proxy for users inside the protected cloud.

Figure 2.9 indicates that for the regular, pass-through router, packets are forwarded through the IP layer without restriction. In the firewall security system, no packets are forwarded. Packets addressed to the firewall are processed locally by the firewall machine.

The basic implementation of a firewall is simple: turn off one of the UNIX kernel parameters and rebuild the UNIX. No outgoing packets will be forwarded after the UNIX is rebuilt.

Filter out packets at the router level. This technique has been adopted by the router industry. This is done in a table. The router administrator may specify the type of user they want to block from access by specifying a host name and the corresponding port numbers. As indicated in the Ref. 8, this defensive technique is just a first step in an overall security policy.

Authenticate at the router protocol level. The newer router protocols such as RIP-2 and OSPF have some rudimentary authentication mechanisms built into them. In RIP-2, there is a 2-octet field (Authentication Type) and a 16-octet Authentication field. In OSPF, another field (in addition to Autype and Authentication fields) performs the checksum.

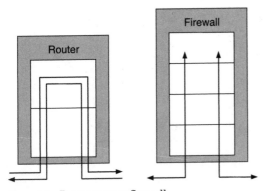

Figure 2.9   Router versus firewall.

Current design, however, falls short of tight security requirements because the "Authentication" fields in both RIP-2 and OSPF protocols are nothing more than a "simple password" procedure. It may not take long for an intruder to figure out the password and simply insert the password string into the Authentication field. The malicious packet then can be masqueraded as an authentic one.

To have better protection at the protocol level, more research should be done to come up with a better authentication algorithm.

2.4 New Developments

2.4.1 Switch-based routing

The router industry has undergone dramatic changes over the past 10 years. Traditional routing is being transformed to the next-generation technologies based on *LAN switching* and *ATM switching*. It is certain that the next wave of attention will be on the switched arena. LAN switching is an evolution of traditional LANs where each user has its own segment; the LAN switch then acts as a multipoint bridge to allow interconnection of all segments. The emergence of *edge routers* and *edge switches*[9] can more efficiently segment LANs when coupled with ATM technology. Here interconnection is supported in large measure by switching; routing tends to occur only when IP subnetwork boundaries have to be crossed.

The edge router, usually located on the customer's premises, differs from a traditional router in its "split personality," in which one side supports *legacy network** traffic through LAN emulation/encapsulation, while the other side looks to a fastpacket wide area network. The edge router converts LAN packets to frames (or packets, cells) such as X.25, frame relay, SMDS, and ATM.

The key application for LAN switches is LAN segmentation. These devices substantially improve performance in medium- to large-size networks that support numbers of user connections. The protocols that LAN switches support can be classified based on the following categories:

- Ethernet
- Token Ring
- FDDI
- ATM

Edge switch is the adjunct switch (adjunct as opposed to the main switch) that can be found in proximity of the user. Edge switches are essentially part of the public network. They serve as the concentration

---

* *Legacy network* means the older, slower technology in a multiplexing scheme.

point for different traffic objects—voice, data, audio, and video. They may also support the conversion from legacy to fastpacket protocols (although this can alternatively be done by the edge router). Some routers now incorporate an ATM switch in their fabric (e.g., Ipsilon's IP Switching equipment).

In the WAN world, the advantages of switch-based routing over the old routing legacy are manyfold. Among them[10]:

- *Effective bandwidth.* The new computing will likely incorporate more multimedia objects. These applications will require more and more bandwidth. Switched networks can manage bandwidth better. Switching-based technology can manage the available bandwidth needed without keeping expensive, high-speed channels open when they are not being used.

- *Cost saving.*[11] The switching router does something no traditional one can do—it merges voice traffic from the PBX onto the same lines that carry the data traffic. This consolidation saves the cost of separate circuits—relieving all the congestion on the campus backbone and providing guaranteed bandwidth.

- *Greater scalability.* A switch-centric model provides smooth scalability up to several gigabytes per second across a wide area. Users have access to media-speed bandwidth on demand.

LAN switching* is still an evolving market segment. Given the advantages of LAN switching technology over the older one, this market no doubt will grow. It is predicted that the LAN switch will prevail in the next few years. The ATM-based edge routing will gradually occupy more market share for the next 10 years. Many vendors have already announced plans to offer the switching-based routing platform. For example, IBM has developed its Switched Virtual Networking (SVN) strategy for migrating router and SNA-based networks to switched ATM networks.[12] SVN supports multiprotocol environments that address both LAN and SNA architectures.

Although ATM technology offers users the aforementioned advantages, the predicted rapid takeoff of ATM at the desktop has not been realized. There has been slow acceptance of ATM on the part of the user community for various reasons[13]:

1. Users have already invested billions of dollars in the traditional routers. The retirement of such a huge investment will not likely happen soon.

---

* Here users are interconnected via a layer 2 Ethernet switch, rather than by a router, except if subnet boundaries are crossed.

2. The long-predicted *bandwidth-hungry* killer applications have not yet arrived. The LAN/WAN applications are, by and large, still limited mostly to the ASCII file transfer and e-mail, which do not require broadband protocol such as ATM. In most cases, T1- or fractional T1-based applications such as frame relay can serve current needs.

We can therefore predict that remote bridges, traditional routers, LAN switching, and ATM switching will be coexisting for the next 10 years. Figure 2.10 depicts the interconnection of those devices.[14]

2.4.2   Routing in software

Another routing trend lies in the *routing software* development. Software routing (sometimes referred to as *source routing*) means that there is no need to have dedicated router hardware to store and update the addresses. The software may reside in a general-purpose PC or within the same host. The software gives the host machine the intelligence to calculate and make routing decisions. Software routers choose the better routes more often because they typically

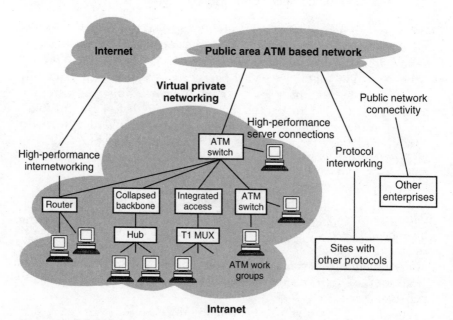

Figure 2.10   Likely interconnection network.

discover all possible routes to the destination before the packet is actually sent.

Traditionally, the routing functionality, such as addressing, multicasting, and packet delivery capabilities, are handled in stand-alone hardware. There is a push to place those functionalities in general-purpose computer software offerings.

The trend of *going software* can be seen by the alliance of the computer/router industries' major players: (1) computer vendor Compaq is developing the network product that will include Cisco System's routing technology; (2) Microsoft is teaming up with Bay Network's routing technology into Windows NT server and Cairo platform. Separately, Novell has been the software pioneer with a highly sophisticated routing product—NetWare Link Service Protocol (NLSP). Cisco also offers a software protocol named LAN2LAN.

There are a few drawbacks to software routing[15]:

- Some of the host (software) routing is housed in the PC, which may not have the necessary processing power to handle the traffic.

- Software routing would not handle all or most of the routing protocols.

- Software routing may not be as configurable as the hardware router.

Another trend is to separate the routing decision from the forwarding decision. This model, evolving under the MuliProtocol Over ATM (MPOA) work of The ATM Forum uses a centralized route server, along with cut-through methods over ATM.

2.4.3 Multicasting

In today's computing, in order to transmit files among machines (such as remote copy or ftp files), the operations are serial in nature. Consider, for example, the simple network topology of Fig. 2.11.

Suppose that we want to send a copy of a file from node C to nodes A, B, D, and E in a serial fashion. We would need transmissions over the following routes: C–B, C–B–A, C–E, C–E–D. Note that nodes B and E have been traversed twice: once as the transit nodes and again as the recipient (destination) nodes. The fact that both nodes are referenced more than once will cause the network unnecessary traffic congestion. "Multicast routing" algorithms do not allow the node to be traversed more than once.[16]

There are a few applications that require multicasting routing features:

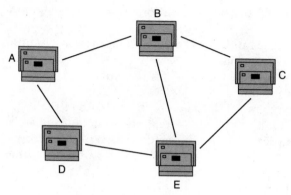

Figure 2.11   A simple network topology.

1. Weather map distribution
2. Credit card authentication (broadcast the lost card number to distributed database sites)
3. Videoconferencing

IETF researchers deployed multicast backbone (MBONE) in experiments conducted in the early 1990s. The MBONE applications include two-way audio and sometimes video transmissions of things such as Internet Talk Radio, IETF member videoconference, NASA coverage of space shuttle activities, and even presidential addresses. The MBONE was a big success among the research community. Since then, many router vendors are including the multicast feature in their product offering.

2.4.4   Mobile routing

The mobile data service concept has existed since 1984. IBM and Federal Express have been using radio channels as the transmission medium to access and retrieve inventory and invoice ordering from their host stations.[2] In fact, the *packet radio* originated from the ALOHA experiment in the late 1970s. The ALOHA project paved the way for carrier sense multiple access with collision detection (CSMA/CD) technique, which is the protocol for the shared-access local networks such as Ethernet.

In this era of portable computer proliferation, computer users may sometimes need to connect to the Internet world while they are traveling. (Do you have the need to retrieve your office e-mail when you are waiting for an airplane? Do you wish to hook up to the Web while you are staying at a hotel on business trips?)

Currently there are some methods of allowing portable computer users to achieve mobile computing. They all involve static technology,* which is unsuitable for the Internet routing. Mobile IP requirements include the following:

1. A mobile host should be capable of continuing to communicate, using the same IP address, after it has been disconnected from the Internet and reconnected at a different point.

2. A mobile host should be capable of interoperating with existing hosts, routers, and services.

3. No weakening of IP security should occur at the router level. If a legitimate mobile user can move around use the same IP address, an intruder might be able to configure his or her address accordingly. Routers at the Internet access path must have a tight authentication process.

4. Multicasting should be possible while the mobile host machine is not stationary (i.e., maintain the location of the mobile hosts at the router level such that broadcasting messages will be delivered).

There are two major phases in the mobile IP protocol:

1. *Beaconing protocol.* When the mobile host moves around, it can "realize" that it is moving by listening to beacons on the radio. At some point it will discover that the beacons from a new base are louder and clearer than those of the previous base; then it is time to switch.

2. *Registration procedure.* Through the beaconing protocol, the mobile host has discovered the IP and "media" address of the new base. It must now register with this new base and obtain its agreement to relay packets.

Currently, the IETF is researching this subject. There are several difficult technical tasks that are waiting to be resolved. In the mobile environment, throughput and delay may vary considerably. Roaming from one cell to another may cause temporary losses of connectivity. TCP will react by reducing its sending rate to a minimum. When the connectivity is reestablished, that sending rate will increase. In the cellular voice world, the quality-inconsistency problem may be acceptable. With the commercialization of Internet, the psychological and legal aspects have yet to be studied. For the technical part, the efforts will

---

* *Static* as opposed to *roaming* technology. Roaming in mobile Internet computing enables mobile Internet computers to keep the same IP address irrespective of the location so that TCP connections can be maintained.

undoubtedly emphasize mobile transmission control and routing algorithm design.

2.4.5 New IP addressing

As discussed, to send messages from one host machine to another, the information must first be *packetized* before the packets are transmitted. During the transmission, packets stop at various "hops." Each hop terminates in a hop or router, which forwards the packet to the next hop based on information recorded in the routing table. A 4-octet IP address is necessary for the router to recognize the next hop. As discussed in Chap. 1, each host machine (computers and routers) on the Internet is assigned a unique IP address* that is used in all communications with that host. IP addresses have five primary classes, as shown in the following format[8]:

The purpose of dividing the 4-octet address into classes was to reduce the router's processing load. In 1978, when the first draft of the

Class	High-order bits	Network portion	Host portion	Number of addresses
A	0	7	24	16,777,214
B	10	14	16	65,534
C	110	21	8	254
D	1110	(Multicast group)		268,435,456
E	11110	(Experimental use)		

Internet protocol was published, 32 bits of IP addressing looked like plenty. It has now been forecast that the current addressing scheme is not enough to accommodate the exponential growth of computers.

Current address assignment allows routers to have Class B addressing. That means each router can theoretically assign up to 65,534 hosts. In reality, however, not too many applications have this many hosts. The favoritism toward routers' processing in assigning the IP addresses is under critical strain from the rapid growth of the Internet. The problems caused by the address depletion are as follows:

1. Class B addresses are becoming depleted. It has been predicted, but has not yet materialized, that the IP addresses will soon be exhausted.

---

* In fact a machine can have more than one address. Typically, each port on that machine could have one or more IP addresses assigned.

2. Routing tables will become ever larger. Because there are more routing nodes to traverse through than there were a few years ago when Internet usage was not as popular, it takes longer to reach the destination host. Thus the *latency* increases.

The Internet could be a victim of its own success. IETF has been charged to do research and propose solutions such that the new addressing format[7]:

1. Alleviates the problem of address depletion

2. Does not accelerate the growth of the routing table

3. Can be implemented in the router, without requiring changes to the hosts

There were several proposals by this work group. One suggestion has been to use Connectionless Network Protocol (CLNP) in the routers. This proposal, known as "TCP and UDP over Bigger Address" (TUBA), would allow for the convergence between the OSI and Internet suites: TCP, UDP, and ISO transport would all run over CLNP.

Another proposal from IETF is a protocol named "Simple IP Plus" (SIPP), which increases the IP address length from 4 to 16 octets, as discussed in Chapter 1.

The design for the new IP address scheme is not complete as of this writing. The new design will be completely compatible with the old IP, so as not to break connectivity.

The transition from the 4-octet IP address scheme to a 16-octet scheme will probably be completed before 2005.

2.5   Router Market

The routing market underwent tremendous growth in the past few years, thanks to the Internet usage and corporations' rush to integrate their distributed computers. As the sales volume increased, the price of routers decreased. Over the previous two years, low-end router shipments have been increasing rapidly. The low-end routers are typically priced at $3000 or less. The growth of low-end applications pushed the demand for high-end routers. The high-end routers can range from $30,000 to $700,000.

2.5.1   Router vendors

In recent years, one of the most noteworthy news items in the routing industry was the move toward joint R&D and corporate mergers. It appears that the distinction between router, bridge, hub, and switches became blurred: hubs and switches add router cards, hubs doing switch-

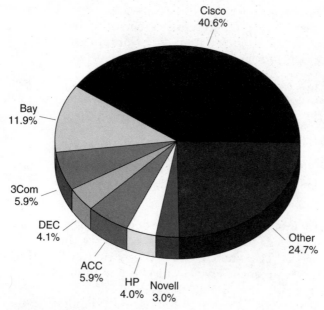

Cisco
40.6%

Bay
11.9%

3Com
5.9%

DEC
4.1%

ACC
5.9%

HP
4.0%

Novell
3.0%

Other
24.7%

**1994 Worldwide router
shipment = 326,000 units**

Source: International Data Corporation

Figure 2.12   1994 router market share.

ing, and routers doing switching. It seems every major router/bridge/
hub vendor is looking to embrace the ATM technology. There has been
a rush for the high-end router vendors to develop ATM, SMDS, and
SONET interfaces.[17] (See Fig. 2.12.)

While the LAN switching is still in its adolescent years, every major
router vendor has been investing more in this area. Although LAN
switch shipments were low just a couple of years ago, it can be expected
that the number will go up during the next five years. (See Fig. 2.13.)

In 1994, the router industry grossed well over $2 billion worldwide.
(Virtually all of the companies are of U.S. origin.) Major router vendors
include Cisco, Bay Networks, Cabletron, Digital, 3Com, ACC, Newbridge, Proteon, and Xyplex.[18] The market share is similar today.

2.5.2   Internetwork at home

Could the routing industry penetrate even lower-end users and appeal
to the critical mass? The answer is "possibly yes." As families across
the nation increasingly own more than one PC, and with the gradual
adoption of microprocessors in home appliances, the need to intercon-

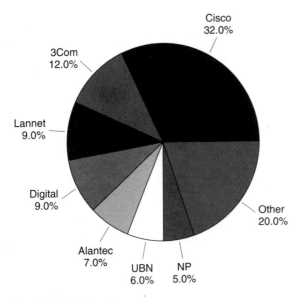

Total = 406,000 ports

Source: International Data Corporation

Figure 2.13   1994 Worldwide LAN switch shipments.

nect will become a necessity. However, the interconnection might come in the form of peer-to-peer networks where computers are simply linked to each other via cables rather than connected to a centralized file server. In this case, terminal-adapter and cable vendors, not routing suppliers, are the biggest beneficiaries of the new trend.

The predicted home PC/appliance interconnection will create a new industry. A new terminology—"HAN"—started to pop out recently in a few trade magazines. HAN is an acronym for *home area network*. Other than for the hardware needed to do home internetworking, software suppliers will be better positioned than the router vendors to provide built-in software for home use. Novell has software called *Powerline* that will allow adapters of home appliances to communicate with each other.[19]

2.6   Conclusion

This chapter briefly described routing technology. The reason for the Internet-focused flavor is because the Internet has radically changed the way corporations do business. Voice communication technology is near maturity, and the major growth area will be in data communication. The Internet allows computers to join together to communicate with humans and for humans. Routing technology is the enabler for this interconnected information highway.[20]

The traditional functionalities of routing have been undergoing changes. The emergence of switched LAN and ATM is the driving force. In order to cope with the changing technology and customer demand, router companies have formed joint development strategies or outright corporate mergers. Examples include the following: Wellfleet merged with Bay Networks; Cisco purchased a number of smaller vendors such as Grand Junction (Fast Ethernet technology), LightStream (ATM technology), and Stratacom (frame relay technology); and 3Com cooperated with ChipCom. The rapid merging of routing/bridging/hubbing companies over the past couple of years will definitely change the industry's landscape. On the ATM switching front, an increasing number of router vendors have been pouring resources into making standards-compliant line cards and software.

With the advent of ATM technology, the traditional networking paradigm involving bridges and routers has begun to shift to switched mechanisms. Switching may gradually replace the routers we see today. However, given the vast investment application users have made over the past 10 years, routers are not going to disappear. For the next five years or so, we might see the coexistence of legacy routers and ATM switches. The router can be attached to the work-group ATM switch. As ATM technology gradually matures and router investment reaches the end of its life cycle, centralized routers might be slowly phased out. ATM switches might eventually replace today's routing technology. However, given that there are already billions of dollars invested in the legacy router technology and that the routing industry is putting R&D resources into new technology areas such as mobile computing, we might see the longevity of routers.

Software routing has been around for at least as long as hardware routing. The IP routing protocol originally came from U.S. Berkeley research labs as public domain software and was freely distributed. Therefore, manufacturers of internetworking devices that incorporated the free software felt they could not charge for it—so they sold their routers mainly as hardware. With the alliance of server workstations and routing vendors, software routing may play an increasingly important role.

References

1. Minoli, Dan, and A. Alles, *Understanding LAN Emulation and Other Related Technologies,* Artech House, Norwood, Mass., 1997.
2. Minoli, Dan, *Telecommunication Technology Handbook,* Artech House, Norwood, Mass., 1991.
3. Tolly, Kevin, "Introduction to FDDI," *Data Communications,* August 1993.

4. Comer, Douglas, *Internetworking with TCP/IP*, Prentice Hall, Englewood Cliffs, N.J., 1991.
5. "Introduction to Cisco Router Configuration, Release 10.3," Cisco Systems Inc., 1995.
6. Baker, Fred, "OSPF Fundamentals," *LAN Magazine*, December 1994.
7. Hunt, Craig, *TCP/IP Network Administration*, O'Reilly & Associates, 1993.
8. Cheswick, William, and Steven Bellovin, *Firewalls and Internet Security*, Addison-Wesley, 1994
9. Tanzillo, Kevin, "It Is Understandable If You're *On Edge* When It Comes to ATM," *CN Communication News*, November 1995.
10. Butt, Tom, "What Is Driving the Switched Network Revolution?," *NetNews*, Issue 3, 1995.
11. Tabke, Bob, "The Switched Network Revolution," *NetNews*, Issue 3, 1995.
12. "IBM Migration Strategy Runs from SNA to Switched ATM," news release published in *Communications Week*, Sept. 18, 1995.
13. Malone, Rick, "Public ATM Services: A Hard Cell," *Business Communication Review*, Oct. 1995.
14. McDysan, David, and Darren Spohn, *ATM Theory and Application*, McGraw-Hill, New York, 1995.
15. Wittmann, Art, "The Soft Route: A Complementary Approach to Hardware Solutions," *Network Computing*, Oct. 1995.
16. Huitema, Chris, *Routing in the Internet*, Prentice Hall, Englewood Cliffs, N.J., 1995.
17. Haber, Lynn, "Routing the Competition," *Communications Week*, September 25, 1995.
18. Miller, Mark, "Which Route for Routers?," *Network World*, August 29, 1995.
19. Kichen, Steve, "Networking," *Forbes Magazine*, November 20, 1995.
20. Gates, Bill, "The Road Ahead," book review excerpts from *Newsweek*, Nov. 27, 1995.

Internet and Intranet Web Server Technology, Access, and Protocols

3.1 Introduction

World Wide Web technology, the combination of Web browsers and Web servers, is being deployed extensively not only on the Internet itself, but also on corporate enterprise networks. As an inter-enterprise infrastructure, the Internet and the Web are stimulating new connections between businesses and their customers, whether the customers are individual consumers or other businesses. The same Web technology is providing an effective way to automate a number of business tasks and processes within the enterprise for use in intranets.

The previous chapters covered the basic communication infrastructure of the Internet and of intranets, including specific networking technologies (Chap. 1) and interconnection equipment (Chap. 2). This chapter begins to shift the emphasis to the application level.* Specifically, server technology, server access, and server applications are discussed.

The WWW is made up of documents of various formats and hyperlinks; these links are known as Uniform Resource Locators (URLs). A document typically contains URLs to other documents. To get to the resource, the user clicks on the URL with a mouse (for graphical browsers) or types in an address string (for text browsers).

---

* Web servers can incorporate the function of a router in the same hardware device. However, we view communication and application support as logically distinct and think of Web servers more as specialized application servers.

The addresses to Web pages that include "http://" in their name are accessed by a Web server that supports this protocol. Through HTTP, the Web client takes this link request and forwards it to the Web server that contains the URL. Once the server receives the request, it forwards the "resource" back to the client that requested it.[1]

The Web is probably the most interesting use of truly distributed client/server technology available today. Web browsers, such as Mosaic or Netscape, can be viewed as the client application. While these clients can stand on their own, they typically depend on Web servers to put them in contact with the information available on the Web. Web servers are software programs that, when running, support the HTTP Web protocol. There are many different Web server programs available. These servers are called HTTP daemon* (HTTPD[†]), or HTTP servers. The most prominent ones are available from the National Center for Supercomputing Applications (NCSA), Conseil Europeen pour la Recherche Nucleaire (CERN), and Netscape Communications Corporation. These are the organizations that helped to create the Web and its most popular browsers. There are also several other server software packages available both commercially and free.

This chapter explores issues related to Web server technology; some discussion of Web clients is also provided.

3.1.1 Web's roots

Chapter 1 described the development of the Internet and the Internet protocol suite from the late 1960s until the present. Work on Web technology took place in the late 1980s as a way to simplify and systematize access to Internet-resident information.

In 1989, Tim Berners-Lee and Robert Cailliau created the World Wide Web (also known as the Web, or W3) at CERN's[‡] Internet facility.[2-4] The project was to be used as a means of transporting research and ideas effectively throughout the CERN organization.[5] It merged the technologies of information retrieval and hypertext to make an easy but powerful global information system. This idea not only worked for the CERN community, but it has spread throughout the world for the benefit of all. The Web is now the newest medium of expression. Its growth rate has been phenomenal, as seen in Figs. 3.1 and 3.2.[6]

The project's goal has been and continues to be to build a distributed hypermedia system. The Web is distributed, interactive, and dynamic.

---

* Daemons are programs that run in a mode awaiting a signal to start performing action, usually under the UNIX operating system.

[†] We use the uppercase (HTTPD) to describe the entity, and the lowercase (httpd) to describe the actual computer code.

[‡] CERN is the European Particle Physics Laboratory in Switzerland.

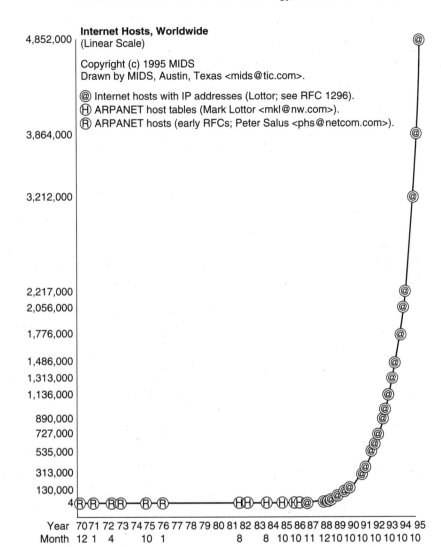

Figure 3.1   Internet hosts, worldwide (linear scale). (*Copyright © 1995 MIDS, drawn by MIDS, Austin, Texas, <mids@tic.com>.*)

The technology consists of client/server software that can understand many information retrieval protocols in use on the Internet (FTP, TELNET, NNTP, WAIS, Gopher, Finger, Rlogin, etc.), as well as the data formats of those protocols (ASCII, GIF, Postscript, WAV, MPEG, etc.), and can provide a single, consistent, user interface to them all.[7] This makes the technology of interest not only for the Internet but also for intranets applications.

The WWW is based on a client/server model where the client and server work independently of the other, both in a technological sense

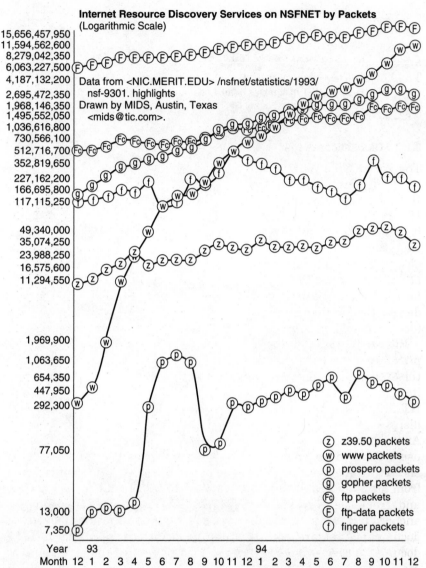

Figure 3.2 Internet resource discovery services on NSFNET by packets (logarithmic scale). (*Data from <NIC.MERIT.EDU> /nsfnet/statistics/1993/nsf-9301.highlights, drawn by MIDS, Austin, Texas, <mids@tic.com>.*)

and in an administrative sense. The Web is made up of the client/server, the URL, and protocols that handle HTML-based documents. There are a number of reasons for setting up a Web server, even for companies not interested in the Internet. A Web server can handle many of the same operations as Lotus Notes; both allow the user to share information with widespread access. The difference lies in where the information is kept. With Lotus Notes, an organization must copy documents to a central repository; however, when using a Web server anyone can access the information from anywhere within a company.[8] The World Wide Web can also allow a company to do away with traditional distributed databases, which carry a costly overhead. The Web gives a company the ability to incorporate graphics and audio.[9,10]

3.1.2 Global access to information

The World Wide Web is a client/server system that integrates diverse types of information on the global Internet as well as on enterprise IP-based networks. Clients and servers on the Web communicate using HTTP. The HTTP protocol is layered on the TCP/IP protocol; therefore it can operate on any network utilizing this suite, whether public or private. The typical Web client is a browser, an interactive application, often with a graphical user interface. A Web browser can display a number of data types, including formatted documents, images, data entry forms, and hyperlinks leading from one document to another. Figure 3.3 depicts the familiar logo of some key browsers.[11] Web servers send data (documents, images, etc.) to clients in response to their requests.

Information integration is the key to the power of the Web. The Web provides three forms of integration. The first form of integration is the Web's ability to link data provided by different servers. Each data item in the Web is addressed by a URL. Web documents, expressed in HTML, can contain the URLs of other documents. Browsers typically display these references (hyperlinks) as special regions called *anchors*. An anchor can be a section of highlighted text or an icon. When the user clicks on an anchor, the browser retrieves the document referenced by the underlying URL. The newly retrieved document can come from a server located across the globe—from both the browsing client and from the server that provided the document containing the anchor.[1,11] HTML is a simple markup system used to create hypertext documents that are portable from one platform to another. HTML documents are documents with generic semantics that are appropriate for representing information from a wide range of applications. HTML markup can represent hypertext news, mail, documentation, and hypermedia; menus of options; database query results; simple structured documents with inline graphics; and hypertext views of

   Figure 3.3 Mosaic and Netscape logos.

existing bodies of information. HTML has been in use by the WWW global information initiative since 1990.[12]

The second form of integration is the Web's ability to provide clients with data from diverse sources in terms of underlying technology. Web servers and Web browsers support this form of integration in different ways. Web servers integrate diverse sources of data by allowing Common Gateway Interface (CGI) programs to run in response to client requests. CGI programs perform general computations, including accepting form data, communicating with other computers, and creating dynamic pages. This way, for instance, a Web server can provide clients with data obtained by running transactions on a "legacy" mainframe system. In such a scenario, the Web server acts as a gateway, translating from the new standard for interactive information access (HTTP) to a previous one (e.g., 3270 terminal protocols). Web browsers integrate diverse sources of data by supporting several Internet data access protocols in addition to HTTP. For instance, a URL can specify the FTP for retrieving data from a file server. Thus, a Web browser is an FTP client as well as an HTTP client. Many Web browsers also support the Gopher (document browsing and indexing) and Network News Transport Protocol (NNTP—bulletin board access) protocols, as discussed in Sec. 3.7.[1,11]

The third form of integration is the Web's ability to encompass new types of data. The HTTP protocol borrows a design for extensible data typing and negotiation from the Multipurpose Internet Mail Extensions (MIME) standard. Browsers are designed to support new data types via *helper applications* that a user can add to the browser. This is how Web browsers deliver audio, video, and PostScript data to users. The Web is capable of being extensible for whatever new data types become important in the future.

3.2 Overview of HyperText Markup Language (HTML)

HTML is intended as a common medium for tying together information from widely different sources. HTML is a means to rise above the interoperability problems with existing document formats and a means to provide an open interface to proprietary information systems. The first version of HTML was designed to be simple, both to an author and for writing browsers. This has played a major role in the rapid growth of the World Wide Web. HTML 3.2 is becoming widely deployed at press time, providing a clean superset of HTML 2.0 and adding high-value features (e.g., tables, text flow around figures and math), while still remaining a simple document format (HTML enhancements have to be seen to be appreciated).

The pressure to adopt (all) the complexities of traditional Standard Generalized Markup Language (SGML) applications has been resisted by the developers. HTML documents are SGML documents with generic semantics that are appropriate for representing information from a wide range of applications. HTML is defined as an *application* of International Standard *ISO ISO8879:1986 Standard Generalized Markup Language*. This specification is being proposed as the Internet Media Type (RFC 1590) and MIME Content Type (RFC 1521) called "text/html; version=3.0."[12]

HTML documents are usually named with the suffix ".html" and are little more than ASCII files with formatting codes that contain information about layout and hyperlinks.[5] It is a language for describing structured documents, since most documents consist of common elements such as titles, paragraphs, headings, and lists. The elements of the document are prefixed and suffixed with HTML tags. HTML tags are typically used in the following way: beginning tag enclosed in brackets (<>), the text affected by the tag, and an ending tag enclosed in brackets (<>) and preceded with a slash (/). Tags are not case-sensitive. Some examples are as follows:

A title tag: `<TITLE> My Home Page </TITLE>`

A link to another site: `<A HREF="http://www.tcg.com/">IBM Home Page</A>`

The Web browsers are HTML formatters. When an HTML document is loaded by a browser, the browser reads the HTML information and formats the text and images on the screen.[13] Each browser has its own way of formatting HTML documents. Therefore, the same Web page may look different on one browser than it does on another. Each new version of HTML comes with new features. The latest version supports tables, the alignment of text and images next to each other, and centered and right-aligned text. HTML is designed to allow rendering on a wide range of devices, from teletypes to terminals, DOS-based systems, Windows-based systems, Macintoshes, and high-end workstations, as well as nonvisual media such as speech and Braille. In this, it allows users to exploit the legacy of older equipment as well as the latest and best of new machines. Figure 3.4 depicts an example of a home page.[11]

3.2.1 HTML 3.0 and higher

The HTML 3.0 specification provides a number of new features, and it is broadly backward compatible with HTML 2.0. HTML 3.0* pro-

---

* The actual release 3 on the market at presstime was Release 3.2.

Figure 3.4   An HTML document with several hyperlinks.

vides for improved support for nongraphical clients, allowing for rich markup in place of the figures shown on graphical clients. HTML can be rendered on a wide variety of screen sizes, using a scrolling or paged model. The fonts and presentation can be adjusted to suit the resources available in the host machine and the user's preferences.[11]

As time goes by, users' expectations change, and more will be demanded of HTML. One manifestation of this is the pressure to add yet more tags. For example, HTML 3.0/3.2 introduces a means for subclassing elements in an open-ended way. This can be used to distinguish the role of a paragraph element as being a couplet in a stanza, or a mathematical term as being a tensor. This ability to make fresh distinctions can be exploited to impart distinct rendering styles or to support richer search mechanisms, without further complicating the HTML document format itself. Scalability is also achieved via URL-based links for embedding information in other formats. Initially limited to a few image formats, inline support is expected to evolve to cover drawing formats, video, distributed virtual reality, and a general means for embedding other applications.

Tables have been one of the most requested features, with text flow around figures and math not far behind. The HTML 3.0/3.2 proposal for tables uses a lightweight style of markup suitable for rendering on a wide range of output devices, including Braille and speech synthesizers.

HTML 3.0 introduces a new element FIG for inline figures. This provides for client-side handling of hot zones while catering to nongraphical browsers. Text can be flowed around figures and the user can control when to break the flow to begin a new element.[12]

Including support for equations and formulas in HTML 3.0 adds relatively little complexity to a browser. Like tables, the format uses a lightweight style of markup, simple enough to type in by hand, although in most cases it will be easier to use a filter from a word processing format or a direct HTML 3.0/3.2 WYSIWYG editor. The level of support is compatible with most word processing software and avoids the drawbacks from having to convert math to inline images.[12]

The Web has acted as a useful exercise in user testing, and a lot of information has been gleaned from the ways people "abuse" HTML in trying to get a particular effect, as well as from explicit demand for new features. HTML 3.0/3.2, as a result, includes support for customized lists and fine positioning control with entities such as horizontal tabs and horizontal alignment of headers and paragraph text. Additional features include a static banner area for corporate logos, disclaimers, and customized navigation and search controls. The LINK element can be used to provide standard toolbar or menu items for navigation, such as Previous and Next buttons. The NOTE element is used for admonishments such as notes, cautions, or warnings, as well as for footnotes.[11] Forms have been extended to support graphical selection menus with client-side handling of events similar to FIG. Other new form field types include range controls, scribble on image, file upload, and audio input fields. Client-side scripting of forms is envisaged with the script attribute of the FORM element. Forms and tables make for a powerful combination, offering rich opportunities for laying out custom interfaces to remote information systems.

To counter the temptation to add yet more presentation features, HTML 3.0/3.2 is designed (but not required) to be used together with style sheets that give control over document rendering and can take into account the user's preferences, the window size, and other resource limitations such as which fonts are actually available. This work will eventually lead to smart layout under the author's control, with rich, magazine-style layouts for full-screen viewing, switching to simpler layouts when the window is shrunk.[12]

The topic of HTML is treated in greater detail in Chap. 4.

3.3 Overview of HyperText Transfer Protocol (HTTP)

HTTP is a protocol with the simplicity and speed necessary for a distributed collaborative hypermedia information system. HTTP has been used by the WWW since 1990, and although it is not an Internet standard, it does give a basis for what is available by a server that is using HTTP. HTTP allows communication between different protocols, which decreases the number of clients necessary to retrieve information from the vast resources of the Internet. A Web server delivers data through an HTTP protocol once the client makes a request. The client sends a URL to the server and waits for the response. Once the response is received, the client translates the information so it is readable.

HTTP is a generic, stateless,* object-oriented protocol, which may be used for many similar tasks such as name servers and distributed object-oriented systems. A feature of HTTP is the negotiation of data representation, allowing systems to be built independently of the development of new, advanced representations. On the Internet, the communication takes place over a TCP/IP connection. This, however, does not preclude the protocol from being implemented over any other connection-oriented protocol on the Internet or other networks. The HTTP protocol is designed for stateless servers, meaning that servers retain no information about clients between connections. Because a Web server is stateless, it can restart and clients will notice nothing more than a delay. This stateless design improves the user-perceived reliability of the Web. Hence, HTTP is a search-and-retrieve protocol. It was created to operate in a fast, stateless way, as is needed for hypertext jumps:

> HTTP was defined in order to allow, like WAIS, document retrieval and index search. HTTP is used for retrieving anything as fast as is needed in response to a hypertext jump. It is a very simple Internet protocol, similar in implementation to FTP and NNTP. The HTTP client sends a document identifier with or without search words, and the server responds with hypertext or plain text. The protocol runs over TCP/IP, using one connection per document request. The browser acts as a pipeline, so that as the bytes arrive from the server they can be presented to the reader as soon as they arrive.[14,15]

Figure 3.5 depicts an example of an HTTP activity.[16]

HTTP transactions consist of a connection, a request, a response, and a close. The connection is made by the client to the server using TCP/IP, the hostname or IP address, and port number. The default port number for HTTP is 80, but other port numbers may be used. The

---

* This means no continuous connection between client and server.

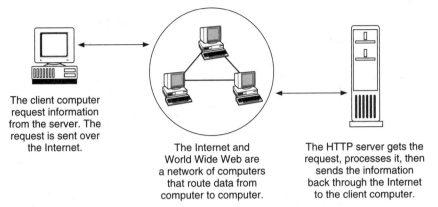

The client computer request information from the server. The request is sent over the Internet.

The Internet and World Wide Web are a network of computers that route data from computer to computer.

The HTTP server gets the request, processes it, then sends the information back through the Internet to the client computer.

Figure 3.5 Sending information between client and server.[16]

client then sends its request to the server. The request is made up of a line of ASCII characters beginning with "GET" followed by a space and then the path and filename of the document. If TCP/IP is not used, the request has to be sent differently. The server responds to the client's request typically with a message in hypertext markup language, which is a stream of ASCII characters. The TCP/IP connection is closed once the document has been sent to the client—unless the client breaks the connection before the request is completely transferred.

The file transfer protocol currently most used for accessing fairly stable public information over a wide area is *anonymous FTP*. This means the use of the Internet File Transfer Protocol without authentication. As the WWW currently operates for the sake of public information, anonymous FTP is quite appropriate, and WWW can pick up information provided by anonymous FTP. Directories are browsed as hypertext. The browser will notice references to files that are in fact accessible as locally mounted and use-direct access instead.

HTTP associates characteristics about the documents being sent, so that the client software interprets the information correctly. If this relationship between the function of the data and protocol did not exist, a viewer would not know if it was supposed to translate the document from its ASCII text format into the intended HTML-code format.[17,18] The Web was conceived with many goals in mind, including the following:

- A distributed information system
- A unified common interface to multiple protocols
- Hypermedia support
- Extensibility, so that any and all data formats would be supported

The existing protocols could not fully support these goals, so a new protocol was needed. The HTTP has been designed with the lightness and speed necessary for distributed, collaborative, hypermedia information systems. It is a generic, stateless, object-oriented protocol that can be used for many tasks, such as name servers and distributed object management. HTTP has six key attributes[18]:

1. *Client/server model.*   HTTP is designed to support communication between clients and servers regarding the transfer of hypertext data. A single server can serve information to large numbers of clients all across the world.

2. *Simplicity.*   HTTP is designed to be a very simple protocol, allowing HTTP servers to handle large numbers of requests efficiently.

3. *Flexibility and content-typing.*   HTTP allows for the transmission of arbitrarily typed data, so it is possible to transfer any kind of object using HTTP and have the client act appropriately on it.

4. *Connectionless.*   HTTP is a connectionless protocol, which means there is a limit of one request per connection. The client connects, makes its request, gets the response, and then disconnects. This is very efficient.

5. *Stateless.*   Without state, the protocol has no memory of the transaction, and the memory of any information needed for a subsequent transaction has to be maintained outside the protocol. Yet the lack of state makes HTTP a faster-running protocol.

6. *Meta-information.*   This is the term used for "information about information." It makes it possible to do more with the HTTP protocol than could be done without it.

The first version of the HTTP specification, known as HTTP/0.9, fell short of achieving all of these goals. Version 0.9 supported only the GET method. It did not allow for meta-information in the request of the response, and it did not provide content-typing. It was no more powerful than previously established protocols like FTP. However, the second version of the specification, known as HTTP/1.0, extended the functionality of version 0.9.[18,19]

Unlike some protocols, the client makes a single request in HTTP, and that request must have all the necessary information. The client and server do not negotiate. Once the client makes a request, the server cannot clarify it or ask for additional information. There are four steps in the flow (see Fig. 3.6[20]):

1. *Open a connection.*   When an HTTP server is running, it is listening via a port, generally 80, and waiting for a connection to occur.

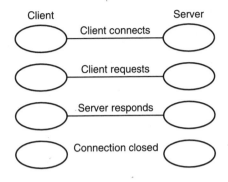

Figure 3.6 Client/server communication interchange—a four-step transaction.

Opening a connection is like picking up the telephone and dialing someone's number. The UNIX file structure makes the implementation of network transfers easy and consistent with the rest of UNIX. Therefore, a socket is a special type of file that allows for network I/O. When a socket is open from the client's point of view, a virtual file is being created. When a user writes to that file, he or she is sending the data across the network. Once that is done, the connection has been established and a request can be made.

2. *Make a request.* The client can make a request by sending the request data string to the server on whichever port the HTTP server resides. An HTTP 1.0 request string is made up of one or more lines, followed by two carriage-return line feeds (CRLFs). The first line is the request line. It includes a method, the URL, and the protocol. The rest of the lines are headers of one type or another. The two CRLFs signal the end of the request.

3. *Server responds.* Once the client makes the request, the server responds. An HTTP 1.0 response string is made up of one or more lines, followed by a blank line and the entity body. The first line is the response line. It includes the server's protocol and status code. The rest of the lines are headers.

4. *Close connection.* When either the client or the server closes the connection, the request is terminated regardless of whether the transaction has been successful or was completed.

3.3.1   Web browsers: HTTP's user-level peer

In order to see what is on the Web, you must make use of a Web browser (also known as Web client). This is the client software piece that was described in the W3 project mentioned earlier. Since the introduction of the Web, several Web browsers have evolved for a wide variety of platforms: Mac, DOS, Windows, UNIX, and VMS, to name a few. Most of these browsers offer a graphical interface such as Mosaic and Netscape. The graphical browsers make using the Internet fun.

They add color, graphics, video, and sound. The interface to the Internet is much more user-friendly with a graphical browser. Information can be obtained by the click of a mouse. A Web browser is all the software needed (plus an Internet connection) to access the World Wide Web from a PC. Web clients are built on top of libwww, the common library, which handles the different communication protocols used in the Web—for example, HTTP, FTP, Gopher, NEWS, and WAIS.[2]

The user tells the browser where he or she would like to go on the Web by typing a URL in the field provided by the browser. The URL is the address, or link, to the information located on a Web server on the Internet. The browser has to do two things based on the URL given: (1) be able to access that piece of information or (2) operate in some way based on the contents of that pointer. The URL can point to several types of servers: HTTP, FTP, WAIS, Gopher, NNTP, etc. Therefore, the browser must be able to understand these protocols and create a virtual HTML document while doing so. The URL consists of three parts: the protocol, the hostname, and the directory path/filename. The following is an example:

```
http://www.hcc.stevens.edu/guide/Paper/EnteringCyberspace/
  guide.mos.ps
```

where http = the protocol (can also be ftp, gopher, telnet, news, etc.)
www.hcc.stevens.edu = the hostname (server)
/guide/Paper/EnteringCyberspace/guide.mos.ps = the directory path and filename

3.4 Web Servers

A server is the basic part that differentiates a provider from a user. To *provide* information on the Web you must either have your own server or rent space on a server. The most common platforms used are Microsoft Windows, UNIX, VMS, and Macintosh. Each platform has a number of programs available to set up a server using different versions of HTTP (see Fig. 3.7). Since the server and client run independently, the server can provide information to other clients and servers on different platforms. Each platform and software has its advantages and disadvantages. For a small provider, however, whichever system is currently being used is usually efficient.[9]

NCSA HTTPD was the most popular and widely used server in a recent survey. The poll surveyed 1722 servers. Of those surveyed, 54 percent stated they use a form of the NCSA HTTPD.[23] This survey corresponds to what newsgroups on the Internet had already been reporting for some time. NCSA HTTPD has different versions for Windows and UNIX. NCSA is a widely supported server on the Internet; there-

Operating system	Program	FTP availability
UNIX	NCSA httpd	Ftp.ncsa.uiuc.edu:/Web/ncsa_httpd (free)
	CERN httpd	http://info.cern.ch/hypertext/WWW/Daemon/Status.html (available from other sources, also, free)
	GN Gopher/HTTP server	http://hopf.math.nwu.edu/
	Perl (Plexus)	http://bsdi.com/server/doc/plexus.html
VMS	CERN HTTP	http://delonline.cern.ch/disk$user/duns/doc/vms/distribution.html (free)
	Region 6 threaded	http://kcgll.eng.ohio-state.edu/www/doc/serverinfo.html
	HTTP server	
Microsoft Windows and Windows NT servers	NCSA httpd	ftp://ftp.ncsa.uiuc.edu/Web/ncsa_httpd/contrib/whtp11ab6.zip (free)
	HTTPS	ftp://emwac.edu.ac.uk/pub/https
	SerWeb	ftp://winftp.cica.indiana.edu:/pub/pc/win3/winsock/serweb03.zip
Macintosh	MacHTTP	http://www.uth.tmc.edu/mac_info/machttp_info.html (shareware)[21,22]

Figure 3.7   Internet addresses for server programs (HTTPDs).

fore it is easy to gain information and expert help when working with the NCSA server. There are a number of experts that deal with only NCSA HTTPD, which is not the case with CERN. Another advantage to using NCSA is that it works well with other applications running on the same computer because it is native to the UNIX system. Some applications that coincide with HTTPD are Gopher, WAIS, and list servers. The third advantage is that it also integrates well with Perl, a programming language used with most CGI. Since Perl was developed to work with UNIX-based systems, NCSA and a CGI work well together.[24]

NCSA HTTPD for Windows is easy to set up and use. Therefore it makes a good server for first-time users to learn the basics of HTTP. It is beneficial for someone who wants to learn by setting up a small system before developing one for a large organization. There are some disadvantages with this server. When running on Windows, it is slower than most servers. NCSA also requires lots of memory and CPU power. NCSA does not have the capability to run as an HTTP proxy client server.[25] NCSA has proved to be a powerful server for UNIX platforms, but is somewhat weak for Windows users.

The second most popular server in the aforementioned survey was CERN HTTP.[23,26] CERN was developed for use on VMS. Although CERN will run on UNIX, it is not recommended. Configuration and setup is more difficult than NCSA for Windows, but it is no harder to learn than NCSA for UNIX.[24] This platform has the ability to serve as a proxy server, which requires less software to access the Web. It also has a scripting language that works well with CGI. It is accessible from the Internet for free, as are most servers.[27]

MacHTTP is one of the few servers available for Macintosh computers.[28] MacHTTP requires a minimum of System 7 and MacTCP to support advanced features. It is a small program that allows almost anyone to establish a server and effectively experiment with the HTTP protocol. This makes it a popular server for first-time and small providers. This server does not have a large handling capacity like NCSA, therefore it is not recommended for large corporations. However, some people have been able to get around this by networking a number of computers, each of which runs a subset of the entire HTML document list from a separate server.[28]

Figure 3.8 depicts a typical server at the functional level. Determining which type of Web server and which computer platform to use is based on a number of factors. These include economic considerations, expected usage, data types that are stored, available hardware, and

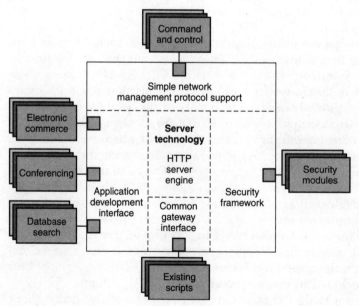

Figure 3.8 HTTP server engine.

experience with specific operating systems.[8] After examining these factors, individually and as a whole, you may decide that a server is not right for your organization, or that you would be better off hiring a company to put information on the Web.

The financial resources required to implement a Web server and maintain it can be significant. Most users will need a direct Internet connection of 56 Kbps or higher, at least a 486 computer (or one comparable in speed and storage), software (the server software is often free), physical space, and technically educated people.[8] A Pentium-based system, a Sun Sparc, or a Digital Equipment Alpha machine would be even better. A server designed mainly for hobbies could be done on a desktop PC with a 28.8 Kbps modem with a SLIP or PPP connection. If a company has been accessing the Internet for a period of time they may already have the required hardware. However, if installing an entirely new computer system is in order, then a company's costs will be greater. Some companies may already have a technical person on hand to deal with computer and Internet problems. If so, few changes will need to be made to the workplace. Large operations will need full-time technical people, but smaller companies may be able to get along with a knowledgeable existing employee.

The data types and their quantities will affect the amount of disk space and maintenance required. If a company plans to distribute only text files, then the space requirement could be small. To utilize graphics or video, the data space will increase rapidly. How you decide to store the data types will affect the amount of CPU that is required. For example, if a company is providing access to a database, the CPU will use numerous resources to fulfill the requests. However, if you are simply providing lists of information via different links, the CPU requires many fewer resources.[8]

The operating system that a company decides to use will influence the steps they need to take. Companies that have been using UNIX and are putting up a large server should have few problems. However, if a company is entering into Internet technology for the first time, it may be appropriate to hire a technical expert to determine the best equipment and to help install and maintain the server. On the other hand, a person who wishes to experiment on a hobby basis should not be discouraged from installing and running his or her own server.

The best way to set up the server is by starting from source code, so that the organization knows the system. However, you can also install a server with a precompiled binary software. Configuring a server can be done in a number of different ways, but there are some things that should be included in every server.[8] For example, a server should be designed in a way that makes it easy to expand and update as needs change. Therefore, it is a good idea to keep everything in one place in a

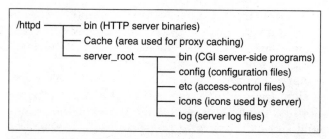

Figure 3.9 Server directory tree.[8]

tree structure so the information can be easily expanded or moved. (See Fig. 3.9.)

At a minimum, the configuration should specify the following information[8]:

- The root (ServerRoot) of the directory tree
- The user identity under which the server will run (for security reasons it is best to give the server as few privileges as possible)
- The path to the log files
- A mapping to executables on the server
- A mapping to HTML source files

As mentioned earlier, there are a number of different protocols that the WWW can access. Each of these protocols has a special function. File transfer is the ability to transfer and locate information that is placed in a public domain. As the Internet grew, so did the needs of the users. Eventually this evolved into new services, such as electronic mail and bulletin boards. These services helped to encourage the growth of the Internet even more. Research then focused on ways to provide services on a higher level.[29]

The WWW brought the concept of a client/server model to the forefront of computing. The client and server each perform different roles. The client handles the user interface, translates into appropriate protocols, sends the request to the server, waits for the response, translates the results back into English, and presents the response to the user. The server, or the provider, waits for a request, processes the request, and returns the results. Gopher was the first protocol to have its structure based on this model. Wide Area Information Server (WAIS) is another protocol that was developed, not to provide access, but as a way to search the masses of information available. The World Wide Web also encompasses this ability and most of the capabilities of all the previous protocols.[29] Later, the WWW became the hierarchy of all the preceding protocols.

The basic advantage of using a Web server over another server is the language it supports and the ability to access many different places on the Internet from a single location. The Web server supports HTML, which allows for a variety of ways to provide information. With a Gopher server the user can access information only in textual format and from lists. The Web server allows the user to insert links, graphics, and sound, thereby making it more appealing and easier for people to use. Another advantage is the Web server's ability to allow links, which makes the server easier to maintain. For example, every "study carrel" of North Carolina State University Library's Web server consists of a single HTML file created with either a public domain editor or from a database program.[28] Each of these files is easier to maintain than the mass of links and lists in the Library's Gopher server. The third advantage is that HTTP allows most of the information processing to be done by the client, thereby allowing the server to work more efficiently and handle more requests. Other servers that do not use HTTP must do all the processing within the server platform. This obviously requires more memory and reduces the number of users the server can handle.[9,22]

3.4.1 Transport issues

HTTP is only a mechanism between sources and typically uses TCP/IP as a transport layer. (However, HTTP is not limited to using TCP/IP.) HTTP allows the client to send a request for a hypertext document, then retrieves any items associated with the document. A user will often request a hypertext link to follow, which is often directed at the same server. TCP is the medium that establishes and transports this three-way handshake between the client and server.[9,30]

TCP transfers the data in a series of PDUs. Every PDU of information does not have to be acknowledged before sending another packet. This form of control may seem to result in errors. There is a system that TCP uses, called Slow Start, to avoid/alleviate the errors. Slow Start opens another window on the server side that keeps track of all received data. This window is opened every time a segment is received, and when a segment is not acknowledged the window is closed. When a window closes, TCP halts the data until the window receives the request it missed.[30]

Analysis shows that HTTP spends more time waiting than receiving or sending data. HTTP is hindered by Slow Start because the URL is often longer than the maximum segment size. HTTP cannot respond until all of the URL has been received, which results in a delay between the initial request and the moment when information is sent. HTTP is also required to hold open resources for every connection that is established in a four-minute period. This level of resources is another major factor in the slowness of HTTP.

New networks are being developed to overcome these and other problems. There are two main factors that affect the performance of a protocol: the latency and bandwidth. *Latency* is a measure of the fixed overhead of a transition (e.g., propagation time) and does not change as documents get bigger or smaller.[30] *Bandwidth* measures how long it takes to send data, this being the message length (in bits) divided by the channel bandwidth (in bps). Bandwidth availability at the metropolitan and wide area level is being improved as time goes by. Faster modems and ISDN are two of the many ways that are increasing the speed of access; higher-speed facilities are also being introduced in the backbone. Unfortunately, reducing the amount of propagation delay is generally impossible (unless a satellite link is replaced with a terrestrial link and/or the processing time through nodal processors is reduced). Therefore, latency due to propagation can become the dominating factor in some environments.

To combat the problems that have become associated with the early versions of HTTP, a new, improved version of HTTP has been proposed. The new version has been called HTTP-NG by some. One of the main differences between HTTP and HTTP-NG will be the basic model each uses when connecting. *HTTP requires each request to open a new connection; each hyperlink / URL needs a separate TCP connection.* HTTP-NG will allow multiple requests to be processed on one connection, thus increasing the speed of the transmission. The client does not have to wait for a response from the server to send out a new request, and the server can respond to requests in any order. So a response for two graphics that were requested could be combined.[31]

HTTP-NG will also set aside one layer of the connection for control-type messages. Each part of the information (text, graphics, or voice) will be sent along its own layer. For example, if the user requested a document that contained three separate graphics and a text document, the connection would be split into five layers. Each layer would carry a different part of the request. This separation of data from control information becomes very relevant when working with protocols such as ATM and RSVP. These two technologies deal with multimedia, which requires more information to be sent than does a simple text document; therefore the improvement is more easily recognized in multimedia applications.[31]

A number of ways have been recommended for implementing this new protocol. The best way would obviously allow for the greatest use of the present resources. For this reason it has been suggested that the best way to move to the new server would be through intermediate proxy servers. This would allow clients and servers to go unchanged while also getting the advancements in HTTP-NG. This works because the majority of the communicating would be done between HTTP-NGs. The HTTP would send the request to the HTTP-NG, which is placed nearby, for any connection done outside the "boundaries" (see Fig. 3.10).

3.5   Web Access

3.5.1   Connection modes

As discussed in Chap. 1, there are several ways to connect to the Internet. You can dial up one of the commercial on-line services such as America Online, CompuServe, or Prodigy (e.g., see Fig. 3.11). Or, if you prefer, you can dial up an Internet service provider (see Fig. 3.12). If you are connected to a LAN, you need a network configuration program. On the other hand, if you are calling an Internet service provider to establish a SLIP or PPP connection, you need a dialer. In either case, you need additional tools to use the Internet once you are connected.

To take full advantage of the Internet, you need a number of pieces of software, a Winsock DLL, a Web browser, an e-mail reader (e.g., see Fig. 3.13), a newsgroup reader, an FTP client, and perhaps a Gopher client and some other search tools.

3.5.2   Accessing a Web server: practical considerations

Getting connected to the World Wide Web is relatively easy. There are actually a number of different ways to go about getting connected to the Web. However, if you want to take advantage of everything on the

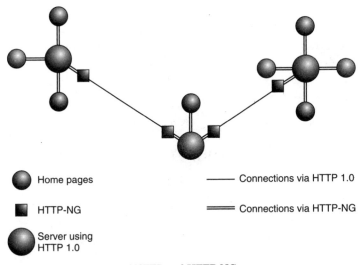

Figure 3.10   Integration of HTTP and HTTP-NG.

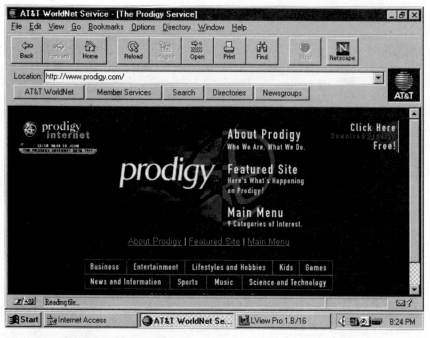

Figure 3.11   Access of Web via Prodigy.

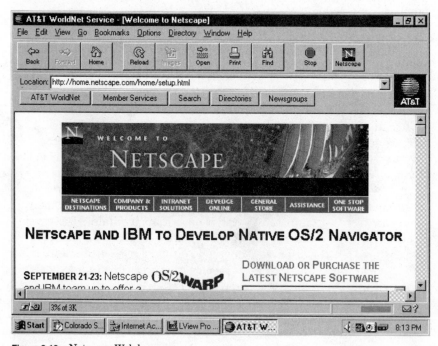

Figure 3.12   Netscape Web browser.

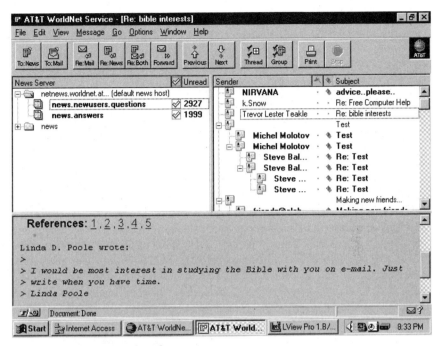

Figure 3.13 Netscape mail reader.

Web, then you need three things: a late-model computer, a minimum 14.4-Kbps modem, and access to a graphical Web browser.[32] You can get a free copy of the Netscape browser by contacting Netscape's home page.

An alternate way is to connect to a Web browser called Lynx, which allows access to the Web on a strictly textual basis.[33] If you only want to see what is on the Web without waiting for all the graphics, then Lynx is a possible way to become connected. All you need is an Internet connection. If the Internet service provider has Lynx, then you are ready to browse. However if the service does not offer Lynx, a user can get there from a number of sites that have Lynx available to the public. One place to try is <www.law.cornell.edu>. Because Lynx is a text-based browser, the user will miss out on the "real excitement of the Web." Graphics range from full-color pictures to simple drawings scanned into home pages. A user will also miss out on the numerous audio clips available.[32,34]

Gaining access to the graphics and audio clips requires better equipment, and this calls for more expensive equipment. This is not to say that it is difficult to get connected. In most cases, if users have a 486

IBM-compatible computer or a recent Performa or Power PC, they basically have everything they need. The only thing missing is a browser. Today there are literally thousands of Internet services that offer a complete package that allows access to the Web and other parts of the Internet.[33] Many companies offer a free trial period.

All services have one thing in common: the way in which the connection is achieved. To be able to connect to the World Wide Web, a SLIP/PPP account must be accessed. This account will allow the graphical browser software to access the hypertext documents on the Web. You can get a connection to a SLIP/PPP account without paying for on-line services. However, full access to the Web in this case does require locating and installing a lot of software programs on your own.[33]

The World Wide Web offers different things to different people and, depending on how much the user wants to do, determines the amount of equipment, time, and money it will take. Whether you wish to browse and enjoy the scenery or provide information to develop the growth of a company, the World Wide Web has something for everyone. For the most part it is easy to access and get your own site. Those who are not computer-knowledgeable can hire a company to put their information on the Web. For those who want to explore and try something new, there are programs designed for the beginner. The World Wide Web contains vast amounts of information, which can be overwhelming, but there are sites such as Yahoo that search the Web. The Web is changing daily.

3.5.3 Publishing on a Web server

In order to publish Web pages on the Internet, it is desirable to have a dedicated computer that runs Web service. In addition to the Web server, a reasonably fast dedicated connection to the Internet is necessary. To be connected to the Internet, Web servers can use TCP/IP over Ethernet. Web servers can also be installed on computers running multiuser operating systems such as Windows NT, UNIX, or OS/2. In the past, Web server technology was available only on a few platforms: UNIX, Macintosh, VM, and VMS. Today, the platforms available also include, but are not limited to, OS/2, Windows NT, and Windows. These systems can be set up to protect certain files from unauthorized access. Web servers can log activity such as the IP address, time, and request made for every connection. It is good practice to keep the logging on a computer separate from the Internet firewall computer. For some Internet Web sites, the logging is kept on a machine separate from the Web server and from the Internet firewall machine. Servers can forward requests for information that neither the client nor the server can access directly to applications called *gateways,* described in the next paragraph. Gateway support, logging, and user authentication are important features to look for when selecting a Web server; logging is needed for both usage statistics and security.[35] The person who administers the Web server has come to be known as the *Webmaster*.

The Web server waits for requests to come from browsers. When a request is made, the server locates the document and sends it back to the browser that originally requested it. Some requests may actually make the server run a script or program. These programs are called *gateway scripts*. The formal standard for these scripts is the CGI. A plain HTML document that the Web server retrieves is static—it is a text file that does not change. A CGI program is executed in real time, so it can output dynamic information.[36]

3.6 Security

Routing sensitive data over the Internet is problematic for two reasons:

- It is difficult to maintain privacy between two computers that are not directly connected.

- Third parties can illegally pose as a computer (known as *spoofing*) in a conversation or transaction and intrude or eavesdrop on the information.[16]

See Fig. 3.14.

At this juncture, the Internet does not provide inherently secure communications between Web browsers and Web servers. Often, this lack of security is no cause for concern, but some applications demand high security. For example, a merchant might want each customer to establish an account by entering credit card information in a Web browser. The customer does not want Internet eavesdroppers to see the credit card information. Web browsers and Web servers can communicate in a secure manner, but only with security enhancements to both browser and server. The browser and server must both use the same

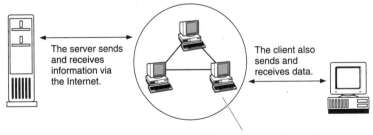

SSL = Secure Sockets Laver

Figure 3.14   Routing between hosts on the Internet.[16]

enhanced-communications protocol; otherwise they will not be able to communicate.[37]

Securing information sent through the Web is a relatively new undertaking. As more banks and commercial sites connect to the Web, the demand to provide secure routing of information increases. A press-time release from Matrix Information and Directory Services states that the Internet now has 20 to 30 million users.[6,38] Of all the host domains, the majority are commercial, with 30,000 commercial hosts reported. (See Fig. 3.15.) This population is very attractive to commercial entities. The demand for secure routing of information is becoming critical. There are several technologies being developed to address this problem. Two different protocols have been implemented for enhanced Web security: Secure HTTP (S-HTTP) and the Secure Sockets Layer (SSL).[11]

3.6.1 Secure HTTP

Secure HTTP (S-HTTP) is an extension of HTTP that provides a variety of security enhancements for the Web. Message protection is provided in three ways: *signature, authentication,* and *encryption.* Any message can use any combination of these three methods. Authentication lets clients make sure they are communicating with the correct server, and allows servers to confirm they are communicating with the correctly authorized client. Authentication is performed using digital certificates issued by certifying authorities. Encryption makes data transferred over the network unintelligible to intruders and eavesdroppers. S-HTTP provides independently applicable security services for transaction confidentiality, authenticity/integrity, and nonreputability of origin.[40] Digital signatures provide two benefits. First, they

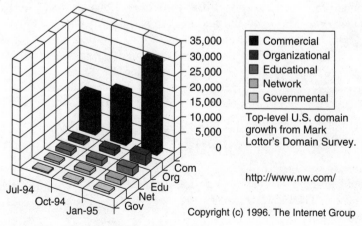

35,000
30,000
25,000
20,000
15,000
10,000
5,000
0

■ Commercial
■ Organizational
■ Educational
□ Network
□ Governmental

Top-level U.S. domain growth from Mark Lottor's Domain Survey.

http://www.nw.com/

Com
Org
Edu
Net
Gov

Jul-94
Oct-94
Jan-95

Copyright (c) 1996. The Internet Group

Figure 3.15 U.S. domain growth.[39]

verify that data transferred over the network was not changed en route. Second, they provide nonrepudiation, where the receiver of data can prove to a third party that the sender really sent the data.

S-HTTP is flexible. It allows each application to configure the amount of security required. A transmission from client to server or server to client can be signed, encrypted, both, or neither. S-HTTP provides a secure communication mechanism between an HTTP client/ server pair in order to enable spontaneous commercial transactions for a wide range of applications.[40] The protocol provides symmetric capabilities to both client and server (in that equal treatment is given to both requests and replies, as well as for the preferences of both parties) while preserving the transaction model and implementation characteristics of HTTP. Several cryptographic message format standards may be incorporated into S-HTTP clients and servers. S-HTTP supports end-to-end secure transactions, in contrast to the existing de facto HTTP authorization mechanisms, which require the client to attempt access and be denied before the security mechanism is employed.[40] A Secure HTTP message consists of a request or status line followed by a series of headers, followed by an encapsulated content. Once the content has been decoded, it should be either another Secure HTTP message, an HTTP message, or simple data. The URL protocol label used for Secure HTTP documents is shttp.[41,42]

3.6.2 Secure Sockets Layer

Secure Sockets Layer (SSL) is a transport layer security technique that can be applied to HTTP as well as to other TCP/IP-based protocols. The SSL Protocol is designed to provide privacy between two communicating applications (e.g., a client and a server). SSL provides authentication, encryption, and data verification. The protocol is designed to authenticate the server and, optionally, the client, but encryption and data verification are mandatory with SSL.[11]

The advantage of the SSL Protocol is that it is application-protocol-independent. A higher-level application protocol (for example, HTTP, FTP, or TELNET) can layer on top of the SSL Protocol transparently (see Fig. 3.16). The SSL Protocol can negotiate an encryption algorithm and session key, as well as authenticate a server before the application protocol transmits or receives its first byte of data. All of the application protocol data is transmitted encrypted, ensuring privacy.

The SSL Protocol is actually composed of two protocols. At the lowest level, layered on top of some reliable transport protocol, is the SSL Record Protocol. The SSL Record Protocol is used for encapsulation of all transmitted and received data, including the SSL Handshake Protocol, which is used to establish security parameters.[41,42]

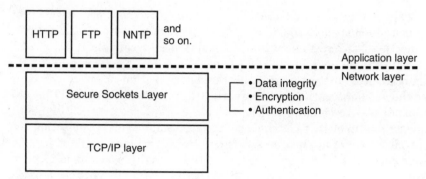

Figure 3.16   How SSL relates to TCP/IP and application protocols.

SSL is a cryptosystem that works at the protocol level and provides authentication (prevents spoofing), encryption (so eavesdroppers cannot read information), and data integrity (notifies parties involved if data was removed or added to packets).[16] In order for SSL to work, both the client and the server must be SSL-enabled and must have obtained a digital certificate from a certification authority. SSL requires a reliable transport protocol such as TCP.

The security process begins when the client sends a request to connect to the server. The server sends a digital certificate to the client. The client authenticates the server by decrypting the digital signature that is within the digital certificate. The client generates a session key and encrypts it using the server's public key from the certificate. The server receives the session key and uses it to encrypt and decrypt the data. SSL uses message authentication codes to ensure the data transferred between client and server has not been tampered with.[16] If for any reason any of these steps fails, the connection between the client and server is closed.

Another technology being developed to secure transactions over the Internet is Secure Transaction Technology (STT). It is being jointly developed by Visa and Microsoft. The point is that with the growth of commercial use of the Internet, more and more ways of ensuring privacy and security will be developed.

3.6.3 Comparison

Two kinds of comparisons of the S-HTTP and SSL protocols are possible: inherent capabilities and current implementations.

Because S-HTTP is an application-level protocol, it can provide nonrepudiation of individual requests or responses through digital signatures. SSL is a lower-level protocol and does not have this capability. S-HTTP, being an application-level protocol, is able to work with firewalls. SSL's transport-level encryption, in contrast, hides the application-level protocol from firewalls. A firewall that relays an SSL connection has no idea what data is being passed back and forth over the connection.[11]

S-HTTP is more flexible than SSL, in that an application can configure the level of security it needs. Encryption and digital signatures can be expensive to compute, so in principle this flexibility can allow a server to handle more connections or respond more quickly. The other side of this trade-off is that SSL, a lower-level protocol, may be easier to optimize. It encrypts more bytes, but might balance this out with a lower cost per byte. Since SSL has fewer options it should be easier to set up and administer than S-HTTP.

Current SSL protocols and implementations are limited in a variety of ways relating to the handling of digital certificates. S-HTTP implementations are considerably more flexible. These SSL limitations are not inherent in the nature of SSL, and will likely be removed as necessary.

3.7   Related Web Capabilities

As alluded to earlier, traditional Internet capabilities are supported by WWW. These are reviewed here briefly from a WWW perspective (you may also refer to Chap. 1).

3.7.1   Network news transport protocol (NNTP) vis-à-vis WWW

The Network News Transport Protocol allows transient news information in the USENET news format to be exchanged over the Internet. News articles make good examples of hypertext, as articles contain references to other articles and newsgroups. Newsgroups appear like directories, but are more informative. (See Fig. 3.17.)

NNTP broadcasts every message to every site, in contrast to e-mail protocols, which send messages to specific sites, and HTTP, which only transfers the information on demand by the reader.[43] Each time a new NNTP server is set up, it has to know about at least one nearby NNTP server. The NNTP servers have an arrangement that they will pass news to each other. Articles can be passed in both directions, and the servers compare article message id headers to see whether they have any new news for each other.[43] The NNTP administrator needs to find another NNTP server that will be his or her news feed. Once this is done, the administrator selects which newsgroups to belong to. Lots of disk space is needed to store all the news articles until they expire, which is usually a few weeks.

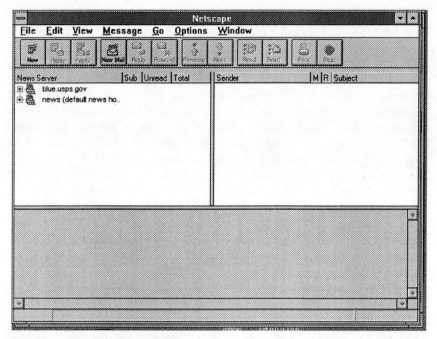

Figure 3.17   Netscape news browser.

NNTP is more efficient than HTTP in the case of articles that are going to be very widely read, because an article is transferred only once onto each site.[43] NNTP servers will allow only local clients to access them directly. Allowing anyone in the world to access the same NNTP server would not be efficient and could lead to heavy loads on the network and on the server. An NNTP server will feed about 10 other servers, which in turn feed 10 other servers, and so on. When an NNTP server feeds another server it sends all its new news articles. The receiving host discards any duplicate articles. The client then can receive a list of new articles from the server. The client receives only articles that are desired and not duplicates. The news server uses a stream connection (like TCP) and SMTP-like commands and responses.[44] It is designed to accept connections from hosts and to provide a simple interface to the news database. The news server is only an interface between programs and news databases.

Web browsers need to be configured to point to the appropriate NNTP news server. Since news articles expire, it is not appropriate to put links to news articles in Web documents.

3.7.2   Gopher vis-à-vis WWW

The Internet Gopher is a distributed document delivery service. It is a lookup tool, similar to a card catalog in a library, that lets the user find information by selecting resources from menus. Gopher menus are easily mapped onto hypertext links. Gopher allows users to access data residing on many different hosts in a seamless fashion. This is accomplished by presenting the user a hierarchical arrangement of documents and by using a client/server communications model.[45] In addition to browsing through hierarchies of documents, Gopher users can send queries to gopher search servers.

Internet Gopher servers accept simple queries sent over a TCP connection and respond by sending the client a document or a list of documents. Since this is a distributed protocol, there can be many servers, but the user sees just one document with the results of the search. The data can reside in several places and may need different commands to access it, but the Gopher knows where and what to do to get at the information, making it easier for the user. In fact, users may never even know they are using a Gopher because the results have the same look and feel as Web pages. Gopher pages just have lots of links to click on.

The Gopher distributed information system uses a "lightweight" protocol similar to HTTP. Therefore, it is now included in every WWW client, so the Gopher world can be browsed as part of the Web. Gopher menus are easily mapped onto hypertext links. It may be that future versions of the Gopher and HTTP protocols will converge.

3.7.3   Wide Area Information System vis-à-vis WWW

WAIS is a service that allows the user to search through a collection of information systems based on a group of words. It was developed by Dow Jones, Thinking Machines, Apple Computer, and KPMG Peat Marwick. Like Gopher, WAIS allows the user to find and access resources on the network without regard for where they really reside.[3] It is a distributed-text searching system and uses TCP/IP to connect client applications to information servers. WAIS uses the Z39.50 protocol to communicate between clients and servers. Z39.50 is a (draft) ANSI standard for requesting bibliographic information. WAIS has been augmented where necessary to incorporate many of the needs of a full-text information retrieval system.

In order to make a document available through a WAIS server, an index must be created for it. For textual information, every word in the document is indexed. The first step begins with a Web user finding access to a WAIS server. A good start is the Web Crawler: http://

webcrawler.com. From here, the user can enter a search request. The Web Crawler searches its libraries and asks each server to search its index for a set of words. It contacts the servers that handle the libraries suggested. It asks each server to search its index for a set of words. The server sends a list of documents that may be appropriate back to the user and places a score next to each one, ranking it in order. The higher the score, the more likely the document will have the information the user requested.

The WAIS protocol is an open protocol, making it easy to adapt to changes in technology. The developers freely distribute the software to encourage more and more WAIS sites.

3.7.4   File Transfer Protocol vis-à-vis WWW

As covered in Chap. 1, FTP allows the transfer of files between any two computers of any type. FTP makes use of the TELNET protocol and runs over TCP. Any kind of computer file, whether it be a text file or a binary file representing software, graphics images, or sounds, can be sent. It uses two connections for each conversation. The FTP control connection is used to send commands that are used to start, stop, and control the session. The data connection is used to move the actual data between systems.

When FTP sends commands, it uses the TELNET Network Virtual Terminal (NVT) standard commands to carry them. The control connection allows for the communication of commands and replies between client and server. The data (or passive) connection listens on a specified port for a connection from the control (or active) connection in order to transfer data. It has a special set of additional commands for transferring, locating, and organizing the files and directories. The FTP protocol allows access to the Internet archives of software and other information. Directories are browsed as hypertext. The browser will notice references to files and access them. README files can also prove useful.

3.8   World Wide Web Proxies

The Web proxy server allows access to the Web from within a firewall. Private subnets typically go through a firewall to get to the Internet. The firewall protects the private subnet from intruders. The proxy server is typically on a separate computer from the firewall. A proxy is a special HTTP server. The proxy waits for a request from inside the firewall, forwards the request to the remote server outside the firewall, reads the response, and then sends it back to the client. Web clients do not lose any functionality going through a proxy—except that the proxy can be set up to restrict access to IP addresses within the subnet or to Web sites that are considered to have no business purpose. Most corporations prefer to have this kind of restricted access.[46]

One of the more robust features of having a proxy server is caching. Documents requested by Web clients are cached to disk on the proxy server. This helps to reduce network traffic, since only the initial request travels over the network, while subsequent requests are retrieved from the local disk via the local network.

There are problems with caching. For instance, how up-to-date are the documents stored in cache? The HTTP protocol allows the author to enter an expiration date in the document summary information. This expiration date is used by the proxy to remove files from cache. However, not everyone puts expiration dates on their documents. Also, most of the documents on the Web are constantly updated. In these cases, it does not make sense to put an expiration date on them.

Proxy support is handled by the client by setting environment variables for each access protocol, such as http-proxy, ftp-proxy, gopher-proxy, and wais-proxy. When Web clients make requests to remote servers on the Web, the libwww code on the client really connects to the proxy server, not to the remote server.[46]

Without using a proxy, HTTP requests made by clients send only the path and keyword in the URL to the remote server. The protocol piece and the hostname are not passed along because the remote server knows it is an HTTP server and it also knows the hostname it is running on. The same is true of a Gopher or ftp request. When using a proxy, the client always uses HTTP for transaction requests; however, the full URL is given. In this fashion, the proxy server has all the information it needs to make the request of the remote server. The proxy acts as a client at this point and retrieves the document requested. When the proxy returns the document to the client, it sends it as an HTTP reply. In other words, the result from a Gopher or FTP request is returned as an HTML document.

The proxy acts as both a Web server and a client. When it accepts requests from clients, it is a server. When it connects to remote servers, it is a client. Another feature of using a proxy is logging. High-level logging of client transactions occurs on the proxy. The information recorded is the client IP address, date and time, the URL, byte count, and success code.

3.9   Future of the Web

3.9.1   Trends

Based on its history, the Web and the Internet will continue to grow at a significant rate in the future. As noted in Chap. 1, some experts speculate that by the turn of the century, there will be an estimated 100 million Internet *hosts.* Microsoft claims this number to be closer to 300 million Web sites. Currently, there are an estimated 20 to 30 million Internet *users.*[47,48] One thing is certain: there will be more users, hosts, and Web sites every year. People are recognizing that Web pages are *another medium.* Whether they will be as popular as books, newspapers, magazines, or TV remains to be seen. There are several issues that need to be addressed in order to make it a successful and heavily accessed medium. The number of hosts will soon exceed the number of available IP addresses. A new approach to addressing is needed to accommodate the growth. (This topic was treated in Chap. 1.)

While there is plenty of information on the Web, it still is not very easy to find the information you're looking for. What is needed is a site-to-site indexing-and-searching mechanism. There currently are intelligent tools that automatically build indexes of the Web continuously and incrementally as it grows. These are called *spiders,* or *robots.* The spiders work by starting with a known list of Web sites and, from these sites, they follow all the links to other sites, and so on. As the spider follows the links, it builds a map of all the URLs. This index can then be stored or sent to other sites. In order to prevent network traffic, spiders need to judge the frequency with which they visit sites: the number of visits must be low enough not to exceed a typical user threshold, but high enough to keep the index reasonably up to date.

Network performance and guarantees of service are also issues that need to be addressed. In order to use audio and video over the network, a minimum bandwidth should be met. Also, there must be steps in place to help handle the network traffic. The network must have adequate capacity for the demands of the Web.

Some feel that users should be charged based on their usage and not on the speed of their connection. During peak hours, it makes sense to charge more for usage. People who need a priority type of service should also be billed more than those who do not. Of course, in order for billing to be successful, security is needed. Even though the technology to secure information sent across the network will be available soon, the challenge will be convincing people to understand and trust these with security mechanisms.

In addition to actual commercial sales over the next few years, Web technology will benefit business-to-business applications. Web servers are good for presenting public information, providing services such as technical support, and marketing. The commercial sector will benefit from implementing Web servers. This topic is treated at length in Ref. 49.

3.9.2   Virtual Reality Modeling Language (VRML)

The Virtual Reality Modeling Language (VRML) is a language for describing multiparticipant interactive simulations. This allows virtual worlds networked via the global Internet and hyperlinked with the World Wide Web. All aspects of virtual world display, interaction, and internetworking can be specified using VRML. It is expected that languages such as these will become more important in the near future as virtual reality applications become more common (see Chap. 9).[50]

It is the intention of its designers for VRML to become the standard language for interactive simulation within the World Wide Web.[11] The designers of VRML decided that it would not be an extension to HTML. HTML is designed for text, not graphics. Also, VRML requires even more finely tuned network optimizations than HTML. It is expected that a typical VRML scene will be composed of many more inline objects and served up by many more servers than a typical HTML document. It was also decided that, except for the hyperlinking feature, the first version of VRML would not support interactive behaviors.

The first version of VRML allows for the creation of virtual worlds with limited interactive behavior. These worlds can contain objects that have hyperlinks to other worlds, HTML documents, or other valid MIME types. When the user selects an object with a hyperlink, the appropriate MIME viewer is launched. When the user selects a link to a VRML document from within a correctly configured WWW browser, a VRML viewer is launched. Thus, VRML viewers are the perfect companion applications to standard WWW browsers for navigating and visualizing the Web. Future versions of VRML will allow for richer behaviors, including animations, motion physics, and real-time multiuser interaction.

At the highest level of abstraction, VRML is just a way for objects to read and write themselves. Theoretically, the objects can contain anything: 3-D geometry, MIDI data, JPEG images, etc. VRML defines a set of objects useful for doing 3-D graphics. These objects are called *nodes*. Nodes are arranged in hierarchical structures called *scene graphs*. Scene graphs are more than just a collection of nodes. The scene graph defines an ordering for the nodes. The scene graph has a notion of state. Nodes earlier in the scene can affect nodes that appear later in the scene.[11,51] This topic is treated in greater detail in Chap. 4.

References

1. Boutell, Thomas, "World Wide Web FAQ," 1995, <URL:http://sunsite.unc.edu/boutell/faq/www_faq.html#intro>.

2. Handley, Mark, and Jon Crowcroft, *World Wide Web: Beneath the Surf,* UCL Press, May 1995.
3. Krol, Ed, *The Whole Internet User's Guide & Catalog,* O'Reilly & Associates, Inc., 1992.
4. Segal, Ben, "A Short History of Internet Protocols at CERN," CERN, April 1995, <URL:http://wwwcn.cern.ch/pdp/ns/ben/TCPHIST.html>.
5. Hughes, Kevin, "Entering the World-Wide Web: A Guide to Cyberspace," Honolulu Community College, September 1993, <URL:http://www.hcc.hawaii.edu/guide/Paper/EnteringCyberspace/guide.mos.ps>.
6. "Finally, 20 to 30 Million Users on the Internet," press release, MIDS, Austin, Texas, August 25, 1995, <URL:http://www.tic.com/mids/press957.html>.
7. Torkington, Nathan, "World Wide Web Primer," December 1994, <URL:http://www.vuw.ac.nz/-gnat/ideas/www-primer.html>.
8. Friesenhahn, Bob, "Build Your Own WWW Server," *Byte,* April 1995, pp. 83–88.
9. Means, Paula, "World Wide Web: Servers, Protocols, and Access," Stevens Institute of Technology, class project, fall 1995.
10. "What Are WWW, Hypertext and Hypermedia?" World Wide Web Frequently Asked Questions, <ftp://rtfm.mit.edu/pub/usenet/news.answers/www/faq>.
11. Smith, H., "Web Server Technology Access and Protocols," Stevens Institute of Technology, class project, fall 1995.
12. HTML Info at http/www.hlp.hp.co.uk/people/dsr/html3/contents.html.
13. Lemay, Laura, *Teach Yourself Web Publishing with HTML in a Week,* SAMS Publishing, 1995.
14. Berners-Lee, T. J., R. Cailliau, J. F. Groff, and B. Pollermann, "World Wide Web: An Information Infrastructure for High-Energy Physics," CERN, January 1992, <URL: http://www.w3.org/hypertext/www/Bibliography/Conferences/A1HEP92/www-for-hep.ps>.
15. Berners-Lee, Fielding, and Frystyk. "Hypertext Transfer Protocol—HTTP 1.0," (work-in-progress memo) October 14, 1995, <http://www.ics.uci.edu/pub/ietf/http/draft-ietf-http-v10-spec-04.html>.
16. *Netscape Commerce Server Installation and Reference Guide (Windows NT),* Netscape Communications Corporation, 1995.
17. Savola, Tom, "Using HTML," Que Corporation, 1995, p. 30.
18. Holicki, D. J., "Building a Web Site," Stevens Institute of Technology, class project, fall 1995.
19. Graham, Ian, *HTML Sourcebook,* John Wiley & Sons, 1995, p. 53.
20. Net.Genesis, Devra Hall, *Building a Web Site,* Prima Publishing, Calif., 1995, p. 150.
21. Vacca, John R., "Mosaic: Beyond Net Surfing," *Byte,* January 1995, pp. 75–86.
22. Vetter, Ronald J., Chris Spell, and Charles Ward, "Mosaic and the World Wide Web," *IEEE Computer,* October 1994, pp. 49–57.
23. Hoffman, Paul E., "Web Servers Survey," September 1995, <http://www.Proper.com/www/servers-survey.html>.
24. Morgan, Eric Lease, "The World Wide Web and Mosaic: An Overview for Librarians," *Public-Access Computer Systems Review,* 1994, pp. 5–26.
25. "NCSA httpd," <http://www.proper.com/www/server15.html>.
26. Luotonen, Ari, "CERN httpd 3.0 Guide," CERN, 1994, <URL:http://info.cern.ch/hypertext/WWW/Daemon/User/Config/Overview.html>.
27. "Httpd from CERN," <http://www.proper.com/www/server3.html>.
28. "MacHTTP from BIAP Systems," <http://www.proper.com/www/server13.html.
29. Schatz, Bruce R., and Joseph B. Hardin, "NCSA and the World Wide Web: Global Hypermedia Protocols for the Internet," *Science,* August 12, 1994, pp. 895–901.
30. Sepero, Simon, "Analysis of HTTP Performance Problems," <http://sunsite.unc.edu/mdma-release/http-prob.html>.
31. Sepero, Simon, "Progress on HTTP-NG," <http://www.w3.org/pub/WWW/Protocols/HTTP-NG/http-ng- status.html>.
32. Hirsch, Peter, "Exercise the Power of the World Wide Web," *IEEE Computer Applications in Power,* July 1995, pp. 25–29.

33. Williams, Margot, "Getting Well Connected to the World Wide Web," *Washington Post* (Washington business supplement), June 5, 1995, p. 19.
34. Notees, Greg, "Lynx to the World Wide Web," *Online,* July 1994, pp. 78–82.
35. Powell, James, "Spinning the Web: Setting Up World Wide Web Servers," September 1994, <URL:http://scholar.lib.vt.edu/reports/Servers-web.html>.
36. Rescoria, E., and A. Schiffman, "The Secure HyperText Transfer Protocol," Enterprise Integration Technologies, December 1994.
37. Stein, Lincoln D., "The World Wide Web Security FAQ," September 1995, <URL: http://www-genome.wi.mit.edu/WWW/faqs/www-security-faq.html>.
38. Bair, J., "Text-Retrieval Software Is Becoming Mainstream on the Web," GartnerGroup, TINFO-1385, 1995.
39. The Internet Group—Statistics 1995, <URL:http://www.tig.com>.
40. McCool, Rob, "The Common Gateway Interface," NCSA, April 1995, <URL:http:// hoohoo.ncsa.uiuc.edu/cgi/intro.html>.
41. Bina, Eric, Rob McCool, Vicki Jones, and Marianne Winslett, "Secure Access to Data Over the Internet," *IEEE Computer Soc. Press,* vol. xii, 1994, pp. 99–102.
42. "Security Considerations," <http://www.w3.org/hypertext/WWW/Protocols/HTTP/ Security.html>.
43. Berners-Lee, T. J., and Hertrik Frystyk, "About News Servers and NNTP," CERN, July 1995.
44. Kanto, Brian, and Phil Lapsley, "Network News Transfer Protocol," Network Working Group, February 1986.
45. McCahill, Mark, "About Gopher," Computer & Information Services University of Minnesota, August 1992.
46. Luotonen, Ari, and Kevin Altis, "World Wide Web Proxies," CERN, May 1994, somewhere under: <URL:http://www.w3.org>.
47. Wheatman, V., "Four Easy Pieces for World Wide Web Deployment," GartnerGroup, TU-119-1386, 1995.
48. "White Paper on the WWW," NetMind Media, Inc., 1995, <URL:http://www. mindnet.com/ref/whitepap/whitepap.html>.
49. Minoli, D., *Electronic Commerce Over the Internet,* McGraw-Hill, New York, 1997.
50. Ang, Cheong, David Martin, and Michael Doyle, "Integrated Control of Distributed Volume Visualization Through the World Wide Web," *IEEE Computer Soc. Press,* vol. xiii, 1994, pp. 13–20.
51. Forzani, Michele, "Web Server Technology, Access and Protocols," Stevens Institute of Technology, class project, fall 1995.

HTML Technology, Applications, and Examples

4.1 Introduction

In the past couple of years, the World Wide Web has exploded into the consciousness of both the general public and of many corporate planners. The WWW distributes information and supports links to resources via Web pages. These documents can incorporate formatted text, color graphics, digitized sound, and digital video clips. HyperText Markup Language is the language used to make these pages become whatever the user intends them to be. HTML is used to display text, graphics, sounds, movies, etc., over the Internet on the WWW. This chapter provides a summarized description of HTML, while supplying enough detail to educate the reader about key features of the language.

4.1.1 Origins of HTML

As covered in the preceding chapters, in early 1989 Tim Berners-Lee and Robert Cailliau at the European Laboratory for Partical Physics (CERN) proposed a new set of protocols for an Internet information distribution system to be used among various high-energy-physics research groups. Since the physicists were located in various organizations and used a variety of computer systems and application software (including various word processing and text markup programs for producing reports), the World Wide Web was developed using the client/server architecture, which ensured cross-platform portability.[1-12] The World Wide Web protocols were soon adopted by other organizations, and a consortium of organizations, called the W3 Consortium, was formed to pool their resources for the continued development of WWW standards. The consortium is led by the Massachusetts Institute of Technology, CERN, and the French National Institute for Research on Computer Science and Control (INRA). This consortium proposes new and more sophisticated features for HTML, evaluates suggestions and alternate implementations, and publishes new levels or versions of the HTML standard.[13,14]

The WWW is officially described as a "wide-area hypermedia information retrieval initiative." It is an information system that links data from many different Internet services under one set of protocols. Web clients, called *browsers* or *viewers*, interpret HyperText Markup Language documents delivered from Web servers.[14,15] The World Wide Web is a distributed, multimedia, hypertext system. It is *distributed* since information on the Web can be located on any computer system connected to the Internet around the world. It is *multimedia* because the information it holds can be in the form of text, graphics, sound, or even video.[1–12]

Hypertext means that the information is available using hypertext technique, which involves selecting highlighted phrases or images that, once selected, retrieve information related to the selected highlighted subject. The information being retrieved can be information located anywhere in the world. The normal way to provide information on the World Wide Web is by writing documents in HTML, the Hyper-Text Markup Language.

4.1.2   Web architecture and usage

With client/server architecture, the user accesses the World Wide Web using a browser client, typically on a desktop machine such as a PC, Macintosh, or UNIX workstation. The client will display hypertext links in some manner, such as underlining the links. Selecting a link (by clicking a mouse button with a graphical client or by typing the number following the link using a simple text-based client) sends a request to the server over the network (which could be a local network, a national network, or the global Internet). The request is sent to a World Wide Web server, which typically runs on a powerful computer system. The server will retrieve the file that has been requested and will deliver it to the client. Once the client has started to retrieve the file, it can display it on the local machine. If the client cannot display the file (many clients, for example, cannot view video clips), the client can pass the file on to an external viewer that can process the file.[1–12]

HTML is designed to specify the logical organization of a document, with hypertext extensions (see Table 4.1 for a snapshot). It achieves that goal by the use of instructions known as *tags*. HTML documents are in plain (ASCII) text format that contains embedded HTML tags. Documents can be created in any text editor (e.g., Emacs or VI on UNIX systems; Edit or NotePad in DOS/Windows systems), including editors in a graphical environment (WYSIWYG). There are also many other tools, including editors, designed specifically to assist in creating HTML documents. To view an HTML document, the user needs a browser. The browser interprets the instructional tags and presents the HTML document. There are many browsers available today (in both text-only and graphical WYSIWYG environments), which operate in a variety of systems, including UNIX, DOS/Windows, Macintosh, OS/2, and others (this topic is discussed in more detail in Chap. 5).

As is now clear, information on the World Wide Web is organized mostly in the form of documents that are written in HTML. HTML defines the structural elements in a document (such as headers, citations, and addresses), layout information (bold and italics), and the use of inline graphics together with the ability to provide hypertext links. HTML documents conform to the ISO standard 8879: "The Standard Generalized Markup Language" format. HTML provides a way to encode document structure with a minimum of presentation information. SGML is a standard way to describe what the markup looks like. The description of the markup is called a "Document Type Definition," usually abbreviated to DTD. Users can view SGML as the architecture behind HTML, which ensures compatibility to DTD in its specifications of Versions 1.0, 2.0 (current), and the proposed Version 3.0.[1] Note: The press-time version in use was Version 3.2.*

4.1.3 Language evolution

Originally, Web pages were written in HTML Level 0. Users saw Web documents on character-based terminals that employed UNIX browsers such as WWW or Lynx (covered in Chap. 3). The Web was not too exciting then. Hypertext was a nice touch, but in 1993 far more people were interested in Gopher access to information than getting on

---

* This discussion is conceptual only. The reader should refer to an HTML 3.2 manual for actual syntax.

TABLE 4.1   HTML: A Snapshot

- HTML is a simple markup system used to create hypertext documents that are portable from one platform to another.
- HTML documents are SGML documents with generic semantics that are appropriate for representing information from a wide range of applications.
- Can represent hypertext news, mail, documentation, and hypermedia; menus of options; database query results; simple structured documents with inline graphics; and hypertext views of existing bodies of information.
- In use by the World Wide Web global information initiative since 1990.
- RFC 1866. Proposed Standard "HyperText Markup Language Specification—HTML 2.0," T. Berners-Lee and D. Connolly, November 1995.
- HTML 3.0 specification provides a number of new features. It is broadly backward-compatible with HTML 2.0.

the Web. Then the National Center for Supercomputing Applications (NCSA) at the University of Illinois produced a graphical Web browser called Mosaic, which was quickly dubbed "the next killer app." Having free versions for UNIX, Windows, and Macintosh helped boost Mosaic's popularity.

Initial releases of Mosaic supported HTML 1.0, essentially the same language as Level 0 plus inline images, but it also proved to be different. Web pages became hyperlinked multimedia publications. Suddenly, everybody wanted a Web site. The popularity of the Web and Mosaic spawned more browsers and a demand for more features.

A working group was formed to develop a standard for HTML 2.0. Much of the effort centered on taking current practice and reformatting it as an SGML Document Type Definition. SGML is a set of codes and tags designed to allow documents to be moved among different computer systems. HTML is a subset and resembles a simplified version of SGML. SGML documents are more complex and programming-like than HTML. The observation that "SGML is to HTML as HTML is to plain text" seems reasonable on the surface. HTML was extended with a few more elements, and fill-out forms and scripts were added. The first beta was released for free in late 1994; the HTML 2.0 standard was finalized soon thereafter.[14,16-20] HTML has been in use by the World Wide Web global information initiative since 1990. The formal HTML 2.0 (RFC 1866) corresponds roughly to the capabilities of HTML in common use prior to June 1994. The "text/html" Internet Media Type (RFC 1590) and MIME Content Type (RFC 1521) is defined by this specification.

There was work under way at press time on higher releases (as covered in Chap. 2 and Sec. 4.6 in this chapter) and other languages (Sec. 4.6). HTML 3.0/3.2 builds upon HTML 2.0. Tables have proven to be important, with text flow around figures and math as runners up. The HTML 3.0 proposal for tables uses a lightweight style of markup. HTML 3.0 introduces a new element: FIG for inline figures. Text can be flowed around figures and you can control when to break the flow to begin a new element. There is also interest in equations. Forms have been extended to support graphical selection menus with client-side handling of events similar to FIG. Additional features include a static banner area for corporate logos, disclaimers, and customized navigation/search controls. The LINK element can be used to provide standard toolbar/menu items for navigation, such as Previous and Next buttons. The NOTE element is used for admonishments such as notes, cautions, or warnings, and also used for footnotes.[21]

Table 4.2 depicts for illustrative purposes the content of the evolving HTML 3.0 standard. Table 4.3 depicts a set of resources that the reader may find on the Internet on HTML (these are only the primary documents—much more is available as secondary documentation).

TABLE 4.2   Contents of HTML 3.0

1. Introduction
    1. How to Participate in Refining HTML 3.0
    2. HTML 3.0 Overview
    3. Transition Strategy from HTML 2.0
    4. Design Guidelines for HTML 3.0
2. Understanding HTML and MIME
3. Understanding HTML and SGML
4. The Structure of HTML 3.0 Documents
5. The HEAD Element and Related Elements
6. The BODY Elements
    1. Banners
    2. Divisions
    3. Heading Elements
    4. Paragraphs
    5. Line Breaks
    6. Horizontal Tabs
    7. Hypertext Links
    8. Overview of Character-Level Elements
        + Information Type Elements
        + Font Style Elements
    9. The IMG (Image) Element
    10. Unordered Lists
    11. Ordered Lists
    12. Definition Lists
    13. Figures
    14. Tables
    15. Math—Missing Entity Names
    16. Horizontal Rules
    17. Preformatted Text
    18. Admonishments
    19. Footnotes
    20. Block Quotes
    21. The ADDRESS Element
    22. Fill-out Forms
7. Special Characters
8. Security Considerations
9. HTML 3.0 Document Type Definition
    1. The SGML Declaration
    2. The Latin-1 Character Entities
    3. Math and Greek Entities
    4. HTML Icon Entities
    5. The HTML 3.0 DTD
10. Terms
11. References
12. Acknowledgments

TABLE 4.3   Primary HTML Documents and Resources on the Internet

- HTML Specifications
  - 3.0 Text, IETF
  - 2.0 Text (RFC 1866)

- General Discussion and Archives
  - HTML-WG Mailing List Archives
  - W3O's collected info on HTML
  - Dave Raggett's Old HTML+ Discussion Document [PostScript] and His WWW94 Paper on HTML+

- HTML Validation
  - HaLSoft HTML Validation Service

- Reference Guides and Test Pages
  - Sandia National Laboratories HTML Reference Manual
  - John Franks' Searchable Version of the HTML 2.0 Specification
  - Tony Jebson's HTML 3.0 Test Page
  - Glenn Trewitt's HTML Form-Testing Home Page (Digital Equipment Corporation)
  - Kevin Werbach's Bare Bones Guide to HTML

- Internationalization and Extended Access
  - Dan Connolly's Paper "Character Set"
  - Gavin Nicol's Paper on the Multilingual WWW
  - Roman Czyborra's Reference List of ISO 8859 Coded Character Sets
  - François Yergeau's List of Web Sites That Serve Documents in Various Languages and Character Sets
  - SGML Extended Reference Concrete Syntaxes (ERCS)
  - Jeff Suttor's Experimental HTML to ICADD Transformation Service

- HTML Style and User Guides (some may be obsolete):
  - HTML Quick Reference by Michael Grobe (U of Kansas)
  - List of HTML Tags by Otmar Lendl (Salzburg U)
  - A Beginner's Guide to HTML by Marc Andreessen (was NCSA)
  - Introduction to HTML Documentation by Ian Graham (U Toronto)
  - How to Write HTML Files by Peter Flynn (UCC Ireland)
  - Composing Good HTML by James "Eric" Tilton (Willamette U)
  - Style Guide for Online Hypertext by Tim Berners-Lee (CERN)
  - Style Guide for Online Hypertext by Alan Richmond (NASA GSFC)

- Related Standards and Drafts
  - RFC 1766 (Language Tags)
  - ISO 639 (Language Codes)
  - ISO 3166 (Country Codes)
  - RFC 1874 on SGML Media Types
  - Jacob Palme's Draft on MIME E-mail Encapsulation of Aggregate HTML Documents

- Related Working Groups
  - IETF HTTP Working Group
  - IETF URI Working Group (now closed)

4.1.4 Key browsers

Mosaic, which supported HTML 1.0, is no longer the leading browser that it once was. *Netscape Navigator,* from Netscape Communications, Mountain View, California, recognizes an enhanced superset for HTML. Because browsers are tolerant of errors, Web pages could be written using Netscape extensions without worrying about breaking other browsers. Web surfers using Netscape would see "fancier" pages than would those using Mosaic. Netscape generated excitement by adding more extensions to each new beta version. It is estimated that roughly 50 to 75 percent of surfers are using Netscape Navigator, giving it the market strength that helps enforce its HTML version. A recent study of more than 72,000 WWW users has found that about four out of five use Netscape Navigator; only 14 percent of the respondents said they used Mosaic as their primary Web browser.[14,22] More recently, Microsoft has been coming on strong with its Internet Explorer 3.0. Microsoft is able to bundle the browser in their office software package for Windows, Windows 95, and NT.

Browser makers have implemented additional features, and HTML 3.0 became a reality even before the draft standard was finalized. For example, in 1995 Netscape Communications announced it would fully support and participate in the HTML 3.0 effort. As the draft standard progressed, Netscape's HTML would converge with that of the Consortium.* The WWW Consortium's test-bed HTML 3.0 browser, called Arena, was available in the summer of 1995 for UNIX platforms and was formally released shortly thereafter.[14,17–20,23]

Since HTML is just a markup language, it does not specify the precise format of the document, but rather offers general suggestions on how the document should be presented. Authors can use HTML tags to specify that they want some text to appear as a bulleted list, but they do not need to specify where the bulleted list will appear on the page, how much indentation should be used, where lines wrap, or what size font to use. These things are all determined by the browser being utilized and the fonts that are available on the system. Not all browsers support all of the HTML features. Some support them but do not interpret them in a sensible way. Unfortunately, this is discovered only by trial and error. *Note:* HTML language is not case-sensitive; except where you link to other pages (when using a UNIX server to host your pages, the UNIX language is case-sensitive, so the links and references must be the same as the filename).

Browsers are discussed in more detail in Chap. 5.

---

* Netscape's home page: http://www.netscape.com/.

4.1.5 Miscellaneous definitions

This section provides some basic HTML terminology.

Home page. A home page is a publicly available World Wide Web document that describes the author, or perhaps a work group or student organization. People who have personal home pages often include information such as their interests, research, publications, and other professional and vocational data. Groups that have home pages tend to describe what they do and how to get in touch with them. Many corporations and institutions now have home pages.

Uniform resource locators. These are "addresses" for Internet resources in the WWW. They use a naming pattern to specify how and where to find any Internet server resource. They behave very much like addresses, not only to actual data, but to any definable resource on the Internet, including the results of application commands. URLs are available for newsgroups on USENET, Gopher servers, TELNET connections, WAIS server files, and World Wide Web server files. Any link from an HTML document to another file or application is written in the form of a URL.

How an author writes a URL is important. A complete (or fully qualified) URL should be similar to this:

```
scheme://host.domain [:port]/path/dataname
```

where the elements are as follows:

scheme	Defines what kind of data the URL points to.
host.domain	Gives the explicit Internet server in which the data or application is located.
:port	Required if the data server is not located at a default port location. For instance, Gopher servers are assumed to reside on port 70.
path/dataname	Defines the specific location and data name of the data on the indicated server (see also Sec. 4.1.6).[14, 24]

Table 4.4 shows URL definition examples. Each example in the table uses fully qualified URLs—every component of the URL is provided to guide any client software to the specific data resource. In HTML, after a document is accessed in a particular path, it can reference other documents on the same server using partial or relative URLs. This simplifies writing links in HTML documents that will point to additional local files.

Partial URLs. A partial URL is the target of the hypertext link as indicated by the anchor attribute HREF, which takes as its value the URL of the target document or resource. *Partial URLs are a shorthand way of*

TABLE 4.4 URL Definitions and Examples

Scheme	Data type	Sample URL
file	Data files	file://ftp.yoga.com/pub/exercises/techniques.txt
http	HTML files	http://www/calendar.com/pub/monthly/january.html
news	USENET newsgroup	news:alt.fan.cecil-adams
gopher	Gopher server	gopher://gopher.toolbox.org/
telnet	TELNET connection	telnet://harbor.piedmont.edu
wais	WAIS server	wais://wais.nectar.gods.com.8080

referring to files or other resources relative to the URL of the document being currently viewed. This is good because the author need not specify entire URLs for simple relative links between files on the same computer. Instead, the author needs only to specify their position on the file system relative to each other. URLs can also point to directories other than the one containing the current document. Specification of these relative directories is done by using a UNIX-like path structure. Note the following example:

```
<A HREF="SubDir/ex2c.html"> hypertext links </A>
```

Notice the UNIX-like directory pathnames in which the forward-slash character indicates a new directory. The specification of the URL syntax uses the forward slash to denote directories or any other hierarchical relationship. The use of back slashes that are used in DOS and Windows and colons that are used with Macintosh are not allowable.[14,17–20,25]

HyperText Transfer Protocol. HTTP servers are designed specifically to distribute hypertext documents. HTTP is a client/server protocol (described in Chap. 3). In the client/server model, a client program running on the user's machine sends a message requesting service to a server program running on another machine on the Internet. The server responds to the request by sending a message back to the client. In exchanging these messages, the client and server use a well-understood protocol. FTP or WAIS and Gopher are other examples of Internet client/server protocols, all of which are accessible to a WWW browser. If such a relationship between the function of the data and protocol did not exist, a viewer would not know that it was to translate the document from its ASCII text format into the intended HTML-coded format. HTTP servers support these important features:

- The ability to return to the client not just files, but also information generated by programs running on the server

- The ability to take data from the client and pass this information on to other programs on the server for further processing

The special server-side programs are called *gateway programs* because they usually act as a gateway between the HTTP server and other local resources such as databases.

An HTTP connection has four stages, as shown in Fig. 4.1. This procedure means that a connection can download only a single document or process a single transaction, while the stateless nature of the transaction means that each connection knows nothing about previous connections (these concepts were covered in Chap. 3).[14,26]

HTML's DTD. This is a document that describes the HTML language, its elements, and their legal uses. The HTML DTD has many levels that pertain to different categories of use or compatibility with the HTML standards. The HTML DTD is written in SGML. The document coding is complex and difficult to read, since it was meant to be read by SGML interpreters. Annotated versions of the HTML DTD make it easier for developers and end users to verify conformity issues.[14,17–20,27]

4.1.6   File-naming issues in HTML

Most people think naming files is as simple as choosing "Save As" and entering a unique name for a data file. For the typical home computer user, that might be true. But HTML requires that users broaden their knowledge of different file-naming schemes and learn how to use and reference filenames for an Internet environment. How does HTML untangle filename allowances and restrictions and provide support for hypertext documents? Through compromise. HTML dictates that filenames, because they are absolute for the platform on which the file is located, must obey all of the local restrictions—and enjoy the benefits as well. UNIX files can be 30 or more characters of mixed cases and underscores between words. DOS files can be cryptic combinations of eight alpha and numeric characters. Macintosh files can use spaces and punctuation.

The compromise comes in the use of extensions. All HTML files and their related data fields (sounds, graphics, and digital video clips) must use a standard set of extensions. Table 4.5 provides a list of common extensions for HTML associated files.[14,28]

Most viewers have a configuration option that defines how the software handles each file type. Some are handled in the application itself, especially the HTM, HTML, and GIF files. Many use external or "helper"

I. Open the connection	II. The request	III. The response	IV. Close the connection

Figure 4.1 HTTP connection phases.

TABLE 4.5   HTML-Associated Files

Extension	File type	Sample filename
html	HTML text	broadway_bound.html
htm	HTML text	broadway.htm
text	ASCII text	sample_output.text
txt	ASCII	text_sample.txt
gif	compressed graphic	pekinese.gif
jpeg	compressed graphic	Damn_Yankees.jpeg
jpg	compressed graphic	damyanks.jpg
tiff	high-resolution graphic	Applegate_Lola.tiff
tif	high-resolution graphic	app_lola.tif
pcx	bitmap graphic	design.bmp
mpeg	digital video	nature_walk.mpeg
mpg	digital video	naturewk.mpg
avi	digital video	nature.avi
wav	digital audio	welcome.wav
au	digital audio	first_visit.au
ps	PostScript data	bibliography.ps

applications to process the other data formats. For instance, the Macintosh version of NCSA Mosaic uses Sparkle to play MPG and MPEG digital video files, and Sound Machine to play AU digital audio files.

4.2   The Nuts and Bolts of HTML

HTML pages are like annotated bibliographies; they give the author the opportunity to expand on an endless variety of topics and present additional factual or thematic resources to further explore a subject. But regardless of how anyone perceives HTML, everyone who uses it speaks the same language. Elements, tags, anchors, hyperlinks, URLs, and attributes: they are all part of the lexicon of the Web's documents.

HTML is not really a language like BASIC, C, PASCAL, or other computer languages. Rather, it is a way of getting a Web viewer such as Netscape, Mosaic, Explorer, or Lynx to display a Web page that still looks roughly like a (human-readable) document. An HTML file still looks like a standard text file, but has extra "tags" added that tell the viewer how to format the text.[14,17–20,29] HTML identifies the structure of the document and suggests the layout of the document. The display capabilities of the browser software determine the appearance of the HTML document on the screen. Using HTML, the home page developer can give instructions for the following:

- The title of the document
- The hierarchical structure of the document with header levels and section names
- Bulleted, numbered, and nested lists
- Insertion points for graphics
- Special emphasis for key words or phrases
- Reformatted areas of the document
- Hyperlinks and associations to other documents

HTML is a simple yet powerful design language. Even the basic HTML tags include common components of an interface language: output language and action language. Both content and presentation tags define the output of a document. Hyperlink tags instruct a computer to respond to users' actions, whether it be connecting to another site in the Web or sending an electronic mail message. HTML's Common Gateway Interface further allows Web designers to create interactive Web pages that include buttons, check boxes, and text input.

HTML consists of formatting commands that adjust the size, shape, color, and position of the text and graphics. To start out in this language, you can give the page a heading and a title when the browser is on that page. Next is the command of <Body>, which is a command for the type of paragraphing you want. There are commands such as <P> (used for a paragraph), <I> (for italics), and many others (such as <B> for bold). Most of the commands end with </, followed by the same formatting character. For example,

<I><B> The WWW </B></I>

gives the following in italics and boldface:

The WWW

Figure 4.2 is a listing of many of the common commands used in the HTML language. These are a good start in laying out a home page and its hyperlinks. Only a few are listed, but they can be combined with others to create various formatting techniques. Figure 4.3 shows an example of the HTML language used to display department members in the MIS Department at Stevens Institute of Technology.

HTML documents are divided into *elements,* which are marked by tags of the form `<NAME> ... some text ... </NAME>`, where the enclosed text is the content of the element. Some elements do not affect a block of text and are hence called *empty elements,* which do not require end tags.

Element names and attributes are case-insensitive. Thus, `<NAME ATTRIBUTE="string">`, `<NamE AtrRiButE="string">`, and `<name attri-`

<A HREF--"Uniform Resource
Locator (URL)"></A> Anchors a hypertext link.

<B></B> Sets bold text.

<Body></Body> Defines the document's body section.

 Inserts a line break.

<Center></Center> or <H1 Align=Center></H1 Align=Center>
Centers the enclosed text and objects.

<H1></H1>to<H6></H6>
Defines heading text (there are six hierarchical levels).

<Head></Head> Defines the document's header section.

<HTML></HTML> Defines an HTML document.

<HR> Inserts a horizontal rule. <I></I> Sets italic text.
<img Src="ImageFile"Align=
alignment> Inserts an image file with specified alignment (right or left).

<P> Inserts a paragraph break.

<Title></Title> Defines the document's title.

Figure 4.2   Key HTML commands.

bute="string"> are equivalent. However, the attribute value (here, the string "string") when enclosed in quotation marks is case-sensitive.

The string <h1> This is the Heading </H1> is then an H1 element, consisting of an H1 start tag, the enclosed text, and an H1 end tag. Sometimes elements take attributes, which are like variables and are usually assigned values that define special characteristics of the element. An example is the *IMG element,* which is used to include an image within an HTML document. An IMG element might appear via the tag: <IMG SRC="filename.gif">. Here, SRC is an attribute of the IMG element and is used to specify the name of the image file, which is actually a URL pointing to the image file to be included in the document.

HTML is a structured language, which means that there are rules for where element tags can and cannot go. These rules are meant to enforce an overall logical structure upon the document. Thus, a heading element, such as <H1> . . . </H>, can contain text, text marked for emphasis, and a few other textlike elements, but it cannot contain elements that mark other headings or lists.[14,30]

4.2.1   HTML elements

4.2.1.1   Approach. As discussed, the interpreted instructions in HTML are called *elements*. Elements are denoted by tags and sur-

```
<!doctype HTML public "-//IETF//DTD HTML//EN">
<HTML>

<HEAD>

<META NAME="GENERATOR" CONTENT="Internet Assistant for
Word ">

<META NAME="BUILD" CONTENT="Feb 10 1995">

<META NAME="AUTHOR" CONTENT="Matthew J. Walls">

<META NAME="CREATIM" CONTENT="1995:5:17:8:">

<META NAME="VERSION" CONTENT="1">

</HEAD>

<BODY>

<P>
5th Floor  Stevens Center Bldg.
<P>
<I><B>Eric Rosenberg</B></I>
<DL COMPACT>
<DT>Director
<DT>201.216.5491
<DT>E-Mail:
</DL COMPACT>

<P>
<I><B>Byron Dolan</B></I>
<DL COMPACT>
<DT>Senior Systems Analyst
<DT>201.216.5147
<DT>E-Mail:
</DL COMPACT>

<P>
<I><B>Gbenga Abimbola</B></I>
<DL COMPACT>
<DT>Systems Analyst
<DT>201.216.
<DT>E-Mail:
</DL COMPACT>

<P>
</BODY>
</HTML>
```

Figure 4.3 Simple HTML script.

rounded by left and right brackets (i.e., <element-name>). Most elements mark blocks of a document for particular purposes or specific formatting. Usually an element tag such as <element-one> marks the beginning of each block or section. The end of the section would then be marked by the ending tag </element-one>.

For example the heading at the top of this section (Sec. 4.2.1) would have been marked by the element H2 (a level-two heading) which would be written as follows:

<H2> 4.2.1 HTML elements </H2>

Some elements are empty, that is, they do not affect a block of the document and therefore do not require an ending-element tag. For example, to draw a horizontal line across the page, a simple element to use is <HR>. To reinforce this, all elements in HTML are case-independent. Thus you can use upper- or lowercase tags as you please. In some cases, elements can have arguments that pass to the interpreter handling this element. These arguments are called *attributes* of the element. An example of an element with an argument in the case of linking the document to another document: the element attribute will be the location of the linked document.[1-12]

The <HTML> container is used to define the extent of the HTML document. Within the HTML document there are two other containers: <HEAD> and <BODY>. The <HEAD> container provides information about the document itself. This can include the title of the document (as illustrated), copyright information, keywords, and expiry dates (for use by caching software). It is important to make use of the tag since, for example, an automatic indexing program that wishes to index the title of HTML documents can parse only the information contained in the container. If the container is not present, the entire document may have to be parsed, which will place an unnecessary extra load on the server.[1-12]

4.2.1.2 List of elements. Elements are the backbone of HyperText Markup Language. The following are elements/tags with examples that are used to make a Web page sensible and attractive while still following HTML coding standards.

HTML. This indicates that the enclosed text is an HTML document. It allows the browser to distinguish between different versions of the HTML language. HTML documents are platform-independent, meaning that they do not conform to any one system standard. When created properly, moving home pages to any server platform and accessing them can be done with any compliant WWW viewer. One reason for this independence is the <HTML> tag. Because HTML documents are not compiled for execution, some applications need a hint to know how to interpret the plain text in a home page. This is the purpose of the ⟨HTML⟩ tag. Although most viewers can handle a home page without the ⟨HTML⟩ tag, it is recommended that all HTML documents us it. Files without the ⟨HTML⟩ tag can be misinterpreted as text-only documents, and the markup tags as just more text on the page. This is particularly relevant as other applications increasingly access existing HTML documents without the presumption that the document is HTML and not a plain-text file, such as mail and newsreaders.[14,17–20,31]

HEAD. This is a container for information about the document, such as the TITLE element. Creating an accurate document head is the first step to writing good HTML. Fortunately, it is also the easiest. The head precedes the main content of the document. The head section is like a quick reference for WWW viewers and other applications that access HTML files. The head supplies the document title and establishes relationships between HTML documents and file directories. HTML provides the HEAD element to define the head section in a document. The ⟨HEAD⟩ tag encloses or contains the head section (which is enclosed by the ⟨HTML⟩ tag). The closing ⟨/HEAD⟩ tag sets the bounds for the head section.[14,32]

TITLE. This element "names" the document. The title does not assign a filename to a document; it defines a text string that is interpreted as the *HTML title* of the document. This information is not displayed as part of the document. The TITLE is displayed separately from the text and usually in a restricted space, such as a window title bar, a small, fixed-size text box, or as a single line at the top of a text screen. It should also be descriptive of the document, as it is often used as a reference to visited sites. Titles serve three purposes:

- They are used by other Internet applications (such as WAIS) for document searches and indexes.

- They act as indicators of what to expect.

- They are the opening text in the document—an easy visual clue for identifying the ASCII source files quickly.[14,33]

Sign and date. Signing and dating documents is a courtesy practice in HTML documents. A signature just displays something, such as an e-mail address, for the reader's benefit. An author should want to be associated with his or her work. The date stamp lets the reader know how current the page is; it is especially handy for evaluating the worthiness of time-sensitive information—for example, a date stamp is crucial on a home page with stock market listings or investment evaluations.

Adding signatures to a document can be done by using the LINK element. This can also be performed by adding a link to a closing ⟨ADDRESS⟩ tag that opens a mail form, allowing readers to send a message to the given e-mail address.[14,17–20,34]

Base. The HTML ⟨BASE⟩ tag acts somewhat like the DOS PATH statement: it provides an additional file directory location for the WWW viewer to refer to when looking up a document link. Specifying a value for ⟨BASE⟩ in the document head shortens the URL statements by using relative URLs in the document's anchor and links. ⟨BASE⟩ protects relative URL links in the document from "breaking" should the file be physically moved.[14,35]

Form. This element collects data. It does not do any processing of the data, so the only way the author can get a form to do anything useful is to send the data gathered by it to a program on the server.[14,36]

Body. This contains all the text and other material that is to be displayed. Everything that does not go in the HEAD goes here. When WWW viewers see the ⟨BODY⟩ line in the document, they know to display the contents that follow and to interpret any HTML formatting or object codes in the contents until they reach the ⟨/BODY⟩ line.[14,17–20,37]

The first element in BODY is an H1 element. H1 stands for a level-one-heading element; in HTML, headings come in six levels, H1 through H6, of decreasing rank. The relationships between each line or item are shown by the level or indentation of the elements; items on the same levels are considered equal to be of equal weight.

One nonstandard use of the heading elements has become a somewhat common practice—using H6 for text that is intended to be "small print." Most viewers display this heading in 8- or 10-point bold characters. The smaller the code number, the larger the text size.

Highlighting. ⟨EM⟩ signifies emphasis and ⟨STRONG⟩ signifies strong emphasis. These are logical descriptions of the enclosed text. ⟨EM⟩ is italicized if possible, while text marked with ⟨STRONG⟩ should be rendered bold.

Paragraphs. The ⟨P⟩ tag marks the beginning of a paragraph and can best be thought of as marking the start of a paragraph container. This is used to avoid compressing all text into one big paragraph. There is no formal ending ⟨/P⟩ tag. A paragraph is ended by the next ⟨P⟩ tag starting another paragraph or by any other tag that starts another block of text, such as a heading tag ⟨H1⟩, a quotation tag ⟨BLOCKQUOTE⟩, list tags, and so on. An initial break is caused by the first heading element. A correct HTML document should have a ⟨P⟩ tag at the beginning of its first paragraph.[14,38]

Line breaks.
 is used to end a line of text at a specific point. It signals the viewer to enter a line feed at the tag and continue with the text on the next line. Netscape has added a new level of functionality to the forced line break as an enhancement to the extensions for the IMG element. The <BR CLEAR> attribute tells the viewer to do the following:

CLEAR=LEFT   Breaks the current line of text and starts the next line of text on the first line available against the left margin.

CLEAR=RIGHT   Breaks the current line of text and starts the next line of text on the first line that has a clear right margin.

CLEAR=ALL   Breaks the current line of text and starts the next line of text on the first line that has both margins clear (there are no images on or overlapping the line).

Unordered lists. An unordered list begins with the tag <UL>. Lists are not empty, and every list must be terminated with an end tag </UL> to define the end of the list. The list will be marked by an indentation of some type and a star or bullet. It is up to the browser to format it nicely.

Ordered list. These are numbered lists beginning with the tag <OL>.

Menu. <MENU> is the element that defines an unordered list consisting of a number of separated, multiline <LI> elements that may or may not be marked by a bullet or similar symbol.

Directory. <DIR> can contain only LI list elements, which have the start tag <LI> and cannot be empty, as every list item must consist of some text. An ending tag is not required, since the end of a list element is implied by the next <LI> or by the </UL> tag that finally terminates the list.[14,39]

Horizontal rule. <HR> simply draws a horizontal dividing line across the page, which is useful for dividing sections. This is an empty element, since it does not act on a body of text.

Anchors/hypertext links. <A HREF="ex2a.html"> hypertext links </A> is the element marking a hypertext link. It is called an A, or anchor, element, and the marked text is referred to as a hypertext anchor. The area between the beginning <A> and ending </A> tags becomes a hot part of the text. Usually displayed with an underline of a different color or in boldface type, pressing on this field causes the client to access the indicated document or other Internet resources.[14,17–20,40]

Comments. Creating HTML documents is often compared to software programming. One habit that good software programmers develop is to include comments and documentation inside the code itself. These sections of hidden text are used to describe the purpose or function of the code that follows, or to leave a notation explaining the programmers' intentions with the code or its methods. HTML documents benefit from this same practice. HTML has adopted the standard SGML container of `<!--` (an exclamation mark followed by two dashes) to begin the author's comments and a tag of `-->` to close the comment container. Comments inside the container should consist of standard text without using any of HTML's special characters.[14,41]

```
<!-- This is an example of a comment. -->
```

4.2.2 Document structure

The most basic element in the HTML document is the paragraph. The Web browser flows all the contents of the paragraph together from left to right and from top to bottom given the current window or display size. This is called *autoflowing*. How the author breaks lines in the paragraph in HTML is immaterial when that page is displayed by a Web browser.[1-12]

The Web browser wraps anything that does not fit on the current line and puts it on the next line. For example, a paragraph that displays 5 lines on an 8-inch-wide window rewraps to about 10 lines if the user resizes the Web browser window to be half as wide. This is called *autowrapping*.

A document will be read by both graphical and character-based Web browsers. Furthermore, there will be display differences with graphical Web browsers due to different screen resolutions. Just because one browser breaks a line at a certain place does not mean others will do so at the same place. It is important to remember that on the Web the world is left-justified and flows from top to bottom.

As implied by the previous discussion, the three basic tagging pairs used to create the highest level of structure in an HTML document are as follows:

<HTML> entire HTML document </HTML>

<HEAD> document header information </HEAD>

<BODY> body of the HTML document </BODY>

The following is a skeletal HTML document that shows the required nesting of these three tagging pairs:

<HTML>
  <HEAD>
  <TITLE>
    Title here

```
</TITLE>
</HEAD>
<BODY>
    Body elements and content
</BODY>
</HTML>
```

Since the physical layout in an HTML document, like indentation and line breaks, is immaterial to Web browsers, you can format an HTML document according to your own preferences.

4.2.3 HTML tags and usages

A simple HTML document is illustrated in Fig. 4.4.

Structural elements in the document are identified by start and end tags. For example the <TITLE> and </TITLE> tags are used to specify the title of the document, which is often displayed by a client. The <H1> and </H1> tags are used to define the first-level heading. Clients will normally display headers differently from the body text. For example, a graphical client could display the header using a larger or different font, whereas a text-based client could display a header as centered text or in all capitals.[1-12]

Figure 4.4 also illustrates the <EM> container. Text held in the container (which is defined by the <EM> start tag and the </EM> end tag) will be emphasized in some way. A graphical browser could show the emphasis by displaying the text in italics, whereas a browser with audio capabilities for the visually impaired could show the emphasis by a change in the tone of the voice output. Figure 4.4 also shows the paragraph container. It is important to understand that the <P> tag is part of a paragraph container and is no longer a paragraph separator. If the </P> tag is not used, the existence of the next <P> tag will imply a </P>. In future versions of HTML it will be possible to specify paragraph attributes: for example, <P ALIGN=Center>.

Although browsers will display the HTML document as shown in Fig. 4.4, for reasons of performance and upward compatibility it is recommended that HTML documents contain additional elements, including the <HTML>, <HEAD>, and <BODY> tags, as shown in Fig. 4.5.

```
<TITLE>The World Wide Web</TITLE>
<H1>Information about the World Wide Web</H1>
<P>The World Wide Web is a <EM>distributed multimedia hypertext</EM> system.
```

Figure 4.4 Simple HTML document.

```
<HTML>
<HEAD>
<TITLE>The World Wide Web</TITLE>
</HEAD>
<BODY>
<H1>Information about the World Wide Web</H1>
<P>Information about the World Wide Web is available
<A HREF="http://info.web.data/htext/World.html"> at TCG</A>.</P>
</BODY>
</HTML>
```

Figure 4.5   A simple HTML document.

Figure 4.5 also illustrates the use of the anchor <A> container. This tag is used to provide hypertext links. In the example, the text "at TCG" that is contained between the <A> and </A> tags will be highlighted in some way by the browser. Selecting this highlighted phrase will cause the client to send a request for "http://info.web.data/htext/World.html." This request will use the http protocol and will be sent to the server running on the system at "info.web.data." Other tags are explained as follows:

<LINK REV="OWNER" HREF="internet-address">

The <LINK> stand-alone tag is used in a special way here to identify the e-mail address of the document owner. This information is not displayed by a Web browser, but is used by some browsers when sending an e-mail message on behalf of the user to the document owner.

<IMG SRC="URL">

The <IMG> stand-alone HTML tag inserts an image into the current autoflow stream. The URL is the location of the image (URL is explained later).

<HR>

The <HR> (horizontal-rule) tag forces the browser to generate a horizontal rule, or line, across the display. It breaks pages into logical sections and is useful when creating forms. There is no equivalent vertical rule.

<ADDRESS>text</ADDRESS>

The <ADDRESS> tagging pair is used to identify addresses. Depending on the Web browser, the text is rendered in a special point size, typeface, or font.

4.2.4 Hyperlinks

One of the most important HTML tagging pairs creates a hyperlink to another document or Internet resource. In general, the anchor tagging pair is used as follows:

```
<A option1 optionN>anchor-text</A>
```

It is called an *anchor* tagging pair because this tag anchors the link to a particular spot in your HTML. Another use of the anchor tag described later marks a point within a document where a link transfers to (it is optional, because by default a link transfers to the beginning of a document). The two variations are called *link-from* and *link-to* tags.[1–12]

The beginning anchor tag always requires at least one option. Although there are several options, the two most important are HREF, which defines a hyperlink, and NAME, which identifies a link-to destination within a file. Let's look at the HREF option first. Here is the syntax:

```
<A HREF="URL">anchor-text</A>
```

The anchor-text is displayed in the browser. When the user triggers the link, the browser retrieves the specified URL. For example, an author signature hyperlink can be enclosed within an <ADDRESS> tagging pair. The initials AC (in the following line) become the anchor text for the hyperlink to another HTML document, called acarmel.html:

```
<ADDRESS><A HREF="acarmel.html">AC</A></ADDRESS>
```

This demonstrates how hyperlinks can be embedded in other tagging constructs. Anywhere you have text within the body of the HTML document, you can create a hyperlink. The text could be in a paragraph, a header, a quotation, or part of an address. However, the reverse is not always true.

Instead of using text as the hyperlink anchor, you can use an image. This is done by enclosing the <IMG> tag with the anchor tagging pair. When the inline image is displayed, it becomes sensitive. If the user triggers it, the browser retrieves the document identified by the associated URL.[1–12]

4.2.5 Linking to areas within documents

By default, links point to the top of a document. But, hyperlinks can be created to jump to other points in an HTML document. For that the link-to point must be identified. This is done with the NAME option of the Anchor tag.

```
<A NAME="anchor-name">anchor-text</A>
```

This tagging pair identifies a link-to point in the HTML document and names that point. The tagging pair provides an alternative entry point into an HTML document. The anchor-text cannot be omitted. This link-to point is then referenced by using "anchor-name." One reason to jump, for example, is to go directly to the appendix of a document. For example,

```
Details are in <A HREF="#Appendix-A">Appendix A</A>
```

If the desired link to jump directly to the appendix section is needed from an external document, the URL must be added:

```
<A HREF="URL#Appendix-A">Appendix A</A>
```

If the syntax of the anchor is incorrect, most Web browsers are forgiving and display the anchor-text or inserted image, but do not make it sensitive as a hyperlink. This can be done intentionally to temporarily disable links without removing all the HTML that defines the link.[1-12]

4.2.6 Uniform Resource Locators

A URL points to a file or directory (the file may be a script or a program rather than a document). There are three types of URLs: absolute, relative, and local. There are also a couple of special-case URLs supported by some browsers. Absolute URLs completely describe how to get a file on the Internet. Relative URLs and local URLs are both ways to specify a file on the same server as the document they appear in.

Absolute URL can be used to reference any resource on the Internet, including local resources. As already noted, the full syntax for an absolute URL is as follows:

```
access-method://server-name[:port]/directory/file
```

The URL of a document that is on a Web server has an access method of *http:*. For example, the master list of public World Wide Web servers throughout the world can be accessed using the following URL:

```
http://www.w3.org/hypertext/DataSources/WWW/Geographical.html
```

This means that by using the HTTP protocol to reach a server called www.w3.org, there is a directory hypertext/DataSources/WWW that contains a hypertext document named Geographical.html. Every file on the Internet is uniquely addressable by its URL, regardless of the type of file or the type of server that provides it.

Besides the *http:* access method, the URL concept also supports other important Internet protocol access methods such as Gopher, FTP, and TELNET. So, for example, to access an FTP server you will type: ftp://ftp.micro.userkits/.

Relative URL assumes the same access method, server name, and directory path as the document the URL appears in. It indicates the relative position of the target URL from the current URL. For example, a URL to a file in the same directory as the document the URL appears:

```
<A HREF="page-7.html">Next Page</A>
```

Relative URLs are also sometimes called *partial URLs*. They are used to point to information resources in the same directory or on the same server. Absolute URLs, on the other hand, are usually used to point to information resources on other servers. In practical terms, this means that you can use relative URLs to direct navigation between documents that you author, and use absolute URLs to direct navigation to resources elsewhere on the Internet.[1-12]

The distinction between absolute and relative URLs is transparent to the Web server. When a user selects a relative hyperlink, the Web browser uses the current URL to determine the access method, server name, port number, and directory path, and sends only absolute URLs to the server.

Relative URLs allow you to author your HTML without worrying about where your final HTML directory structure will be placed on the Web server or even which system the server will run on. Relative URLs also give the flexibility to move HTML directory structure anywhere on the Web. Relative URLs also work when files are read directly from the file system by a Web browser without the intervention of a Web server.[1-12]

4.2.7 Lists

Another key HTML construct is the list. There are three types of lists:

- Unordered (bulleted) list: <UL>list</UL>
- Ordered (numbered) list: <OL>list</OL>
- Definition list: <DL>list</DL>

In the first two types of lists, the elements of the list are designated with the <LI> list-item tag. A simple bulleted list with three items would be tagged like this:

<UL>

<LI>First bullet

<LI>Second bullet

<LI>Third bullet

</UL>

It would look like this:

- First bullet
- Second bullet
- Third bullet

As you might expect, if a list-item phrase is wider than the display width, the Web browser autowraps the phrase and aligns the next line to indent under the previous line. Lists can also be nested:

<UL><LI>First bullet

   <UL><LI>First sub-bullet

   <LI>Second sub-bullet

   <LI>Third sub-bullet</UL>

<LI>Second bullet

<LI>Third bullet</UL>

The preceding code produces this result:

- First bullet
  - First sub-bullet
  - Second sub-bullet
  - Third sub-bullet
- Second bullet
- Third bullet

The third type of list, the definition list, is used when the list items do not need to be bulleted or numbered and can stand on their own. An example might be a glossary, which lists terms and their definitions. Definitions do not use the <LI> tag to mark a new list entry. Instead they use the <DT> and <DD> tagging pairs. The <DT> tagging pair identifies the primary text and the <DD> tagging pair identifies the text associated with and indented below the <DT> tagging phrase. For example, the following is a definition list of publications:

<DL>

<DT>Action Plan for African Primate Conservation</DT>

<DD>Compiled by J.F. Oates, the IUCN/SSC Primate Specialist Group, 1986, 41 pp.</DD></DL>

This will appear as follows:

Action Plan for African Primate Conservation

Compiled by J.F. Oates, the IUCN/SSC Primate Specialist Group, 1986, 41 pp.

4.2.8 Graphics

There are two different ways to present graphics: inline images and external images. *Inline images* are displayed by the Web browser as part of the document and are automatically retrieved along with the document. *External images* are displayed by a separate viewer program (started by the Web browser when needed) and must be specifically requested by triggering a hyperlink.

Inline graphics involve the transfer of a lot of data, so retrieving them can be slow. Fortunately, many Web browsers let users optionally delay downloading the inline images. With delayed downloading, inline images must be triggered by a hyperlink before they will be downloaded. When triggered, they still appear inline, not in an external viewer.[1-12]

Inline image is just one more piece of information that is included in the autoflow and autowrap of your HTML on the Web browser screen. So, an image is treated just like a word. For example, an image can appear in the middle of a paragraph.

For inline images, the two supported graphics types are the Graphics Interchange Format (GIF) and the X Bitmap (XBM) format. GIF images support 256 colors and are the more common of the two image types. X Bitmap is black and white. When inline images are autoflowing as part of a paragraph, you can explicitly control the alignment of the image with the text line by using the optional ALIGN option of the <IMG> tag. The three values for ALIGN are:

<IMG ALIGN=TOP SRC="filename.GIF">

<IMG ALIGN=MIDDLE SRC="filename.GIF">

<IMG ALIGN=BOTTOM SRC="filename.GIF">

TOP alignment places the top of the image even with the top of the current line of text, and so on. If ALIGN is omitted, bottom alignment is the default. In terms of image placement and autoflow, both image formats normally provide square outlines. It is possible to develop images in either format that have translucent (or clear) backgrounds to eliminate the square outline. With a translucent image background, the background color of the main window display can show through the translucent areas of the image.

In browsers running on color graphics systems, images might be sharing the color map with other applications. Mosaic, in particular, allocates a color-map table with only 50 entries. If an inline image has more colors than can be displayed, it still is displayed with the available colors, but it will not look as good as the full-color image. With these color-map issues in mind, it is probably better to reduce the number of colors used in GIF files to less than 50.

Also, performance must be considered. It takes a lot longer for a Web browser to retrieve an HTML document that has inline images than to retrieve one that does not. The larger the inline image, the longer it takes. In fact, the time is proportional to the square of the dimension (a four-inch-square image takes almost twice as long as a three-inch-square one). Many graphically based Web browsers cache inline images, so if the inline image has been used in previous HTML documents in the user's navigation chain, that image might still be cached. Caching also happens when the same inline image appears multiple times in the same HTML document. It is retrieved only once.[1-12]

One method that is used to solve the performance problem of large images is to use thumbnails. A *thumbnail* is a small version of a figure displayed inline, which is a link to the full-size image displayed externally. With image manipulation tools, it is easy to create a smaller version of an image.

External images are images that are not displayed inline as part of a document, but in a separate window, by an external viewer program. This is the technique to use with non-GIF images, such as TIFF, JPEG, RGB, or HDF. This technique is also useful for displaying very large GIF images, instead of using the <IMG> HTML tag described earlier. For example, to display a JPEG image in an external window: <A HREF="filename.jpg">anchor-text</A>.

4.2.9 An example of HTML page preparation

Here is an excerpt of HTML used to create Diane Holicki's home page with the *vi editor* (in a class project run by the author at Stevens Institute of Technology). FTP was utilized to copy the .htm file from UNIX.

The code shows several elements covered above. The page can be found at the following address:

http://www/esaas.att.com/personal/diane/home.htm.

```
<HTML>
<HEAD>
<TITLE>Diane J. Holicki</TITLE>
</HEAD>
<BODY>
<A> <img align= right SRC= "oliver.gif"></A>
<H2>Diane J. Holicki</H2>
<H4>Member of Technical Staff</H4>
<H4>Environment and Safety Systems Development Group</H4>
<P>
<A HREF="hi.wav">Hello</A>, Welcome to my home page!!!
(Continuously Under Construction)
<P>
<HR>
EDUCATION:
<LI>1994 BS Computer Science,
St. Peter's College, Jersey City, NJ
<LI>Presently pursuing Masters in Telecommunications
  Management,
<A    HREF="http://menger.eecs.stevens-tech.edu/">Stevens
  Institute of Technology, Hoboken, NJ</A>
</UL>
WORK:
<LI>Programmer/Analyst
<LI><A HREF="http://www.powersoft.com">Powerbuilder</A>
<LI><A HREF="http://www.informix.com">Informix-4gl</A>
<LI>Source Code Administrator
</UL>
FUN:
</A> <img align= right SRC= "friends.gif"></A>
<LI><A        HREF="http://www.lehigh.edu/j114/public/www-
  data/pooh.html">Winnie the Pooh and Tigger, too!!</A>
<LI><A
HREF="http://www.teleport.com/~celinec/yanni.htm">Yanni</
A>
<LI>Jersey Shore
<LI>Rollerblading
<LI><A HREF="bstart.au">Banana Splits?!?!?!?!?!</A>
<P>
This is my <A    HREF="http://www.post.att.com/cgi-
  bin/htpq?qtype=mult&name=diane_holicki&org=nw4801100&loc=n
  j0117">POST entry</A>:
</UL>
```

```
<A HREF="mailto:diane@esaas.att.com">Send Me Mail!!!</A>
<P>
</BODY>
</HTML>
```

Figure 4.6*a, b,* and *c* shows how pages look once the HTML is properly coded.

4.2.10   Displaying preformatted text in its original form

The question arises: Is there an easier way to re-create a specific section of text without having to use <BR> and <P> tags? Preformatted text tags is the answer. They are containers that tell the WWW viewer to display HTML code in its original format, possibly including line feeds and multiple blank spaces as well. This can simplify having to cut and paste while trying to retain the original text layout. There are three such containers:

PRE. This is used to enclose preformatted text for presentation as is, preserving the space characters and carriage returns typed into the HTML document and displaying the characters using a fixed-width typewriter font. Use PRE to display computer codes, text examples, or

(a)

Figure 4.6   HTML home page for student (Diane Holicki).

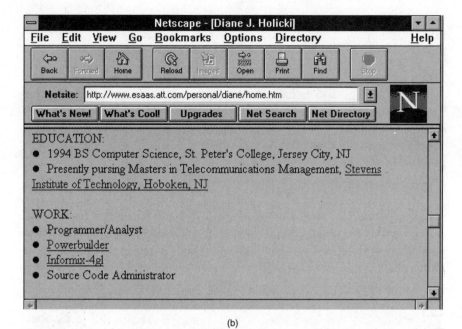

(b)

Figure 4.6   (*Continued*)

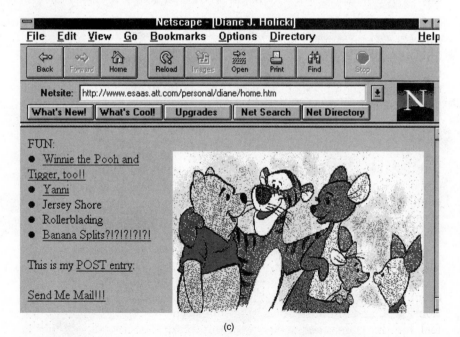

(c)

Figure 4.6   (*Continued*)

verbatim text sequences. This is also the only way to currently create tables for display in an HTML document, since this is the only element that preserves the horizontal spacing needed to align columns.

XMP. This works like PRE except in the following ways:

- HTML tags cannot be used in an XMP container.
- Viewers display the text in a proportional font, typically the default body-text font.
- The </XMP> closing tag does not force a line break.
- Not recommended for tables or columns.

PLAINTEXT. An element of the original HTML specification, this will soon be obsolete. The current WWW viewers display PLAINTEXT text in varying ways, which may be confusing. Using this tag is not recommended.[14,42]

4.2.11 Collections of hypertext documents

There are several design issues to consider when developing large document collections.

1. Each document should be small, usually no more than two or three screens full of data. The advantage of the hypertext model lies in linking various components of the documentation package. This advantage is largely lost if the author is viewing a single, huge document containing hundreds or thousands of lines of displayed text. Although hypertext links can be built within a document to other points inside the same document, this is generally more difficult to navigate than a collection of smaller files.

2. Each document should have navigation tools in the form of hypertext links that connect the document to other documents in the hierarchy and to general navigation points within the collection. Thus, each page should have links to *next* and *previous* documents and to a table of contents or the section heading. If the document is large—more than two or three screens full of text—then it might be a good idea to place the navigation icons at both the top and bottom of the document, making them easier to find.

3. Documents should show a consistent presentation style. Each document should have the same heading structure, the same navigation icons, and similar contents outlines. This makes it easy to get a feel for the collection, using programs that take advantage of this structure.[14,17–20,43]

4.2.12   Advantages and disadvantages of using HTML

HTML has its pros and cons.

4.2.12.1   Advantages

1. *Speed and ease.* Applications are quickly developed, requiring substantially less time than is required when creating stand-alone programs with languages such as C and Pascal. Web applications are easy to maintain and update without disrupting the network data traffic (or requiring users to install new software on their desktops).

2. *The client/server relationship.* As a Web viewer requests a document from a Web site, its server sends the data, and the connection between the two computers is dropped. The client application does all processing and manipulation of data, conserving the server's CPU processing power. This relationship reduces the amount of time a server spends serving a client, freeing it to serve other users or let the host system perform other tasks.[14,17–20]

Also, it allows businesses with tight budgets to invest in hardware with less horsepower (based on the size of the intended audience and the anticipated amount of document traffic). These smaller servers are cost-effective and work well serving closed environments, such as a company's intranet.

3. *HTML as common ground.* Developing applications in HTML takes advantage of HTML general compatibility. Web applications can access other company data servers, such as FTP and WAIS databases. Web viewers are also an interface to TELNET sessions, allowing users to run external command-line programs from within the HTML application. Developers can also use HTML documents to distribute Web viewer updates or revisions of software to users at their convenience, reducing support costs. HTML applications become the common interface for the audience, regardless of its platform and operating system. There are no portability issues to tackle.

4. *Collecting information with HTML.* HTML 3.x officially introduces support for forms, although most popular viewers have already implemented this support. Forms collect data from author-defined input fields and buttons, and send the results to either an e-mail address or to a Computer Gateway Interface script to be processed in the background. Forms allow Web sites to retrieve data such as customer mailing and payment information. Scripts can perform functions such as verifying user authorizations and generating an output to be displayed in an HTML document based on user inputs. An example of a site for reference that incorporates forms, CGI scripting, and external application and

dynamic HTML display is the Interactive Graphic Generation page at http://www/engg/ksu.edu:8872/. The HTML document acts as a front end for a do-it-yourself, 3-D graphics renderer. Web authors can use prewritten commercial scripts to assist in collecting on-line purchasing information.[14,44]

4.2.12.2 Disadvantages. There are disadvantages to creating applications in HTML and distributing them over the Internet.

1. *Locking.* Because HTML is not a compiled data format (HTML is text-based), Web pages cannot be locked. Users have free and open access to look at HTML sources; many popular viewers provide a "view source" option; HTML fields are easily displayed with any ordinary text editor. In the WWW model, the server delivers HTML-marked documents to Web clients, which interpret the coding and display the document according to their own configuration. Using HTML means giving up control over exactly how a document will look to end users and which HTML features the viewer will support (e.g., forms, tables, URLs).[14,17–20]

2. *Security.* Using the Internet and the WWW is easy—few network hosts require anything more than an anonymous login. Information is easily accessible and travels unimpeded between hosts and desktops. The cost of this freedom is lack of inherent security. For, just as an author can log on to the port of a remote Web site to retrieve an HTML document for his or her viewer, so can an unscrupulous user run software to monitor the traffic into and out of that port. These applications are called *sniffers,* and all they do is collect data packets. Hackers can then utilize these packets and steal unsecure information from them. The only solution to this problem requires encrypting the data before it leaves a computer (refer to the discussion in Chap. 3).

3. *Speed.* On the WWW, there are two types of speed: data transmission performance and Web page development cycle. If you are interested in high-speed data access, there is a limited number of choices, except for business applications. The current infrastructure is undergoing a series of upgrades to higher-speed data hardware, but chances are that any complex HTML documents are not going to be instantaneously on the users' desktops. The amount of graphical data and how it is incorporated into the Web pages also affects the speed of the Web. For HTML applications on LANs, performance is markedly better.

4.2.13 The server side of HTML

The NCSA Web server can incorporate information from files and environment variables into an HTML file just before the file is sent to the user. It can also automatically include the last-modified date, current date, document size, and a few other useful pieces of information. For example, adding the following to an HTML document will automatically have the document's most recent modification date entered (from the file system):

Creation Date: <EM><! --#echo var="LAST MODIFIED"--></EM>

Another example will be to add the following to a document:

<!--#include file="owner.txt"-->

This include creates a file, in this example called owner.txt, that contains a single line:

<ADDRESS><A HREF="acarmel.html">AC</A></ADDRESS>

All HTML documents with such a line will have the owner of the file included by the Web server whenever a user requests that file.

Another #include tag is virtual, which specifies a file relative to the document root. To have standard boilerplate such as a copyright notice used with every document on a Web server, independent of the document tree structure, the virtual tag should be used instead of the file tag.

4.2.14 HTML standards

The HTML standard is constantly under development. Users and developers from around the world contribute to the ongoing discourse and testing of new ideas, concepts, and uses for HTML and its component elements. The initial draft for the HTML 3.0 specification was published in March of 1995 as an Internet draft. The work on the specification was progressing at press time as a number of smaller documents covering the following areas[1-10]:

Tables	Considerable work has been undertaken in this area, and its draft has been circulated. The draft provides full backward-compatibility with Netscape Communication version 1.1N and provides additional control over visibility of borders, as well as simplifying tables importing.
Figures	Figures and embedding objects into HTML documents are covered by a new tag, FIG which is an extension to the IMG tag. FIG tag improves HTML's image-handling capability, as well as how to embed active objects into HTML documents.
Forms	Fill-out-forms improvements, together with standard hooks for scripting languages, include field labels, grouping related

fields into frames, nested forms, and a new database record entry mechanism.

Banners   Toolbars, banners, and subsidiary windows are all new to HTML 3.x. There is ability to define document-specific toolbars and static banners that don't scroll with the document, plus ways for specifying relationships between a number of document "windows."

Math   Refinement of the HTML 3.0 representation for mathematical formulas is being designed with regard to the ability to render HTML math into graphical and textual displays.

The version available at press time was Version 3.2. One user who provides time and energy in this process is Daniel Connolly (connolly@w3.org) of the W3 Consortium at MIT. He outlined standards for the standards, providing the following guidelines for the HTML development team to assist them in writing the current and upcoming specifications for HTML. The goal of any HTML specification should be to promote confidence in the fidelity of communications using HTML. This means specifications should adhere to the following standards:

- Make it clear to authors that idioms are available to express their ideas.

- Make it clear to implementers how to interpret the HTML format so that authors' ideas will be represented faithfully.

- Keep HTML simple enough that it can be implemented using readily available technology and then processed interactively.

- Make HTML expressive enough that it can represent a useful majority of the contemporary communications idioms in the WWW community.

- Make some allowance for expressing idioms not captured by the specifications.

- Address relevant interoperability issues with other applications and technologies.

There is other work under way. For example, currently, HTML forms allow the producer of the form to request information from the user reading the form. These forms have proven useful in a variety of applications in which input from the user is necessary. However, this capability is limited because HTML forms do not provide a way to ask the user to submit files of data. Service providers who need to get files from the user have had to implement custom user applications. Since file upload is a feature that will benefit many applications, RFCs (specifically RFC 1867, experimental "Form-based File Upload in HTML," E. Nebel and L. Masinter, November 1995) propose an extension to HTML to allow information providers to express file-upload requests uniformly, and a MIME-compatible representation for file-upload responses. RCF 1867 also includes a description of a backward-compatibility strategy that allows new servers to interact with the current HTML user agents.

Initially, the application of HTML on the World Wide Web was restricted by its reliance on the ISO-8859-1 coded character set, which is appropriate only for Western European languages. Despite this restriction, HTML has been widely used with other languages, using other coded character sets or character encodings at the expense of interoperability. The issue of the internationalization of HTML by extending the specification of HTML is also being addressed.

More information regarding the ongoing HTML standards process from Daniel Connolly's Web page can be found at:

http://www/w3org/hypertext/WWW/People/Connolly

4.2.15   Outstanding issues in HTML

The HTML language is officially under the control of an IETF (the Internet Engineering Task Force) Working Group. HTML has been in use by the World Wide Web global information initiative since 1990. Significant developments with HTML have and will take place with HTML 3.x, which provides additional capabilities over previous versions, such as table definitions, text flow around figures, and mathematical equations. HTML 3.x builds upon HTML 2.0 and is fully backward-compatible.

Netscape Communications, authors of the most popular browser of the mid-1990s, Netscape Navigator, has released its own extensions to HTML, which do not conform to HTML 3.0. They are under considerable pressure to conform to HTML 3.0. Yet, if Netscape will not give in to the pressure, it might affect the acceptance of HTML 3.x, since Netscape still controls a significant portion of the Web browser market.

The goal is that future developments with HTML or any future languages will not replace HTML in the sense that HTML will no longer be supported. They will coexist side by side with HTML and will be as backward-compatible as possible.

4.2.16   Which Web development language should you use?

HTML is not the only markup language available. At one time there was little choice. HTML, chosen as a standard by the Internet Engineering Task Force (IETF), was the de facto standard for creating Web pages. While HTML Version 1.0 and especially 2.0 served their purpose, users clamored for more flexibility, so the IETF began work on HTML 3.0. Then, in 1995, Netscape Communications introduced its Netscape Navigator 1.1 Web browser, which incorporated some of Netscape's own HTML extensions. These extensions may or may not end up in HTML 3.x. However, there is hope for convergence if all the information on the Internet and on a corporate intranet is to be readily available. Developers now typically utilize HTML 3.2.

Complicating matters further, in the fall of 1995, Microsoft was talking about introducing Blackbird, originally in conjunction with the Microsoft Network (MSN). This is a development tool to enable a new generation of interactive multimedia applications. Unfortunately, many of its commands are not compatible with HTML. Pages designed using Blackbird will not look the same when viewed with a Web browser that does not support that standard. Here is a quick comparison of the two.

HTML 3.x is designed to be platform-independent, usable on teletypes, Windows, or even high-end workstations. This need for platform independence weighs against the need for information provided to control the final appearance of documents. Other advantages of HTML 3.x are highlighted in Table 4.6. Since HTML documents are designed to be readable on a variety of computer platforms and Web browsers, one of the design guidelines for HTML 3.x is "content, not presentation markup"—that is, providing a way to put information on the Web without too much concern for how pretty it looks. Most of Netscape's HTML extensions, however, broaden the presentation tags to define structural elements of a document. For instance, the text will appear in the headline of a document or page. Presentation markup, on the other hand, gives the document a particular look and feel. For example, a browser will display the command ⟨HR⟩ as a horizontal rule on the page. Several new tags have been added to ⟨HR⟩ in Netscape's extensions. ⟨HR SIZE=number⟩, ⟨HR WIDTH=number|percent⟩, and ⟨HR ALIGN=left|right|center⟩ all allow Web designers to specify the height, width, and position of horizontal rules. Netscape's presentation extensions—particularly the ability to center type on a page, change the color of the type, or add a colored or textured background to the page—have distinguished Netscape navigators from other Web browsers.[14]

Blackbird is based on an object-oriented approach. Blackbird supports MS Object Linking and Embedding (OLE). OLE is a powerful concept that eases data exchange between different types of software programs. Under Microsoft's plan, OLE's links between documents, sounds, images, and movies will help a suite of computer applications appear to

TABLE 4.6   HTML 3.x Advantages and Goals[21]

■ *Interoperability.*   HTML is intended as a common medium for tying together information from widely different sources, a means to rise above the interoperability problems with existing document formats, and a means to provide open interfaces to proprietary information systems.

■ *Simplicity.*   HTML 1.0 was designed to be simple, both to author and to write browsers for. HTML 3.x provides a superset of HTML 2.0, adding high-value features such as tables, text flow around figures, and math, while still remaining a simple document format.

■ *Scalability.*   New features are easily added.

■ *Platform independence.*   HTML is designed to allow rendering on a very wide range of devices, from teletypes to terminals, DOS, Windows, Macs, and high-end workstations, as well as nonvisual media such as speech and braille.

■ *Content not presentation markup.*   HTML 3.x is designed for use with linked style information that defines the intended presentation style for each element. Style sheets can be expressed in a platform-independent fashion or used to provide more detailed control for particular classes of clients or output media.

■ *Support for cascaded style sheets.*   For the Web, it is valuable to allow for a cascading of style preferences.

be one program to the user. Until now, only a few Windows applications supported OLE-Visual Basic and Microsoft Publisher among them.

HTML's simplicity played a major role in the success of the Web, making writing a Web page easy for anyone who knows word processors. Sticking to HTML standards would be the wisest choice for Web designers.[14,45]

4.2.17   Putting it all together

To summarize this discussion, HTML is a markup language with which World Wide Web hypertext documents are written, and it allows an author to create hypertext links, fill-in forms, and clickable images. Writing good HTML documents involves both technical issues (proper construction of the HTML document) and design issues (ensuring that the information content is clearly presented to the user). These formatting tasks make the document aesthetically pleasing. HTML contains commands, called *tags,* to mark text as headings, paragraphs, lists, quotations, emphasized text, and so on. It also has tags for including images within the documents, for including fill-in forms that accept user input, and, most important, for including hypertext links connecting the document being read to other documents or Internet resources, such as WAIS databases and anonymous FTP sites. It is this last feature that allows a surfer to click on a string of highlighted text and access a new document, an image, or a movie file from remote computers. The HTML document specifies the location of a document through a URL, which is included in the HTML markup instructions and which is used by the browser to find the designated resource.[14]

The best way to learn HTML and create a Web page is to practice. A good reference for people who basically understand how HTML works and just want to see the tags and how they are used may be found at http://kuhttp.cc.ukans.edu/lynx_help/HTML_quick.html.

HTML requires the construction of documents with sections of text marked as logical units (such as titles, paragraphs, or lists), and leaves the interpretation of these marked elements to browsers of different abilities viewing the same HTML documents. There are browsers for everything from UNIX graphics computers to plain-text terminals, such as VT-100s or old 8086-based DOS computers. As an example, in viewing the same document, a graphical UNIX browser may present major headings with a large, perhaps slanted and boldfaced, font, while a VT-100 browser may just center the title, using the single available font. Both presentations will look different, but both will reproduce the logical organization that was built in with the HTML tags.

An HTML document can be prepared with a simple text editor such as NotePad editor on a Windows PC, TeachText on the Macintosh, or vi on a UNIX workstation. There is no obligatory need for a special word processor or fancy HTML editor to create HTML documents. There are editors that an author can use to put together a page. One such editor is the HTML Editor 1.0 by Rick Giles, which is not quite a WYSIWYG editor. It shows the text with a rough approximation of the chosen HTML attributes, and it does not display "on-line" GIF at all. It also lacks some of the fancier HTML features. It is, however, a fast way to input tags and view them under a Web browser. It includes a button that automatically invokes the Web browser of the author's choice, handing off the current document for display and allowing the author to edit and view the results dynamically. Another editor, Murray Altheim's HTML Edit, has no WYSIWYG capability, but offers a more complete HTML implementation than HTML Editor.[14,17–20,46]

With the current diversity of clients for the Web, it has become important to write HTML that will look good on any client, not just on the specific client to which the author may have access. If these guidelines are followed, the document may not look the best on a particular browser, but it will not look bad on any browser, which is the risk taken by disregarding these recommendations and tweaking the HTML for, say, Mosaic. Unfortunately, Mosaic may render things differently from Lynx, which in turn may render things differently from any other browser.

4.3 Tools and Guides

HTML is only six years old (at press time), and therefore most of the HTML tools are much younger. Usually, for software packages, this short period of time is not sufficient for them to reach maturity. Yet there are some good tools for HTML that succeeded in providing many powerful yet easy-to-master features, such as HoTMetaL Pro from SoftQuad and some integrated tools within the browser software such as Netscape Navigator Gold (Version 2.0) from Netscape Communications. The following is a short description of the different types of tools available for publishing on the World Wide Web with HTML.

4.3.1   HTML authoring tools

Initially, information providers on the World Wide Web used standard editors such as vi and emacs to create HTML documents. As WWW expanded in popularity, authoring tools were developed to assist information providers.

4.3.2   Word processing tools

Another approach is to develop authoring tools that work within a word processing environment. These tools are normally implemented as macros for popular word processing packages such as Word for Windows or WordPerfect.

4.3.3   Browser editing tools

Another approach to editing HTML documents is provided by browsers that are integrated with editing tools, as explained in the beginning of this section.

4.3.4   HTML document conversion tools

Authoring tools are normally used to create new HTML documents. Document conversion tools, on the other hand, can be used to convert existing documents to HTML format.

4.3.5   HTML quality tools

The HTML specification states that "HTML parsers should be liberal except when verifying code. HTML generators should generate strictly conforming HTML." This means that browsers should be capable of displaying documents that contain invalid HTML, but HTML authoring tools and document converters should generate HTML that conforms strictly to the standard. A number of HTML validation tools are available that can validate HTML documents.

4.3.6   HTML Check Toolkit

The HTML Check Toolkit is an HTML validation program. The software can be installed using a WWW browser. There are several programs for that purpose.

4.3.7   Writing style

Writing styles for WWW documents are still developing. However, there are a number of guidelines that can be provided. The following are some basic good practices to adopt that will save you a lot of grief:

- Avoid using "Click on the option." This is browser-specific: with a command-line browser, such as Lynx, it is not possible to click to select hypertext links.

- Avoid using "Back to home page." If the reader has gone directly to the page, the word *back* is not appropriate.

- Avoid using "University home page." Which university? Try to give the reader some context.

4.4   Browsers

In order to access the World Wide Web and to view an HTML document, another software package is required: a browser (or a client). A wide range of clients is available for many different platforms. Browsers allow people to treat the data spread across the Internet as a cohesive whole. Web browsers integrate the function of fetching the data with figuring out what it is and displaying it. One of the most important file types that browsers understand is HTML. HTML allows text data objects to embed simple formatting information and references to other objects. The most popular browser today is from Netscape Communications, called Netscape Navigator.[1] Microsoft's Explorer is also making inroads.

There are many publicly available TELNET browsers that can be accessed using the TELNET protocol. These browsers can be accessed by giving the command TELNET address (for example, TELNET dir.mcc.ac.uk). In some cases you will automatically be logged in; in other cases you must enter a username (which is often Lynx).

Text-based browsers, sometimes referred to as command-line browsers, run in a text-based operating system environment (e.g., DOS rather than Microsoft Windows, or UNIX rather than X Windows).*

---

* Text-based browsers are sometimes used with a Windows environment simply because they let the user access the Internet without overtaxing the corporate LAN, with all the graphics material otherwise being received. For example, Hofstra University chose this approach using Lynx under Microsoft Windws to preserve resources.

Command-line clients place fewer demands on the local computer system, but they do not provide the ease of use or range of functionality provided by graphical clients. The most widely used text-based browser is probably Lynx. Lynx was developed at the University of Kansas, originally for UNIX. Lynx has also been ported to the MS-DOS environment, which provides access to the World Wide Web from an entry-level PC with the appropriate networking capability.[1]

The most popular types of browsers today are graphical browsers. As the popularity of the global Internet and especially the World Wide Web grows so rapidly, graphical workstations such as PCs are the most common way to access the Web. These workstations use a graphical interface (such as Microsoft Windows), and therefore they use graphical browsers. Although it was not the first graphics browser, NCSA Mosaic helped to popularize the Web with its first version to X-Windows. NCSA Mosaic for Windows and for the Macintosh made it available to a much larger number of people.

One of the first browsers developed for the Microsoft Windows environment was Cello. It was written by Thomas R. Bruce of the Legal Information Institute at Cornell University. Another browser, the EINet, has developed the WinWeb and MacWeb browsers for the PC and Apple Macintosh platforms.

As mentioned, Netscape Communications Corporation, which was set up by Jim Clark, founder of Silicon Graphics, recruited the developers of NCSA Mosaic to develop a WWW browser. A beta release of Netscape was released in October 1994. It generated a tremendous amount of interest because of its speed and functionality. However, it also caused concern, since it included extensions to the HTML standard that had not been part of the HTML standardization process at that time. In less than one year Netscape succeeded in becoming the leader in the browser market.

Another popular browser is Air Mosaic, a commercial browser that is based on the NCSA Mosaic source code. Air Mosaic was developed by Spry, today part of the largest on-line service provider, CompuServe, which uses it to provide its customers with a common, easy way to access its own services and the World Wide Web.

Microsoft, the desktop software powerhouse, provides the Explorer browser along with its normal suite of office applications.

There are many new software packages today for the Web that blur the lines between browsers and HTML authoring and management tools. These new products, such as FrontPage from Vermeer, Page Mill and Site Mill from Ceneca, NaviPress from NaviSoft, and Netscape's new Navigator Gold, are all adding new functionality to their software. These new functions include authoring tools that let users publish on the Web without having to learn HTML, plus management tools that often offer hierarchical views of a Web site, making it easy to identify documents. By taking much of the complexity out of building and managing Web sites in-house, such products could bring even more mainstream businesses onto the Web. These topics are covered in greater detail in Chap. 5.

4.5 Practical Considerations for Internet and/or Intranet Pages

For most companies, the process of putting information on the Internet consists of a computer technician consolidating all the stories into one big file on the computer. He or she runs a program that translates the stories into HTML and then makes this information available on the WWW by opening up a server at the company's site. Every business on the Web has a home page; this can be thought of as what can be seen when a user "pulls up in front of a particular address on the superhighway." This usually appears similar to a brochure or news article, with text and graphics filling the screen. On the first page are hyperlinks, which are text or pictures that, when clicked on, bring the user to another page. These hyperlinks are a way of breaking down business information as if you were going into another folder, and then hyperlinking into another folder, and so on. These hyperlinks can also take you to other home pages on the Internet. All of this is achieved through HTML.[47]

You can do all this formatting of the information in a text editor (emacs for UNIX). Or you can utilize programs that convert your text into the HTML language, which formats it for the user. These programs give companies the ability to publish Web pages as fast as they can write them, and they also reduce the time factor for programmers working on publication. It reduces the computer technician's time spent importing information, and gives him or her the ability to creatively format the overall home page and how it will look through the eyes of the browser.[47]

Microsoft has come out with a browser/HTML generator for their Microsoft Word 6.0, called Internet Assistant. It is installed into Word and allows the user to switch back and forth from word processing to an Internet browser. This program converts Word documents into the HTML language. Hypertext links, pictures, and so on are available for insertion at the click of a mouse.[47]

This is only one of many HTML generators on the market, but they are all of similar design. They give people, businesses, and large corporations the ability to advertise on the Internet. These generators do not invalidate the need for a computer specialist. A specialist is still needed if your site has a server on location that must be constantly monitored for traffic. Also, the fact remains that someone needs to understand the language in order to effect the small changes that give pages an acceptable appearance on browsers such as Netscape and Explorer, and text browsers such as Lynx.

Many of the tools and techniques described in this chapter apply to both the Internet and intranets.

4.5.1 Entry requirements

You do not need a full-time Internet connection with a dedicated computer to establish your Web site. It is more practical for most individuals and small companies to rent Web space—disk space that holds Web information and supplies it to the Internet via a commercial provider, generally an Internet service provider. If you have browsed the Web, you probably have everything you need to publish a home page. The most important ingredient is access to a direct Internet connection, typically via a PPP or SLIP account that includes an allowance of disk space on the provider's Web server. Most ISPs offer this service, often through a UNIX shell account, a command-oriented adjunct to your PPP or SLIP account, which you access through a terminal emulation session. Alternatively, you can use an independent Web-space provider on the Internet. Such providers let users maintain Web pages remotely on their high-speed servers. In either case, you generally pay a monthly fee based on the amount of data in the page and the traffic volume or number of hits it incurs.[47]

When using a Macintosh, in addition to software to connect to the Internet, you need the following: a text editor, such as Apple's Simple-Text, for composing the Web page; a TELNET terminal-emulation utility, such as NCSA TELNET, for setting up personal Web space on the ISP's Web server (which involves typing commands under your UNIX shell account); an FTP utility (for uploading its components to your Web space); and a Web browser, such as Netscape Communications' Netscape Navigator or Microsoft Explorer.

4.5.2 Designing your Internet/intranet page

When creating your home page, keep in mind three design principles: simplicity, brevity, and functionality. The page should lead the reader clearly through its message, without distracting ornamentation.

4.5.3 HTML application example

An example of an HTML application is a program that asks for information about a Web site and has the user pick out correct information and then send it back to the serving home page.

This page is designed to give the providing home page useful feedback about the information that it provides, so it can adjust accordingly. This page is designed just like all the other pages, but with a few additional formatting commands. The nice thing about this page is the ability to set up pull-downs and create Yes/No fill-in boxes. This will limit the range of feedback and will give greater control over receiving appropriate feedback. An additional information box can be included as a way to get more information about questions that did not have appropriate answers.

After this information is filled in, the person will click on a Send button, which sends the information to the server through a CGI gateway and can be viewed by the sender. This information can be e-mailed to people throughout a corporation and then compiled to give additional information to their company. An example of this is a graduate school that puts an on-line application page on the WWW to be filled in by potential students and then sent to the server. This application can be e-mailed to advisers and then reviewed for possible acceptance of the applicant.

Refer to Fig. 4.7. This shows an actual page on Stevens Institute of Technology home page. The information that is filled in is sent via e-mail to one of the admissions counselors and then processed through a preliminary inquiry. This lets the admissions department reach out to a greater number of potential students. (If interested, access http://Mis01.adm.stevens-tech.edu/~mwalls/start.httml.)[47]

4.6   Beyond HTML

Although HTML is the main focus of this chapter, it would not be complete without exploring the future of some of the aspiring new languages that extend the use of the World Wide Web and the functionality of HTML. Today's development is occurring at such a rapid pace that it is difficult to predict where things will go from here. However, there are some directions that seem inevitable. The following is an in-depth examination of three new areas of development.

4.6.1   VRML

Virtual Reality Modeling Language (VRML) is considered by some the next step in presenting graphical embellishments to World Wide Web sites. VRML works much like HTML, except it works in three dimensions (3-D). It is a language for describing multiuser interactive simulations, or virtual worlds networked via the global Internet and hyperlinked with the World Wide Web.[1] This discussion elaborates on the introduction provided in Chap. 3.

```
<title>Undergraduate Admissions Inquiry Form</title>
<h1>Undergraduate Admissions Inquiry Form</h1>
<form method=POST action="http://web.cc.stevens-tech.edu/cgi-
bin/undergrad">

Last name:<INPUT TYPE=text NAME=Last_Name SIZE=15>
First name:<INPUT TYPE=text NAME=First_Name SIZE=15>
M.I.:<INPUT TYPE=text NAME=Middle_Initial SIZE=2>
<p>
Street Line 1:<INPUT TYPE=text NAME=STREET_Line_1 SIZE=30><br>
Street Line 2:<INPUT TYPE=text NAME=Street_Line_2 SIZE=30><br>
City:<INPUT TYPE=text NAME=City SIZE=25>
State:<INPUT TYPE=text NAME=State SIZE=5>
Zip:<INPUT TYPE=text NAME=Zip SIZE=12><br>
Country:<INPUT TYPE=text NAME=Country SIZE=30><br>
Phone:<INPUT TYPE=text NAME=Phone SIZE=30>
<p>
High School/College (If Transfer):<INPUT TYPE=text NAME=HS_College
SIZE=50><br>
City/State:<INPUT TYPE=text NAME=HS_C_Where SIZE=25>
Year of Graduation: <INPUT TYPE=text NAME=Year_of_Graduation SIZE=6
VALUE="19">
<P>
Cumulative GPA:<INPUT TYPE=text NAME=Cumulative_GPA SIZE=10>
<p>
PSAT Scores: Verbal<INPUT TYPE=text NAME=PSAT_Verbal SIZE=5> Math<INPUT
TYPE=text NAME=PSAT_MATH SIZE=5>
<p>
SAT I Scores: Verbal<INPUT TYPE=text NAME=SAT_Verbal SIZE=5> Math<INPUT
TYPE=text NAME=SAT_MATH SIZE=5>
<p>
ACT Composite:<INPUT TYPE=text NAME=ACT SIZE=5>
<p>
Social Security #:<INPUT TYPE=text NAME=SSN SIZE=11>
<p>
Sex: Male<INPUT TYPE="radio" NAME="Sex" VALUE="Male"> Female<INPUT
TYPE="radio" NAME="Sex" VALUE="Female">
<p>
Major: (Select one)<dl>
<dd><INPUT TYPE="radio" NAME="Major" VALUE="Engineering"> Engineerin.
```

(a)

Figure 4.7   Stevens Institute of Technology home page.

On a VRML site, you navigate a three-dimensional world that contains different objects and places—a world where you can interact with
the objects and even communicate with them. For instance, a VRML
site might look just like a supermarket, and the user could walk the
aisles looking at different products. "Touching" one of the products
might take the user to another VRML site, or even to a regular HTML

Undergraduate Admissions Inquiry Form

Last name: First name: M.I.:

Street Line 1:
Street Line 2:
City: State: Zip:
Country:
Phone:

High School:College (If Transfer)
City/State: Year of Graduation

Cumulative GPA

PSAT Scores: Verbal Math

SAT I Scores: Verbal Math

ACT Composite

Scoial Security #

Sex: Male Female

Major (Select one)

    Engineering
    Science/Mathematics
    Computer Science
    Humanities/Liberal Arts
    Pre-Law
    Pre-Med

(b)

Figure 4.7   (*Continued*)

---

site about the company that produced the product, much the same way that HTML hyperlinks work today. VRML is still new and under development.

4.6.1.1 VRML background. Late in 1993, Mark Pesce and Tony Parisi developed a three-dimensional interface to the Web that embodied many of the lessons learned in several years of research in both virtual reality and networking. Upon communicating these innovations to Berners-Lee, Pesce was invited to present a paper at the First International Conference on the World Wide Web in Geneva, Switzerland. During a session to discuss virtual reality interfaces to the Web, attendees agreed there was a need for a common language to specify 3-D scene description and WWW hyperlinks, an analog of HTML for virtual reality. The term Virtual Reality Modeling Language (VRML) was coined, and the group (headed by Pesce and Brian Behlendorf, of *Wired* magazine) began work on a VRML specification immediately following the conference.[1]

The team members proposed several worthwhile candidates, and after much deliberation they came to a consensus: the Open Inventor ASCII File Format from Silicon Graphics. The Inventor File Format supports complete descriptions of 3-D scenes with polygonally rendered objects, lighting, materials, ambient properties, and realistic effects. It has all of the features that professionals need to produce high-quality work and an existing tool base with a widely installed presence. A subset of the Inventor File Format, with extensions to support networking, forms the basis of VRML.

VRML is designed to meet three criteria: (1) platform independence, (2) extensibility, and (3) the ability to work over low-bandwidth (14.4-Kbps modem) connections. Early on, the designers decided that VRML would not be an extension to HTML, which is designed for text, not graphics. The next generation of Web browsers will understand and interpret VRML.[1]

4.6.1.2 Language basic. When the user selects an object with a hyperlink, the appropriate viewer is launched. When the user selects a link to a VRML document from within a correctly configured WWW browser, a VRML viewer is launched. Thus, VRML viewers are the perfect companion applications to standard WWW browsers for navigating and visualizing the Web. Future versions of VRML will allow for richer behaviors, including animations, motion physics, and real-time multiuser interaction.

At the highest level of abstraction, VRML is just a way for objects to read and write themselves. Theoretically, the objects can contain anything (e.g., 3-D geometry, MIDI data, JPEG images). VRML defines a set of objects useful for doing 3-D graphics. These objects are called *nodes*. Nodes are arranged in hierarchical structures called *scene graphs*. Scene graphs are more than just a collection of nodes: the scene graph defines an ordering for the nodes. The scene graph has a notion of state. Nodes earlier in the scene can affect nodes that appear later in the scene. For example, a rotation or material node will affect the nodes after it in the scene. A mechanism is defined to limit the effects of properties (separator nodes), allowing parts of the scene graph to be functionally isolated from other parts.[1] This topic is revisited in Chap. 9, which covers Internet and intranet applications of virtual reality (VR).

4.6.2 Java language

The Java programming language and environment was designed by Sun Microsystems to solve a number of problems in modern programming practice. It started as part of a larger project to develop advanced software for consumer electronics. These devices are small, reliable, portable, distributed, real-time embedded systems. When Sun started the project, it intended to use C++, but encountered a number of problems. Initially, these were just compiler technology problems, but as time passed, the company encountered other problems that were best solved by changing the language.

Java is a simple, object-oriented, distributed, interpreted, robust, secure, architecture-neutral, portable, high-performance, multithreaded, and dynamic language.

Most programmers these days use C, and most programmers doing object-oriented programming use C++, which requires a lot of training. Java was designed to be as close to C++ as possible in order to make the system more comprehensible; yet it is very simple and easy to program with. Java omits many rarely used, poorly understood features of C++ that in many cases bring more grief than benefit. A good example of a common source of complexity in many C and C++ applications is storage management: the allocation and freeing of memory. By virtue of having automatic garbage collection, the Java language not only makes the programming task easier, it also cuts down on bugs. Another aspect of being simple is being small. One of the goals of Java is to enable the construction of software that can run as stand-alone in small machines. The size of the basic interpreter and class support is about 40 KB.[1]

Object-oriented design is very powerful because it facilitates the clean definition of interfaces and makes it possible to provide reusable "software pieces." Simply stated, object-oriented design is a technique that focuses design on the data (objects) and on the interfaces to it.

Distributed, Java has an extensive library of routines for coping easily with TCP/IP protocols such as HTTP and FTP. Java applications can open and access objects across the net via URLs with the same ease that programmers are used to when accessing a local file system. Java is intended for writing programs that must be reliable in a variety of ways. Java puts a lot of emphasis on early checking for a possible problem, later dynamic (run-time) checking, and eliminating situations that are error-prone.

Java is intended to be used in networked/distributed environments. Toward that end, a lot of emphasis has been placed on security. Java enables the construction of systems more resistant to viruses, tampering, or infiltration (but it remains to be seen if these techniques are totally tamperproof). The authentication techniques are based on public-key encryption.

4.6.2.1 Architecture-neutral. Java was designed to support applications on networks. In general, networks are composed of a variety of systems with a variety of processor and operating system architectures. To enable a Java application to execute anywhere on the network, the compiler generates an architecture-neutral object file format. The compiled code is executable on many processors, given the presence of the Java run-time system. This is useful not only for networks but also for single-system software distribution. With Java, the same version of the application runs on all platforms. The Java compiler does this by generating bytecode instructions designed to be both easy to interpret on any machine and easily translated into native machine code on the fly.[1–10]

Being architecture-neutral also means being portable. The new Java compiler is written in Java, and the run time is written in ANSI C with a clean portability boundary. The portability boundary is essentially POSIX.

The Java interpreter can execute Java bytecodes directly on any machine to which the interpreter has been ported. And since linking is a more incremental and lightweight process, the development process can be much more rapid and exploratory. While the performance of interpreted bytecodes is usually more than adequate, in situations where higher performance is required, the bytecodes can be translated on the fly (at run time) into machine code for the particular CPU on which the application is running.

In summary, the Java language provides a powerful addition to the tools that programmers have at their disposal. Java makes programming easier because it is object-oriented and has automatic garbage collection. In addition, because compiled Java code is architecture-neutral, Java applications are ideal for a diverse environment like the Internet.[1–10]

4.6.2.2 HotJava. HotJava is a Web browser that makes the Internet "come alive." HotJava builds on the Internet browsing techniques established by Mosaic and expands them by implementing the capability to add arbitrary behavior, which transforms static data into dynamic applications. The data viewed in other browsers is limited to text, illustrations, low-quality sounds, and videos.

Using HotJava you can add applications that range from interactive science experiments in educational material to games and specialized shopping applications. You can implement interactive advertising and customized newspapers.[1]

In addition, HotJava provides a way for users to access these applications in a new way. Software transparently migrates across the network. There is no such thing as "installing" software. It just comes when you need it. Content developers for the World Wide Web do not have to worry about whether or not some special piece of software is installed in a user's system; it just gets there automatically. This transparent acquisition of applications frees developers from the boundaries of the fixed media types like images and text and lets them do whatever they like. HotJava has these dynamic capabilities because it is written in the Java language.

The central difference between HotJava and other browsers is that while other browsers have a lot of detailed, hard-wired knowledge about the many different data types, protocols, and behaviors necessary to navigate the Web, HotJava understands essentially none of them. This essential difference results in flexibility and the ability to add new capabilities easily.[1]

One of the most visible uses of HotJava's ability to dynamically add to its capabilities is called *interactive content*. For example, someone could write a Java program following the HotJava API that implemented an interactive chemistry simulation. People using the HotJava browser on the Web could easily get this simulation and interact with it, rather than just having a static picture with some text. They can do this and be assured that the code that brings their chemistry experiment to life does not also contain malicious code that damages the system. Code that attempts to be malicious or that has bugs cannot breach the walls placed around it by the security and robustness features of Java.[1-10]

HotJava's dynamic behavior is also used to understand different types of objects. For example, most Web browsers can understand a small set of image formats (typically GIF and X11 bitmap). If they see some other type, they have no way to deal with it directly. HotJava, on the other hand, can dynamically link the Java code from the host that has the image, allowing it to display the new format. If someone invents a new compression algorithm, the inventor just has to make sure that a copy of the Java code is installed on the server that contains the images the inventor wants to publish. All the other browsers in the world will have to be upgraded to take advantage of the new algorithm. HotJava upgrades itself on the fly when it sees this new type.

4.6.3 WebObjects

WebObjects is an object-oriented language, designed by Next Corporation for use in both Web applications and relational database applications. WebObjects allows the user to do the following[1-10]:

- Build Web-based applications 5 to 10 times faster.

- Build object-oriented applications that are compatible with all Web browsers.

- Run Web server applications on major server operating systems.

- Leverage the power of object orientation: reusability, maintainability, scalability, and distributability.

- Work with existing HTML and forms-generation tools.

- Dynamically generate HTML.

- Distribute applications with the first OLE-compliant Web server.

- Integrate with NeXT's PDO and the Enterprise Objects Framework to add distributed objects and database independence to your Web-based applications.

WebObjects provides an environment for rapidly building and deploying Web-based applications on top of many popular operating systems, including Windows NT, Solaris, SunOS, HP-UX, Digital's UNIX, and NeXT's MachOS. WebObjects adds a dynamic HTML presentation layer to data stored not only in object-oriented applications but also in industry-standard relational databases. Combining the capabilities of object-oriented technology with the Web's ubiquitous availability, corporations can now build real-world applications that can be deployed not only on the Internet, but on corporate LANs where cross-platform application deployment is essential. This allows companies to gain all of the advantages of object-oriented programming: rapid application development through object reuse, transparent distribution, simplified maintenance, and scalability using the common interface of Web browsers.[1–10]

Web security is handled at two levels. Today's sophisticated network equipment creates firewalls to block all unauthorized requests to machines on the network. WebObjects will also support security standards such as SSL and S-HTTP (discussed in Chap. 3) to enforce security when exchanging sensitive data such as credit card numbers.

Object interoperability is achieved through NeXT's DOL for Windows product. WebObjects can communicate with OLE/COM objects, allowing Windows applications to share information with Web-based applications. Web applications can now leverage existing data that is computed and stored in spreadsheets such as Excel.

WebObjects allows organizations to create distributed Web servers. Typical Web servers come to a halt when they cannot handle the number of requests they receive, resorting to the familiar "service unavailable" message to the browser. WebObjects can distribute requests across multiple machines, thereby creating a virtually unlimited ability to service Web requests. And the multiplatform compatibility of WebObjects allows these server requests to be distributed across a variety of operating systems.

WebObjects is database-independent. Web-based applications can access industry-standard databases such as Oracle and Sybase without writing database-specific code. This allows developers to create WebObjects applications that display HTML pages containing data from multiple databases.[1-10]

4.7   Future Direction in HTML

Despite all the new technologies that deliver new possibilities to the World Wide Web, HTML is now, and will most likely remain, the fundamental way of providing information to the Web.

The development rate of HTML was and still is very fast, and that is even more extraordinary when we consider the naturally long time it takes to develop any specification. From HTML 1.0 in 1990, we are today in an advanced stage of HTML 3.2 usage. This kind of initiative is most likely to continue in HTML's future development and will reinforce its use.

Yet some of the new languages will do well on their own, enriching the HTML and the World Wide Web. Sun's Java is an example of a new technology that will most likely succeed in the future. Supported by Netscape Communications, Java is already built into the new Netscape Navigator 2.0 (currently in a beta). HotJava, Sun's own browser, although in beta testing at the moment, will also penetrate many of the Web sites that are using Sun's computers, the leading manufacturer of UNIX computers.

Another technology that is bound to succeed is VRML. Its virtual reality and strong support from graphics vendors such as Silicon Graphics, a leader in superfast graphic workstations and servers, and by some companies in the movie industry will definitely push it forward. Furthermore, acceptance will be assured by the adoption of VRML by the forceful and vigorous Microsoft in its new browser (Internet Explorer 3.0) and also in its four new Web servers (currently in a beta) that support both HTML version 3.0 and VRML specification.

These new languages will work side by side along with HTML and will provide many new ways to benefit from Internet connectivity.

References

1. Carmel, A., "HTML and Beyond," Stevens Institute of Technology, class project, fall 1995.

2. Ayre, Rick, and Don Willmott, "Beyond Browsing," *PC Magazine*, October 10, 1995, p. 151.
3. Connolly, W. Daniel, "Toward Closure on HTML," *World Wide Web* at www.w3.org, April 7, 1994.
4. Graham, Ian, "HTML Documentation," *Computing and Communications*, University of Toronto, Ontario, Canada.
5. Grobe, Michael, "HTML Quick Reference," *World Wide Web*, Academic Computing Services, The University of Kansas.
6. Lentz, Robert, "Web Documentation/Resources," *World Wide Web*, Northwestern University Astronomy, May 2, 1995.
7. Mendelson, Edward, "No Experience Required," *PC Magazine*, October 10, 1995, p. 203.
8. Netscape Communications Corporation, "Netscape Extensions to HTML," *World Wide Web* Netscape home page, 1995; "Netscape Navigator 2.0 Data Sheet," *World Wide Web* Netscape home page, 1995.
9. Pesce, D. Mark, "VRML Virtual Reality Modeling Language," *World Wide Web* at www.w3.org; "Java Language Overview," *World Wide Web;* "HotJava Overview," *World Wide Web,* Sun Microsystems, June 9, 1995.
10. Raynovich, R. Scott, "Microsoft Web Browser Makes Waves," *LAN Times,* October 23, 1995, p. 49.
11. Taylor, Charles, "Really Quick Guide to Good HTML," *World Wide Web,* U.S. Navy, August 8, 1995; "Intermediate HTML Functions," *World Wide Web,* U.S. Navy, August 3, 1995.
12. Tilton, James, "Composing Good HTML," *World Wide Web,* June 2, 1995.
13. Savola, Tom, *Using HTML,* Que Corporation, 1995, p. 30.
14. Holicki, Diane J., "HTML Technology, Applications, and Examples," Stevens Institute of Technology, class project, fall 1995.
15. Savola, Tom, *Using HTML,* Que Corporation, 1995, p. 30.
16. Wood, Lamont, "Coming Up to Speed on HTML," *Interactive Age,* July 3, 1995, p. 24.
17. Cody, Glee Harrah, and Pat McGregor, *Mastering the Internet,* Sybex, California, 1995.
18. Karpinski, Richard, "Help Make Web-Page Creation Easier," *Interactive Age,* April 10, 1995.
19. Karpinski, Richard, "Moving Beyond HTML," *Interactive Age,* April 24, 1995.
20. Peck, Susan B., and Linda Mui, *Building Your Own Web Site,* O'Reilly & Associates, California, 1995.
21. http:/www.hlp.hp.co.uk/people/dsr/htlm3/contents.html.
22. Savola, Tom, *Using HTML,* Que Corporation, 1995, p. 32.
23. Aronson, Larry, "Which HTML Is 'Real?,'" *NetGuide,* October 1, 1995, p. 91.
24. Savola, Tom, *Using HTML,* Que Corporation, 1995, p. 144.
25. Savola, Tom, *Using HTML,* Que Corporation, 1995, p. 151.
26. Mui, Linda, and Susan B. Peck, *Building Your Own Web Site,* O'Reilly & Associates, May 1995, p. 11.
27. Graham, Ian, *HTML Sourcebook,* John Wiley & Sons, Inc., New York, 1995, p. 32.
28. Graham, Ian, *HTML Sourcebook,* John Wiley & Sons, Inc., New York, 1995, p. 68.
29. Graham, Ian, *HTML Sourcebook,* John Wiley & Sons, Inc., New York, 1995, p. 57.
30. Graham, Ian, *HTML Sourcebook,* John Wiley & Sons, Inc., New York, 1995, p. 4.
31. Savola, Tom, *Using HTML,* Que Corporation, 1995, p. 160.
32. Savola, Tom, *Using HTML,* Que Corporation, 1995, p. 160.
33. Pfaffenberger, Bryan, *Netscape Navigator Surfing the Web and Exploring the Internet, AP Professional,* 1995, pp. 76–77.
34. Pfaffenberger, Bryan, *Netscape Navigator Surfing the Web and Exploring the Internet, AP Professional,* 1995, p. 139.
35. Pfaffenberger, Bryan, *Netscape Navigator Surfing the Web and Exploring the Internet, AP Professional,* 1995, p. 163.
36. Graham, Ian, *HTML Sourcebook,* John Wiley & Sons, Inc., New York, 1995, p. 62.
37. Graham, Ian, *HTML Sourcebook,* John Wiley & Sons, Inc., New York, 1995, p. 9.
38. Graham, Ian, *HTML Sourcebook,* John Wiley & Sons, Inc., New York, 1995, p. 11.
39. Savola, Tom, *Using HTML,* Que Corporation, 1995, p. 133.

40. Savola, Tom, *Using HTML,* Que Corporation, 1995, p. 21.
41. Savola, Tom, *Using HTML,* Que Corporation, 1995, p. 199.
42. Savola, Tom, *Using HTML,* Que Corporation, 1995, p. 183.
43. Yamada, Ken, "Converting to HTML," *Computer Reseller News,* September 11, 1995, p. 57.
44. Savola, Tom, *Using HTML,* Que Corporation, 1995, p. 125.
45. Zhang, Bruce, "Language Barriers—Which Web Design Standard Is the Safest Bet?," *NetGuide,* August 1, 1995, p. 59.
46. Levitt, Jason, "To Learn How to Do a Web Page, Just Jump Right In," *Information Week,* November 28, 1994, p. 63.
47. Walls, Matthew, "HTML Technology, Applications, and Examples," Stevens Institute of Technology, class project, fall 1995.

5

Browsing Systems for the Web, the Internet, and Intranets

5.1 Overview

Today the Internet is a connection to all parts of the world. Servers on the Internet can be considered an enormous library of information and ideas, both old and new, an arena of communication among all generations and cultures all over the world. The Internet connects people of all ages and of many professions. It suits the purposes of many kinds of people. Whatever your interests, the Internet can help—check out the latest fashions in Milan, find out what's new in sports, catch a weather forecast in China, plan a vacation, write a term paper, get the latest gossip and pictures of pop singer Madonna, shop for gift ideas, explore new innovations or technologies, chat with a friend in Australia, obtain a recipe for morels, or find help choosing a play. The possibilities are nearly endless.[1] The Internet has become a playground of the mind, a place where anyone with the time and inclination can travel the globe, grab a portrait of the "First Cat" during a tour of the virtual White House, listen to digitized songs from little-known bands, or obtain guides to cities and countries the world over.

Today surfing* the Internet is accomplished via a service and a set of tools that make the Internet easy to navigate; this service is the Web. The World Wide Web is the fastest growing communications system in human history. The Web does not exist in any physical sphere. The Web is redefined every day by the people who use it. It is loaded with useful

---

* The process of navigating and exploring the Web is often called *surfing* instead of searching, browsing, or cruising.

information, and it is educational. The Internet will become a significant asset to corporations, particularly given the global nature of today's economy. Corporate America is just beginning to realize the tremendous business potential of the Web. The Web is a way for businesses, from newspapers and record houses to high-tech vendors such as Microsoft and Sun, to reach out to customers.

For companies, it is a way to publish documents, to communicate with potential customers and partners, and, increasingly, to handle businesses transactions. For businesses professionals, the Web is a way to gather information from all over the globe. Most professionals call it a "global hypermedia system." For the average individual, it is an interesting way to jump from one computer to the next, just by clicking on an underlined word or phrase that is "hyperlinked." After clicking the hyperlink, the Web goes to work, accessing the information requested. This information can range from an article to a book to an animation to a sound or even to a movie clip. All of this information is simply stored on all the servers connected to the global inter-enterprise network that is the Internet. The request may link to large amounts of information that may be located on a computer across the street or around the world. But for traditional corporate MIS, providing Web access has meant learning a whole new vocabulary and adopting a far more open and user-centered way of working. It has also meant having to work out new security schemes, new support abilities, and new approaches to increase the bandwidth needed for serious Web access.[2-6] Life in the post-Web world will never be the same again for users or MIS: the Web is to the Internet what the Macintosh interface was to the personal computer—a whole new way of seeing and interacting with information.

One of the Web's many emerging identities is as the world's largest hypertext publishing enterprise, a vast panoply of interconnected pages and graphics. In fact, the World Wide Web is considered the manifestation of the global information superhighway, which consists of knowledge that will be required of any educated person.[2] At its simplest, the act of publishing on the Web requires little more than the ability to format documents with HTML. Acquiring a publication is as simple as pointing the Web browsers in the direction of the document. Users no longer need to understand how their data is getting to them or where on the Internet it resides; they just need to know how to point and click on hot buttons, and the browsers and servers work out the details among themselves.

The Web is rapidly transforming every industry it touches. People who never could have been expected to handle the intricacies of command-level TELNET and anonymous FTP sessions can easily launch these applications from some of the Web browsers just by clicking on HTML documents.[3-8] Small business can set up a presence on the Internet by publishing a World Wide Web site page with a local Internet service provider, as discussed in Chap. 4. Then, using a browser, a customer can have direct, on-line access to the company, its products, and any current information included in the company's Web home pages.

Perhaps a corporate planner might consider this populist interest (and the description herewith) to be tangential to their computing and networking requirements. To the contrary, corporate America cannot expect to employ computer scientists at every level of every organization in order to face the telematic requirements of today's global economy; it would be like hiring mechanical engineers to drive corporate cars, astronomers to tell time, or scholars to read a business document. Corporate planners must therefore capitalize on the interest in Internet access.

This chapter focuses on browser systems and technology. This discussion does not in any way sanction any company or product but simply discusses a few of the current exemplars of GUI-based access to the Internet (e.g., Netscape Navigator and Spyglass' Enhanced Mosaic). As discussed in Chap. 3, a number of new languages and technologies are being introduced; hence, browsers will certainly evolve, and new ones will grab the industry's attention. In addition, the discussion of features is intended more to describe the requirements of a typical browser than to be a product review.

Some of the information contained herein will evolve over time. This chapter is intended to educate the planners as to the kinds of functions, the kinds of issues, and the kinds of directions that browsers are taking. It is not intended to be a source of the latest features and functions on specific products.

5.2 Browser Features and Capabilities

5.2.1 Background

Sampling the wealth of the Web requires a browser. NCSA Mosaic launched the Web as a popular source of instant data and brought it to the masses. As a by-product, it spurred development of thousands of home pages that can be read by anyone with Internet access. For example, to find the portrait of First Cat Socks, you merely point your browser to the White House URL http://www.whitehouse.gov and the network handles the task of connecting to the White House home page. The user's browser then renders those elements in text, graphics, and possibly sound or video, and presents them as a printed document.[3–7] (See Fig. 5.1.[8])

A browser decodes the HTML symbols in Web documents, turning them into richly formatted documents with graphics and other media. In addition, browsers also originate messages that locate and retrieve documents every time you click a hyperlink. These links tell the browser

Example of a Web database query

Filling out a form requesting information

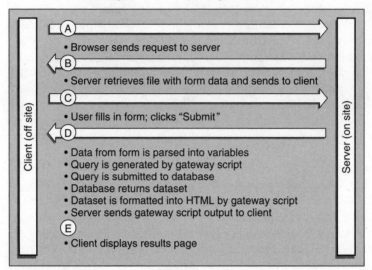

Figure 5.1 Example of a Web database query. Filling out a form requesting information.

where on the Internet to look for a particular piece of information.[2] Hypertext is familiar to anyone who has used a Windows' Help File; double-clicking a highlighted phrase on one page summons a second page explaining the phrase more fully.[3–7,9] On the Web, hyperlinking allows a user to follow ideas and themes from one Web page to another, regardless of whether those pages are stored on a single computer or Web server or scattered on servers around the world. And these programs now do more than just let the user view Web pages. Many also give the user access to other Internet services, including e-mail, Gopher, FTP, USENET news, and WAIS. In other words, a Web browser could be the only software tool you'll need to make the Internet easier than ever to access.

Mosaic is freeware that translates HTML coding into interactive Web pages. By making the Web accessible to a large new audience, Mosaic quickly became the killer application of the Internet.[3–7,10] It also spurred competition. Two years after Mosaic was introduced, there were only a few Windows-based browsers. Today there are hundreds of browsers in the market. The users (and/or corporate planners) choose a browser based on appearance, ease of use, design, and features. The one chosen will be the browser that most closely coincides with the user's needs. In some situations, the users will not settle on a single browser—they may discover that they will use one browser for some tasks and another for other tasks. It is simply a matter of activating the browser on the PC that serves their needs at a particular moment. There are benefits to using browsers in addition to "browsing the Web." For example, users can save printing costs by publishing electronic information both domestically and internationally. A user can use the browser to reach a company's servers for the latest information. Furthermore, facts and data can be updated immediately, without ever having to reprint outdated items. Any kind of data can be made available to people on the Internet through the use of browsers, even a combination of graphics, text, video, and sound that will present a full multimedia experience to the people accessing the information.

To use these new tools, however, you need workstation/PC communications software that supports TCP/IP (see Chap. 1). TCP/IP software is sometimes bundled with the Web browser; if not, it is available for free over the Internet. Browsers also require an Internet connection, either through the local area network or via modem to an Internet service provider (ISP) using SLIP or PPP. Access at 9600 bps is impractical; even at 14,400 or 28,800 bps, cruising the Web can seem slow. Higher speeds are really needed (see Chap. 8). For users who would rather not deal with acquiring TCP/IP and SLIP or PPP accounts, IBM offers a relatively easy Web connection as an option in its OS/2 Warp operating system, and Microsoft has done the same in the second generation of Windows 95. By press time, the major commercial on-line services, including Prodigy, CompuServe, and America Online, have already made, or will soon make, Web access a standard part of their offerings.[3–7,10] (This topic will be revisited in Chap. 6.)

The first Web clients' readers were text-mode line browsers able to follow hyperlinks from one document to another. Eventually, Web publishers began creating their pages using HTML. In addition to text hyperlinking, HTML also supports high-resolution graphics and lets page designers recognize text as hierarchical elements, such as titles, heading, and body text (see Chap. 4). The widespread use of HTML means Web pages can look and feel more polished and varied than the content typically found on commercial on-line services up to this time.[3,10] As users have added richer data types to their documents' images, sound and video protocols have been developed to handle the presentation of those types, and text browsers began to evolve into GUI multimedia tools.

NCSA's Mosaic was the first Window-based Web browser. Today, largely as a result of its success, the browser field is very active, with new products released weekly and existing ones updated, sometimes hourly. As noted, browsers are even making it into PC operating systems. Browsers are distributed in a variety of ways. For example, both the freeware NCSA Mosaic and the commercial Netscape are given away for free over the Internet. Other browsers are components of full-featured Internet software bundles, such as WebSurfer with NetManage's Chameleon.

5.2.2   Basic functionality

The following list describes the functions of the Mosaic browser, which is typical of most graphical browsers in the market today. New browsers that are coming to the market add many exciting new functions and tools, including smart document management, HTML authoring tools, e-mail capabilities, and even support for some of the new languages, such as VRML (in Microsoft's Explorer V2.0) and Java (in Netscape Navigator V2.0). The functions of the Mosaic browser include[11-24]:

- A consistent mouse-driven graphical interface
- The ability to display hypertext and hypermedia documents
- The ability to display electronic text in a variety of fonts
- The ability to display text in bold, italic, or strike-through styles
- The ability to display layout elements such as paragraphs, lists, numbered and bulleted lists, and quoted paragraphs
- Support for sounds (Macintosh, Sun audio format, and others)
- Support for movies (MPEG-1 and QuickTime)
- The ability to display characters as defined in the ISO 8859 set (including languages such as French, German, and Spanish)
- Interactive electronic-forms support, with a variety of basic forms elements, such as fields, check boxes, and radio buttons
- Support for interactive graphics (in GIF or XBM format) of up to 256 colors within documents
- The ability to make basic hypermedia links to and support for the network services such as FTP, Gopher, TELNET, NNTP, WAIS
- The ability to extend its functionality by creating custom scripts (comparable to XCMDs in HyperCard on Macintosh computers)
- The ability to have other applications control remotely its display
- The ability to broadcast its contents to a network of users running multiplatform groupware, such as NCSA's Collage
- Support for the current standards of HTTP and HTML
- The ability to keep a history of traveled hyperlinks
- The ability to store and retrieve a list of viewed documents for future use

There are many new software packages for the Web that blur the lines between browsers and HTML authoring and management tools. These new products, such as FrontPage from Vermeer, Page Mill/Site Mill from Ceneca, NaviPress from NaviSoft, and Netscape's new Navigator Gold, are all adding new functionality to their software. These new functions include authoring tools that let users publish on the Web without having to learn HTML, plus management tools that often offer hierarchical views of a Web site which make it easy to identify documents. By taking much of the complexity out of building and management Web sites in-house, such products could bring even more mainstream businesses onto the Web, in ever greater numbers.

Browsers today are available to all platforms and operating systems, from PC, Macintosh, DOS, Windows, NT, OS/2, UNIX, and X Windows, all the way to VAX, AS/400, and the VM mainframe operating system.

When a browser starts, it loads the default document that is specified as the "page" in the configuration. The full URL for the home page is displayed at that time. Most browsers contain the following screen capabilities[25]:

- The title bar containing the usual window function buttons (control menu box and maximize/minimize buttons). In addition, it has the name of the application and the name of the WWW document the user is viewing.

- The menu bar allows access to all the functions pertaining to retrieving documents to view, print, and also to customize the look of the navigation tool.

- The URL bar shows the URL of the current document.

- The document viewing area is the area of the window where the text of a document and any inline images it may contain appear.

- The status bar serves two functions:

  —Displaying the progress of the files being loaded

  —Displaying the URL of the hyperlink under the cursor

The following list gives a basic description of Web browser functionality:

- *Open* opens a URL.

- *Save / Save As* saves the current document to disk.

- *Back* displays the previous document in the history list.

- *Forward* displays the next document in the history list.

- *Reload* reloads the current document.

- *Home* goes to the default page.
- *Add Current to Hotlist* adds the URL of the current document to the end of the current hot list.
- *Copy* copies the current selection to the Clipboard.
- *Paste* pastes the content of the Clipboard to the active window.
- *Find* locates a text string in the current document.
- *Print* prints the current document.

These browsers can be used for both Internet and corporate intranet applications.

5.2.3   Features to look for

What makes a good browser? First, the software should come with an easy-to-use, interactively-customizable installation and setup routine. At a minimum, it should make it easy to mark the user's place and return quickly. It should facilitate viewing documents and files in various formats and should give the user options for handling multimedia objects like sound and video files. It should, of course, render graphical elements accurately and interpret HTML appropriately. Web browsers are windows onto the Internet's emerging world of electronic publishing. Though all browsers display text and graphics and follow hypertext links, some are easier to contend with than others.[3-7]

5.2.3.1   Installation.   Some browsers completely automate the setup process. They establish an account with an access provider and configure the bundled TCP/IP software in the process of installation. Other browsers leave it up to the user to set up an account and secure TCP/IP software.

5.2.3.2   Security.   A browser should also support some form of security. Most browsers offer basic authentication, a simple password, and user name scheme. But for transactions such as credit card purchases, the browser should also support either S-HTTP or SSL security standards.

5.2.3.3   Navigability.   Most browsers have text boxes for entering a page's address (URL), links, toolbars, hot lists (customizable compendia of a user's favorite sites), and history logs (automatic lists of the sites visited in a given Web session). How well does a browser report on the progress of a download? Some programs show the number of bytes transmitted, some indicate the percentage of pages that have arrived, and others use a thermometer-style gauge.

5.2.3.4   Data capture.   Data-capture capabilities control how easily you can download text and graphical data. Some browsers are set up to make capturing information easy, letting you download data in the background while you continue to search the Internet for more. Others allow you to turn off the display of graphics, which usually saves download time, because displaying the download requires more computing resources than just capturing it. A quality browser also lets you view as many graphics formats as possible. Most browsers come with their own internal viewers for the most common graphics formats, including GIF, JPEG, and BMP. Most also let you use third-party viewers for formats they cannot view themselves.[3-7]

5.2.3.5 Interoperability. If a remote Web site presents an FTP interface or news hyperlink, can you use the Web browser with it? At a minimum, a product should support Web-based FTP, mail, and Gopher sites. Additional features include Web-based news support, useful HTML extensions, support for additional stacks out of the box, and the capability to import bookmarks from other browsers.

5.2.3.6 Performance. This is a key issue when one accesses graphics-intensive Web sites. Unfortunately, there is no analytical way to compare browser speed. So many variables come into play (conditions at the access provider as well as traffic on the Net as a whole and at the page you are visiting) to allow for accurate benchmarking.[3,26] But you can check to make sure a browser is doing everything it can to maximize performance. First, it should let the user turn off the graphics, which take longer to download than text. Second, it should download text first, so the user can start reading while the graphics load. Third, it should let the user load more than one page at a time. Finally, it should cache pages in memory or on disk, so the user can reload a previously visited page quickly during the current session.

5.2.4 Sample of available browsers

There are many Web browsers available on the market and on the Internet. The user or corporate planner has to decide which features are most important and which ones the user is most comfortable using. Popular commercial products include Netscape's Navigator, Spyglass Enhanced Mosaic, Spry's Air Mosaic, and NetManage's WebSurfer. Other browsers available at press time are Cello, WinWeb, HotJava, NetCruiser, Internet Explorer, and many more.

The remainder of this chapter discusses some of the popular browsers as the current exemplars of state-of-the-art, GUI-based access to the Internet. As noted, the discussion of features is primarily intended to describe the requirements on a typical browser, not as a product review. Feature information is time-dependent. This material represents only a base of capabilities, which the user or corporate planner should find indispensable in future browsers.[73]

5.3 Netscape

5.3.1 The history of Netscape

Today, the Internet provides millions of users with access to information from around the globe. This "Web" of networks will ultimately link educational institutions, corporations, and most public and private businesses with one another. These complex networks have gone as far as connecting consumers' PCs in their own homes. Navigating successfully through the complex networks of data available on the Internet will be one of the significant challenges of the future. Recognizing this challenge, a team of staff and students at the University of Illinois' National Center for Supercomputing Applications (NCSA) in 1993 simplified Internet navigation by creating a graphical user interface.[27] This first edition of NCSA Mosaic was a research prototype and gained penetration of an estimated 2 million users in a single year. In addition, it was offered free. There is no doubt that the success of NCSA Mosaic, which was widely acclaimed as the *killer application* for the Internet, created a demand for software packages that would allow users to explore and surf these global networks with the simplicity of point and click. It is this growing demand that sparked the creation of Netscape Communications Corporation and its products.

According to a recent Web survey, more than 75 percent of those who access the Web use Netscape Navigator to do so.*[3–7,28] As stated on its home page, "Netscape Communications Corporation intends to be the premier provider of open software that enables people and companies to exchange information and conduct commerce over the Internet and other global networks." The company, based in Mountain View, California, was founded in April 1994 by Dr. James H. Clark, founder of Silicon Graphics, Incorporated, and Marc Andreessen, creator of the NCSA Mosaic software for the Internet.[29]

The Netscape software line includes Netscape Navigator products. All of these products provide security features, perceptive graphical layout, high performance, and adherence to standards (to various degrees). When products are based on industry standards and protocols, they are compatible with existing World Wide Web browsers and servers. They help deliver secure communications with point-and-click ease for everyone wanting to access information for the Internet or private networks.

---

* Market-share figures were time-dependent. Over time these shares change, particularly as venerable companies such as Microsoft target the market.

This discussion does not in any way sanction the company or its product, but simply reviews, for pedagogical purposes, this browser as an exemplar of a GUI-based access to the Internet.

5.3.2 Netscape Navigator browser

On September 18, 1995, Netscape Communications introduced Netscape Navigator 2.0 (logo shown in Fig. 5.2). This release of an already popular Internet client browser was said to bring "a new level of interactivity to users on enterprise networks and on the Internet." It accomplishes this by "increasing performance, adding a host of new browser features, and extensibility via plug-ins and programming languages, combining the capabilities of the World Wide Web, electronic mail, threaded discussion groups, chat, and file transfer services together in a integrated package."[30] Some claim that "Navigator 2.0 may well prove to be a full applications platform, a Swiss army knife of desktop client software."[30]

This navigator purports to offer performance up to 10 times that of other browsers by optimizing the navigator to run smoothly over 14.4-Kbps modems as well as higher-bandwidth lines.[31] (A modem operating at a minimum speed of 14.4 Kbps is required when using SLIP or PPP protocols.) A user may use this high-performance feature to access company and product information ranging from software updates to "what's on the horizon" and company financial records. Furthermore, the Netscape Navigator provides a common look-and-feel feature set and a standard GUI across noncompatible platforms such as Microsoft Windows, Macintosh, or X Windows operating environments, thus making itself convenient for all types of users. According to a number of studies "Netscape Navigator is the most widely used Internet client in the world today."[32] However, as noted, market shares change over time.

Figure 5.2 Netscape Navigator logo.

5.3.3 Basic key features

The basic features that come with Netscape Navigator include a configurable GUI where users can set color and font preferences for their viewing pleasure. Assigning fonts will not affect any headings. Furthermore, a user can choose colors for hyperlinks, hyperlinks already visited, text, and the background. In addition to these features the Navigator provides the following:

- *File transfer support* for both sending and receiving files

- *Context-sensitive help* both on-line and through the Netscape Web pages

- *Dynamic documents,* where a server can push new data down to a Netscape Navigator window for continuously or regularly updated information, such as stock quotes and weather maps

- *Native AU and AIFF sound support* (AU and AIFF are sound file formats[33])

An advanced toolbar is another feature, with easy point-and-click navigation allowing for quick accessibility to most any function. This feature helps to minimize the use of the menu bar options. In addition the browser includes the following:

- *Bookmark facility.* Allows users to maintain, index, and search a hierarchical list of favorite sites. A bookmark is a URL that can be saved to a user-maintained list of Web sites. Whenever users run across a Web site they like, they can set a bookmark.

- *Pop-up, object-specific context menus.*

5.3.4 The Navigator's performance

Netscape Navigator offers "support for new features such as the Progressive JPEG graphic format (existing GIF and JPEG files will have to be converted to take advantage of this), and client-side image mapping, a proposed HTML 3.x feature in which image maps are downloaded to Navigator instead of remaining on the server."[34] It supports multiple, simultaneous loading of text and file downloads. It also supports multiple, simultaneous streaming of video, audio, and other data formats due to a variety of integrated plug-ins (described later). The outcome is that the user begins to experience the effect before the entire object has been downloaded.

The progressive JPEG file format loads images up to three times more quickly than the previous GIF format and provides faster intermediate image recognition so users on slow connections can view color-rich images quickly. In fact, with Native Progressive JPEG Decompression, less than 10 percent of the image needs to be loaded to be recognizable.[34] (See Fig. 5.3.)

Figure 5.3   Progressive scanning.

As stated previously, Netscape Navigator is optimized to run over 14.4-Kbps modems as well as higher bandwidths. This helps ensure a quick and secure easy-to-use environment for all transactions such as communicating and transferring data between the multiple networks on the Internet. Other features that enhance performance are as follows:

- *Three-level caching.*   A cache is a part of a computer's memory that Netscape sets aside for recently accessed documents. When reaccessing documents stored in memory, the documents are redisplayed much faster.

- *CD-ROM caching.*   Allows quick, seamless access to CD-ROM-based media.[35]

5.3.5   Secure e-mail

Netscape Navigator offers fully functional e-mail. A user can embed Internet URL links and complete Internet hyperlinks into mail messages, enabling them to both read and send e-mail. Other functions include: list, view, sort, drag and drop messages; create hierarchical message folders; read messages off-line; or enhance mail security using the secure "Secure MIME" (S/MIME) protocol for encryption and digital signature. In addition, the e-mail client is "a conventional POP3 (Post Office Protocol 3) and SMTP (Simple Mail Transport Protocol)."[35] Netscape Navigator e-mail includes a personal address book and supports MIME attachments for multimedia messages.[1] MIME is a standard specifying how Internet applications should handle multimedia. Figure 5.4 shows how this e-mail feature allows users on the Internet and company Webs to send and receive secure messages with embedded HTML, live objects, and images. With the new Netscape Navigator, the mail option can be accessed from the file menu which activates the new mail window.

5.3.6 Security

Netscape allows its users to create their own digital identities by getting an on-line Digital ID from VeriSign, which proves the user's on-line identity as an "Internet driver's license." With a Digital ID, Navi-

Figure 5.4 E-mail capabilities.

gator users are able to communicate via secure e-mail, positively identify others, be authorized to access information, ensure privacy, and enable digital signatures.[36]

VeriSign provides Digital ID products and services for the electronic commerce marketplace. The digital IDs play a key role in ensuring the privacy and authentication of electronic transactions and communications. VeriSign, founded in 1995 as a spin-off of RSA Data Security (an encryption company), is working with its inventors, including Ameritech and Visa International, and partners such as Netscape and Apple, to open the electronic marketplace to consumers. VeriSign's goal is to provide consumers with the confidence necessary to conduct electronic commerce worldwide.[37]

To provide secure transactions via the World Wide Web, Netscape Navigator takes advantage of the Secure Sockets Layer open protocol. This *proposed* Internet, standard discussed in Chap. 3, seeks to provide secure public-key encryption capabilities so that people can exchange information securely via any established Internet protocol.[38] This type of security will enable customers to take advantage of available features such as on-line publications, financial transactions, and interactive shopping.

Much of the Web's confidentiality and security problems can be solved with the use of encryption. In essence, encryption is the process of converting a *plain-text message* (a message that could be read by anyone) into an unreadable *ciphertext* (encrypted text) by means of a *key* (a method of transforming the message so that it appears to be unintelligible).[39] Netscape Navigator applies encryption to hide sensitive information from all except the users intended to receive it.

The Doorkey icon shown in Fig. 5.5 indicates whether Netscape is accessing a secure server. If a secure site is not accessed, then the key is broken. It is wise not to give credit card numbers to any vendors unless the connection is secure. If the connection is secure, then the key is unbroken. A dialog box will also appear when a secure server is accessed, indicating that a secure document was requested. In addition, a secure server is identified by a URL beginning with *https / /:.*

Netscape Navigator includes the following additional features to help protect data:

- *Authentication.* This helps to ensure that the user trying to access the server is who he or she claims to be. This is provided for both

Figure 5.5 Security icon.

servers and clients with integrated access to VeriSign's Digital Identification services.

- *Secure Courier Payment Protocol Support.*   Provides payment support from the desktop to the financial institution. With this protocol, a user sends an encrypted credit card number to the merchant, who forwards it to the bank, which then authenticates the credit card.[40]

- *Encrypted USENET news/conference capabilities.*   Via SSL support for the Network News Transfer Protocol.

- *Encrypted transfer of Web pages and forms data.*

- *Ability to route SSL-based connections.*

5.3.7   Threaded Discussion Groups

Threaded Discussion Groups allow users to sort and list messages from subscribed folders. "It provides fully threaded and MIME-compliant newsreading and posting for multimedia news articles and it supports multiple news servers."[41] It also shares a common user interface with Netscape mail for a consistent look and feel. Newsgroups can be accessed from the file menu within Netscape. This option will open the newsgroup window without ever having to leave the application. Figure 5.6 is a glimpse into the new window.[1]

5.3.8   Frames

The new frames feature offered with Netscape Navigator is a "sophisticated page-presentation capability that enables the display of multi-

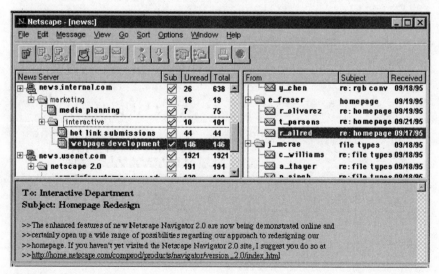

Figure 5.6   News via Navigator.

ple, independently scrollable frames on a single screen, each with its own distinct URL."[42] Within the same screen, frames can point to different URLs and be targeted by other URLs. Users can "incorporate banners, legends, tables of contents, and display panels into their designs, allowing users to scroll through multiple sites simultaneously, submit database queries in one frame and receive back results in another, and even freeze regions of the screen in place while the user scrolls through information on a page."[42]

The page shown in Fig. 5.7 is divided into different frames or sections. Since each frame contains its own URL (Web address), the user is browsing through multiple pages at the same time.

A frame can function as a constant area of the screen, which is referred to as a *ledge*. This allows important information to be kept in constant view while the user scrolls through pages. Page setups for ledges can be both horizontal or vertical. In addition, the size of a ledge can be adjusted or remain fixed. Furthermore, requests executed in one frame can generate a new outcome in another frame. This function helps to simplify the browsing of different sites by minimizing the need to jump back and forth between screens.

There were several dozen companies using frames at press time. Companies include 7th Level, BASIS, BellSouth Network Solutions,

Figure 5.7 Frames.

CMP, Discovery, Federal Express, and Silicon Graphics. Figure 5.8 is an example of how Atlantic Records is using frames.

5.3.9 Inline plug-ins

Netscape Navigator supports a new feature that enhances functionality by providing support for a large range of Live Objects. "With Live Objects, developers can deliver rich multimedia content through Internet sites, allowing users to view that content with plug-ins such as Adobe Acrobat, Apple QuickTime, and Macromedia Director seamlessly in the client window."[43] This is completely functional and there is no need to access any other external application. (See Fig. 5.9.)

"Plug-ins are dynamic code modules, native to a specific platform on which the Netscape client runs."[44] Plug-ins are expected to be compatible with existing platforms and new programming languages such as Java. The current version of the plug-in supports four broad areas of functionality. Plug-ins can do the following:

- Draw into, and receive events from, a native window element that is a part of the Netscape window hierarchy
- Obtain data from the network via URLs

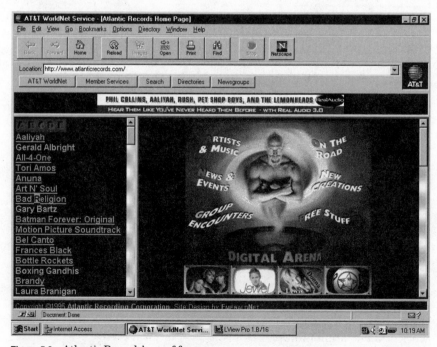

Figure 5.8 Atlantic Records' use of frames.

Figure 5.9   Utilization of plug-in modules.

- Generate data for consumption by Netscape or other plug-ins
- Override and implement protocol handlers[44]

5.3.10   Java support

Netscape Navigator supports Sun's Java, which, as discussed in the previous chapter, is "a new programming language based on C++ and designed for secure two-way, real-time interaction."[45] This programming language is an object-oriented language developed by Sun Microsystems to provide a programming language for the Internet. Using Java, users can write custom mini-applications called "Java applets." When integrated into Web pages, Java applets can enable expert graphics rendering, real-time interaction with users, live information updating, and instant interaction with servers over the network.[46] Java applets support server or platform. They are designed to be easily downloadable and provide additional security on public networks, with multiple safeguards against viruses, tampering, and other threats.

5.3.11 Programming with the Netscape scripting language

Netscape Navigator provides additional programmability with the use of the Netscape scripting language, "which is a programmable API that allows scripting of events, objects, and actions across all the platforms."[47] This language is also Java-compatible and allows the user to access events such as "start-ups, exits, and user mouse clicks." In addition, the Netscape scripting language uses the programming capabilities of Netscape Navigator to extend to a wide range of users and "is easy enough for anyone who can compose HTML. Use the Netscape scripting language to glue HTML, inline plug-ins, and Java applets to each other."[47]

This scripting language will allow nondevelopers to guide responses from a variety of events, objects, and actions. Users can change or incorporate any JPEG images, play a variety of different sounds, and be more responsive to events that take place with simple navigation. Some of these events include the number of mouse clicks or the number of times the user exits and enters the screens.

In Fig. 5.10, a script was used to check time of day and display the appropriate background to the photograph.

5.3.12 HTML support

HTML[48] is the markup language used to create Web documents, as discussed in Chap. 3. Netscape Navigator decodes the HTML instructions and displays the documents on the screen. Netscape works with the Internet Engineering Task Force and the World Wide Web Consortium. "W3 Consortium plans to develop the Web into a global information infrastructure capable of supporting commercial activities."[49] Any recommendations that were covered and gathered from HTML 2.0 were reviewed and, if found useful, incorporated into the new HTML 3.x version.

Navigator 2.0 supports HTML 3.x. Some of the recommendations that seemed useful and that would obviously be approved were already implemented in the release. In doing so, Netscape is striving to get a jump start on technology in order to be the main browser that supports more of the HTML 3.x specifications. Furthermore, Netscape added some additional HTML functions to the Navigator that are not currently in the HTML 3.x specification.

Some of the basic HTML functions that Netscape provides are backgrounds, tables, subscript and superscript, and extensive paragraph-

Figure 5.10   Use of scripting.

alignment control. In addition, Netscape Navigator will also support implementation of new HTML proposals. With this new browser, some of the additional proposals that will be implemented are frames and targets that help create multiple frames on a single screen and control which frames are reloaded, inline scripts (previously mentioned), auto-scrolling frames, and also object embedding that helps to receive new audio and video streaming technologies.[50]

5.3.13 Standards

The following are some additional standards with which Netscape Navigator complies. These standards help existing software packages such as plug-ins, Internet servers, and also many platforms to be compatible with one another. Any package adhering to these standards will remain essential to the use of the Internet.

- *Native support.*   Available for HTML, HTTP, FTP, NNTP, SMTP, MIME, S/MIME, S/MIME POP3 standards.

- *Comprehensive cross-platform support.* Provides a common interface and common behavior among the different platforms. (See Sec. 5.3.15.)
- *Open environments.* Works in environments that support HTTP-compliant network clients, including Winsock.

5.3.14 Product information

To help increase the usage and demand of Netscape Navigator 2.0, Netscape Corporation is offering an upgrade program from previous versions. This upgrade program is compatible with both Windows 3.1 and Windows 95 versions of Netscape Navigator, and therefore allows users who have not upgraded to Windows 95 to continue using Netscape Navigator 2.0.

Final release of version 2.0 was planned for early 1996.[51a,b,c] The product will initially be available in English, Japanese, German, and French. All public beta versions for Macintosh, Windows, and X Window System operating platforms are available for downloading via FTP from ftp.netscape.com.[52] These beta versions are available only in U.S.-style English. "This beta software is *free* to all students and staff of academic institutions and charitable nonprofit organizations, and for 90-day evaluation by individuals and commercial users."[53] When the final release of Netscape Navigator 2.0 is available, users can purchase supported, licensed copies of Netscape Navigator either directly from Netscape Communications or from a Netscape vendor. The pricing for this new version starts at $49.[54]

5.3.15 Supported platforms for the Navigator

The following is a listing of support platforms for the Navigator.

Apple Macintosh	Macintosh System 7 or later
	MacOS
	PowerPC
Intel-based	(x86) Windows 3.1 and 3.11
	Windows for Workgroups 3.11
	Windows 95
	Windows NT (3.5 or higher)
UNIX	Digital Equipment Corp. Alpha (OSF/1 2.0)
	Hewlett-Packard 700-series (HP-UX 9.03)
	IBM RS/6000 AIX 3.2
	Silicon Graphics (IRIX 5.2)
	Sun SPARC (Solaris 2.4, SunOS 4.1.3)
	386/486/Pentium (BSDI)

The platform requirements are shown in Table 5.1.

TABLE 5.1   Platform Requirements

Platform	Processor (minimum)	Disk space (MB)	Memory (min. MB)	Memory (recommended MB)
Windows	386sx	2	4	8
Macintosh	68020	2	4	8
UNIX	N/A	3	16	16

5.3.16   Other utilities

The following are products that are available with Netscape Navigator (as of press time). We include them here for illustrative purposes.

5.3.16.1   Netscape Chat. Netscape Chat opens up a range of applications that were not possible or that were ineffective in text-based chat. For instance, you can use Netscape Chat to host your own Internet talk show or to participate in the same types of social chat and special chat auditoriums on the Internet's IRC (Internet Relay Chat) networks that were previously available only on commercial on-line services. For business applications, Netscape Chat can be used to deliver training sessions, communicate with partners and resellers, or to answer on-line customer questions about your company's products and to take customers on a guided tour of the company's "electronic store."[55]

Customers who have purchased support contracts can dial up a chat channel with a support engineer to resolve a problem. Netscape Chat lets you communicate with customers in real time while using Netscape Navigator to show them how to download new patches, get answers to frequently asked questions (FAQs), or obtain information about new products. You can also take advantage of the multimedia-rich contents of the World Wide Web with Netscape Chat. This allows you to share URLs with other Netscape chat users. A Web site access can be automatically shared, without others having to manually enter the URL of that site. In addition, Chat offers multiple chat communication modes: Netscape Chat supports personal conversations (one-to-one), group conferences (many-to-many), and moderated auditoriums (one-to-many).

Netscape Chat offers simple point-and-click access to the most important chat functions. It enables users to join existing chat rooms or create new rooms. There is also extensive on-line help and documentation for needed information.

Standards.   Netscape Chat supports standards-based IRC chat:

- Connects to any standard IRC chat server
- Connects to the Netscape Community System Chat Server
- Supports access to IRC "Slash" commands as defined in RFC 1459.[55]

Additional features. Netscape Chat enables chat users to customize their environment and access advanced chat features:

- Customizable phone book for frequently accessed chat rooms
- Customizable address book keeps track of frequently visited chat users
- Customizable list of URLs that can be shared with others
- Connects to any standard IRC chat server including Netscape Community System Chat Server
- Supports major IRC commands including bidirectional exchange of URLs with Netscape Navigator
- Fully compatible with all Windows 3.1, Windows 95, and Windows NT versions of Netscape Navigator 1.1 or later
- Supports resizable and multipaneled windows[55]

5.3.16.2 Netscape Navigator Gold. Netscape Navigator Gold 2.0 is a next-generation software tool that enables users of all experience levels to easily create, edit, and navigate live on-line documents. In addition to World Wide Web capabilities, electronic mail, threaded discussion groups, and file transfer features included in Netscape Navigator, Netscape Navigator Gold also integrates WYSIWYG document-creation capabilities into the Navigator environment, which makes composing for the Web, e-mail, or newsgroups a simple cut-and-paste, drag-and-drop process.

The document-creation capabilities in Netscape Navigator Gold are designed to provide both experienced and beginning content creators with a simple solution for editing and publishing on-line documents. WYSIWYG editing allows first-time users to create dynamic on-line documents easily and publish them to local file systems and remote servers with a single push of a button. For more experienced content creators, Netscape Navigator Gold offers capabilities for creating complex HTML documents, including one-click image and Live Object insertion, a raw document and script editor, and document and image format conversion. Additionally, professional developers can custom-design Internet sites with Java applets. Netscape Navigator Gold also supports inline plug-ins for Adobe Acrobat, Macromedia Director, Progressive Networks RealAudio, and many others, allowing rich multimedia content to be incorporated into Internet sites.

5.3.16.3 Netscape Power Pack. Netscape Power Pack is a suite of add-on applications that extends the capabilities of Netscape Navigator for Windows. Combining Netscape SmartMarks, Netscape Chat, and multimedia add-on applications from Adobe Systems, Apple Computer, and Progressive Networks on a CD-ROM, Netscape Power Pack lets customers easily take advantage of five leading add-on applications that enhance the capabilities of Netscape Navigator. Programs such as Power Pack enrich the visual and audio experience of the Internet as well, with Adobe Acrobat Reader, Apple QuickTime, and RealAudio Player opening up still and moving images and real-time audio.

5.3.17 Assessment by given categories

5.3.17.1 Installation and setup. Netscape Navigator comes on two 1.44-MB floppies. The product can be simply configured to run over both a LAN and a TCP/IP network. To configure it for dial-up services, SLIP or PPP, you need to configure the TCP/IP stack, which can entail some work.

5.3.17.2 Security. As discussed, Netscape Navigator contains built-in SSL security support, which uses public-key encryption to ensure secure document and data transfer. It comes embedded with Certificate Authority keys that let it check the servers to which it connects for server-side Certificate Authority. The browser and server then agree on the right level of security for the transaction. Once the session is established, SSL handles encryption of all transfers, including requests, responses, forms, and all other data. Support for Socks, a common security-testing product, is also built into Netscape. Socks acts like a proxy in that it can run on top of the organization's firewall to allow Internet access for the protected host. S-HTTP support, which involves message-based encryption at the application level, is not currently available in Netscape, although Netscape has announced that it was planning to support S-HTTP. Proxy support is also built into the Netscape browser. It is simple to make the proxy entries in Netscape: specify your own proxy server name and the port number of the proxy next to the service to be used. These include FTP, Gopher, HTTP, security, and WAIS. To bypass proxy for any servers, "no proxy" can also be specified.[3,8]

5.3.17.3 Navigability. Bookmark features in Netscape are easy to find and use, and the product also gives the user editing power. A bookmark can be added with one click. A find feature is essential when the list grows too long to easily scroll. The default name entry can be changed; this quickly becomes important when saved Yahoo searches keep getting saved under "Yahoo." The list can be organized by URL, the date the site was last visited, and the date it was first created. Netscape also includes quick buttons for newsgroups and e-mail, but none for FTP or Gopher.[3,8]

Netscape includes other navigational tools. The "What's New," "What's Cool," "Net Search," and "Net Directory" buttons move the user to ever changing, live, on-line hot links, to the latest on the Internet, and to various sites that specialize in proving easy searches for Internet information. Netscape maintains these live on-line hot links on its own WWW server, to which Netscape connects by default on start-up.[3-7,56]

5.3.17.4 Data capture. Netscape Navigator presents hypertext links first, because graphics images are drawn line by line. The ability of turn off autoloading of graphics is available. With autoloading deactivated, an icon is placed where each graphic element would be. You can click on only the icon representing the graphic that you want to view, which saves download time. Netscape includes a viewer that will display GIF, JPEG, and XBM graphics files.[3-8] The viewer is activated when you click on a link or icon that downloads one of these file types. In Netscape, you can easily set up either disk or RAM caching to increase performance and speed. If you have turned off graphics but then want to see a page in full, a button on the toolbar will reload the page with graphics. It loads graphics in eight sequential renderings, so you can preview images as well as text.[3,28,56] In documents with multiple graphic images, up to four images can be downloaded in round-robin fashion, so those who page ahead through the document are more likely to see at least a partial graphic image.[3,56]

5.3.17.5 Interoperability. Netscape Navigator is compatible with a variety of software. For instance, Netscape supports all of the extensions to the HTML specifications included in HTML 2.0 and also includes support for a number of specs for HTML 3.x.[3-8] Netscape Navigator provides a built-in mail application with its interface. You can include single file attachments, including multimedia files. Unfortunately, this mail application does not let the user receive mail, and the mail server name has to be entered manually during the first-time setup. Neither does the product have an FTP button or other method of launching an applet from within the Netscape browser. However, you are able to perform FTP downloads by clicking on links within HTML documents that support this feature. The product's new feature is activated once the user enters the news server name. You can click on View All News Groups to build a list or view the previously saved list of groups available from the user's specified server. Subscribing and unscribing is also an easy task. Netscape also supports forms. Netscape will let you know if you are about to send off information that will be unsecured, and it then gives you the option of canceling the transfer. This is a concern when the site to which you are submitting the form does not have a secure method of data transfer.

5.4   Mosaic

5.4.1   History

The early method of obtaining and viewing documents from the Internet was anonymous FTP. In late 1992 and early 1993, NCSA staff members were looking for a way to make information on the Internet more accessible to the average computer user. The search for tools that would lend themselves to the sort of graphical, point-and-click interface that has proven so effective over the past decade for PCs led eventually to the World Wide Web.

The first release of NCSA Mosaic, in April 1993, was a client for X Window System platforms. Clients for the Macintosh and Microsoft Windows platforms soon followed in the fall of 1993. In 1994, the following versions were released: NCSA Mosaic for Microsoft Windows Version 2.0, NCSA Mosaic for the Macintosh Version 1.0.3, NCSA Mosaic for the X Window System Version 2.4.

Mosaic's influence has been recognized with a considerable amount of coverage in the mass media and on the Internet. From a *NetGuide* article: "The subject of almost as much media hype as the Internet itself, Mosaic has been called—and with some justification—the Internet's first 'killer application.' "[57] Many new information providers ask, "How can I set up a Mosaic home page?" What they are referring to is a Web home page or a home page on a server.

5.4.2   Spyglass Enhanced Mosaic

Today, Mosaic is facing competition from many of the other browsers that have followed in Mosaic's footsteps. To position Mosaic to better meet the increasing competition and a growing market demand for easy Internet access tools, Spyglass, Incorporated, and the University of Illinois announced in 1995 "a master license agreement assigning to Spyglass all future commercial licensing rights for the university's NCSA Mosaic graphical Internet browser."[58] Spyglass, of Savoy, Illinois, develops and distributes graphical software applications and commercially enhanced versions of Mosaic, called Enhanced NCSA Mosaic, for Windows, Macintosh, and UNIX computers.

The University of Illinois–Spyglass agreement was expected to create a broader, more practical distribution channel for commercial versions of NCSA Mosaic. NCSA Mosaic traditionally has been available in two ways: (1) for free with copyright to individual users who must download it from the Internet and (2) through a limited number of commercial licensees. The company indicates that "This new agreement solves the problem of getting solid, commercial-quality copies of Mosaic to people who want to tap the rich resources of the World Wide Web and the Internet. It will give vendors stable, standard and feature-rich versions of Enhanced NCSA Mosaic that they can incorporate immediately into their products—with little or no additional development work, if they so choose. By 1996 there should be more than 20 million copies of Enhanced NCSA Mosaic from Spyglass in use on desktops."[58]

Subsequent releases of Enhanced NCSA Mosaic from Spyglass were expected to include features enabling Mosaic and the World Wide Web to be used for more sophisticated electronic publishing as well as electronic commerce. Release 2.0 was to include enhanced security and viewers for the most popular document, as well as image and audio file formats. Future enhancements will include additional multimedia support, compatibility with other applications using standards such as OLE 2.0 and AppleEvents, and full and secure payment-processing capabilities and other features for true electronic commerce on the Internet.

The new Spyglass Enhanced Mosaic looks much like that of the NCSA Mosaic. Some items have changed, however. For example, with the new Enhanced Mosaic, the lower left-hand side of the screen contains a status bar. This status bar shows Mosaic's process when loading long pages or images. The command buttons have changed as well. Spyglass eliminated tiny buttons, making more space for the Web pages themselves. Figure 5.11 shows an example of a Mosaic window.

NCSA Mosaic 2.0 was made available on the Internet in late 1995. It offers simple but powerful features that have not been seen in previous Internet clients. Text and images can appear adjacent to each other within the same window. Mosaic also offers important navigation aids. For example, it shows selectable links in a particular color, and it remembers which links a user has selected previously, depicting them with another color. It also provides a "hotlist" feature, which allows the ability to add an item to a list of interesting documents for quick reference with a simple click of the mouse.

Enhanced Mosaic version 2.0 contains almost identical feature sets as the Netscape Navigator 2.0 browser. The following paragraphs will explain in brief detail some of Mosaic's features.

5.4.3 Features

5.4.3.1 The globe. Whenever Mosaic attempts to access a Web address, a colored globe in the left- or right-hand corner of the screen moves. The movement tells the users that Mosaic is trying to make a connection. "The spinning globe offers reassurance and demonstrates activity."[59]

5.4.3.2 Basic capabilities. The basic features that come with the new Mosaic browser include a configurable GUI that lets users set color and font preferences for their viewing pleasure.

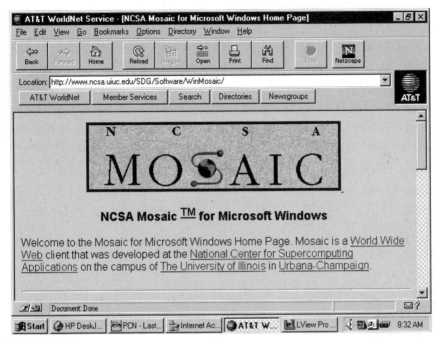

Figure 5.11   Mosaic's home page.

- *Bookmark facility* allows users to maintain, index, and search a hierarchical list of favorite sites. A bookmark is a URL that can be saved to a user-maintained list of Web sites. Whenever users run across a Web site they like, they can set a bookmark.

- *Pop-up, object-specific context menus.*

- *Advanced toolbar* allows complete access of functions with minimal use of the menu bar options.

5.4.3.3   Visually enhanced documents.   With Spyglass Mosaic, you can view documents formatted with widely accepted, HTML extensions— tables, centered and right-aligned text and images, text wrapped around images, background colors and bitmaps, and colored text. Multimedia capabilities for viewing JPEG and GIF image files and listening to AU and AIFF audio files are included as well. These will help make interaction with the Web more eye-pleasing.

5.4.3.4   Secure electronic payments.   Secure transactions technology is crucial for customers supplying applications that involve the passing of proprietary information across the Internet. Enhanced Mosaic allows the user to purchase goods and services on-line through the use of safe and easy-to-use payment systems. Systems include the "EBC Electronic Wallet" and the "First Virtual Wallet." Each provides a safeguard for ensuring that payment transaction information is carried out securely. These systems eliminate the need to add complicated security designs that are activated once users start shopping on-line. Additional information about e-cash was provided in Chap. 1.

5.4.3.5 Global history. Mosaic maintains a global history of visited Web sites, newsgroups, etc. Mosaic offers the option to set an expiration date for the visited sites. Mosaic also offers the ability to change the color of a site from the visited color to the unvisited color. Configurations option for these sites can be found under the Options, Preferences, Anchors menu.

5.4.3.6 Access to information. Significant improvements in performance have been made to the new browser. The following are some features that help increase the performance of Mosaic.

- Smart Maps, a Spyglass innovation, are a way to configure *image maps,* clickable images frequently used to navigate the Web. Smart Maps allow users to link to new documents more quickly because they reduce the need for server intervention. And because server communication is not required, Smart Maps work in CD-ROM applications as well as across the Internet.[60]

- Advanced Display Technology "instantaneously" displays text and progressively displays images, enabling users to follow hyperlinks before a document finishes downloading.[60]

- Local Disk Cache restores recently retrieved documents without making an Internet connection.

5.4.3.7 Compatible languages. Mosaic hopes to help reduce language barriers on the Internet by providing users with the ability to display documents in their preferred language. Upon encountering a server that also supports language negotiation, Spyglass Mosaic displays documents in the language the user selected. This feature is available in both French and German.

5.4.3.8 Security. Spyglass Mosaic features the ability to choose from and add a variety of levels of security by providing compatibility to users for any plug-in security system they want. To meet username/password security needs, Spyglass Mosaic offers two preinstalled modules: Basic Authentication and Digest Authentication.[60]

5.4.3.9 Integration of popular applications. Specialized applications that enhance the functionality of the Web, such as search engines, document viewers, authoring tools, and 3-D viewers, can be configured to be compatible with Spyglass Mosaic. Developed to work with the Spyglass Mosaic Software Development Interface (SDI), applications such as RealAudio Player, Adobe Acrobat, SoftQuad Panorama, and WebSpace are among the growing group of SDI-enabled applications.

The RealAudio Player software enables users to access RealAudio programming and play it back instantaneously. Key features include the following:

- Full control of RealAudio streams much like a VCR, with start, stop, and pause options

- Ability to instantly jump to any part of an audio program, much like a CD player

- Inserts bookmarks and hot-list entries into Web browsers to allow the user direct access to the RealAudio home page and other sites of interest

Acrobat Reader 2.1 accepts some specially enabled plug-ins, such as Weblink and Movie. This allows Acrobat Reader users to take advantage of new capabilities in PDF files created with Acrobat Exchange; for example, following World Wide Web (URL) links or viewing QuickTime and AVI (Windows only) movies within a PDF document. Also the printing quality has been improved to non-PostScript printers.

Panorama PRO is the commercial version of Panorama, the first SGML browser for the World Wide Web. It is fully supported and comes with many features that include broader presentation capabilities, more powerful context-sensitive searching, and enhanced hypertext linking. Panorama PRO allows publishers to create SGML documents and users to view SGML documents on the Web. It also allows greater control over the display of documents, with the power to create multiple personal link layers, annotations, and bookmarks. It also provides rich presentation capabilities, powerful searching capabilities, and enhanced hypertext linking capabilities.

5.4.4 Platform requirements

Table 5.2 depicts hardware requirements.

Supported Platforms for Mosaic are similar to those of Netscape.[61]

TABLE 5.2   Hardware Requirements

Platform	Processor (minimum)	Disk space (MB)	Memory (min. MB)	Memory (recommended MB)
Windows	386sx	2	4	8
Macintosh	68020	2	4	8
UNIX	N/A	3	16	16

5.4.5 Comparison between Netscape Navigator and Enhanced Mosaic

Netscape Navigator 2.0 and Enhanced Mosaic 2.0 are both powerful browsers that enable surfing of the Internet to be as easy as navigating a local PC environment through Microsoft Windows. Each browser combines performance and style to complete the task at hand. In general, both browsers offer the same set of features. On a lower level, there are some functions that one browser may perform better than the other. Mosaic might not be as speedy as many browsers, but the ability to add Web sites to its menu bar for quick recall is desirable.[62a,b,63] In the final analysis it is simply a matter of taste and preference. Most average users will not note the differences in speed, yet a simple, fun, graphical look may lure them into purchasing the browser.

5.5 Other Browsers

This section covers other browsers on the market. This discussion does not in any way sanction any company or its products, but simply discusses, for pedagogical purposes, these browsers as exemplars of a GUI-based access to the Internet.

5.5.1 Spry's Mosaic

Mosaic from Spry and its accompanying suite, Internet Office, are the next logical step in Spry's Internet-based product line, which includes the popular Air for Windows, one of the first packages to give Windows users full Internet access.[3-8] Spry's Mosaic offering is different from the Air series in its emphasis on its Mosaic interface as the primary way for its users to interact with the Internet. All normal Internet functions are accessible from Spry's Mosaic interface. You can send e-mail messages, download files, read and post to newsgroups, and enter information into forms. An e-mail reader is included.

5.5.1.1 Installation and setup. Spry's installation package supports five different IP stacks out of the box, including those for SLIP/PPP, generic Microsoft, LAN Manager, Windows 3.11 virtual device driver, and Novell's LAN Workplace.

5.5.1.2 Security. Spry's Mosaic supports proxy servers for FTP, HTTP, news, WAIS, and Gopher. It also supports S-HTTP, which is based on public-key encryption. This means it is quite difficult for intruders to eavesdrop on the Web session. New users can log in to RSA's authentication server to receive a certificate for use with S-HTTP. This certificate, or key, is then added to a file to which Spry's Mosaic refers whenever you attempt to connect to a secure HTTP site. You can define a number of users who are authorized to use the key on your computer by adding them to a local database file. In addition to encryption, authentication is provided by a specific remote site set up as the trusted root.[3,8]

5.5.1.3 Navigability. Spry has added several navigability features to NCSA Mosaic, including a toolbar at the top of the screen. You can use the toolbar buttons and menu selections to help the user launch the newsreader and Spry Mail from within the browser. This is more than most Windows-based Web browsers offer. For a more manageable structure, Spry Mosaic lets you categorize documents into folders, which can be added to the menu bar. You can create up to 15 hot-list folders, each of which can handle approximately 200 URLs.[3,64] You can access them through the file menu. They are arranged by topic, and each one comes preconfigured with the URLs of related Web sites. To access a desired URL, you just double-click on its folder and select it from an alphabetized list. To save a bookmark, you either create a new folder for it or add it to an existing folder. You cannot annotate bookmarks as you can using NetManage's WebSurfer, but you can rename hot-list folders and site names or change URLs for each entry.[3-8] The one drawback to multifolder storage of URLs is the potential for being overwhelmed by the number of folders. Spry's Mosaic counteracts this problem to some extent by making your favorite sites more readily accessible. The folder name becomes the menu item, and the drop menu displays all sites stored in it. Even better, you can also export hot lists as HTML files, so you can easily publish interesting or related Web sites on the user's Web server for others to access.

A feature unique to Spry is the kiosk mode, which allows the user to view the full screen without the obstruction of the menu. This is particularly handy if you wish to view a home page in its entirety, but the feature is somewhat limiting. You can only travel forward using hyperlinks in kiosk mode, and you cannot use the menu selections. You have to exit kiosk mode to toggle between pages or navigate backward.[3-7,64]

5.5.1.4 Data capture. Spry Mosaic allows the user to scroll through the current documents while documents are being gradually loaded. You can also click on hyperlinks and move on before the current document finishes updating, which saves time. Many other browsers allow you to start multiple connections concurrently or move on to new pages while others are updating, but Spry's Mosaic does not. When either of these actions are tried, a dialog box instructing the user to wait or cancel the current operation is displayed. Spry Mosaic's capability to drag and drop URLs to other windows applications is handy.[3,8] Click and hold the mouse button on a hyperlink and drag it to the desired application to copy the document in HTML format.

Spry's Mosaic presents a common placeholder graphic for each Web page graphic, and the graphic is displayed when it is fully downloaded. It does not display interlaced GIF graphic images with increasingly higher resolution; this leads to slower perceived performance in some cases.[3,56] Spry's Mosaic supports 25 assorted graphic text, audio, and video formats. Text files, as well as AU and AIFF sound files, are also supported, and a viewer is included, but the viewer does not read all of these formats.[3–8] Therefore, you will need to use the viewer and players and use Spry's Mosaic to associate these with the appropriate type of file format. These viewers and players will then be automatically launched when a supported file type is selected via hyperlinks.

5.5.1.5 Interoperability. Spry's Mosaic provides the ability to send E-mail messages, download files, read and post to newsgroups, and enter information into forms.

5.5.2 NetManage's WebSurfer

WebSurfer is an addition to NetManage's well-known Internet Chameleon package. NetManage's WebSurfer is part of a connectivity package. The suite gives the user network file system capabilities over TCP/IP. But it also supports some interesting extensions, such as floating images, which can be left-, right-, or center-justified, word wrap and flow, and inline, MPEG-based video. It also contains some useful administration tools for system configuration and software distribution.

The browser is of decent quality. Some press-time limitations are as follows (but features change rapidly over time). You cannot save Web documents as text files, although you can save them in HTML format; you will have to use the Edit HTML command to load the document into Notepad first, but the program does not properly convert the UNIX documents found on the Web into DOS documents (the line-break character is not properly converted). WebSurfer also does not display some graphics correctly. Simple inline images that appear correctly in other browsers appear murky and dithered in WebSurfer. WebSurfer can save hypermedia documents via an option called Save Cached Documents Between Sessions. You are saving the entire document, including the inline images and not just the basic HTML text. That means that if you return to a document in a later session, it will be pulled from your hard disk, not from the Web itself. There is also a document-style configuration system that lets the user change attributes such as document color, margins, line spacing, text sizes, fonts, colors, indents, and so on.[25,65–72]

5.5.2.1 Installation and setup. The suite completely automates the process of setting up an Internet account. You can immediately establish an account with one of five default vendors or set up an account of your own.[3–8,28] Fonts and colors are also conveniently customizable. The product's SLIP configuration is "slick." Its custom application handles multiple interface installation well, keeping separate copies of configuration information for each interface defined and a dial-up SLIP connection by simply highlighting the user's selection. WebSurfer makes it easy to configure a SLIP connection because of the flexible way it lets the user create a serial-line connection. You can either make the connection manually via the include SLIP terminal program or create a modem script to automate the entire process.[3–8]

5.5.2.2 Security. As of press time WebSurfer supports neither SSL nor S-HTTP security. This means that on-line business transactions must traverse the Internet unencrypted. However, WebSurfer works well with an Internet firewall and Netscape proxy servers. Both daemons can be set up on the server and accessible through different ports. All you have to do to enable proxy support within WebSurfer is to plug the port number for each proxy server into WebSurfer's preferences dialog box and check the enable proxy box in the Web configuration section.[3,8] Full access to the Internet still exists, even with the security products acting as intermediaries.

5.5.2.3 Navigability. The program's lack of feedback is somewhat frustrating. When you click on a link or type in a URL or select a page from the hot list, you have no way of knowing whether the next page was actually loading or how long it would take to finish.[3–7,28]

WebSurfer's interface provides a toolbar right below the menu bar that can be turned off if desired. You can also display icon descriptions for each button. You cannot customize the toolbar with different icons; the selection provided is fixed, although it does represent the most commonly used functions. You can also change the appearance of HTML documents by selecting style schemes under the setting menu option. Among the things you can change are font size, colors, and style for each HTML element or heading, as well as background colors and margin settings.

WebSurfer provides a hot-list function that lets the user save favorite sites to an easily accessible list. That way, you can add URLs to your hot list and pull down the list from the same page currently being displayed, as well as annotate hot-list entries to distinguish between two similar sites.

It would be desirable to be able to perform all Internet activities from one application interface, even if the applications are not built into the browser itself. Unfortunately there are not any menu items to let the user launch IP applications such as FTP or e-mail from the WebSurfer interface.[3,8] (Some links automatically launch some of these applications, but users cannot configure these.)

5.5.2.4 Data capture. WebSurfer provides the user with different models for displaying graphics within the HTML document. By default, graphics are depicted as icons, and you can move around the Web without waiting for a downloading image to relinquish control of a frozen screen. When each image has complete downloading in the background, the screen refreshes very briefly and the picture is displayed. You can elect to defer image retrieval altogether by selectively clicking on icons to view the associated images. One of WebSurfer's features lets the user define caching preferences on a per-document basis. This way, system resources can be devoted to frequently accessed Web pages, thus giving the user a performance boost.

Another desirable feature is a simple click box that allows the user to copy HTML pages to the local disk between Web sessions or write them to a disk cache during the current session, letting you speed up your work. In the first case, you can access popular pages off-line at a later time, thus eliminating reconnection and downloading overhead. Clicking on a hyperlink will then reconnect the user to the Internet. In the second case, you store documents in temporary cache, which is cleared from the disk when the current session is closed. If you are concerned about a cached document being stale, you can manually refresh it or deselect the current session cache to force a download of revisited sites.

WebSurfer works with NetManage's include file viewer and sound player, but only after you manually associate the supported file with the viewer and the player through the Windows File Manager. Third-party utilities should work with Chameleon NFS if configured similarly. The viewer should launch automatically whenever you click on a graphic image link. This lets the user view pictures before deciding to download them. Without associations, you are informed by WebSurfer that an associated viewer was not found and given the choice to download it sight unseen or cancel the operation.

WebSurfer can connect to more than 10 concurrent Web sites.[3-8] The history function and the arrows on the toolbar can be used to move between the cached and live documents. Because of caching, performance is not greatly affected by the number of concurrent connections when browsing. As you would expect, though, downloading a file in one session does slow screen updates and page jumps in other sessions.

Another feature in WebSurfer is the ability to view or edit the HTML code for the page currently being viewed. This is useful for training and/or publication purposes. Simply find a page you would like to mimic and modify, and you can view the code immediately or save it locally for later modification.

5.5.2.5 Interoperability. WebSurfer provides the capability to perform Web-based actions such as downloading files with FTP, sending mail using forms found at remote Web sites, and even posting and reading news entries. WebSurfer supports floating images—meaning that you can justify an image left, right, or centered. Word wrap works in tandem with this feature, allowing text to flow around the sides of the images rather than just on top or beneath them.[3,8] This is a standard feature of desktop publishing and most word processing packages. It also supports inline video by letting the user click on a still MPEG image and watching it come to life on the page.

5.5.3 DOSLynx (DOS)

For non-Windows-based PCs, the key alternatives are to run DOSLynx or to use a service provider's Web browser. DOSLynx is an easy-to-use, text-based browser from the University of Kansas. DOS TCP/IP software is required to run the browser. Links are selected by double-clicking on them or by using the keyboard. Multiple windows can also be opened, enabling running multiple Web sessions at once, something only a few other browsers allow.[25,65–72]

DOSLynx has all the usual browser functions: defining a home page, opening an HTML document on the hard disk, printing a document, and searching the current document. Unlike most browsers, which automatically display the URL in some kind of status bar, DOSLynx uses a menu command. A feature of DOSLynx is its ability to save rendered text, stripping out all the HTML tags so the user is left with plain ASCII. Although this is not that difficult technically, most PC browsers do not have that flexibility.

DOSLynx does not have a history list, but it has a hot list; entries are placed into a special document, viewed by pressing F1. This provides a quick way to create your own home page, too. The easy-to-use DOSLynx can do most of what you need. However, few people have TCP/IP connections in DOS, and most users want the pictures and colors that graphical browsers display.

5.5.4 InternetWorks (Windows)

InternetWorks is a quality Windows browser developed by BookLink (now acquired by America Online). InternetWorks is not really part of a suite of software, although it comes with e-mail and newsgroup programs. InternetWorks is fast. Reading the first part of a document while the program continues transferring the rest of the text along with any inline images in the background is available. Initiating multiple sessions is possible; window splitting into two panes is also feasible.[25,65-72]

There is drag-and-drop OLE support that allows dragging a document into Word for Windows and turns the word processor into a Web browser, for example. In addition, a Web-like hyperlinked e-mail message can also become a Web browser. You could use OLE to store Web documents inside Word documents and launch InternetWorks from within Word.

InternetWorks has a caching system that stores every document it can (as much as disk space and memory will allow). It makes the documents available through tabs at the bottom of a window and in its Card Catalog system. By splitting the display, you can view a current document as well as one the user viewed half an hour ago.

Not only does InternetWorks provide a kind of history list, but its Card Catalog is used to create hot lists. You can drag entries from the "history" Card Catalog onto another Card Catalog, then save the new one. In this way, you can create catalogs for different subjects—for music, politics, books, and so on. You can save any session's Card Catalog for future use.[25,65-72]

Web documents can be saved as HTML (but not as plain text) as well as in a "hypermedia" format with graphics. Thus, you can save a document on your hard disk and view it in the future with all its graphics.

5.5.5 Microsoft Internet Explorer

Although Microsoft was slow to join the Internet tools market, it now offers, with Internet Explorer, a strong, feature-rich, Web browser with extensive support for Windows 95, HTML 3.0/3.x, and VRML. It is based on SpyGlass Mosaic. Version 2.0 of the Internet Explorer is an update to the software that was included in the Plus! Pack and on Microsoft's Web site. The new version is a no-cost extension to Windows 95 and is available as a download. Installation is fairly simple, by downloading the file from the Web site. The browser is simple to use. It has all the HTML 2.0 features and most of the 3.0 proposed characteristics. The most notable of the "Designed for Internet Explorer" features include color-table support, color-highlighted text, in-line sounds, in-line animation, a centralized search page, and a customizable starting page (all features not found on the majority of the other browsers). Although it does not support full plug-ins, as does Navigator 2.01, a VRML module is available as a free plug-in (however, other vendors have plug-ins that manipulate 3-D files more expeditiously than Explorer). Version 3, to be available at press time, was expected to support Java, Object Linking, and Embedding Custom Controls for running Visual Basic and Visual C++ applets, HTML 3.0 frames and style sheets, JavaScript, and VBCScript.[73]

5.6 Next-Generation Web Browsing

Today's Web browsers are limited by HTML specifications, which are good for two-dimensional page layout but not necessarily for truly interactive browsing. VRML and Java are two new languages (discussed in Chap. 4) designed to enhance the Web browsing experience and to take the on-line world to another level. VRML offers a method of describing three-dimensional space so users can navigate in three dimensions. Java is an object-oriented language that adds animation and real-time interaction through inline applications called *applets*. These emerging Web technologies include graphics layout animation and special effects that include automatic application updating—for example, a running stock ticker inside a financial analysis Web page, 3-D virtual reality for Web browser walkthroughs of architectural models' prototype office buildings, and virtual worlds.

These new languages are being implemented by SGI's Webspace (VRML) and Sun's HotJava (Java). Both browsers were available in pre-release form at press time to demonstrate the technologies. Webscape will be commercially available from SGI and Template Graphics. Other browsers, such as Netscape Navigator, are planning to support one or both technologies.

5.6.1 SGI's WebSpace

SGI and Template Software have teamed up to create WebSpace, an interactive 3-D Web browser that uses VRML to allow browsing of VRML sites in three dimensions.[3–7,74] WebSpace is currently used as a helper application under Web browsers. While browsing the Web with Netscape, a jump to a VRML document will launch WebSpace. The center of control is a graphical joystick in the middle of the screen. The view resembles what you would see looking through a camcorder to navigate around a neighborhood. WebSpace is very demanding for hardware and is power hungry. For now, there are only emerging applications for VRML. Some implementations could include molecule modeling or touring vacation spots.

5.6.2 Sun's HotJava

As an object-oriented programming language, Java lets sophisticated animation and special effects run inside Web pages. Java is the first to provide a comprehensive solution to the challenges of programming for the Internet, providing portability, security, advanced networking, and reliability without compromising performance. The Java language supports a complex networked environment of clients and servers and can link in new forms of code without requiring anything of the user. The first Web browser to use the Java technology is HotJava, which at press time ran only on Sun Solaris. Sun plans to port HotJava to major platforms such as Windows NT and Mac OS System 7.5. Netscape will integrate Java technology into its own Web browser products, which stands to make Java the most popular development technology for the Web.[2,37]

Java offers a very flexible environment for developing interactive applications for the World Wide Web. Using a pseudocompiler, object code is converted into a format that the Java interpreter can understand. You can add these applets inline on a standard HTML page. Applets can be programmed to do almost anything that a standard C++ program can, with equal difficulty in writing code. The Java language is flexible, but writing applets is an order of magnitude more difficult than HTML code.

While Sun's HotJava works well on a Sparcstation 20 and Windows NT, it may soon be available on platforms such as the Power Macintosh and Windows 95. Because of the interpreted applets, they can be written independent of the platform with only the interpreter being specific to the hardware and operating system.[3-7,75]

5.7   Using Browsers for Commercial Gain

5.7.1   Opportunities and motivations in the Internet and intranets

The advent of Mosaic has accelerated the shift of Internet usage from scientists and academics to commercial users and consumers, and it has spurred the creation of hundreds of thousands of Web pages—and the numbers are expected to rise quickly into the millions. Who's creating all these pages? Art galleries, museums, schools, magazines, civic organizations, and cities; even the Library of Congress is on the Web. Recently, Californians used the Web to broadcast election results before the television stations did.[3-7,9]

Businesses are especially interested in the Web, seeing it as the modern cyberspace equivalent of an exotic trade route to new markets. Every day, dozens of new businesses set up home pages or electronic storefronts on the Web, hoping to snare new customers through the personal computer. In addition, many large corporations have already built intranets to make a lot of the corporate information available to the employees in uniform GUI and indexable form.

To establish a presence on the Web you need to create the HTML files. Microsoft and Novell will be offering add-ons for Word and WordPerfect that translate word processing documents into HTML, enabling virtually everyone who uses a PC to become a Web publisher. Third-party utilities from Interleaf and Quarterdeck, among other companies, will

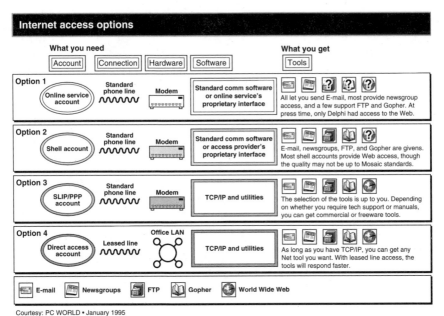

Figure 5.12

do the same thing.[3,9] Before long a "save as HTML" command will be standard in many business applications.

Once you have created HTML documents you need to put them on a Web server where Web users can get at them. You could do it yourself, but you would need a PC running Web server software along with a router and some kind of high-speed phone line. It may be better in some cases to let somebody else handle Web services. This can be as simple as renting some space on your local ISP's Web server and a portion of the provider's high-speed phone line. (See Fig. 5.12.[5])

To establish intranets you need only upgrade the enterprise network to TCP/IP (if it is not already), and then add Web-based servers accessible by users' PCs that are equipped with any of the browsers described in this chapter or that may evolve in the (near) future. The use of ATM-based or switched Ethernet networks in the corporate environment may prove beneficial to support the data rates that Web servers can generate.[76,77]

5.7.2 Some issues needing resolution

Before commercial planners rush out to sign up for a PPP account or space on a server, they should consider that the growth of the Internet and the potentiality of millions of new users coming aboard the WWW from commercial on-line services is causing concern that the Web may tax Internet's current transmission capacity. While graphics and multimedia pages look and sound nice, they also take up large amounts of bandwidth.

Can the Internet handle all this extra traffic? Experts have mixed opinions. While some argue that the Internet's resources are expanding to meet the growing demand, others argue that it is getting more difficult to get connected to popular sites. For example, logging onto Netscape Communications' Web site to get a copy of Netscape Navigator[78] can be an ordeal, given the thousands of users who try to access the site every day.[3-9] Some WWW search tools reported 22 million URLs per month (April 1996). As discussed, the Internet consists of the access network, the backbone networks, and the servers connected to these networks. Network capacity must be engineered by the carriers. Server capacity must be tracked by the organization setting up the server.

Security is another big issue. S-HTTP and SSL are competing to be adopted as the standard for financial transactions over the Web. The decision as to which to use was expected imminently at press time. Following this, it is expected that even more businesses will likely set up Web pages.[3,10] But news accounts of hackers grabbing passwords and credit card information on-line have made some businesses justifiably wary about joining the rush to the Web.

In the meantime, the Web is becoming easier to use than ever for publishers and end users. It is the 1990s equivalent of desktop publishing except that the audience is global, the medium is interactive, and you do not need paper. Thanks to its ease of use, multimedia capabilities, and interactivity, the Web has been hailed by some as the most important advance in publishing since the printing press. Others, however, have called it a great productivity drain and the most overhyped technology since pen-based computing or ATM.[3,10]

5.7.3   Access from on-line services

The major on-line services—America Online, CompuServe, Delphi, Prodigy, and Microsoft Network (MSN)—now offer Web browsers of their own.[3-7,79,80] Prodigy was the first on-line service with graphical access to the Web. Prodigy has maximized performance by caching popular Web pages on your local server so you do not have to fetch the pages over the Internet or copy frequently requested graphics (such as company logos) on the user's local hard disk.

America Online was planning to debut a Web browser based on InternetWorks. According to AOL, users will access the Web from the service's existing Internet Center (which already offers FTP, Gopher, USENET newsgroups, e-mail, and WAIS). More recently, they have joined forces with AT&T.

Instead of incorporating a browser into its existing on-line, Compu-Serve was planning to offer PPP access over its network. You can dial a local CompuServe access number, then log in to the Internet using TCP/IP. As for software, CompuServe recently acquired Spry and will presumably make Spry's software readily accessible to its subscribers.

Delphi has offered Internet access longer than any other on-line service, but its interface has not kept up. At press time, Delphi offered a text-based Web browser that gives the user hypertext links but does not support graphics. This situation should improve; Delphi has licensed browser technology from Netscape and plans to incorporate it into a new interface debuting later this year.

Finally, if you decide to upgrade to Windows 95, you will have two more Web options: (1) You will be able to get at the Web through a standard Internet account, using TCP/IP drivers built into Windows 95 and a browser based on Spyglass Enhanced Mosaic. Or (2) you will be able to access the Web through Microsoft Network. Microsoft indicates that this new on-line service will have full Internet access by early 1996, including Web access based on Spyglass technology.

On-line services are discussed further in Chap. 7.

References

1. Pane, Antoinette, "Browsing Systems," class project, Stevens Institute of Technology, fall 1995.
2. Pfaffenberger, Bryan, *Netscape Navigator—Surfing the Web and Exploring the Internet,* Academic Press, Inc., 1995, p. 14.
3. Wong, Suk Yee, "Browsing Systems for Web and Internet," class project, Stevens Institute of Technology, fall 1995.
4. Ayre, R., "Making the Internet Connection," *PC Magazine,* October 31, 1994.
5. Abernathy, J., "The Internet: How to Get There from Here," *PC World,* January 1995.
6. Fleishman, G., "There's More to Web Server than Meets the Eye," *Infoworld,* June 19, 1995.
7. The Internet, various resources.
8. Stapleton, L., et al., "A Tangled Web Unsnarled," *InfoWorld,* June 19, 1995.
9. Barr, C., "All You Need to Go On-line," *PC World,* June 1995.
10. Lewis, P. H., "Web Browsers," *PC World,* June 1995.
11. Carmel, A., "Building a Web," class project, Stevens Institute of Technology, fall 1995.
12. Boutell, Thomas, "World Wide Web FAQ," *World Wide Web* at http://sunsite.unc.edu/boutell/faq/wwwfaq.txt, 1995.
13. Collins, E. Stephen, "Internet Server Kitchen," *World Wide Web,* The University of Minnesota.
14. Colomb, Chris, and Paul Jones, "How to Be a Server Daemon," *World Wide Web* at http://sunsite.unc.edu/chris/daemons/.
15. CyberGroup Inc., "Building Internet Servers," *World Wide Web* at http://www.charm.net/~cyber/, October, 1995.
16. Graham, Ian, and Michael Lee, "Browsers, Viewers, and HTML Preparation Resources," *World Wide Web,* August, 1995.
17. Hughes, Kevin, "Entering the World Wide Web," Enterprise Integration Technologies, May 1994.
18. IETF, "IETF Home Page," *World Wide Web* at http://ietf.cnri.va.us/ and, ftp://ds.interic.net/ietf/1ietf-description.txt.

19. Kriz, M. Harry, "TCP/IP Technical Details," *World Wide Web* at http:/leaming.lib. vt.edu/wintcpip/technical.html, September 1995.
20. Management Technology Association, "Internet: The Basics," *World Wide Web,* July, 1995.
21. Stein, D. Lincoln, *How to Set Up and Maintain a World Wide Web Site,* Addison-Wesley Publishing Company, April 1995.
22. The Internet Society, "NSF Press Release," *World Wide Web* at http://www.isoc.org/ adopsec/nsf-naine-fees.html.
23. "The Internet Society," *World Wide Web* at http://www.isoc.org/standards.
24. "The World Wide Web Consortium (W3C) Overview," *World Wide Web* at http://www. w3.org/pub/WWW/Consortium.
25. Muhammad, S., "An Assesment of Internet Browsers," class project, Stevens Institute of Technology, fall 1995.
26. Dern, D. P., "Navigating the Web Navigators," *Network Computing,* April 1, 1995.
27. Levitt, Jason, "A Matter of Attribution: Can't Forget to Give Credit for Mosaic Where Credit Is Due," *Open Systems Today,* issue 149, May 9, 1994, p. 71.
28. Symoens, J., "Window's Web Browsers," *PC World,* June 1995.
29. "Netscape's Mission," Netscape Communications Corporation, Copyright 1995, located at home.netscape.com/comprod/netscape_mission.html.
30. Levit, Jason, "New Net Navigator—Netscape Charts Bold Course with Latest Browser," *Information Week,* issue 550, Oct 23, 1995, p. 28.
31. Pfaffenberger, Bryan, Ibid. p. 48.
32. Karpinski, Richard, "Testing the Browsers: Netscape 1.1 vs. Enhanced Mosaic 2.0," *Interactive Age,* issue 210, March 13, 1995, p. 10.
33. Pfaffenberger, Bryan, p. 77.
34. Levit, Jason, "New Net Navigator—Netscape Charts Bold Course with Latest Browser," *Information Week,* Oct. 23, 1995, issue 550, page 28.
35. Pfaffenberger, Bryan, p. 190.
36. Bronson, Gail, "Head of Spin-off Reveals Marketing Plans—VeriSign's Strategy," *Interactive Age,* issue 222, August 28, 1995, p. 27.
37. "VeriSign," VeriSign Corporation, Copyright 1995, located at www.verisign.com/ vs_info/about_vs.html.
38. Pfaffenberger, Bryan, p. 306.
39. Pfaffenberger, Bryan, p. 305.
40. Santo, Brian, "Netscape Execs See Success on Horizon," *EE Interactive Times,* issue 865, Sept. 11, 1995, p. 30.
41. "Netscape Navigator 2.0 Data Sheet," Netscape Communications Corporation, Copyright 1995, locate at www.netscape.com/comprod/products/navigator/version_2.0/ datasheet.html.
42. "Frames," Netscape Communications Corporation, 1995, located at home.netscape. com/comprod/products/navigator/version_2.0/frames/index.html.
43. "Plug-Ins," Netscape Communications Corporation, 1995, located at home.netscape. com/comprod/products/navigator/version_2.0/plug-in.html.
44. "Netscape Software Development Kit—Inline Plug-Ins," Version 1.0, draft 3, Aug 29, 1995.
45. Rohan, Rebecca, "The New Programming Language," *NetGuide,* issue 210, October 1, 1995, p. 24.
46. Kohlhepp, Robert J., "Next Generation Web Browsing," *Network Computing,* issue 609, Aug. 1, 1995, p. 48.
47. "Script" Netscape Communications Corporation, 1995, located at home.netscape.com/ comprod/products/navigator/version_2.0/script/index.html.
48. Gunn, A., "Internet Front Ends to Watch For," *PC Magazine,* October 11, 1994. p. 235.
49. Schultz, Beth, "W3 Consortium Eyes Commercial Web Activities," *Communications Week,* issue 529, Oct. 31, 1994, p. 31.
50. Aronson, Larry, "Which HTML Is 'Real'?—The Language is Evolving to a New Version, with Some Exciting Features to Come," *NetGuide,* issue 210, Oct. 1, 1995, p. 91.
51a.Press release, Netscape Communications Corporation. Copyright 1995. Located at home.netscape.com/newsref/pr/newsrelease56.html.

51b."Netscape's Stock Wows the Market," MulQueen, John T., *Communications Week,* Aug. 14, 1995, issue 570, page 5.

51c. "Netscape to Make Internet a Callaborative Apps Platform," Baron, Talila, *Communications Week,* issue 576, Sept. 25, 1995, p. 5.

52. Wilder, Clinton, "Netscape Offers Applications Development—Navigator Pushed as the Platform of Choice," *Information Week,* issue 547, Oct. 2, 1995, p. 98.

53. Santo, Brian, "Netscape Execs See Success on Horizon," *EE Interactive Times,* issue 865, Sept. 11, 1995, p. 30.

54. Wilder, Clinton, "Netscape Offers Applications Development—Navigator Pushed as the Platform of Choice," *Information Week,* issue 547, Oct 2, 1995, p. 98.

55. "Netscape Navigator Chat," Netscape Communications Corporation, Copyright 1995, located at home.netscape.com/comprod/chat.html.

56. Gerber, B., "Browsers on the Wild, Wild Web," *Network Computing,* April 1, 1995.

57. "Browsing the Wild, Wild, Web—Nine Ways to Cruise the Web," *NetGuide,* issue 203, March 1, 1995, p. 41.

58. "Spyglass Press Release," Spyglass Inc., August 24, 1995, p. 1, located at www.spyglass.com/one/press_mosaic.html.

59. "Browsing the Wild, Wild, Web—Nine Ways to Cruise the Web," *NetGuide,* issue 203, p. 41.

60. "About Our Browser," Spyglass Inc., 1995, located at www.spyglass.com/products/browser.html.

61. "Spyglass Reports Third Quarter Results," July 19, located at www.spyglass.com/archive/july 1995_1.html.

62a."Prosaic, Mosaci E, and More," Jerome, Marty, *NetGuide,* issue 210, October 1, 1995, p. 33.

62b.Santalesa, Rich, "Simply Hyperactive—The Big Three Online Services Offer Easiest Way to Access the Web," *NetGuide,* issue 208, Aug. 1, 1995, p. 63.

63. Haight, Timothy, "James Clark and Marc Andreessen, Chairman and Vice President of Technology, Netscape Communications," *Network Computing,* issue 611, Sept. 15, 1995, p. 76.

64. Ayre, R., and K. Reichard, "The Web Untangled," *PC Magazine,* February 7, 1995.

65. Cronin, Mary J., *Doing Business on the Internet, How the Electronic Highway Is Transforming American Companies,* Van Nostrand Reinhold; New York, 1993.

66. Krol, Ed, *The Whole Internet: User's Guide and Catalog,* O'Reilly & Associates, Inc., Cambridge, Mass., 1992.

67. Pike, Mary Ann, *Using the Internet,* 2d ed., Que Corporation, 1995.

68. Thomas, Brian J., *The Internet for Scientists and Engineers, Online Tools and Resources,* SPIE Optical Engineering Press, Bellingham, Washington, 1996.

69. Galvin, Christopher J., "The Wide World of Web," *Compuserve Magazine,* June 1995.

70. Miller, Benjamin F., and Neil Randall, "Create Your Own Web Page," *PC Computing,* Sept. 1995.

71. Miller, Benjamin F., and Neil Randall. "Rating Web Browsers," *PC Computing,* Sept. 1995.

72. Miller, Benjamin F., and Neil Randall, "The Web Awaits," *PC Computing,* Sept. 1995.

73. J. Linder, Web Browers, Network Computing, May 1, 1996, pages 59ff.

74. Raucci, R., "Extending the Web," *InfoWorld,* June 9, 1995.

75. Khthepp, R. J., "Next Generation Web Browsing," *Network Computing,* August 1, 1995.

76. Minoli, D., and M. Vitella, *ATM and Cell Relay in Corporate Environments,* McGraw-Hill, New York, 1995.

77. Minoli, D., and A. Alles, *Understanding LAN Emulation and Other Related Technologies,* Artech House, 1997.

78. http://home.netscape.com.

79. Miller, D., "Online Services Get Webbed," *PC World,* June 1995.

80. Gunn, A., "Internet Front Ends to Watch For," *PC Magazine,* October 11, 1994.

6

Building a Corporate Web Site: Practical Issues on Servers and Application Software

The previous chapters provided Web information from an abstract point of view. This chapter pulls together this information from a practical perspective. It aims to provide practical information related to actually producing a corporate Web site for both Internet and intranet applications.

6.1   Background: Using the WWW for Business

There are several thousands (5000+) public and private sites on the Internet serving information over the WWW, at least 10 percent of which are commercial.[1] Each of these sites runs Web server software, which delivers information over the network as it is requested. The Web is made up of a collection of servers and clients, programs running on the computer, also called *browsers,* which exchange information. A client usually sends a request message over the Internet (access and backbone components) to a computer running a Web server. The server sends the requested document back to the client, which then displays the document on the user's computer screen. The protocol is HTTP/FTP. There are many reasons why people access the Internet and the World Wide Web.[2–11]

- *Electronic mail service.*   It is very convenient to use electronic mail service that can deliver messages to places anywhere in the world in seconds.

- *Extensive library.*   It contains publications on every and any subject. Books have been placed on-line and can be retrieved and read.

- *Source of news.* It is the world's most dynamic—and complete—newsstand, with news and analysis on business, economics, sports, entertainment, and the arts.

- *Community gathering place.* It is a place where you can "rest and relax," engaging in informal discussions with friends and colleagues.

- *New business opportunities.* It is a source for new business, including electronic shopping malls.

- *Educational resources.* Educators have been using the Internet for a long time, setting up e-mail discussion groups on curricula, newsgroups that report on educational trends, and servers that help teachers with specific problems.

Almost everyone benefits from Internet services. Some take advantage of cost savings and quick delivery. The Internet improves their interdepartmental communications by exchanging documents and designs for research. Some businesses use the Internet to enhance customer support or to find ways to reach new customers. Many organizations are taking a more active role, opening up their own corporate servers to provide product information, business information, or business transactions to the outside world. Others use the network as the central source of all company information. Some use World Wide Web or Gopher services, for example, to present company newsletters, stock quotes, announcements, press releases, competitors' actions, organizational charts, orientation materials, company goals, product or service info, sales successes, promotions, employee successes, and ethics. Intranet-based information is even more extensive.

A corporation can start a home page and take advantage of a whole host of opportunities[2–11]:

- *Increase the customer base.* A user base of more than 30 million people can offer individuals access to products or services. As with any marketing project, however, companies must use judgment and market research to reach appropriate prospects for products or services. Sending e-mail to 20 million people is not exactly practical.

- *Get expert help.* Many Internet participants are university professors and corporate professionals—often at the top of their field. The Internet encourages friendly discussions. Answers to difficult questions may be available without paying a consulting fee.

- *Test-market new products.* Some users are willing to answer surveys. Product analysts can ask Internet users for input, and also for feedback about products already on the market.

- *Recruit employees.* Advertise job offerings as one of the topics on a home page.

- *Use for customer support.* Publish updated versions of product manuals on a service. This reduces the load on technical support personnel. Technical companies have used the World Wide Web for technical support for several years. It is more convenient to handle queries via FAQs or forums than to shuffle phone calls among product experts. And some customers prefer searching a Web site to the time and expense incurred for phone calls to technical support departments. This updated version of a BBS can return real cost savings, cutting down on live requests for support. World Wide Web servers replaced the crude BBS with a superior user interface and a better information delivery tool. Perhaps Web manuals can be designed to be multimedia documents rather than just hard copies of documentation.

- *Get customer feedback or bug reports.* Giving customers the means to provide feedback empowers them. In turn, this gives an organization a means of immediately satisfying customer needs, as well as up-to-the-minute beta testing that allows companies to correct a problem before it becomes widespread.

- *Provide search lists of foundations for sources of grant money.* Entire libraries of foundations are now available. The job of finding foundations to which you can apply without using the Internet can be difficult. Computer-assisted searching takes the pain out of finding appropriate foundations to which to apply.

- *Allow customers to buy products and services on-line.*

For people both internal and external to a company, the Internet is a means of increasing the company's visibility, product services, and sales. Figure 6.1 depicts a modern Internet network-access-point architecture being put in place (by companies such as Teleport Communications Group—TCG).

6.1.1 Examples of businesses on the Internet

Many companies and organizations have set up World Wide Web servers, which lets them distribute documents all across the Internet. Some companies have created Internet networks running Web servers that allow their employees to search for and retrieve any documents they are interested in. There are many reasons why companies should have local information networks, and there are equally many reasons why they should have Internet connectivity. Web servers and clients can run on either local networks or over the Internet. They offer a number of benefits for organizations that wish to get connected, as follows[12]:

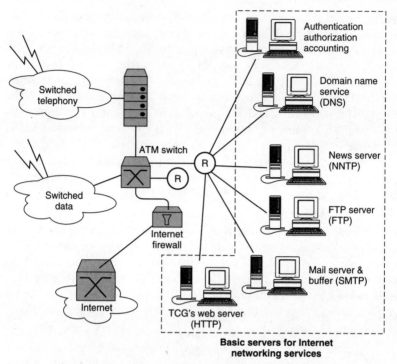

Basic servers for Internet networking services

Figure 6.1   TCG Internet network-access-point model (approximate view).

- Hypermedia documents can be shown on many different types of computers. The Web was designed to convey information in a device-independent manner. This means that HTML documents on the Web are shown to users in a way that is best suited to their display. Documents with graphics and formatting information might be shown in full color on an X terminal, while only basic formatting and text within the same document might be shown on a text-only screen. Companies with different types of computers will find that the Web offers a good way to display the same information on many platforms.

- Information navigation is fast, interactive, and intuitive. Documents on the World Wide Web often contain mouse-driven "hot spots" in the form of hyperlinks forms and menus that allow users to search quickly through archives and documents. Multimedia presentations, on-line forms, and database interfaces can be created so that users have the ability to interact with and control information rather than just view it. This is well suited to organizations that need interfaces for data entry or customer support.

- The Web works on standards. Most Web clients and servers have been designed to communicate using TCP/IP. If someone can connect to the Internet, he or she can also connect to the Web. If someone has a protocol that the Web client cannot speak, hooks are provided in servers so that gateways can be created in many programming languages.[13]

Table 6.1 suggests just how committed companies are to doing business on the Internet.

The following examples give an idea of how (a few) companies are using the Internet.[2-11]

Federal Express: http://www.fedex.com. Ships packages all over the world. On its home page, a user can

Track a FedEx package

Find out FedEx service availability

Learn what's new at FedEx

Hewlett-Packard: http://www.hp.com. Offers a service, called Access HP, that tells users how to effectively use the Internet. The company views this project as an extension of its customer-relations support services. In addition a user can

Download new and updated software

Receive on-line technical support through forums and FAQs

Find out about products

TABLE 6.1   Use of Internet by Corporate America

Company	No. of networks registered with Internet
Exxon	263
Transamerica	260
GTE	254
Unisys	216
Texas Instruments	188
Boeing	140
Motorola	140
Hewlett-Packard	137
Commonwealth Edison	130
Sprint	102
Johnson Controls	85
Loral	85
Pacific Bell	74
Martin Marietta	69
SmithKline Beecham	67
Lockheed	66
Ford Motor	61
Bell Atlantic	58
General Electric	52
Intel	51

Paramount Pictures: http://www.paramount.com. You can see previews of upcoming *Star Trek: Voyager* TV shows (in a video clip), listen to the captain and the holographic doctor talk to you, and examine previous episodes of *Star Trek: Voyager.*

Canadian Airlines: http://www.cdnair.ca. Canadian Airlines can help arrange travel plans. Home page offers

News updates

Airline services

Maintenance and engineering server

These are just a few examples. Organizations are benefiting by developing Web servers accessible through the Internet and by providing timely and accessible information, using low-cost marketing and customer support, and beginning business transactions via forms.

6.1.2 Case study

This section provides a case study of Web development in an organization, based on Ref. 2. AMS is available at http://www.amsinc.com.

Release 1 of the AMS World Wide Web server is currently available internally to AMS users over the internal worldwide network (AMSWAN). Internal users use TCP/IP to access the World Wide Web server running on a 486-based personal computer under the Windows NT operating system. AMSWAN has been connected to the Internet using UUNET as the service provider. Anyone on AMSWAN with TCP/IP access has access to most Internet capabilities.

6.1.2.1 Implementation issues. After initial prototyping efforts, development of the AMS World Wide Web server proceeded over about a three-month period. During that time, AMS dealt with a variety of technical and management issues. However, even the technical issues sprang from management concerns. Once these were dealt with, the actual implementation was fairly straightforward. Two key types of concerns were expressed in meetings of an internal Internet Task Force:

- How to maintain network security while opening a link to the outside world

- How to deal with the various issues of ownership, timeliness, and quality of the material to be presented on the server

The first issue could be dealt with by appropriate technical architecture of the Internet gateway, but the second would require an ongoing effort as well as the establishment of new policies. Both the design of the technical architecture and the discussion of policy were carried out primarily on-line via Lotus Notes with the sponsorship of AMS's Center for Advanced Technologies.

6.1.2.2 Technical architecture. The technical architecture team considered several approaches to ensuring that outside users had acceptable access to the server while other aspects of the internal network were protected. After several design sessions and consultation with UUNET, AMS designed a two-tier firewall system using a single leased line into UUNET. This would allow having both a World Wide Web server and an FTP server, which was intended to be used primarily for updating the contents of the World Wide Web server.

The two-tiered firewall system is built using two Ethernet segments and one IP router. The IP router is used to link AMS to UUNET, providing minimal packet filtering on an unsecure Ethernet segment and full packet filtering on the secure segment. The combined World Wide Web/FTP server resides on the "unsecure" network. The secure segment is configured with appropriate IP packet filtering to prevent inbound Internet requests from passing onto the secure Ethernet, which could then compromise AMS's wide area network.

6.1.2.3 Management issues. Most of the discussions in designing the Web server were focused on a broad range of management issues. It is impossible to bring up a new corporate communications mechanism such as a Web server without addressing many of these issues. While not all were solved, an acceptable degree of protection was provided without unduly hampering the ability to create a complete Web server.

6.1.2.4 Overall network security. Security of the internal network was of primary concern. One approach considered was to create a totally separate Internet connection for externally accessible servers, but it was felt that this was not sufficiently flexible. The two-tiered firewall described above provided the right combination of security and flexibility for AMS.

6.1.2.5 Copyright and intellectual property. Some of the issues were still awaiting legal precedent and court resolution at press time. It is believed that appropriate legal rights over any AMS-copyrighted material is maintained. Securing permission is necessary in order for other organizations to put it on-line.

6.1.2.6 Trade secrets. The simplest way to protect trade secrets is to keep them secret. Arrival of secure communications on the Web is sought before dealing with this type of information. Two-way communication (e.g., allowing people to request that they be sent more information) is an important capability provided via a Web server. The issue is how to control access to this capability. If thousands of requests for information come in, for example, this would present a significant problem (AMS's business is focused on doing larger projects with a small number of client organizations, perhaps only a few hundred in total). With a potential Internet audience of millions, most of whom are neither potential partners nor clients, this causes a great deal of concern.

The initial approach is to provide e-mail addresses for requesting further information. If this results in an acceptable response rate, data entry forms will be added to Web documents. Also, it is imperative to carefully monitor requests and the ability to respond to them in order to provide good service to legitimate requests.

6.1.2.7   Consistency of user interface.   AMS is a decentralized organization, and many different groups will be preparing information to be included on the Web server. A mechanism was needed to ensure quality and consistency of presentation across services and across areas of the company. The approach was to treat information on the Web server the same way it would treat a marketing brochure or even the annual report. These types of documents go through stringent review processes within the company and are subject to all Web server content to that same level of scrutiny.

An ad hoc Internet Task Force has become an ongoing group, discussing issues, reviewing policies, and coming up with new ideas for additional Web services. The group was able to deal with each of these issues, at least to some degree, and has been able to establish AMS on the World Wide Web.

6.1.2.8   Conclusion, case study.   Having the opportunity to create a new business medium for your company does not happen very often. The Internet, the World Wide Web, and browsers like Mosaic, have provided an opportunity to the developers that has enormous potential for changing the way in which many business interactions occur. The ability to set up a World Wide Web server for AMS in a relatively short time is just one indication of why thousands of organizations are flocking to the Web as a potential marketplace. AMS plans to continue the evolution of its server with new materials and new services. AMS fully expects that all customers, vendors, business partners, employees, and recruits will find something of interest and importance on its Web server.

6.2   Getting Connected

The first challenge to overcome in using the Internet is getting connected to it. There are many Internet providers, many categories of service, and many pricing structures. As discussed elsewhere in this book, a corporation can connect to the Internet in one of two ways: (1) dial-up account and (2) leased line.

6.2.1 Dial-up

With dial-up, the user uses a modem to call the Internet provider to connect to the Internet. When finished, the user hangs up and terminates the connection to the Internet. The cost is either metered out on an hourly basis, a flat fee, or a combination of the two. For example, you might get the first 40 hours per month included in the monthly Internet bill and then pay $2 per hour thereafter.

When you connect to the Internet through a modem over ordinary telephone lines with a dial-up account, the data transmission rates vary between 2400 and 28,800 bits per second (bps).* This transmission rate works fine for e-mail, running processes on remote machines, and even moderately well for WWW browsers handling hypertext (less so for hypermedia). A dial-up line can handle one call per telephone line. To minimize costs, a small company that needs only company e-mail or other text-based access should use a dial-up shell account to connect to the Internet.†

6.2.2 Leased lines

A leased line (also known as a *dedicated* or *private* line) is a communications facility (channel) that connects the company to the Internet provider. The organization does not need to dial; a company is always connected to the Internet through the provider. The organization pays for the leased line according to the volume of Internet traffic that crosses the wires. Whereas individuals and small companies can choose to use dial-up Internet accounts, medium to large companies should use leased lines. Speeds vary from 56 Kbps to 10 Mbps (e.g., via an ATM link).

6.2.3 Categories of service

There are three categories of Internet service, as covered in Chap. 1:

1. Shell
2. SLIP/PPP
3. Direct

A shell Internet account provides a UNIX command line as a user interface when you connect to the Internet through dial-up. You

---

* If the ISP supports ISDN and you yourself have access to ISDN, then speeds up to 128 Kbps (residence) or 1.544 Kbps (business) can be achieved.
† There also are several trials to deliver Internet access over cable TV at 10 Mbps.

can use FTP, WAIS, and Gopher to connect to remote services and retrieve documents. Now that the graphical browsers, such as Explorer, Netscape, Netcruiser, Mosaic, and Chameleon, are becoming widely renowned, what at one time seemed "enough" will no longer suffice. Because the shell account cannot use graphical browsers, it may soon fall from favor.

Two faster kinds of connections that provide full Internet access are SLIP and PPP, also available through dial-up (see Chap. 1). With these connections, you can use graphical browsers, such as Mosaic, Explorer, and Netscape, along with all of the other Internet tools, such as WAIS, FTP, and Gopher, to explore the Internet. Since this type of connection still supports only limited throughput, it may not by itself be appropriate for a large company. This is fine for individuals and small business.

Direct connection provides full Internet access to the Internet using a dedicated communications line. Because a direct connection is made through a dedicated line of specified speed, the company can attain much greater transmission rates and thereby service a greater number of employees. A leased connection provides between 9600 bps and 45 Mbps; lines operating at 155 Mbps (OC-3) are now also appearing (actual throughput, however, was around 10 Mbps at press time). Companies that use a leased line from a local telephone company can have a permanent Internet address. This kind of connection is appropriate for medium- to larger-sized companies. Such a setup requires some extra machinery: one or more servers, a router, a firewall host, and a CSU/DSU or a modem, as shown in Figs. 6.2, 6.3, and 6.4, which depict Internet access options.

A *server* is a dedicated computer that handles incoming Internet requests. It stores e-mail from the Internet and Internet services, such as Gopher, Archie, or the World Wide Web. A *router* (Chap. 2) supports IP protocol peers, which are required for direct Internet access. Routers contain tables of information about Internet servers all over the world and use that information to direct Internet messages to correct destinations across the intricate path of Internet connections. A *channel service unit/data service unit* (CSU/DSU) is (digital) line termination equipment.

Standard bandwidths for Internet services follow: 9600 bps, 14.4 Kbps, 28.8 Kbps, 56 Kbps, 128 Kbps, 384 Kbps, DS1 (1.5 Mbps), DS3 (which ranges up to 45 Mbps). At this time, DS3 connections are usually only used by Internet service providers to connect, for example, the networks at one end of a state to another with their backbone networks. The reason for this is that DS3 is very expensive. Only the very largest companies can justify the expense of a DS3 connection (the actual throughput may be somewhat lower).

One attractive feature of getting a leased line is that the Internet service provider generally gives the company a permanent Internet

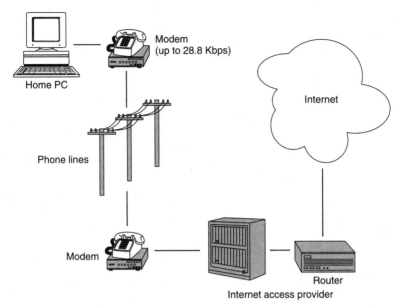

Figure 6.2   Connecting to the Internet from home (least expensive).

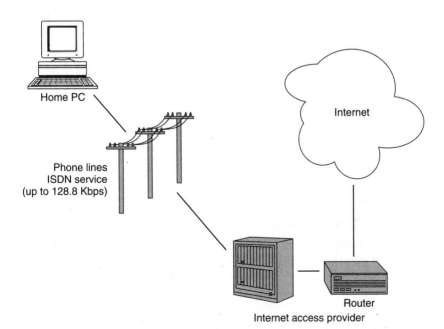

Figure 6.3   Connecting to the Internet from home (more expensive).

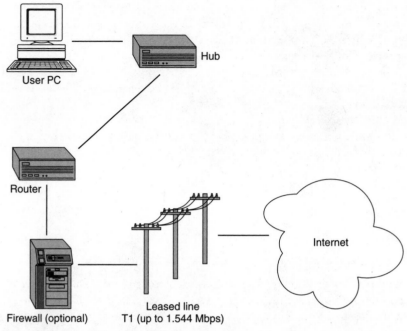

Figure 6.4 Connecting to the Internet from work.

address and a domain name (see Sec. 6.2.4). If the company wants a permanent presence on the Internet (e.g., a WWW service), a permanent Internet address is required. InterNIC Registration Services provides an Internet registration template from the agency that assigns Internet addresses and domain names. Its Gopher site is rs.internic. net. As covered in Chap. 1, there are three classes of Internet addresses: A, B, and C. A Class C address can handle up to 255 nodes on a single segment, whereas a Class B address can handle up to 65,535 nodes per segment. If the company has less that 255 addressable computers on a local network, use Class C (Class A is now of limited import). CIDR is increasingly being used to preserve address space by abandoning these (older) class rules.

6.2.4 Domain name services

As briefly discussed in Chap. 1, domain name is a service intended to simplify the access and the use of the Internet. It is implemented using the Domain Name System (DNS-RFC 1034) and appropriate DNS servers. It is a service for any host or user on the Internet, not just for the HTTP (a Web server), and it is an important option to consider when building a Web site. A DNS server is a computer which translates numeric IP addresses to and from user-friendly names (domain names) to identify hosts and networks on the Internet. As interest in the Internet grows, the demand for domain names has gone beyond the National Science Foundation's ability to continue completely funding the service. Domain names are Internet "addresses" and the registration process creates a database that maps the names to the numbers used for Internet routing. When NSF began operation in 1993, new domains were being registered at a rate of 400 per month; it is estimated that by the end of 1995, the figure will top 20,000 per month. This demand has created up to a five-week delay in registering new domain names. That is also the reason NSF decided to start an annual fee for domain names and registering.[14-27]

Section 6.5.5 provides some additional information related to communication issues.

6.3   Elements of a Web Service

6.3.1   Client software: practical factors

The various World Wide Web browsers are mostly free, and some are reborn commercial products. More in-depth information on browsers was provided in Chap. 5. A synopsis follows, to set the stage for the discussion.

Browsers allow people to treat the data spread across the Internet as a cohesive whole. Web browsers integrate the function of fetching the data with figuring out what it is and displaying it. HTML allows text data objects to embed simple formatting information and references to other objects.

Months after CERN's original proposal, the National Center for Supercomputing Applications (NCSA) began a project to create an interface to the World Wide Web. The NCSA's Software Design Group began work on a versatile, multiplatform interface to the World Wide Web. It is called Mosaic. Because of the number of traditional services it could handle, and due to its easy, point-and-click hypermedia interface, Mosaic soon became a popular interface to the Web. Current versions of Mosaic can run on UNIX-based machines such as Sun, Silicon Graphics, and DEC workstations, as well as IBM-compatibles running Microsoft Windows and Macintosh computers.[14-27] Netscape's Navigator and Microsoft's Explorer are two commercially important browsers to be considered in any Internet access/intranet deployment decision.

Web browsers offer many services throughout the Internet besides access to HTML documents and multimedia services. As can be seen from the following list, it is easy to add other files and services (such as FTP) to Web sites and to use a browser to access them[14-27]:

Anything served through Gopher

Anything served through WAIS (Wide Area Information Servers)

Anything served through anonymous FTP sites

Full Archie services (an FTP search service)

Full Veronica services (a Gopher search service)

Full CSO, X.500, and whois services (Internet phones book services)

Full finger services (an Internet user lookup program)

Anything on USENET

Anything accessible through TELNET

Anything in hytelnet (a hypertext interface to TELNET)

Anything in techinfo or texinfo (forms of campuswide information services)

Anything in hyper-g (a networked hypertext system in use throughout Europe)

HTML-formatted hypertext and hypermedia documents

A document is available listing many browsers and other tools for many different platforms. Originally written by Ian Graham and revised and updated by Michael Lee (August 1995), it is available on the Web at the following address:

http://www.utirc.utoronto.ca/HTMLdocs/intro_tools.html

6.3.2 Client software functions

This section covers functions of Web site software.

- If a browser supports user authentication, you can authenticate browsers with a username and a password.

- It enables you to create HTML catalogs of your directories. Catalogs describe what is in the directories.

- You can write your own service scripts that generate documents on the fly.

- You can move document files to different directories and different servers without having to rewrite the HTML and without having to advise users of the move.

- You can write scripts to handle form requests. Form requests are documents that have one or more fill-in text fields that are often used for entering search criteria.

- You can limit user actions and connections. You can prevent users from specific hosts from connecting to your service. You can also require user authentication to gain access to your service if the World Wide Web client supports user authentication.

6.3.3 Pointing to the server

As covered elsewhere, URLs provide a means of identifying the location of resources on the Internet. In order to retrieve a resource from the Internet, you must know how to find it. Identifying a resource on the Internet requires not only specifying its physical location but also the protocol that should be used to retrieve the data. URLs provide a single means of describing the locations of resources on the Internet.[12,28] In order to determine which naming scheme you should use to identify a resource, you must know what type of resource it is and which protocol is the most appropriate for retrieving that type. While the format of all URLs depends on the protocol used to access a resource, many protocols share a common URL format known as the Common Internet Scheme Syntax (CISS). The general format is shown in Fig. 6.5.

URLs look like these examples (file: and ftp: URLs are synonymous).

```
file://wuarchive.wustl.edu/mirrors/msdos/graphics/gifkit.zip
ftp://wuarchive.wustl.edu/mirrors
http://www.w3.org:80/default.html
news:alt.hypertext
telnet://dra.com
```

The first part of the URL, before the colon, specifies the access method. The part of the URL after the colon is interpreted specific to the access method. In general, two slashes after the colon indicate a machine name (machine:port is also valid). To find a service, you need the following URL:

```
http://serverName[portNumber]
```

In this example, serverName is the name of the server and portNumber is specified only if you have your service running on a port other than 80. If that is all the browser provides, HTTPD* returns

---

* HTTPD is an HTTP/1.0-compatible server for making hypertext and other documents available to Web browsers.

Format	schemename://username:password@host.port/path
scheme	URL format for a particular protocol. In general, schemes correspond to the various protocols used to access data. For example, FTP, HTTP, and Gopher are three protocols that have schemes defined in the URL specification document.
path	Identifies the resource. It does not necessarily reflect a hierarchical structure or physical location as it does in DOS or UNIX.

Figure 6.5   URL format.

the contents of ServerRoot/index.html if it is defined. When browsers want specific documents, they use an expanded URL of the following form:

```
http://serverName/[Alias \ (or ScriptAlias)/][pathName/]fileName
```

Both Alias and ScriptAlias are path names defined in the configuration file srm.conf. If neither an Alias (or ScriptAlias) nor user prefix is in the URL, the httpd daemon inserts the path defined by document Root in srm.conf.

The biggest advantage of URLs is that they provide a single, uniform method of identifying resources that are available via many different protocols, including Gopher, WAIS, FTP, TELNET, and HTTP. In the original specification, *U* in URL stood for *Universal*. The ability to identify resources was a requirement of the specification for Uniform Resource Identifiers (URIs). Not all existing protocols have an established URL scheme, but it is reasonable to expect such schemes to evolve in the future (NFS is a good example of this potential).

Table 6.2 shows the standard URL format most commonly used and the defaults associated with each scheme.[29]

Coming up with *new* URL schemes is fairly straightforward. According to the URL specifications, the proponent needs to demonstrate the

TABLE 6.2   URL Formats and Defaults

Scheme	URL format	Defaults
FTP	ftp://user:password@host:port/path	Username=anonymous Password=user's e-mail address Port = 21
HTTP	http://host:port/path/searchpart	Port = 80
Gopher	gopher://host:port/path	Port = 70
Mailto	mailto:local-address@host	None
News	news:newsgroup-name news:message_id	None None
NNTP	nntp://host/newsgroup-name/article-number	Port = 119
TELNET	telnet://user:password@host:port	Port = 23 If omitted, user prompted for username and password
WAIS	wais://host:port/database wais://host:port/database wais://host:port/database	Port = 210
File	file://host/path	None
Prospero	prospero://host:port	Port = 1525

"utility and operability" of a new URL scheme. In addition, the new scheme should be similar to URL formats already in place. New prefixes need to be defined and agreed to by the Internet Assigned Numbers Authority, but anybody can come up with new URL schemes and suggest them to IANA. The protocol with an explanation of how it works must be submitted.[30]

6.3.4   Creating a home page for the Web server: practical issues

It is nice to have a point of entry for users who have decided that it would be interesting to learn more about a company. This can be accomplished with home pages. The organization might also provide a hyperlink in each Web page to the home page so that users can start over easily.

The standard name of the home page is home.html. You put it at the top of the source tree, for example: http://www.corp.sgi.com/home.html. It is also a good idea to copy home.html into index.html or to set directory index in srm.conf to home.html. These provisions send out a company's home page with even the most minimal URL address. There are no conventions for home pages; however, users have come to expect several elements, as follows:

- What's Hot hyperlink, with the date it was last revised, publicizing your company's latest and greatest.

- Hyperlink to the system administrator, often called the Webmaster, for user feedback.

- Hyperlinks to major topics on the service, for easy navigation and an overview of your idea of what your company does best.

- The date the home page was last updated.

HTML lets the user do hypertext links, interactive buttons (which are links), and clickable, inline pictures, as discussed in Chap. 4. There are a number of HTML editors available to help organizations create the "applications" that run on the Web server. These are discussed here only to document desirable features and capabilities (this discussion is not meant to recommend any products or to attempt to provide an up-to-the minute review of release features).[2-11]

HotDog.   An application that guides the user through the entire process of creating documents to publish on the Web. HotDog Editor includes ways to easily incorporate HTML 1.0, 2.0, and many of the HTML version 3.x features into your on-line creations. Other features of HotDog Editor include quick TABLE and FORM code generation, easy font-size editing, and the ability to drag and drop text and graphics into a document directly from Windows File Manager. This editor is downloadable and the file is about 700 KB.

HoTMetaL PRO 2.0.   This application aims at making the creation of HTML documents as easy as using a word processor. Though experienced authors may miss the file-formatting control afforded from other editors, many will be happy to give up a little to know they are creating documents that follow the rules. This editor complements the capabilities of the text-style editors and should be considered—unless you need complete control over the files you create. It is a Microsoft Windows–based stand-alone program. It is a hybrid between text-style and WYSIWYG HTML checking—during editing and importing. Features found in this package include the following:

- There are a large number of import options. The package can import a large number of file formats and attempt to create HTML from them (including Word and WordPerfect).

- Display is easy to read. Tags are shown using an iconlike representation. This simplifies discerning tags from the text in the document. When working with a document that contains many similar sections, this feature is useful. The package also gives a feel for what the document may look like when you hide the tag display (headings stand out, images are shown, etc.), but as always the browsers have the final say (user can change the display style if desired).

- Tables in the document are easily edited. Specifically, the program makes it easy to insert a table. In addition, the table can easily be edited after creating it using a table format similar to those found in word processors. This is important if the information changes in the table frequently, because searching through a series of tags can be very frustrating.

- Using the package is much like using a word processor that shows formatting. The package is intelligent to simplify some operations, such as creating a new list element.

- It supports Netscape and HTML 3.x.

HTML Assistant.   Features found in this package include the following:

- User-definable text. A dialog box for defining text is present. This text can be scrolled through and selected for placement into a document.

- All the normal URLs are supported in the simple dialog. Browsing local files is supported, which really is a must. A simplified dialog for creating named anchors is supported.

- A good editor with a reasonable interface.

Ken Nesbitt's WebEdit 1.2. Features found in this package include the following:

- HTML 3.x/Netscape extensions support.
- Friendly interface. The toolbar is uncluttered, with each icon representing a class of tools. Clicking on a button brings up a list of appropriate items.
- Complete link and inline-image dialogs.
- The program offers a link dialog box which includes a URL-building (with a very complete listing of URL types) dialog and file-browsing capability. The image dialog includes every possible option (including Netscape-specific ones).

6.3.5 Supporting forms

In terms of usefulness, forms provide a key aspect of the Web. It is not enough to present the person running a site with information on the surfer who browses the site. A business wants to be able to generate qualified leads by knowing more about the person visiting the site. Forms helps the planner accomplish this. The basic information provided in the log files from the CERN and NCSA HTTPD Web server programs contain generic information that is provided to the HTTPD process by the browser. In general, that information is limited to what the browser chooses to tell the HTTPD process. The information provided to the HTTPD includes the time and date that a person visited the site, what they took (get) or sent (put) to the site, and the resolved name of the site that made the contact (or an IP address if the name could not be resolved). Newer versions of HTTPD programs also contain two additional log files. The first is a file that details the types of browsers that were used to access data at the site. The second one tells where the reference was when someone connects to one of the site's pages.[2–11]

There is no way to obtain from a browser or HTTPD process a trusted user's name. Also, there is no way to obtain a trusted e-mail address. To obtain the information that marketing people call "qualifying the lead," there must be a proactive method of getting a visitor to provide that information.

Forms provide a key way to obtain a more detailed description of the person coming to a site. An example of the use of forms is the way you obtain access to the Wall Street Journal Money and Investing Update. Browsing http://update.wsj.com/ provides a view of the offerings of the WSJ Money and Investing Update, but to access it requires registration. In the registration process, a form is used that seeks to obtain a more detailed perspective of the visitor to the site.

This information can be used to show advertisers who the WSJ site is attracting. It can be used to determine article style and direction. It can be used to help define content or offer hard copy to the visitor. Essentially, it provides the site with information about the visitor: information that only the visitor could provide. It is not enough to be able to get the message out. A business also wants to get feedback and information about the site's customers or visitors.[2-11]

6.4 Security Issues: Practical Considerations

Currently, most Web sites are simply vehicles for disseminating information, such as corporate profiles, descriptions of products and services, and instructions on how to go about obtaining these products/services. For owners of such sites, the greatest concern is keeping unauthorized users from accessing the site and corrupting their data. But as businesses increasingly embrace true electronic commerce—taking orders on-line, accepting credit card info and digital-cash payments, even conducting EDI—the stakes will rise, and both companies and their customers will demand higher levels of security.

In this context it is worth noting that the hacker profile is changing. Thrill-seeking young people who characterized the first wave of computer intruders are not so young anymore, and as they have matured, hacker culture has grown more malevolent. While there are still many who simply wish to scrutinize the corners of the Internet to see what is there, others are deliberately attempting to read privileged information, perform unauthorized modifications to data, or disrupt entire systems. Benign intruders may be tolerable, although just barely; after all, they do consume resources and slow performance for legitimate users. But serious attacks—the kind that cost money, either through damage inflicted on internal systems or by leaking critical information—are a real and growing problem.[2-11] Some developments are fueling this trend. Facing the pressures of international competition, more companies are resorting to electronic industrial espionage. There is evidence that some of these organizations are aided by "hacker clubs" that sell such services. In addition, companies have traditionally kept most of their data either on mainframes, which can be guarded with sophisticated security software, or on stand-alone PCs, which are rarely accessible remotely. In the increasingly popular client/server model, however, most servers run UNIX, which is notorious for its lack of mainframe-style security features.

Hackers like to share information, using underground BBS to exchange dial-in port phone numbers, compromised passwords, security holes, and intrusion techniques. Security and systems personnel, on the other hand, are reluctant to share security-related data. (And when they do, attackers often eavesdrop and exploit holes before they can be plugged.) For that reason, intruders are better able than their adversaries to stay abreast of the latest tricks of the trade and corporate vulnerabilities.[2-11]

6.4.1   Vulnerabilities of the Web

Businesses are looking to the Internet to achieve a global presence and become more accessible to catering to customers. The Web is new, but the mechanics are old and familiar: Web sites consist of (1) an application (the server) running on a local operating system and (2) data (Web pages) stored in a local database or file-management system. As such, Web sites are vulnerable to all the techniques that intruders have been developing for years to attack operating systems and databases.

There are four principal threats: unauthorized alteration of data; unauthorized access to the underlying operating systems; eavesdropping on messages passed between a server and a browser; and impersonation.

At first glance, the chances of the first two breaches occurring may appear negligible. After all, if a server is dedicated to Web site access, what can potential intruders really do, aside from executing relatively simple commands allowing them to view information and fill in forms? But, already, weaknesses are becoming apparent. For example, many versions of Mosaic browser running on UNIX machines have been found vulnerable. An intruder could conceivably put bad code on a Web server by overrunning a software buffer. Once in place, that code could give the intruder access to the operating system in the account under which the server is running. Alternatively the intruder could embed a UNIX command into a Web request so that the server is tricked into passing that command on to the operating system. This could be used to introduce a virus.[2-11]

Eavesdroppers on messages between a Web server and client present another security risk. For example, companies expecting repeat business sometimes use Web applications that set up customer accounts to facilitate future ordering. If intercepted, the hacker can change the shipping address by signing on with that account and then buy merchandise using the stolen information.

6.4.2   Securing a Web site

Given these threats, how secure can you actually make a Web site? The answer: as secure as you want, provided you are willing to pay for the requisite hardware, software, and personnel, and to put up with increased inconvenience for users. As things now stand, companies can achieve a very high level of security by taking a few reasonable—and not prohibitively expensive—steps. There are two basic lines of attack to improving Web security: (1) securing the site itself and (2) securing the applications running on that site. Both are essential.[2-11]

1. *Securing the site.*   Install all operating system security patches recommended by the vendor, the Department of Energy's Computer Incident Advisory Capability (CIAC), and the Computer Emergency Responses Team (CERT). After that, it is a matter of keeping up with the latest security advisories and promptly installing patches as flaws turn up.

2. *Securing the application running on it.*   Install the Web server software with minimal system privileges. If full privileges are given, anyone who gets past the server and into its file directory has access to everything on the system, including additional applications, password files and other critical information.

There are several new technologies that can be used to improve user authentication. With these technologies, you do not need to send passwords across a network. The technologies include the following:

- *Message digest.*   A calculation performed on a message. The calculation is based on a secret key. Message digests are used in a login authentication scheme called the "Challenge Handshake."

- *Public-key encryption.*   A method of encryption for which the key used to encrypt a message is different from the key used to decrypt the message. The public key is made available to anyone who needs to communicate with you. They encrypt the message to be sent with that key, but only you can decrypt it. This is based on practical methods used to encrypt order entry forms and e-mail.

- *Use of a firewall.*   This offers the most common and effective approach by far. A firewall is an application software that sits on a computer between your LAN and the Internet. All Internet messages must pass through the firewall. To reach the server from the Internet, you must have a firewall account that defines your user ID, password, group ID, and system-administrator-given permissions. Permissions include any combination of reading, writing, or execution of files in the network.

Chapter 3 discussed the issue of a secure transport mechanism in terms of S-HTTP and SSL.

6.5   Management Issues Related to Web Server Setup

6.5.1   What is a Webmaster?

Just as *postmaster* is the name given for someone who manages the e-mail system on computers, *Webmaster* is the name given to the person or persons responsible for the administration of World Wide Web sites. The Webmaster's duties are typically to set up and maintain the local Web server and handle any type of support and questions regarding the site. A Webmaster might also install other Web-related programs, as well as clients, and usually coordinates site activity and performs quality-assurance checks on server information.[12]

The personnel required to set up and maintain a Web depends greatly on the organization and how much information is being served. For example, a small college may have one person doing all the administration and coordination, while a large company may divide tasks among a number of people, such as a systems administrator to handle network problems and program installation, an advertising group to handle HTML look and feel, an information resources group to gather and convert documents and a master Webmaster to coordinate it all.

A small company or organization can set up a good site with one part-time Webmaster. Average-size sites should have someone doing full-time work on the Web and related information resources. For large organizations, setting up a professional, well-maintained site may require a few people sharing duties and coordinating skills.

6.5.2 Getting the software

Server software is available for many operating systems, including the following: SunOS 4.1.x, Solaris, Iris 4.x, VMS, OSF/1, AIX 3.2, HP/UX 9.x, NextStep 3.0, Windows, and Macintosh OS (see Chap. 3). Two of the most popular server packages are NCSA's httpd and CERN's httpd.[31]

To set up and compile the server on whichever computer you may have, you should follow the directions on configuration and compilation that accompanies the software. In configuring the server, you will probably need to tell it the TCP *port* to listen to (the standard port for HTTP is 80), the location of the user's HTML files, access control options, and contact information for the person who maintains the system. On UNIX machines, server software is usually installed under the /usr/local/httpd or /usr/local/etc/httpd directory.[12]

Although it is possible to run servers under inetd (the port monitor that TCP/IP uses), many usually run in stand-alone mode. Although inetd may add more security in running a server, it can also add overhead and can be somewhat tiresome to configure. To run a server in stand-alone mode, simply execute the program with the proper command-line options.

Web servers depend on a minimum set of files in order to run. A typical server will have an external configuration file; a place to store external programs, often called *scripts,* which may execute during its operation; a place to log its activity; and a directory of HTML files to serve to users. A user would want to make sure that the server is able to read and write to these places as needed.

6.5.3 Server establishment

Much of setting up a Web server has little to do with the actual server itself. As was discussed in Chap. 3, document creation and organization play a key part in creating a good World Wide Web service. HTML files, related media (such as sound and image files), and files in other formats that will be distributed by the server are usually put in a single directory hierarchy. On UNIX machines, the root directory for such files is often /usr/local/www or /www below the system root directory or folder. A user will want to keep file names consistent and easy to type. Always use suffix conventions for files, such as .html for HTML files, .txt for text files, etc., and keep to names consisting of lowercase letters with periods as separators.[12,32]

In setting up a server, the root directory of the Web tree is usually specified in the configuration. A developer will have to tell the server what his or her home page is. As already discussed, a home page is the default HTML file that is displayed when a user connects to someone's site. This page may contain an overview of the site with a menu of options and links to other places. It is a good idea to name the home page something like foo.home.html.

It is important to take the time to make a good directory hierarchy. Often, root directories contain the home page, a page to point to when a document is "under construction," a page or directory containing the latest news and announcements, and subdirectories with other information. Splitting up files in a logical order will ease site maintenance.

The average amount of traffic the server gets will depend on the nature of the organization and who the audience will be. Keep in mind that the speed of the local network will affect the server's performance. There are a number of things every good Webmaster should do[12]:

- *Create a proper alias for the machine.* Web servers are typically named in the machine's name. For instance, if the machine is machine.foo.com, create an alias called www.foo.com that also points to that machine.

- *Ensure that the machine is properly networked.* Many problems can be caused by bad network connections or unstable hardware.

- *Analyze the logs every now and then.* By reading the logs of the server's activity, you can detect errors, bad links and files, and get a good idea of who is looking at your site. Many log analysis programs are available to analyze and graph Web server activity in a variety of ways.

- *Create proper mail aliases and support services.* Create a mail alias for "Webmaster" at the site as well as other services to ensure that users have someone to give feedback to if needed.[33]

6.5.4 Anticipating usage patterns

In order to determine the physical requirements of a Web site, the developer must anticipate how much use the site will experience. Usage affects the network connection and the software and hardware needs of the system. Different sites on the Web experience different loads. Some sites average hundreds of connections (*hits*) a day, while others average tens of thousands a day. There are ways to get a rough estimate for how popular a site will be. The first is to consider the size and composition of the target audience. Next, consider the uniqueness of the information to be posted. If this site is one of only a few that provide a certain type of information, then this site will be more valuable. If the site is one among many that offer the same information, it is necessary to create a unique slant or way to make this site stand out from the others. Also, consider the connection options and choose hardware and software that will best suit the needs of the developer.

6.5.5 Network connections: practical issues

As covered in Sec. 6.2, a Web site to be accessible to the public, the host computer must have an Internet connection in the form of either a direct connection or one made through an Internet gateway on a LAN. The first major consideration to take into account is continuous connectivity. Users of the Web must be able to reach a site 24-hours a day, regardless of their location. For this reason, users who access the Web from behind a firewall usually are unable to provide Web sites. A firewall is a device that separates a local network from the Internet for security purposes. The basic idea is to restrict all outgoing and incoming traffic through this one machine, which is good at looking for suspicious connections and stopping them from getting through to a system. Additionally, Web sites that use intermittent dial-up SLIP or PPP connections are only available sporadically.[34]

Another significant factor in the performance of a Web site is deciding what size of a network connection is necessary. A Web site can be run over a 9.6-Kbps connection, but the data transfers are very slow, and multiple connections can easily overload the link. The company may have to consider dedicated access. Sites that experience heavy traffic (e.g., to transmit image-intensive pages) often require fractional DS1 dedicated lines to the Internet.[35]

The communications bandwidth determines the amount of information that can flow through the network at any given time, so the size of the connection places a limit on the amount of data being transmitted from the server at one time. Sometimes, other factors besides the size of the connection determine whether the system can transmit the maximum amount of data. The amount of data that gets through in a specified amount of time is called *throughput*. A crucial problem of having a low-bandwidth network connection is the length of time it takes to deliver documents to clients. This is called *latency*. For example, a 56-Kbps line takes a minimum of 14.3 seconds to transfer a 100K file (100K = 800 Kbits = 56 Kbps).* On the other hand, it would take a minimum of half a second to send the same file across a 1.544-Mbps T1/DS1 line.[35]

Another crucial measure of a site's performance is determined by the network's message loss, which happens when one or more of the IP packets (the unit in which data is transmitted) does not arrive at its destination within the accepted amount of time and has to be resent. An average document takes several seconds to transfer over a 14.4-Kbps connection, about a second over a 56-Kbps line, and a fraction of a second over T1/DS1. These times increase as usage of the site goes up and users retrieve multiple documents simultaneously.

While faster is certainly better in terms of network connectivity, faster is also more expensive. People usually obtain an Internet connection from an Internet access provider. The bandwidth, cost, and terms vary widely among providers. Higher-bandwidth services are expensive. Regional DS1 lines typically are priced at $2000 to $5000 per month depending on mileage, plus a $3000 to $8000 installation charge (metropolitan-level lines cost around $500 to $1000 per month). A 56-Kbps connection is about $300 to $400 per month, plus a $500 start-up fee.† The average price for dial-up SLIP and PPP connections is only $35 to $40 per month, plus a $40 start-up charge—but these are not dedicated (continuous) connections.[36] Most major metropolitan areas are covered by local providers.

---

* On an asynchronous line, each 8-bit byte is transmitted with a Start and Stop bit; 100 KB equates to 1 Mbit of transmitted information; this results in a 17.8 second transfer time. On a synchronous line the time is about 14.3 seconds, without considering the data link layer overhead.

† As an example provided by the reviewer of this text: In the Long Island "metropolitan network area," April 1996 costs for T1 lines are $1000 per month, and 56-Kbps lines are advertised at between $100 and $200. The monthly price for Prodigy with annual subscription is under $15; Netcom charges $19.99 for up to 40 hours of time usage and 200

Besides considering the bandwidth and cost of a network connection, it is also necessary to examine network service providers' performance statistics. Whether T1/DS1 has the potential to carry 1.544 Mbps is meaningless if the network is being slowed down by large amounts of packet loss or long delivery times. The network service provider can easily become the bottleneck. When evaluating network providers, note the following criteria.[12]

Performance/reliability. One of the easiest ways to evaluate a network service provider is to ping several hosts on the network and evaluate the statistics that are returned. A ping generally returns four important numbers: the minimum, average, and maximum latencies, and the percentage of packets that were lost. Between 1 and 3 percent is an acceptable packet-loss range. Depending on how far away the remote host is, latency times should not be more than 100 to 200 milliseconds (ms). Quality network service providers should have latencies significantly lower than this. By checking these statistics at various points during the day and over the course of a few days, it is feasible to obtain a reasonable profile of the kind of service given by the provider.

Customer references. Talk to a few of the service provider's customers to check out the quality of service. Ask if they have had problems with network outages, how quickly the network service provider responded, how receptive the service provider is to customer questions and problems, and if they have noticed any lag time in their connections. A customer can give you a feel for how a provider has performed in the long term.

Available bandwidth. Ask network service providers *how they are connected to the rest of the Internet.* Most have substantially more bandwidth to the rest of the network than a single T1/DS1. If they have only one T1/DS1 line and they are trying to sell a T1/DS1, then that T1/DS1 will have to be shared with other customers. Sharing a T1/DS1 line should not be a problem with the major national network service providers, but it can be a very real problem with small Internet service providers that attempt to support as much over-

---

hours of non-prime-time usage. AT&T charges $19.99 for unlimited time usage. However, these are individual use rates and may or may not be identical to corporate rates. It should also be noted that providers may bundle their prices and charge a higher premium just because the line is used for Internet access. For example, whereas a simple 10-mile T1 line may cost $4000, a T1 line accessing the Internet may be priced at $1200. Naturally there are network management advantages in bundling the service.

booking as possible. A top-of-class backbone provider will have a network operating at DS3, OC-3, or OC-12. A high-end ISP will provide access at T1/DS1 and/or T3/DS3 rates.

Consider the possibility of future upgrades when obtaining network service for the first time. It usually does not cost much to upgrade from a fractional T1/DS1 to a greater fraction of a T1/DS1, but going from a 56-Kbps line to a fractional T1/DS1 costs a lot, because the installation fee needs to be paid again. You should get terms for upgrade options from the network service provider. Also, consider how quickly upgrades can be made. Some kinds of lines, fractional T1s/DS1s in particular, take one or two days to upgrade, but other upgrades involve installing new lines and can take weeks or months.

For intranets, many of the same considerations come into play, but these relate to the corporate enterprise network. Sufficient bandwidth must be available to transfer Web pages over the intranet network, particularly when a large number of users access the information at the same time. Both technology selection and network design/teletraffic considerations come into play.[37-39] New LAN technologies such as switched Ethernet/Token Ring systems, 100-Mbps and switched 100-Mbps Ethernets, and eventually ATM-based LANs may be required. Company internetting equipment (routers, bridges, gateways, etc.) may need to be upgraded for higher throughput. For telecommuters, dial-in-access networks (for example, based on ISDN or ADSL) may be required.

6.5.6 Server hardware selection

The chief hardware component of the Web site is the host computer, which houses the site's information content. The software program that runs on the host is called a Web server or HTTP server. An HTTP server interprets incoming requests and returns documents, objects, or other files. As covered earlier, server programs are available for most major operating systems, including UNIX, VMS, VM, Macintosh System 7, Windows (3.1, NT, and 95), and even LISP machines.

The question comes down to whether a PC, Macintosh, or UNIX-based system, is wanted.[40] The major considerations in choosing a Web host computer are platform stability, performance, and RAM. Platform stability is most important. If the operating system routinely crashes under nominal loads, the Web site often will be inaccessible. In general, UNIX computers have the most stable and robust operating systems, but they also cost more and have more advanced technical requirements. Macintosh and Windows machines are usually good for handling light loads, but they are not recommended for heavy loads. Load is a measure of how many users there are, as well as of how many processes the machine is trying to do at one time. To provide a fully functional Web server that can handle a reasonable load and provide all the features that users expect from a professional site, the only real option at this time is a UNIX-based machine.

A Web server should have a minimum of 8 MB of RAM; 16 MB is very good; 32 MB is even better. For a really intensive server, 64 MB of RAM is ideal.[41] This is because having the application and data in memory makes the server work that much more quickly than it would if there were a need to swap out to read from disk. *Swapping out* means copying data from memory into a space on disk. The server process should never have to swap out of memory, except perhaps during peak loads.

To support heavier loads, the host computer should be a dedicated World Wide Web machine, one that is used exclusively for the Web site. Under low loads, a host can be used for tasks in addition to its Web server duties. A low load is an average connection rate of about 750 connections per hour, with peak usage below 1500 connections per hour.[12]

Until very recently, selecting the platform for a Web server was not a significantly complex issue. The obvious choice was (and in many cases still is) a UNIX file server. UNIX is a mature multitasking operating system. In addition, UNIX provides a wide range of tools that can be used to assist in system administration. Servers are also available for the PC and Macintosh platform, but due to the inherent deficiencies in the operating system environments that are currently used on the platform, such servers are probably not recommended if you wish to run a large-scale, stable service.

However, in today's ever changing and advancing computing technology, there is a new contender to UNIX that successfully succeeded in penetrating this arena and has now taken the lead in the number of new installations of Web servers. It is Windows NT. Its robustness and simplicity over UNIX, together with a very low price, helped establish this operating system as a good choice in new Web server sites.[14-27]

Another main reason for the acceptance of Windows NT servers is the robustness of microcomputers nowadays. The following list supports the Windows NT choice:

- There are robust implementations of HTTP and other protocols available.

- The cost of a microcomputer capable of adequate performance as a server is well within the reach of many organizations and individuals.

- Today, new high-end machines such as Digital's Alpha and Intel's Pentium offer the performance and scalability formally found only on a UNIX platform.

- Support costs (e.g., people costs) for microcomputer servers are significantly lower than those found in the UNIX environment.

- More mature, robust, and stable implementations of TCP/IP are available on microcomputers.

There is a lot of server software available in the market today. From free software to commercially, powerful with strong security packages. Server software is available for many platforms, from UNIX (which dominated that market until very recently) to a PC with or without a Windows system. One good resource for available servers can be found in the World Wide Web FAQ written by Thomas Boutell:

http://sunsite.unc.edu/boutell/faq/wwwfaq.txt

The following is a short list of the names of some of the server software that is available today. New server software, with new capabilities (especially for secure commerce), is becoming available almost daily.[14-27]

UNIX servers
CERN httpd

NCSA httpd

EIT httpd

GN Gopher/http

Plexus perl server

WebWorks Enterprise server

Macintosh servers
MacHTTP

Novell NetWare servers
httpdnlm

Microsoft Windows and Windows NT servers
https

NCSA httpd for Windows

SerWeb

A complete list of available servers (httpd) may be found at

http://www.netgen.com/book/server-list.html

The widest variety of stable World Wide Web server programs are for UNIX platforms. The two most popular are from CERN and NCSA. The NCSA server is relatively small and fast. The CERN offers a wide array of features, including the ability to run as a proxy server (on a firewall host) with caching. Both servers support most UNIX platforms. Each includes features for server-side executable scripts, image maps, and some degree of access control.[12]

Both the CERN and NCSA servers are public domain software. Netscape provides another UNIX option with its Netsite Commerce and Netsite Communications servers. Netscape's servers are not in the public domain, so they are not free, but they provide features that the CERN and NCSA public domain servers do not.[42]

6.5.7   Server software installation

Once a hardware platform is selected, a *download* and the *configuration* of Web server software can begin. After obtaining the server software, decompress it with a decompression utility, review the documentation, and proceed with the installation. When the server software is installed, the configurations should be modified to include information such as the name of the server, server port, and the top-level directory or folder from which files are to be served.

6.5.8   Installing and configuring the CERN
HTTPD Web server

By now, it is obvious that there is a need for a server part and a client part in order to build a World Wide Web site. But there is also a need for some other software tools to assist in building, searching, maintaining, and adding contents to a Web site. The first issue to deal with is the server software. Since a Web browser (the client side) is very straightforward and is becoming more and more standard, the main consideration is to choose the right server platform and its software (i.e., the machine and its operating system, as well as the HTTP software).[14-27]

The best way to illustrate how to install and run a Web server is to follow a step-by-step explanation of such an installation. For illustrative purposes, a system based on the CERN server for a PC platform will be an excellent example of how easy it is to install a Web server. The following four steps will do that[14-27]:

1. The first step is to get the software for the PC environment. The file is called whtpl3pl.zip.

2. The next step is to create a directory called C:\HTTPD on the C: drive of the PC. Then, uncompress the file by giving the command PKZUNIP -D whtpl3pl.zip.

3. At this point, you can run Microsoft Windows and create a program icon using the New option on the File menu. The icon should point to the file C:\HTTPD\HTTPD.EXE.

4. The last step is to set the time zone in the AUTOEXEC.BAT file so that TZ=GMT and to run the server program.

This concludes the installation of the server. Now it is time to connect to the server with a client software. For that purpose, you run a World Wide Web browser, and then enter the URL containing the IP address of the server PC. For example, if the server PC has an IP address of 192.11.1.1 you will enter http://192.11.1.1/ at the Web browser.

6.5.9   Setting up the NCSA HTTPD

The discussion in this section is based on a UNIX implementation using NCSA httpd. The NCSA Web server was designed to be simple and fast, but at the expense of additional functionality.

6.5.9.1   Downloading the NCSA software.

The first step is to decide which directory you desired to be the root directory for the server. If it does not yet exist, create it. Then move to it. For this sample implementation, /usr/local is the root directory. Next, there is a need to transfer the software to the machine using anonymous FTP. Finally, change directories to NCSA's current directory, use the ls command to list the files, and prepare for a binary transfer using the bin command.

Once in this directory, download the correct file for the machine. Table 6.3 shows the appropriate file for the operating system being used. If the machine type that interests you is not listed, download the source file httpd_source.tar.Z and read the instructions on compiling it into a binary (a binary is an executable file).[43]

For this example, assume that a Sun machine is being used. Use the get command to download the file to the system and then quit, as follows:

```
ftp> get httpd_sun4.tar.Z
200 PORT command successful.
```

TABLE 6.3   NCSA Files for Various Operating Systems

File	Operating system
httpd_decaxp.tar.Z	Digital Equipment Corp. OSF/1.13
httpd_decmips.tar.Z	Digital Equipment Corp. Ultrix 4.2 Rev. 96
httpd_hp.tar.Z	Hewlett-Packard HP-UX 9.01
httpd_rs6000.tar.Z	IBM AIX 3.2.4
httpd_sgi.tar.Z	Silicon Graphics IRX 4.0.5c
httpd_sun.tar.Z	Sun Microsystems SunOS 4.1.3

```
150 Opening BINARY mode data connection for httpd_sun4.tar.Z
(211981 bytes).
226 Transfer complete.
211981 bytes received in 6.9 secs (33 Kbytes/sec)
ftp> quit
221 Goodbye
```

Once the file has been downloaded, uncompress it and use the tar command to unarchive the file so that you can edit the configuration files:

```
> uncompress httpd_sun4.tar.Z
>tar -xvf http_sun4.tar
```

6.5.9.2   Editing the configuration files.   In the process of unarchiving the files, the tar command also created the httpd_1.3/conf subdirectory. Move to that subdirectory using the cd command, and use the ls command to list the files located there. httpd.conf-dist and srm.conf-dist are the two files that have to be modified. Httpd.conf-dist is the main configuration file for the server and srm.conf-dist maps user requests to files on the server. Access.conf-dist is the configuration file that handles access control, and mime.types maps file extensions to content types. These last two files do not need modification. Make copies (using the cp command) of the distribution files for use with the server (distribution file names end in dist):

```
> cd httpd-1.3/conf
>ls
acces.conf-dist httpd.conf-dist mimie.types srm.conf-dist
> cp access.conf-dist access.conf
> cp httpd.conf-dist httpd.conf
> cp srm.conf-dist srm.conf
```

After the httpd.conf file is downloaded and modified, changes must be made to several settings:

ServerType. The ServerType option determines whether the server is a stand-alone mode or through the Inetd system process. Inetd is a standard UNIX process that acts as a superdaemon: it listens for requests for many Internet services and then launches the correct daemon. Inetd is commonly used to handle other servers, such as the FTP and finger daemon. However, for Web server services, it really does not make sense to run a server under inetd. Therefore, the setup is as follows:

```
Server standalone
```

Port. The server uses a specific port to listen for clients, and this line specifies that line number. The standard port for http connections is port 80.

```
Port 80
```

Username, Group. These two options are used to set the server's user and group identification. If the developer has root access to the machine on which the Web will be run, the defaults will remain as follows:

```
User nobody
Group #-1
```

If you do not have root access, set the User option to your own username. For example,

```
User minolid
Group #-1
```

ServerAdmin. The ServerAdmin setting specifies the address that is sent when the NCSA httpd reports errors to users of the system. It should be sent to the e-mail address of your Web server administrator:

```
ServerAdmin webmaster@your.site.com
```

ServerRoot. The ServerRoot option describes the root directory of the server, the root directory in which the configuration files and access logs are stored. Remember that this setting will depend on the root directory and server version being used. With the server in/usr/local, this setting should be as follows:

```
ServerRoot /usr/local/httpd_1.3
```

If these are not set properly, the server will not run. There are other settings that may need modification, but those are optional (the default values are acceptable unless you are trying to do something sophisticated). These options include the following:

- TimeOut (does not appear in default server configuration file)
- EfforLog
- TransferLog
- PidFile
- ServerName
- AccessConfig, ResourceConfig, and TypesConfig (does not appear in default server configuration file)
- IdentityCheck (does not appear in default server configuration file)[44]

6.5.9.3   Running NCSA HTTPD.   After all configuration files have been taken care of, the httpd server can start running. If running in stand-alone mode, the binary must be executed. Some systems do not automatically look into the current directory, so it is always safest to provide a full path to the current directory:

```
> /usr/local/httpd-1.3/httpd
```

After running the server, kill it by typing the following command in the server's root directory:

```
>kill 'cat logs/httpd.pid'
```

6.5.10   Information architecture and content

Information refers to the actual content, how the data is represented, and how those representations are organized. Because of the interactive nature of the WWW, a site's information architecture has much to do with its quality. In general, navigational pages should be made as brief as possible. Ideally, they should present all relevant information on one screen. A site's overall structure should be logical. The interface should be intuitive to make navigation easier for the user. To make site navigation simple, include a site "map" and search functions. A site's content will be better received if it is formatted nicely and properly organized.

As covered in other chapters, HTML is a relatively simple language, and a number of programs are available to assist in HTML generation and documentation conversion. As a general rule, document-conversion tools do a poor job; often the output ends up looking quite different from what is intended. Be sure to check the output of the converters used and clean up documents before making them available.[12] Editors were described earlier. A list of HTML editors can be found at

http://www.netgen.com/book/html_editors_list.html

Establishing the content of the site is very important. Content is what attracts people to a site and keeps them there. There are factors to consider when establishing a Web site's content. There is a literal web of documents and other objects that are interconnected and accessible by way of hyperlinks. Providing content for a Web site means completing two related tasks: (1) converting content into HTML documents and objects and (2) linking those documents and objects into coherent WWW structure.[12] Another application is on-line catalogs via database connections. Refer to Section 6.7.3 for a discussion of server-based application software.

The on-screen presentation of Web documents is controlled by the quality of the document's HTML and the manner in which browsers display the HTML to users. Compatibility between software systems is also an issue. What is intended by the developer is not always interpreted the way it is intended by the users' browser software, because browsers on different platforms interpret HTML differently. For example, a Web page that appears one way on the NCSA Mosaic browser for UNIX X-Window platforms might appear another way on the MacWeb browser. Therefore, if a page's HTML is correct with respect to the specification, the page should appear uniformly over a wide range of browsers.

6.5.11   Server configuration files

Installation is only the first stage of building a Web site. It provides the platform for the server and the connectivity to the server. But World Wide Web server software will normally have a configuration file that is used to do the following[14-27]:

- Specify an area on the server machine from which files can be retrieved.

- Restrict access to certain files.

- Specify caching, which enables remote files to be stored on the local server for a period of time.

- Act as a proxy gateway, which provides a means for unauthorized machines to access resources on Web.

As the Web develops, additional features will be provided in the server software, and the configuration files are likely to grow in complexity.

Figure 6.6 shows a simple configuration file for the CERN httpd server. Line 2 specifies that files located under the directory /apps/ WWW should be available to the WWW server software. Line 1 specifies that file /apps/WWW/homepage.html is the default file to be displayed when the WWW server is accessed. Usually, a configuration file will include additional setup information, some of which is described in the following list.[14–27]

- Provides a mechanism for ensuring that the proxy gateway cannot be accessed from outside the local domain. Without these options it would be possible for a browser on an external system to use the proxy gateway to gain access to files that are restricted to local use.

- Passes requests for the httpd, Gopher, WAIS, and FTP protocols.

- Specifies the location for CGI files (discussed later).

- Specifies the area of the file store that can be accessed by the server.

- Describes the location and format of the server log file.

- Specifies that server caching is to be available, and gives the location of the cache and the cache log files, together with the size (in MB) of the cache.

- Specifies the purging frequency for files in the cache.

Another aspect of a Web server is a Log file. The Log file intends to provide information about all the files that are being accessed with the date and time. The log file can also provide information on the files that used the caching system, allowing for a better tune-up of the caching system.

6.5.12 Caching

Many clients provide client-side caching. This means that if you retrieve a file and then retrieve another file, when you return to the

```
map / file:/apps/WWW/homepage.html
map /* file:/apps/WWW/*
pass file:/apps/WWW/*
fail *
```

Figure 6.6   A simple httpd.conf configuration file.

initial file it will be retrieved from the client's cache, thus saving a subsequent network transfer. A number of servers also support caching by the server.[14-27] Caching can improve the performance of a Web service by ensuring that frequently requested files will tend to be stored in the local cache. In order for a client to make use of a cache on a server, the client's configuration file must be suitably configured. When considering the caching strategies, there is also a way of using national caching service. An institution will need to decide whether to use a caching service and, if so, whether to have caching services running on a number of departmental systems. In the future it may be possible to chain caches. The possibility in the long term of having institutional, metropolitan, national, and continental caches should be considered.

Another approach is to mirror sites. Many organizations that are visited by international Internet users have files that are often downloaded. To reduce the overseas telecommunications transmission burden, mirror sites are set up in two or three continents. This is also being used on an East Coast–West Coast basis, within the United States.

6.5.13 Firewalls

In many organizations, access to the Internet is restricted to authorized computers for the security reasons described earlier. Depending on the institution's local policy, authorization may be restricted to computers located in offices in which there is an individual who is responsible for use of the machine. Such a policy may be enforced in order to provide some means of security against hacking remote services.[14-27] The httpd server also handles a number of security issues, as discussed earlier in this chapter. It is common practice to restrict access to a certain area of the file store. For example if the server configuration files contain the lines shown in Fig. 6.7, then clients will only be able to access files held under the directory /apps/WWW/.

Additional levels of security can also be specified[14-27]:

- Restricting access to specified computer systems
- Restricting access by username and password

```
map /* file:/apps/WWW/*
pass file:/apps/WWW/*
fail *
```

Figure 6.7   Server configuration file.

The method of implementing such security tends to be server-dependent. One approach that addresses the security issue, especially considering the rise of commerce on the net, is the use of a firewall. A firewall is a system that enforces an access control policy between two networks. The actual means by which this is accomplished varies widely, but in principle the firewall can be thought of as a pair of mechanisms: one that exists to block traffic, and another that exists to permit traffic. A system administrator must have an idea of what needs to be blocked and what should be permitted access (i.e., to have a policy). A firewall can protect a company's private network from the Internet while allowing employees to access the Internet from within the company safely.[14-27] The intranet resides inside the firewall.

6.5.14   Proxy gateways

In practice there is a technique known as *proxy gateways* that can be used to provide access to services off-site without compromising local security. With a proxy gateway, a trusted system (typically UNIX or NT systems that are more secure from hacking than PCs) will have Internet access. Machines in open access clusters can point to the proxy gateway, which will then retrieve information from off-site services. Many providers of Web servers (HTTP software) are including a proxy gateway built into their product, some of which can work on the same machine as the HTTP software, saving the need for another machine.[14-27]

6.5.15   Server strategies

An institution needs to decide on its server strategies. For example, should it support a central server or number of departmental servers? If the second option is chosen, then issues such as how to achieve indexing across servers and which caching strategy to adopt are very important. What skills levels are needed by the server administrator? Any organization needs to recognize that adopting a server strategy is more than simply installing the server software.[14-27]

6.5.16   Maintenance and housekeeping utilities

There are many utilities that enhance and ease the use and maintenance of a Web server. A number of useful utility programs have been developed that will assist systems managers and information providers. For example,[14-27]

w3new is a program that will extract a list of URLs from the Mosaic client hot-list file or extract URLs from an HTML document. It will then retrieve the modification dates for each document listed and output an HTML file with the URLs sorted by their last modification date.

wusage is a Web server usage meter that produces weekly activity reports in HTML. In addition, it provides graphical displays of server usage.

weblint is a UNIX utility for checking the syntax of HTML documents. The checks include illegally nested, overlapped, unclosed, and obsolete tags.

Verify_links is a robot that performs link verification.

MOMspider (Multi-Owner Maintenance spider) is a tool that can be used to help information providers and system managers maintain links to documents.

Hypermail is a program that converts a file of e-mail messages to a hypertext.

6.6 Novell's WWW Service Alternative

Novell facilitates turning a NetWare server into an Internet publishing server for publishing information on the company's network and on the Internet. NetWare Web Server software lets the organization publish documents on internal corporate networks and on the World Wide Web, enabling your company to establish an Internet presence easily and cost-effectively. Implemented as a set of NetWare Loadable Modules (NLMs), NetWare Web Server converts your NetWare 4.1 server into a platform for publishing HTML pages. It leverages existing systems to integrate your NetWare network with the Internet, giving your business a powerful new way to communicate.[2-11]

With a simple installation, NetWare Web Server gives a company a Web publishing solution. It runs on your existing NetWare 4.1 servers, so you get all the capabilities you need to create, publish, and browse Web documents with a minimal investment.

Because this solution is based on NetWare 4.1, the user does not have to learn or invest in any UNIX-based operating systems and tools to participate in the world of the Internet. Simply use WordPerfect 6.1 Internet Publisher to create Web documents from your WordPerfect word processing software. The documents are automatically converted to HTML, eliminating the need to learn the HTML authoring language. Documents can also be embedded with links to other documents with related information. You then "publish" the documents by copying them to the Web server, limiting access to certain users if desired.

WordPerfect Internet Publisher also includes a copy of Netscape Navigator, so users can easily browse any Web document. This solution allows companies to publish Web documents whether the NetWare network is connected to the Internet or not. The organization may choose to start by publishing documents for internal company use only, then publish documents for Internet users later on when the company acquires an Internet connection.

NetWare Web Server supports all the common features of the World Wide Web. It includes support for forms, the Remote Common Gateway Interface (R-CGI), access controls, and logging, as well as BASIC and PERL* script interpreters.

6.7 Extensions and Applications on the Web

There are many ways to extend the functionality and services offered by your Web server. New standards and languages now allow a full range of applications, including forms with tables and different types of files (other than HTML).

6.7.1 External viewers and other file types

As explained, access to the Web can be achieved by using a client such as NCSA Mosaic to display HTML documents and inline images in GIF format. However, the World Wide Web is an extensible system: clients can access information that is in formats other than HTML. When a client receives a file from a server, it checks on the file type. If the file type indicates that it is an HTML document, the file will be displayed by the browser. Otherwise, the browser's configuration file can specify an external viewer that can be used to display the file. The following is a list of widely used external viewers:

---

* Quoted from Ref. 45 with some amendations:

Perl, created, written, developed, and maintained by Larry Wall (lwall@netlabs.com), is a language for processing text. Sounds pretty harmless, doesn't it? Perhaps at one time it was pretty harmless, but in its present state, with its sophisticated pattern matching capabilities, straightforward I/O, and flexible syntax, Perl is anything but harmless. In fact, by borrowing heavily from C, sed, awk, and the Unix shells, Perl has become the language of choice for many I/O, file processing, and management, process management, and system administration tasks. "Perl" is an acronym for "Practical Extraction and Report Language." Information on the subject abounds online. The kind folk at comp.lang.perl.misc, for instance, are always happy to share advice and anecdotes. But please read the FAQ so that you do not trouble them with questions whose answers you should already know (the list is available both as vanilla ASCII and as hypertext). And for those of you who prefer to figure things out on your own, the perl4 page comes in a handy hypertext form (courtesy of rgs@cs.cmu.edu). It is also a great place to get the latest version of Perl, browse the Perl newsgroup archives, and find a whole bunch of Perl-related stuff.

File format   *Viewer*

JPEG   LVIEW (MS Windows) xv (X Windows)

Postscript   Ghostview

DVI   xdvi (X Windows)

MPEG   mpeg_play (X Windows and MS Windows)

The association between the file type and the viewer is given in the browser's configuration file. New browsers that include the newest e-mail standards built into the software can easily allow many new types of files due to the MIME capability. MIME was designed to service many of the variations of SMTP, UUCP, and other mail protocols such as BITNET. It is capable of a full multimedia mail, and at the same time it allows you to view many different types of files.

6.7.2 Running client applications

If a Postscript file is retrieved from a Web server, the browser program normally responds, "I don't know what to do with a Postscript file—but I know a program that does. I'll pass the Postscript file onto the Ghostview program." If, for example, an Excel spreadsheet is retrieved from a Web server, the client could be configured to respond, "I don't know what to do with an Excel spreadsheet file—but I know a program that does. I'll pass the spreadsheet file onto the Excel program." This technique extends the functionality of the World Wide Web from acting as a distributed file viewer to acting as a distributed program manager.

6.7.3 Common Gateway Interface (CGI) programs

To accomplish what has been described requires another system: Common Gateway Interface (or simply CGI). This script language allows an administrator to create a sophisticated procedure that can automate many tasks for the end users. This kind of a procedure is also known as a CGI program. CGI is a standard that has been adopted by a number of server developers (primarily developers of the CERN and NCSA server software) for running programs on the server machine. CGI programs are executed in real time, so they can output dynamic information. There are many ways to use CGI to connect the Web server to a database. Almost all relational-database vendors are offered ways to connect their databases to the Web, very often with CGI extensions. A definition of CGI is available at the following URL[14-27]:

http://hoohoo.ncsa.uiuc.edu/cgi/examples.html

Microsoft has become very aggressive regarding the Internet market and is coming out with a number of Internet servers. For example, Gibraltar is a World Wide Web server that has a new application programming interface (API) called ISAPI (Internet Services API), which replaces CGI completely and allows an easy connection to many other Microsoft programming tools and databases.

6.7.4 Forms

Forms, mentioned earlier, are often used to collect from a user the information that is used as input to a CGI program. Creating a form involves areas of the screen in which the user can input data. The data is sent to the HTTP server, which can run a script or program to process the data in some way. One common use of forms is to provide feedback on a Web service. Input to the form can be e-mailed to the service administrator. Forms can also be used to input search criteria to be input to a search engine or to specify parameters for distributed teaching and teaming services.

A form is defined by the <FORM . . . > and </FORM> HTML tags. The <FORM> tag has the following syntax:

```
<FORM METHOD="method" ACTION="url">
```

For example,

```
<FORM METHOD="post" ACTION="http://www.tech.il/cgi/mysrpt">
```

will send the input data to be processed by mysrpt. Once the form is submitted, the data that has been entered is appended to the end of the URL given in the ACTION attribute of the FORM tag. This information is then processed by the script.

6.7.5 Searching and indexing

The growth in the numbers and extent of information services on the Web has made "blind" surfing an ineffective way of finding useful information. Fortunately, sophisticated indexing tools are being developed. The following list represents some of the known searching tools.

Alta Vista	http://altavista.digital.com/
Yahoo	http://akebono.stanford.edu/yahoo/
Globewide Network Academy	http://uu-gna.mit.edu:8001/cgi-bin/meta/
EINet's Galaxy	http://galaxy.einet.net/

Aliweb	http://web.nexor.co.uk/public/aliweb/ aliweb.html
Lycos	http://fuzine.mt.cs.colorado.edu/mlm/ lycos-all.html
WebCrawler	http://webcrawler.com/

As this list implies, a number of software developers produced software that automated this process, so that a program went from server to server indexing information, such as contents of the <TITLE> tag or the contents of server home pages. Such programs became known as *robots*, or *spiders*. One robot was called WWWW, the World Wide Web Worm. There are a number of problems with this approach to global indexing:

- *Server performance.* When a robot arrives at your server it can place a significant load on the server.

- *Network performance.* Robots can place heavy loads on the network infrastructure.

- *Volume.* Quality robots index all files. They are unable to differentiate between valuable information resources (such as a collection of research reports) and low-quality, transient information (such as an undergraduate's personal interests).

- *Maintenance.* The robot will not know if an information source that has been indexed is withdrawn from service.

The following is a list of some of the robots that are available[14-27]:

- With Aliweb (Archie-Like Indexing in the Web), each site is responsible for indexing files. The server administrator is responsible for choosing the files to be indexed. Archie-Like Indexing in the Web, which was presented at the WWW 94 in CERN is available at http://web.nexor.co.uk/mak/doc/aliweb-paper/paper.html.

- SWISH (Simple Web Indexing System for Humans) was announced on November 16, 1994. It is a program that allows you to index your Web site and search for files using keywords in a fast and easy manner.

- WAIS is another mechanism for indexing resources. The following command demonstrates its use:

```
waisserver -p 210 -d /apps/info/WWW/WAIS
```

This command is used to start the WAIS server software. The -p 210 argument specifies the name of the port on which the server runs, while the -d argument gives the name of the directory that will contain WAIS databases. The WAIS database can be accessed by a dedicated WAIS client or by a WWW browser that contains support for the WAIS protocol. A number of utilities are available which can postprocess the output from WAIS. wais.pl is a CGI script that is distributed with the NCSA httpd server. Son of wais.pl is a CGI script that is based on the wais.pl script. SFGate is a CGI script that interfaces to WAIS servers. SFGate provides a forms interface that can be used to access a number of WAIS databases.

6.8 Legal and Ethical Issues

There are many legal issues to consider, and even more ethical issues in regard to information that is placed and/or is accessible via an Internet connection: Is the Web service legal? Who is legally responsible for the contents of a Web service? Is nudity pornography? Is pornography acceptable on a Web service? If not, who defines pornography versus art? The following are some points to consider regarding those issues. Some of these can be answered by thinking of the Web as a newspaper (an electronic one), and then asking the question in that context.

Liability. It could be argued that the contents of a Web service are the responsibility of the organization that runs the service. If so, a university may be held legally responsible for an undergraduate student who publishes libelous information under its auspices.

Pornography. Are nude pictures acceptable on the Web? The answer is probably yes from a freedom-of-speech perspective, as long as it is not *legally* pornographic. A lot of emotion goes into this issue. (What is the definition of pornographic material?) In the end, it is a matter for the courts to decide what is *legally* pornographic or obscene, based not on people's differing opinions of these concepts but on operative legislation. Nudity as found in magazines purchasable at the newsstand and in R- and NC/X-rated movies is by definition *not legally pornographic;* otherwise it would not be purchasable at legitimate places of business. Naturally, this material cannot be legally purchased by underage people. There is material in circulation that could be legally qualified as pornographic (e.g., sexually explicit material of underage people). Such material should be prohibited on the Web. A complicating factor, however, is that the Web is a global network; hence, what may be considered pornographic in one nation may or may not be considered so in another. Based on published reports, there is material on the Web that is legally (in the United States) pornographic and/or in poor taste.

Copyright issues. In general, copyrighted material requires permission from the owner of the intellectual property before any use of it is made. A Web manager may have the responsibility to ensure that copyrighted material is not used unless the copyright holder has granted permission. This may affect research papers that have been submitted for publication. It may also affect the use of photographs, drawings, and maps that are copyrighted.

Data protection. Information about individuals that is available on the Web may have to be registered with the Data Protection Officer. The information provider may have to abide by regulations to ensure the accuracy of the information.

Equality of access to information. The Web can provide global access to a wide range of information services. However, including large logos and graphical icons on pages can act as a barrier to accessing the information, especially for readers in developing countries with limited network access. In some developing countries, access may be provided over local telephone lines. A health worker in a hospital in Africa who wishes to retrieve information about public health services may have to pay the additional costs of retrieving unnecessary graphics. If the local telephone company is owned by a multinational telephone corporation, then accessing the information will result in a transfer of money from the developing country to that of the multinational corporation.

6.9   Final Observations

Building a Web site requires understanding the Internet and the Web—their operations, functions, and usage. It also requires knowledge of HTML and the tools to build and support the Web site. The following list summarizes the steps needed to build a Web site once those preliminary tasks have been achieved.[14–27]

Site concept planning. To ensure that the Web site supports the overall marketing objectives and effectively communicates the message of the organization, careful planning is a must. Issues such as single server or multiple servers will affect the site planning.

Selecting, installing, and setting up the server. Server software selection is based on the planning of the site, according to the organization's goals for the site. Installation is typically straightforward, but configuration and setting up require more in-depth planning to maximize the objectives of the Web site.

HTML page creation. The opening of an HTML document is the gateway to the organization. The amount of information and graphics elements should be given consideration according to the user's characteristics.

The home page should be edited and refined to maximize the communications impact—not merely recycled with hypertext links.

Customizing the Web site. Create forms to enable interactivity with users, thus providing them a means to request more information, purchase products or services, or offer general information. Add clickable image maps of the organization to enhance and increase the effectiveness of the Web site and the organization's image.

Site promotion. Let the organization's target audiences in the Internet community know about the site.

Additional services. When the Web site is active, it is time to look for other services, such as a search engine for the site to assist users in finding the information they want and an e-mail list to establish two-way communications that will enhance the relationship with the audiences.

Ongoing maintenance. Keeping the Web site dynamic is important. The home page should be constantly updated and enhanced to reflect the organization's growth and objectives. Update existing pages to remain current with organization changes, objectives, and activities. Also, you should find new and better ways to promote the Web site to current and new users in order to expand the visitors' base.

References

1. Hughes, Kevin, "Everything You Need to Know to Build Your Own Web Server," *Open Systems Today,* June 6, 1994, p. 56.
2. Muhammad, S. Y., "Building a Web Site, from Servers to Application Software," class project, Stevens Institute of Technology, fall 1995.
3. Cronin, M. J., *Doing Business on the Internet, How the Electronic Highway Is Transforming American Companies,* Van Nostrand Reinhold, New York, 1993.
4. Eckel, G., and C. Hare, *Building a Linux Internet Server,* New Riders Publishing, an imprint of Macmillan Computer Publishing and Simon & Schuster, publishing arm of Viacom, New York, 1995.
5. Feit, S., *Accessing the Internet,* DATA-TECH Institute, 1994.
6. Hahn, H., and R. Stout, *The Internet Yellow Pages,* 2d ed., Osborn, McGraw-Hill, New York, 1995.
7. Stallings, W., "Working with the Net," *Webmaster,* November/December 1995, pp. 22–26.
8. Cortese, A., "The Software Revolution," *Business Week,* December 5, 1995, pp. 78–90.
9. Egan, R., "Going Online," *PCTODAY,* November 1995, pp. 104–107.
10. Koch, C., "Electronic Commerce—Mutable Markets," *CIO,* December 1, 1995, pp. 68–76.
11. The Cobb Group, "HotDog! An Excellent Windows Program for Creating Web Pages," *Inside the Internet,* October 1995.
12. Holicki, D. J., "Building a Web Site," class project, Stevens Institute of Technology, fall 1995.
13. Hughes, Kevin, "Everything You Need to Know to Build Your Own Web Server," *Open Systems Today,* June 6, 1994, p. 57.
14. Carmel, A., "Building a Web," class project, Stevens Institute of Technology, fall 1995.

15. Boutell, Thomas, "World Wide Web FAQ," *World Wide Web* at http://sunsite.unc.edu/boutell/faq/wwwfaq.txt, 1995.
16. Collins, E. Stephen, "Internet Server Kitchen," *World Wide Web,* The University of Minnesota.
17. Colomb, Chris, and Paul Jones, "How to Be a Server Daemon," *World Wide Web* at http://sunsite.unc.edu/chris/daemons/.
18. CyberGroup Inc., "Building Internet Servers," *World Wide Web* at http://www.charm.net/~cyber/, October 1995.
19. Graham, Ian, and Michael Lee, "Browsers, Viewers, and HTML Preparation Resources," *World Wide Web,* August 1995.
20. Hughes, Kevin, "Entering the World Wide Web," Enterprise Integration Technologies, May 1994.
21. IETF, "IETF Home Page" *World Wide Web* at: http://ietf.cnri.va.us/ and ftp://ds.interic.net/ietf/1ietf-description.txt.
22. Kriz, M. Harry, "TCP/IP Technical Details," *World Wide Web* at: http://learning.lib.vt.edu/wintcpip/technical.html, September, 1995.
23. Management Technology Association, "Internet: The Basics," *World Wide Web,* Management Technology Association, July 1995.
24. Stein, D. Lincoln, "How to Set Up and Maintain a World Wide Web Site," Addison-Wesley Publishing Company, April 1995.
25. The Internet Society, "NSF Press Release," *World Wide Web* at http://www.isoc.org/adopsec/nsf-naine-fees.html.
26. The Internet Society, *World Wide Web* at http://www.isoc.org/standards.
27. "The World Wide Web Consortium (W3C) Overview," *World Wide Web* at http://www.w3.org/pub/WWW/Consortium.
28. Graham, Ian, *HTML Sourcebook,* John Wiley & Sons, New York, 1995, p. 31.
29. Net.Genesis, Devra Hall, *Building a Web Site,* Prima Publishing, Rocklin, Calif., 1995, p. 117.
30. Net.Genesis, Devra Hall, *Building a Web Site,* Prima Publishing, Rocklin, Calif., 1995, p. 110.
31. Hughes, Kevin, "Everything You Need to Know to Build Your Own Web Server," *Open Systems Today,* June 6, 1994, p. 57.
32. Hughes, Kevin, "Everything You Need to Know to Build Your Own Web Server," *Open Systems Today,* June 6, 1994, p. 58.
33. Hughes, Kevin, "Everything You Need to Know to Build Your Own Web Server," *Open Systems Today,* June 6, 1994, p. 59.
34. Net.Genesis, Devra Hall, *Building a Web Site,* Prima Publishing, Rocklin, Calif., 1995, p. 65.
35. Net.Genesis, Devra Hall, *Building a Web Site,* Prima Publishing, Rocklin, Calif., 1995, p. 66.
36. Net.Genesis, Devra Hall, *Building a Web Site,* Prima Publishing, Rocklin, Calif., 1995, p. 68.
37. Minoli, D., *First, Second, and Next-Generation LANs,* McGraw-Hill, New York, 1994.
38. Minoli, D., and A. Alles, *Understanding LAN Emulation and Other Related Technologies,* Artech House, 1996.
39. Minoli, D., *Broadband Network Design and Analysis,* Artech House, Norwood, Mass, 1993.
40. Net.Genesis, Devra Hall, *Building a Web Site,* Prima Publishing, Rocklin, Calif., 1995, p. 73.
41. Cady, Glee Harrah, and Pat McGregor, *Mastering the Internet,* Sybex, Calif., 1995, p. 304.
42. Net.Genesis, Devra Hall, *Building a Web Site,* Prima Publishing, Rocklin, Calif., 1995, p. 78.
43. Net.Genesis, Devra Hall, *Building a Web Site,* Prima Publishing, Rocklin, Calif., 1995, p. 84.
44. Net.Genesis, Devra Hall, *Building a Web Site,* Prima Publishing, Rocklin, Calif., 1995, p. 88.
45. The University of Florida Perl Archive.

On-Line Services: Technology, Applications, and Vendors

7.1 Overview

The on-line industry is now taking a giant leap forward in order to remain viable. The Internet has had profound impact on on-line services. The Internet, especially the World Wide Web, has transformed the industry and awakened it to the future possibilities of information, entertainment, and communications technologies. Proprietary networks have had to reinvent themselves and learn to live with, if not embrace, the Internet's World Wide Web. All on-line markets have benefited from increases in personal computer performance and declining prices for memory, processors, and peripherals. Both the consumer and business segments of the market were "drawn" by the Internet and quickly forced to devise new ways of doing business.[1-5] The on-line services industry has had to adjust to the exploding interest in the Internet. This chapter provides some information about commercial on-line services to give a perspective vis-à-vis direct Internet service that an organization may contemplate. This information is presented only to provide a snapshot of the field as of press time, particularly in reference to the *kinds* of services that are available. No recommendation of any kind is implied herewith. You should refer directly to the vendor for more time-dependent information.

7.2 Definition of On-Line Services

On-line services provide access to information, entertainment, communications, and/or transaction services via telecommunications. The telephone network is the typical distribution system for on-line services. Cable TV networks, satellite, wireless networks, and the unused portion of FM radio or television signals may also be used. A PC and modem are the most common devices used for accessing on-line services. However, on-line services can also be accessed via dumb terminals, screen phones, video-game machines, and handheld wireless devices. Television cable "boxes" may also be used to interact with on-line services, although this technology is mostly in test mode.

Companies that operate on-line services are called on-line service vendors. They are also sometimes called *system operators* or *hosts.* Content providers offer the services that are available through on-line service vendors. Content providers are segmented into two groups: (1) companies that create information, called database producers, information providers, information service providers, or publishers; and (2) marketers that provide advertisements, transaction services, promotional services, or product information services.[1-5]

Many companies are both on-line service vendors and content providers; that is, they supply the host computer system and some of the information that is distributed through the system.

One key distinction between on-line services and the Internet is that on-line services companies either provide content or have a close association with a content provider, while the Internet relies on distributed, usually nonaffiliated content providers, including individual corporate entities.

7.3   History of On-Line Services

On-line services have their roots in computer time-sharing. From the mid-1960s to the late 1970s, computers were so expensive that the only economical way to use them was to conduct all processing at a central site. Users in remote locations, using terminals with no computer power of their own, were connected to a central computer via telephone lines. Independent computer time-sharing companies were created to serve firms that did not buy in-house systems.

This infrastructure was the foundation of the on-line industry. Publishers realized that loading information onto time-sharing services provided them with instant potential users. Early on-line services, such as LEXIS, were based on the time-sharing model. The proliferation of personal computers in the 1980s provided another base of potential users for collection of information. Consumer on-line pioneers such as CompuServe began allowing personal computer owners with modems to access on-line services.[1-5]

7.4   The On-Line Services Market: Trends

Growth of the Internet's World Wide Web affected both the consumer and business on-line services. However, the most immediate action was taken by consumer services providers to protect themselves against this new competitive force. The consumer services feared that masses of on-line users would secure Internet connections via local access providers, bypassing their services altogether. Therefore, the on-line services quickly made moves to position themselves in all facets of on-line/Internet publishing. This led to these companies integrating the Web into their commercial on-line services. Via acquisition, partnerships, and business development, the leading on-line services—America Online, Prodigy, and CompuServe—now provide full Internet access to their subscribers and Web site development services to content providers.

The World Wide Web, the most commercial part of the Internet, which is searchable by hyperlinks and which supports multimedia, has become an attractive publishing platform for both content providers and marketers alike.[1-5] SIMBA estimates that the number of households with direct Internet access was 250,000 in 1994, 600,000 in 1995, and 1.3 million in 1996. The majority of consumers who use the Web will access the Internet from commercial on-line services, including the Microsoft Network and America Online, over the next few years.[6]

7.5   On-Line Services Industry Makeup

The on-line service industry is estimated at $12.5 billion in the United States, consisting of consumer and commercial segments. The consumer segment is in its infancy but is growing rapidly. Estimates by SIMBA Information put industry revenues at $708 million and growing at a 39 percent annual rate. SIMBA Information predicts that the subscribers are increasing at a 42 percent annual rate.[6]

- The consumer on-line service segment targets the home PC user. Consumer on-line service subscribers can access a wide variety of content and services targeted at the consumer. Examples are newspapers, magazines, entertainment games, personal finance information, and value-added services such as travel information, discussion forums, electronic chat areas, and e-mail.

- The business on-line service segment is much larger—$11.8 billion; but it is growing more slowly (9 percent per year) and includes such business services as brokerage, credit, and financial information. (See Fig. 7.1.[3])

Three major players in the industry control 88 percent of the market: America Online (the only pure player, with 2.0 millions U.S. subscribers), CompuServe (a division of H&R Block, with 2.0 million U.S. subscribers), and Prodigy (a partnership of Sears and IBM, with an

1995 Estimate ($ billions)

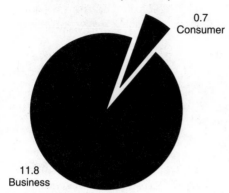

0.7
Consumer

Figure 7.1   The on-line services market.

11.8
Business

estimated 1.35 million U.S. subscribers). (See Table 7.1.[6]) America Online had 36 percent of the market share in 1995; CompuServe had 32 percent; Prodigy had 20 percent; MSN had 3 percent; and other providers had 9 percent.[2]

At press time there were just over 5 million subscribers in the United States. Penetration is low, at only 5 percent of television households (HHs),* 14 percent of the 36 million PC HHs, and 30 percent of the PC/modem HHs. Industry penetration is expected to reach 16, 33, and 60 percent, respectively, by 1998, as consumer on-line subscribers reach 16 million in the United States.[1-6]

Growth of consumer on-line service subscribers has been rapid, amounting to 73 percent in 1994 (over the previous year). But there is still plenty of room for expansion given penetration of only 5 percent of TV households. (See Table 7.2.[6]) However, the impact of direct Internet access may somewhat temper future growth.

There are three groups that make up the on-line industry: subscribers, information aggregators, and information providers. *Subscribers* are the users who dial up from home on their PCs. The *information aggregators* are the service providers themselves. They

---

* Note: TV households are used as a measurement of media penetration and nearly equivalent to total U.S. households.

TABLE 7.1   Three Major Players

Service	Current U.S. subscribers* (millions)	Launch date	Owner
America Online	2.00	1985	America Online
CompuServe	2.00	1979	H&R Block
Prodigy	1.30	1988	IBM/Sears

* As of mid-1996.

TABLE 7.2   Three Major Players

	1993	1994	1995
Total U.S. subs	2,631,000	4,578,000	5,350,000
Percent change	27	73	

package content from the information providers in an easy-to-use format on their own computer systems. The services are generally icon-driven. The *information providers* contribute content. The most important variable in this industry is the content being offered. Seven segments make up the business/professional on-line services group[1-5]:

- *Brokerage information services* provide information necessary to trade financial instruments. These services distribute real-time market information to financial services firms and banks.

- *Credit information services* help credit grantors assess the risks of lending to individuals and businesses by collecting and selling payment histories.

- *Financial news/research services* are decision-support and news-alert services for professional investors. This segment includes financial information and services that deliver business newswire feeds to corporate electronic mail systems.

- *Marketing information services* sell targeted mailing lists, list-enhancement services, and information that enables marketers to assess the effectiveness of promotions.

- *Professional services* are database services that automate retrieval of a variety of business, scientific, medical, and technical information. Librarians and other information professionals are the typical users of this service.

- *Legal/regulatory services* provide access to information produced by government, including access to laws and legal decisions, corporate records, and real estate transactions histories.

- *Vertical market services* are specialized services that are not covered by the six business/professional segments. They serve niche markets with information pertinent to particular user groups. They are used mostly by end users within the markets they serve.

The end-user/consumer segment of the on-line services industry has two segments[1-6]:

- *General-interest services* provide access to an assortment of databases, communications, and transactions services. Communications services and special-interest groups are the most popular of the general-interest services.

- *Individual investor services* offer access to information and databases to help personal investors make investments. Some services permit investors to conduct trade.

Growth in the consumer on-line service segment has been driven by the increase of PCs purchased for home use, which is expected to continue at a 20 percent annual rate (according to Dataquest) for the immediate future.

The increase in PC sales to the home, particularly modem-equipped multimedia PCs, coupled with aggressive marketing efforts have caused the consumer segment of the on-line services industry to become the fastest-growing part of the business in recent years. A combination of factors is driving consumer acceptance of on-line services. Some of the significant market drivers include[1-6]:

- Availability of less-expensive multimedia PCs for home use. At the end of 1994, consumer PC penetration in the United States was 36 percent. This is being driven by leading PC vendors such as Compaq and Packard Bell.

- Prevalence of Windows-based graphical interface, making on-line services easier to use, especially for first-time PC owners.

- An optimized on-line product due to technological developments. Improved memory and multimedia capabilities have made on-line services much more appealing to consumer tastes. Entertainment values, a key component of the interactive experience, which is lacking in text-based services, is now possible. Current on-line services offer acceptable-quality still photos, audio clips, and animations.

- The emergence of recreational applications, such as real-time chat, which are broadening the demographics of on-line user profiles.

- The extension of branded content to on-line networks through alliances with established TV- and print-based media. Examples of branded on-line content from such alliances include *The New York Times* on AOL; ESPN on Prodigy; and *U.S. News & World Report* on CompuServe.

- Transition to affordable pricing, which reflects decreasing communication costs and heightened competition between on-line services for market share.

- An increased pool of qualified potential subscribers because of improved computer literacy.

- Growth of consumer Internet use driven by the availability of easy-to-use browser software. Currently, the top-three on-line services offer comprehensive Internet and World Wide Web access.

- Improved multimedia capabilities, such as real-time audio and the implementation of full-motion video, delivered at faster access speeds.

- Growth of the installed base of mutlimedia-capable machines.

- New players in the market—AT&T, Microsoft, MCI, as well as cable companies such as Cox Cable, Tele-Communications Incorporated, and Time Warner.

- Billions of dollars invested by media companies, on-line providers, and telecommunications, hardware, and software companies.

- The National Information Infrastructure, a government initiative to create a nationwide information-services infrastructure through private industry. Plans by Clinton Administration and Congress to overhaul existing telecommunications policies and deregulate the industry are expected to result in lower telecommunications costs.

7.6   Technology Trends

The graphical capabilities of on-line services have been limited by available distribution technologies. The narrowband public-switched telecommunications network now in place to deliver on-line services has limited capacity to deliver multimedia elements such as sounds, pictures, animation, and video. The Internet has increased modem-speed requirements. To access the graphic-intensive services of the World Wide Web, for example, minimum 14.4-Kbps modem speeds are required. Increased processing speeds and faster modems have allowed on-line services to offer more multimedia elements, such as graphics. Many on-line services have taken advantage of this trend by offering newer and better graphical user interfaces that support improved graphics, pictures, and sound.[1-6]

Cable TV companies, telephone companies, hardware and software providers, and on-line services companies are all experimenting with even faster speeds than the 28.8-Kbps modem for on-line services delivery. Cable modems and ISDN promise faster speeds and real-time multimedia via on-line services, but these are still in the early phase.

Cable modems will enable users to download sound files, video clips, or large text files in seconds rather than in minutes or hours. By using a combination of coaxial cable lines and high-speed telephone lines, cable modems can distribute information at 3 Mbps, compared with 28.8 Kbps for the best modems currently in the market. Cable modems will be one of the primary drivers that will bring the on-line services industry to the next level. Manufacturers include Motorola, Zenith, Intel, General Instrument, and Digital Equipment. On-line services such as Prodigy, CompuServe, and America Online are all experimenting with on-line delivery through cable modems. Another option, ISDN, is based on upgrades to the standard telephone network (see Chap. 8 for additional discussion of ISDN).

Until higher bandwidth can be delivered through telephone networks or cable modems become the norm, on-line services are using CD-ROMs to deliver graphics and sound presentations to customers. CompuServe was the first on-line service to offer a CD-ROM product to its on-line members. The CD-ROM (which contains paid advertising) allows users to seamlessly enter the on-line service from the CD-ROM. (See Chap. 8 for a more extensive discussion of this topic.)

7.7 Profiles of Major On-Line Service Providers

7.7.1 America Online

7.7.1.1 Overview. America Online (AOL) is the largest for-profit on-line service in the United States. The company has the highest growth rate of any paid-access on-line service, including the Internet. The service is currently available for MS-DOS, Microsoft Windows, Apple, and Macintosh operating systems, and for Personal Digital Assistants (PDAs).

AOL currently maintains its operations through three primary business units: AOL Enterprises, AOL Services, and AOL Technologies. AOL Enterprises represents the company outside of North America, and it is now negotiating to bring AOL service to Japan and Europe. AOL provides all basic services, including Internet access. The AOL technologies unit is responsible for developing new technologies for use on AOL both domestically and internationally.[1-7]

AOL has been aggressive in building its international operations. AOL established AOL International in 1994 to develop potential international services. The first major program developed is AOL Away From Home, which provides U.S. subscribers with a way to access the service from more than 140 cities in 42 nations worldwide.

In addition to introducing its own service to the international market, AOL is also establishing a new European Online service with partner Bertelsmann AG, a German media conglomerate. Under an agreement struck by the two companies, AOL and Bertelsmann will jointly own 90 percent of the service. The remaining 10 percent will be offered to European investors. The new service will offer the same basic service as AOL, but with a European feel. Bertelsmann's music, video, and publishing interests will all be featured on the service. The two companies plan to launch the service in France, Great Britain, and Germany. AOL and Bertelsmann expect to expand the service throughout Europe after it has been established in its three core markets.[1-7]

7.7.1.2   Service offerings/applications.   AOL offers numerous basic services covering a variety of topics. It also offers electronic messaging services that range from e-mail to Instant Messages (IMs) that can be sent while on-line. AOL also sponsors special events on-line, including guest appearances by politicians, movie and television celebrities, and musicians, among others. AOL's newest offering is the limited Internet connectivity, with Internet e-mail support and access to Internet news sites, mailing lists, WAIS, and Veronica.

7.7.1.3   Electronic messaging.   On AOL, all screen names are assigned an Internet address, which enables AOL users to receive mail from and transmit mail to the Internet as well as to other services with Internet links, including CIS and Prodigy. E-mail can be sent while on-line or in the course of a "Flash Session," which allows users to write and read mail off-line, and therefore save on-line time.

In addition to e-mail communication, AOL members can send messages to other users on-line in real time using the "Instant Message" option. With this option, a message is sent to another member regardless of the AOL service he or she is using at that moment. Instant Message cannot be delivered if the addressee is not on-line at the time the message is sent. If the message fails to reach the desired party, the sender is informed immediately.[1-7]

7.7.1.4   General services.   AOL's general services are divided into several "departments." Each department includes a download and upload section, a chat room, and message boards that allow users to post messages that can be read at any time by other members. In addition, each department now spotlights popular sites on the World Wide Web that reflect the department's primary interests. For example, the Sports department now offers advice on where to find the top sports site on the World Wide Web. The following is a review of the general services offered.[1-7]

Clubs & Interests.   The Clubs & Interests department features activities and chat rooms dedicated to special interests, hobbies and clubs, careers, and sports.

Computing.   More than 250 hardware and software manufacturers maintain a presence in this area in order to answer consumer questions and respond to comments concerning their products. Articles concerning the computer industry and written by computer user group members are also available on-line for downloading.

Education.   The Education department enables subscribers to reach outside research resources, including the Library of Congress, Electronic University Network, *National Geographic,* and the Smithsonian.

Entertainment. The Entertainment department encompasses most of the entertainment resources available on-line, including chat rooms dedicated to specific movies, television shows, sports, and books. Several networks also have established on-line sites in this area, including ABC, MTV, Comedy Central, Lifetime Television, and E! Entertainment Television.

Internet Connection. The Internet Connection provides full access to the Internet, including an Internet e-mail gateway and access to newsgroups, FTP (file retrieval), and mailing lists. AOL subscribers can also download the company's World Wide Web browser directly from the service. The browser can be used to view WWW pages from throughout the world. The browsers feature compression technology that displays graphics faster than most browsers.

Kids Only. The Kids Only department is dedicated to children's interests. This section features news and sports information geared toward youngsters, with computer games, Disney Adventures, etc.

Marketplace. The Marketplace department features on-line shopping through several outside sources, such as Computer Express, 800 Flowers, etc.

Newsstand. The Newsstand department features electronic versions of several popular publications, including *USA Today, The New York Times,* the *San Jose Mercury News,* and the *Chicago Tribune.* The latter three have established area-specific services that offer reviews, a calendar, and other features via AOL that are not offered in their print version.

People Connection. The People Connection includes "The Lobby" chat session where AOL members can mingle and discuss whatever topics come to mind. There is a limit of 20 people per lobby, but a new lobby is automatically created as an existing one overflows.

Personal Finance. The Personal Finance department features financial information, including stock quotes (updated hourly), financial news, *Investor's Business Daily,* and various other services.

Reference. The Reference department offers access to every reference outlet on AOL, including *Compton's Encyclopedia,* Software File search, a Directory of Services, a Member Directory, the Bible, and CNN Newsroom news.

Sports. The Sports department provides up-to-date sports information culled from Headline News and *USA Today* Sport. Other sports services include the Odds, Standings, and Scoreboards section, which features general sports information on teams and individual players.

Today's News. The Today's News department includes the PR newswire and Reuters newswire services, as well as general news stories culled nationwide from magazines and newspapers.

Travel. The Travel department features several travel-related information outlets, including Traveler's Corner (offering general advice to travelers), Bed & Breakfast USA, State Travel Advisories, etc. Subscribers can make reservations on-line for both airlines and hotels through American Airlines' Sabre service.

Special events. In addition to its departments, AOL offers members the chance to "meet" special guests on-line in the "Center Stage Auditorium." Questions are sent by pressing a special icon that calls up a line to the AOL moderator, who then passes the questions on to the guest.

7.7.1.5 Technological developments. AOL's rapid growth has resulted in a number of service problems, including a dramatic half-a-day outage. The most common subscriber complaints include busy signals during peak hours and being dropped from the network due to heavy calling volume. The growth has also taken a toll on the company's primary mail system. The substantial mail volume has led to mail delays of hours and sometimes days. Additionally, in the past, mail sent via the Internet has been occasionally returned unsent, or "bounced," because the AOL mail system could not handle the load. These and other problems led the company to announce a series of changes in 1994 and 1995. The solutions that are now being implemented include the following[1-7]:

- *Acquisition of Advanced Network & Services (ANS), BookLink Technologies, and Navisoft.* AOL acquired ANS, the company that built the backbone of the Internet, in early 1995 for $20 million in cash and $15 million in stock. AOL purchased BookLink Technologies and NaviSoft, both Internet service companies, in 1995 for more than $35 million in stock. The three companies are now refining AOL's Internet access software as part of the company's Internet Service unit.

- *Acquisition of WAIS Incorporated and Medior Incorporated.* This move is designed to improve AOL's ability to help information sources get on the Web. AOL has confirmed deals with several software companies to allow "one-button" access to AOL services.

- *Additional support staff.* AOL has expanded its Technical Service and Member Services & Billing staffs in Vienna, Virginia, and has also established a new-member support site in Tucson, Arizona.

- *Expanded access capabilities.* SprintNet, AOL's primary network service provider, now offers 14.4-Kbps service in almost every market that also has 9.6-Kbps service. SprintNet has also increased its overall modem base and expanded AOL's network capacity. In addition to these changes, AOL has introduced alternate methods of accessing the service. Subscribers that have Internet access outside of AOL can now TELNET to the service. Additionally, AOL now offers AOLNet, a data-carrier network owned and operated by the company itself. AOLNet currently offers 28.8-Kbps service in major cities nationwide.

- *WebShark.* AOL plans to offer InterCon's WebShark World Wide Web browser to its Macintosh-based customers in the near future. AOL released its Windows-based WWW browser in May. AOL officials say the company will be the first of the major services to offer a WWW browser for the Macintosh.

Multimedia. AOL is dedicated to introducing the latest technologies, including multimedia, as they become available. The company already offers "multimedia press (movie) kits" for downloading, and is participating in interactive trials being conducted by Intel, General Instrument, Viacom Cable, and Comsat Cable. The trials are designed to test the delivery of on-line services via cable directly to PCs. AOL's interest in multimedia led the company to join forces with LANcity, an equipment manufacturer. The companies plan to jointly support the distribution of PC-based multimedia on-line services via cable television lines. LANcity will provide broadband cable modem technology necessary to provide cable access to AOL. AOL's interest in multimedia also led to its involvement in 2Market. 2Market's home-shopping services are delivered via CD-ROM (for Macintosh and Windows-compatible machines) as well as via AOL and Apple Computer's on-line service, eWorld. The CD-ROM and on-line services both deliver detailed information about goods for sale, and they feature color photographs of the items.[1-7]

CD-ROM deals. To broaden its multimedia content and offer "one-button" access to its service, AOL struck deals with several CD-ROM publishers. Alliances were formed with Broderbund Software, Compton's NewMedia, Hachette-Filipacchi Magazines, Novell, SoftKey, Virgin Interactive/Entertainment, 2Market, Midisoft, and MindQ Publishing. AOL plans to create companion CD-ROMs highlighting partners' content to further enhance the publisher-to-consumer connections. The CD-ROMs will be designed to provide members with an enhanced multimedia experience blending the CD-ROM with the on-line services to offer real-time content updating and interactivity.

Internet software. AOL's Internet service unit will offer two new software products, NaviServer and NaviPress, as part of an integrated World Wide Web publishing system. The software will enable content creators and providers to easily establish and maintain Web applications. While NaviServer and NaviPress can serve as stand-alone products, they are part of a client/server application development system. NaviServer, the server product, is designed to offer a powerful architecture to support applications by servicing requests and managing content. NaviPress, the client product, offers a point-and-click interface for creating, editing, and linking content.

High-speed, dial-up network. In 1995, AOL signed a deal with Bolt Beranek and Newman (BBN), provider of Internet technology and services, in which BBN will build, maintain, and operate a portion of AOL's nationwide, high-speed, dial-up network. AOL established its own nationwide network, AOLNet, to provide members with improved high-speed access. AOLNet was formed through ANS (Advanced Network & Services), the corporate Internet access provider and builder of the Internet's backbone, which AOL acquired earlier. AOLNet is a high-speed network that enables users to access AOL at 14.4 Kbps, 28.8 Kbps, and ISDN.

7.7.2 Compuserve Information Services

7.7.2.1 Overview. Compuserve Information Services (CIS) is the oldest and second-largest on-line service in the United States, with more than 3 million subscribers worldwide (2 million in the United States). CIS officials say that the service's actual membership base is approximately 40 percent larger than the numbers released in the press due to the way multimember accounts are managed.

The CIS client software is available for the MS-DOS, Windows, and Macintosh operating systems. Additionally, CIS is offered via cable lines to customers in Exeter, New Hampshire, under a trial being conducted in cooperation with Continental Cablevision. At this time, cable access is provided on a trial basis only.

All CIS subscribers receive the same basic services, regardless of the transmission method or type of computer used. CIS's package of basic services, like those of most on-line services, includes on-line news, e-mail, reference materials, on-line shopping, and free software that is available for downloading. CIS's basic services are the same in the United States and abroad. Its international markets include Austria, Belgium, Canada, France, Germany, Italy, the Netherlands, Spain, Sweden, Switzerland, and the United Kingdom.[1-6,8] CIS offers a variety of domestic and international news and information outlets that are primarily business-oriented. Additionally, CIS offers its service in several languages, including English, French, and German, and provides national headlines for some international markets, including France and Germany.

CIS's services are designed with adult users in mind. CIS's strategy is to transform itself from a primarily residential service to one that meets the business user's needs.

Although it is targeting business users, CIS recognizes that even business users want to relax, and therefore the company has retained many of its more popular non-business-oriented services. These include Roger Ebert's movie reviews, Hollywood gossip columns, biorhythms, and assorted games that can either be downloaded or played against other users in real time. In addition, CIS features an on-line travel service and an electronic restaurant guide. These services are intended to appeal to business travelers and residential users alike.

CIS also features live on-line chat areas that enable users to meet and discuss a variety of topics with other users worldwide. CIS was planning to offer a graphically enhanced chat option, dubbed WorldsAway, in 1996. Once the service is available, CIS subscribers will be able to assume a character on-line and chat with others using that character. Whenever a participant types, his or her words will appear in a balloon above the corresponding character's head. The service will be compatible with 486 PCs equipped with Windows operating systems and Apple Macintosh computers running System 7.5 or better. Additionally, the service will accommodate modems running at speeds of 2400 bps or higher.[1-6,8]

CIS is also developing a new client interface, code-named "Shamu," that will be easier to learn than the existing interface. The new client will rely more heavily on icons and graphics than does the existing CIS Interface. The Shamu client will also feature a questionnaire concerning the user's interests. After a subscriber completes the questionnaire, the CIS server will automatically suggest some areas on-line that may be of interest, and it will offer links to those areas. CIS officials note that Shamu is still in the conceptual stage, and therefore all elements are subject to change before the interface is introduced. The Shamu client will be offered as an alternative to the existing interface, but will not replace the current CIS interface outright, CIS officials say. The Shamu interface will be recommended primarily for individuals who are venturing into cyberspace for the first time and those who simply need help on CIS.

7.7.2.2 Service offerings. CIS provides a wide variety of basic services, as well as an "Executive Services Option" that offers expanded news coverage and other special deals for business customers. CIS also maintains a roster of additional services that are available on a fee-per-use basis.[1-6,8] Basic services offered by CIS follow.

Entertainment and games. CIS maintains a number of entertainment offerings, including current movie reviews, gossip columns, the "Hollywood Hotline," biorhythms, and soap opera summaries. Other services include a Science Trivia Quiz and other quizzes. Current games include CastleQuest, Blackdragon, Adventure, and Hangman.

Financial information. CIS offers current stock quotes, issue/symbol reference guides, and major foreign currency exchange rates. Also available is "Fundwatch Online," a mutual fund screening and report service. Additionally, CIS offers a mortgage-calculation service that enables users to determine monthly payments for specific mortgage amounts.

Internet. CIS currently offers users access to USENET newsgroups, a World Wide Web browser, and an Internet e-mail address. CIS subscribers also have the option of TELNETing in via a separate Internet account. The USENET newsgroups are message boards on a variety of topics, including politics, entertainment, and lifestyles. CIS also offers TELNET access to its customers. This service enables subscribers with personal Internet accounts to access CIS via the Internet, thus avoiding modem surcharges. CIS users can also use the TELNET gateway to access databases worldwide. In addition to offering Internet access, CIS maintains an Internet discussion forum. The forum is used to explain these and other Internet services, as well as to answer questions concerning Internet access. In addition to USENET and WWW access, all CIS customers are assigned an e-mail box and are entitled to send and receive messages. The current CIS mail is capable of receiving and transmitting mail to individuals at any of the following locations: Internet (includes access to most on-line services), MCI Mail, AT&T 400, AT&T Easy Link, cc:Mail, Infonet, Advantis, Telebox 400 (Deutsche Bundespost Telekom), Netware MHS, Spring Mail, and others.

Membership support services. CIS offers various support services from its staff members, who are available on-line to help users get the most out of the service.

News, sports, weather. CIS maintains a roster of both domestic and international publications, columns, newswires, and other access points to provide the most comprehensive news coverage possible. Its current information resources include everything from electronic newspaper and magazines to specialty services.

Reference library. CIS maintains a reference library that includes *Grolier's Academic American Encyclopedia,* Peterson's College Database, Handicapped Users Database, *HealthNet* (medical reference text), *American Heritage Dictionary,* and *Consumer Reports.*

Shopping. CIS offers 24-hour access to the Electronic Mall, which features more than 100 retail stores, specialty shops, discount wholesalers, and catalog companies on-line.

Travel and leisure. CIS offers access to the Sabre, and WORLDSPAN Travelshopper services. Both services offer airline, hotel, and rental car information and are capable of accepting reservations for all three services on-line.

7.7.2.3 Executive Service Option. CIS offers an "Executive Service Option" membership that provides all basic CIS services plus additional discounts on optional services and extra services not available to its basic members.

Executive News Service. Provides specialized newswires that feature any topic selected by the customer. For example, a customer can request a wire that includes stories on the telephone industry only. CIS then calls all relevant stories from its assorted resources and delivers them to the customer.

Supersite. Provides comprehensive demographic reports on any requested location in the United States.

Company Analyzer. Provides in-depth analysis on companies, including strengths and weaknesses.

Disclosure II. Provides corporate information.

Discounts. Provides various discounts on specific CIS premium databases and purchases of most CIS merchandise.

7.7.2.4 Additional services. In addition to its basic and executive services, CIS offers a number of extra services that carry fees based on the amount of time spent on-line and the modem speed used while on-line. Some of the services include computer support forums, extended electronic communications, special-interest forums, computer graphics, and others.

7.7.2.5 Technological developments

Network upgrades. Most of CompuServe's investment will be to upgrade its network of 420 POPs worldwide to 28.8 Kbps from 14.4 Kbps. CompuServe expects to complete the upgrades of 360 U.S. POPs and 60 international POPs and to double its ports to over 85,000 in 1996. This means that customers can access the network with a local phone call at speeds of up to 28.8 Kbps. The total cost will be around $201 million.[8]

Distribution strategy. CompuServe is looking for new ways to expand distribution through new media platforms. CompuServe began distributing its software for mobile users through Geowork's GEOS operating system and Sony's Magic Cap personal communicator. Other tests include delivery over ISDN and high-speed cable networks.[8]

One-button Web access. CompuServe plans to introduce fully integrated one-button Web access with its WinCIM release. CompuServe users will be able to hot-link to several new CompuServe content areas that reside in the Web, including IAC's new Cognito, an HTML-based database.

Commerce on the Internet. CompuServe joined CommerceNet, a consortium of technology-oriented companies and organizations conducting market trials of commerce on the Internet.

7.7.3 Prodigy

7.7.3.1 Overview. Prodigy is the third-largest subscription on-line service in the United States, with approximately 1.3 million subscribers. Prodigy's basic services include e-mail, bulletin boards, newswires, entertainment resources, and multimedia services (available for Windows only). Prodigy software currently is offered for the MS-DOS, Macintosh, and Windows operating systems. Prodigy currently is available at modem speeds of up to 14.4 Kbps, and 28.8 Kbps is expected to be coming soon.

Prodigy has announced plans for an improvement in both the GUI and the process by which services are developed, and a plan involving direct links between the three leading on-line services. The direct links would allow users to access information from any of the three on-line services (CompuServe, America Online, and Prodigy) and may lead to development of enhanced services.[1–6,9]

To combat subscriber attrition and to attract new subscribers, Prodigy has introduced several service changes in recent years. In 1993, the company offered a GUI option; this has increased Prodigy's attractiveness to graphics-based computer users. Prodigy has also added full-color photographs to certain sections of its service. And in 1994 Prodigy debuted a new version of its software that offers access to multimedia services.

Prodigy's multimedia package requires a Windows interface (a Macintosh version is expected soon), a sound card, and speakers. The service primarily adds sounds to the various portions of the Prodigy service, including a two-minute spoken news update that accompanies the photos and newswire stories on-line.

7.7.3.2 Service offerings. Prodigy was established primarily to be a source of information. As such, the service offers substantial reference materials, including magazines and newspapers. In addition, Prodigy offers a number of information outlets to its users, including encyclopedias, travel guides, and restaurant reviews. In 1995, Prodigy, along with Berlitz Publishing Company began offering e-mail in foreign languages. This service also provides users access to language-related publishing, translations, and language training products.

Although Prodigy is still primarily an information resource, the company has begun offering other services. Bulletin boards are now available on various subjects for users to post questions and comments to one another, and live chat areas are now available.

All Prodigy users are assigned an e-mail address. Prodigy's standard e-mail service includes a Mail Manager service that, at the push of a button, goes on-line, sends any mail to be transmitted, and retrieves unread mail from the subscriber's mailbox. The Mail Manager then logs off. This grants customers the freedom to leave the room and attend to other tasks as mail is being exchanged. A similar service is now available on AOL.

In addition to these communication services, Prodigy offers several specialty services designed to meet the interests of its customers. Current topics of interest include the following.[1-6,9]

Investments. Prodigy offers stock advice in the strategic investor section; current advisers include Graham & Dodd and CANSLIM. Prodigy also offers access to the nation's largest discount on-line stockbrokers: PC Financial Network. Therefore, users can purchase or sell stock any time of the day or night via computer. Also, Prodigy offers an additional feature, "Quote Track," which automatically calculates the loss or gain of any number of stocks in a user's portfolio while on-line.

Sports. Prodigy signed a deal with cable channel ESPN to develop an exclusive service, ESPNET, for distribution via Prodigy. ESPN has already taken over Prodigy's regular sports services, which include statistics, news, trivia, photographs, polls, and the chance to interact with ESPN personalities. Prodigy and ESPN plan to add sound and video clips to the service at a later date.

Children's interests. Prodigy offers a variety of educational resources, including an on-line encyclopedia. In addition, Prodigy offers real-time adventures, polls, and interactive games for children. Other features include NOVA experiments and science discussions, and an interactive version of the popular children's television show *Sesame Street*.

News and weather. Prodigy maintains a newsroom that constantly scans the top national and international news resources and edits stories for transmission on Prodigy.

Travel. Prodigy offers access to Sabre travel service, which can be used to make travel arrangements, including booking flights, on-line. Sabre also offers free overnight delivery of tickets booked through the agency.

Politics. Prodigy offers access to congressional biographies, voting records, and campaign contributions information through its "Political Profile" section.

The Cable Guide. Prodigy offers an on-screen, interactive version of *The Cable Guide*'s television listings, where customers can scan program listings for the following seven days. Listings can be called up through several categories, including day, time, network, and type of program. Prodigy is now developing enhancements for the on-line Cable Guide, including the possible addition of pictures, sound bites, and video clips from shows listed in the guide.

America's Talking. Prodigy offers on-line subscribers a way to converse with the hosts of several new programs presented live each day on "America's Talking," a cable network owned by NBC.

7.7.3.3 Technological developments

Internet strategy. Prodigy is very involved in the Internet. Prodigy introduced USENET newsgroup access in 1994. Prodigy's Web server was introduced in 1995. By press time, more than 600,000 people have subscribed to Prodigy's World Wide Web browser. Additionally, Prodigy was the first commercial on-line service to establish a Web page of its own, called AstraNet. Prodigy is also adopting an HTML-based protocol for its core service. This will facilitate providers' transition to the Web, which also uses the HTML format. Previously, content for Prodigy had been developed with a closed, proprietary language called North American Presentation Level Protocol Standard.[9]

Prodigy, which is jointly owned by IBM and Sears, is the first of the big three on-line networks to provide World Wide Web access. Prodigy plans to divert the bulk of its 28.8-Kbps Internet access from Sprint, Tymnet, MCI, and AT&T to the IBM Global Network. IBM will also be instrumental in converting Prodigy's proprietary network to the Internet standard TCP/IP protocol. The best indication of IBM's commitment to pursue the Internet access business is its network upgrade plan. IBM network upgrade expenditure will exceed $200 million over the next three years. IBM's Advantis unit is the U.S. arm of the IBM Global Network. IBM expects to increase its number of POPs from 167 to 450 by press time. The company will increase the number of high-speed digital ATM nodes to 83.[1–6,9]

IBM's dial-up Internet access pricing is competitive. IBM is also drawing on its diverse set of subsidiaries to assemble a full-service Internet access business for businesses and consumers. In addition to providing dial-up access and high-speed connections, its various subsidiaries will offer electronic commerce, transactional security and encryption, application integration, content hosting, and Web services.

New transmission methods. In addition to enhancing the services provided on-line, Prodigy is researching new transmission methods. One promising new way to deliver Prodigy is via cable, which also would provide the opportunity to add interactive services. Prodigy and partner Cox Cable were testing a cable delivery service in California at press time. Participants in the cable delivery trial receive regular Prodigy service and are the first to receive new services, including photograph and video images on PCs.

Prodigy was also planning a separate trial with Media General Cable. Prodigy plans to deliver its service to approximately 200,000 cable subscribers in Fairfax County, Virginia, during the trial.

In addition to cable-based access, Prodigy is planning to offer ISDN access through an agreement with partners IBM, BellSouth, NYNEX, and Pacific Bell. The higher-speed access will be available only to Prodigy members using the IBM 7845/ISDN WaveRunner modem. The faster speed is already available to subscribers in San Jose and Woodland Hills, California.

7.7.4   GEnie

7.7.4.1   Overview. GEnie is a subsidiary of General Electric Information Services (GEIS) and is the fourth largest for-profit on-line service in the United States with approximately 200,000 subscribers in the United States and Canada. The service is also available in Japan, Germany, Austria, and Switzerland. GEnie's interface is compatible with the Apple Macintosh and IBM-compatibles equipped with any operating package. A GUI also is available.

GEnie offers personal e-mail, games, files for downloading, on-line message boards, and live chat areas. The company's services appeal to a diverse subscriber base, including business users and home users of almost all ages. The service is geared primarily to users in their mid-20s and older. GEnie's current growth rate is averaging approximately 20 to 30 percent annually.

GEnie took one major step toward catching up to the current on-line standards in late 1994, when it introduced its GUI for Macintosh and Windows users. In addition to the new interface, it also debuted its first Internet access services in late 1994. The company offers an e-mail gateway and other text-based services, such as USENET newsgroups. A basic knowledge of UNIX is required to navigate GEnie's Internet service at this time. However, GEnie plans to add GUI-based Internet services, including WWW access.[1-6]

7.7.4.2   Service offerings. GEnie offers numerous basic services covering a variety of topics and full Internet access. It also maintains additional services that are available on a fee-per-use basis.

GEnie's basic services are bulletin boards, business and news resources, chat lines and roundtables, computer-assisted learning, center download library, GE mail (e-mail), on-line games, on-line shopping and travel services, real-time conferences, and Internet access.

GEnie also offers "premium" services for an additional charge, which varies according to the service selected. Current premium services are as follows

Dun & Bradstreet's Company Profiles.   Provides access to a comprehensive database covering top U.S. businesses.

Charles Schwab Brokerage Services.   Provides discounted brokerage services on-line. Users can trade, change, cancel, and view the status of investments made through the broker.

Dow Jones News/Retrieval.   Provides access to more than 500 business publications, including *The Wall Street Journal* and the Dow Jones newswire.

GE Mail to FAX.   Provides the means to transmit messages to any fax machine worldwide.

The Official Airline Guides Electronic Edition Travel Services.   Provides full travel agency services.

ANALY$T.   Provides current and historical stock quotes, analytical reports, stock charts, market indicators, and financial news.

Internet strategy.   GEnie's Internet offerings still lag behind those available through Prodigy, CompuServe, and America Online. The browser it introduced has met with only moderate success because it lacks sophisticated functionality. To fix this, GEnie intends to license a third-party browser to distribute to its members.

GEnie launched its own World Wide Web home page to promote its service in 1994, but has no immediate plans to migrate its content to the Web. The reasons are largely due to the technical limitations of its mainframe network, which is still being converted to a UNIX-based system.

7.7.5   Microsoft Network

7.7.5.1   Overview.   Microsoft has provided point-and-click access to the MSN's client software built into the Windows 95 desktop. The service is available via a local telephone number in 47 nations worldwide, with support for 20 different languages. Microsoft plans to expand the service's accessibility within the first year of operations and expects to introduce a Windows NT version of the MSN software. An Apple Macintosh version of the software is also in development and was expected to be available by press time. Microsoft does not plan to import the MSN client for IBM's OS/2 platform. Microsoft's expansion plans also include improved modem-access speeds. The service currently supports 14.4 bps (and lower). Microsoft expected to introduce 28.8-bps and ISDN access by press time. Additionally, Microsoft and partner Tele-Communications Incorporated (TCI) plan to begin testing cable-based delivery of the service in 1996.[1-6]

7.7.5.2 Service offerings.

MSN's basic service includes e-mail, live chats, file and software libraries, newswires, Internet access, arts and entertainment, news and weather, business and finance, sports/health and fitness, and science and technology. Each of these areas feature message boards, live chats, information resources, and software areas. In addition, some areas feature on-line sites established by Microsoft's partner companies. Each company is responsible for designing and setting up its own site. More than 40 companies have already signed up to create on-line sites.

Microsoft is charging a 30 percent commission on all sales completed on-line. Microsoft claims that the 30/70 split is the best deal available to vendors seeking an on-line partner. (Some on-line services take as much as 40 to 50 percent, depending on the company.)

7.7.5.3 Technological developments

ISDN bundle. Microsoft and partner Pacific Bell and CompuUSA are negotiating to bundle and distribute a software and hardware package that would enable subscribers to access the MSN via ISDN lines. As planned, the bundle would include Windows 95, an ISDN adapter, and ISDN telephone service (through Pacific Bell). The bundle will be sold in CompuUSA stores throughout California. (Microsoft is hopeful of similar agreements with other telephone carriers nationwide.)

NBC partnership. Microsoft and partner NBC are joining forces to develop entertainment resources, including CD-ROMs, interactive games, and on-line offerings. NBC has agreed to withdraw its sites from other on-line services, thus offering MSN subscribers exclusive on-line access to the network.

Internet strategy. Microsoft has positioned the Microsoft Network as an on-line service offering seamless integration with the Internet. It has also portrayed its development tool, Blackbird, as a robust multimedia tool that will allow developers to implement full motion and sound. Microsoft is counting on Blackbird to deliver content providers and electronic merchants richer and more compelling multimedia features than the Web's HTML programming language or programming languages of existing consumer on-line services.

According to Microsoft, Blackbird is a development platform with broad applications, including on-line, CD-ROM, broadcast, and interactive TV. The tool includes a strong search engine, called The Find, which allows users to create personal profiles. Other Blackbird features include drag-and-drop design, information retrieval, and open extendability, which allows third-party developers, such as Adobe or Macromedia, to integrate Blackbird into their tool sets.

By mid-1996, any user with a Windows/Mac-based client was expected to be able to access MSN through the Internet. Internet access providers will be able to resell MSN, allowing customers to access MSN through the Internet. Microsoft's Web browser—Microsoft Internet Explorer—is designed specifically for the Microsoft Windows 95 operating system. The program includes built-in RealAudio technology, providing real-time audio capabilities. The Internet Explorer supports Windows 95 shortcuts to the Internet and supports full drag-and-drop text and graphics.

References

1. Krishnamurthy, Allen, "Report on Online Services Industry," class project, Stevens Institute of Technology, fall 1995.
2. *Successful Marketing Strategies for Online Services,* LINK Resources Corporation.
3. Industry Analysis (Online Services), J. P. Morgan Equity Research.
4. Forbes (August 1995 Issue)—Computer/Communications.
5. "Online Marketplace," *Interactive Transaction Monthly,* Jupiter Communication, New York.
6. "Online Services Trends & Forecast," SIMBA Information Inc.
7. America Online company material.
8. CompuServe company material.
9. Prodigy company material.

8

Broadband Communications for the Internet and Intranets

8.1 Introduction

As discussed in other parts of this book, the popularity of the Internet is growing, along with the number of users and applications. As more and more people use the Internet, and as the Web applications available on it increase in complexity, the underlying end-to-end communications technologies will need to be upgraded. Otherwise, the Internet may eventually become an ineffective means of global communication. It is already apparent when downloading a large file or a high-resolution graphic that speed is not one of the Internet's greatest assets at this time. By upgrading to higher speeds and/or broadband communications technologies end to end, the Internet will be able to support a multitude of production-level users and complex multimedia applications.[1] Higher-speed facilities are needed for both the *access portion* of the network (whether you reach the Internet over a dial-up or over a more elaborate service) and *internally* to the Internet itself, namely, in the set of backbones that comprise it. (See Fig. 8.1.) The need for higher speeds is also evident for intranet applications now evolving, as discussed throughout this text.

This chapter discusses the technologies available for this required upgrade, as well as the issues surrounding the need to support the expected growth in requirements and grade of service. The focus of this chapter is on increasing actual bandwidth by utilizing existing and evolving communication services such as Integrated Services Digital Network (ISDN)—for access—and Asynchronous Transfer Mode (ATM)—for access and for backbone requirements. Although the typical corporate planner has little influence on what is inside the Internet in terms of communication facilities, the planner has a lot of control on

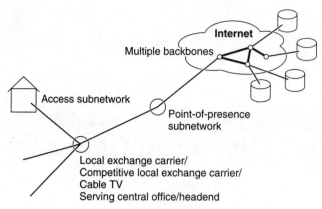

Figure 8.1 Components of Internet communication.

the access facilities. The planner does have some control by selecting an ISP that has paired with an NSP that has a high-capacity backbone. However, for a specific Internet session, the actual end-to-end network performance also depends on the ISP that the target server has chosen—hence the overall performance is beyond the direct control of the planner. In addition, there is a short discussion of broadband initiatives as they relate to the Internet and to other networks.

8.2 Services and Requirements Driving the Need for Broadband

8.2.1 New services desired on the Internet

Table 8.1 lists some of the services that are currently of interest, or may become of interest, to users over time. Some of these services are realized outside of the Internet, but many do utilize the Internet, at least in some form (e.g., to obtain educational materials, publications, or technical specifications).[2]

A number of the services listed in Table 8.1 may find a reasonably high level of market penetration. These include interactive television, video-on-demand, home shopping, videoconferencing (e.g., for training, education, medical consultation, business meetings), remote monitoring and security, government service delivery, and Internet surfing. Many people want these services in the context of the Internet.

Many of these services utilize hypermedia and GUIs to make it easier for users to access information and to navigate between elements of the distributed repository. Hypermedia/multimedia is emerging as an effective way to communicate, but traditional telephone lines and modems cannot effectively deliver multimedia to homes. To overcome this hurdle many on-line services and service providers are migrating to higher-speed data links such as ISDN, ATM, and Syn-

TABLE 8.1   Typical Services Driving Broadband Requirements

Government	Health services
Electronic form lodgment	X-ray and CAT scan transfer
Document and data transfer	Video consultation
Videoconferencing	Medical records transfer
Electronic access to government	Remote monitoring of outpatients
information	**Education**
Electronic voting and public consul-	Remote interactive teaching
tation	Access to local and overseas libraries
Video libraries	International classrooms
Business	**Home services**
Videoconferencing, including "virtual	Video-on-demand
meetings"	Home shopping and banking
Electronic commerce	Interactive multimedia
Remote interactive training	On-line information services
Computer-aided design and manu-	Video mail and video phones
facturing	Security services and utility metering
Multimedia communications	Telecommuting*

* Internet source—Broadband Services Expert Group, Australia.

chronous Optical Network (SONET).* As consumers desire more of these bandwidth-intensive services, there is going to be a need to install high-speed communication lines and services in their offices and homes, and to upgrade the speed of the Internet backbones.

People spend much of their lives producing or consuming information—through work, conversations, watching television, or reading newspapers. Almost every home in America now has a telephone connection. People receive radio and television services, and in some places, satellite services. A rapidly increasing part of the population has mobile telephones; around 40 percent of homes have personal computers; and a vast majority has videocassette recorders. There is a growing household use of telephone-line modems, and the on-line services industry in the United States is also growing at a significant rate. All of this sets the foundation for increased demand for on-line services in general, and Internet services in particular.[2]

On a going-forward basis, networks must be able to do the following: support broadband services such as high-quality video; allow people to create and distribute their own material; support and interconnect both fixed and mobile systems through a combination of cable, satellite, and local wireless services; enable multiple parties to be connected to an interactive multiparty, multimedia, multiconnection high-speed service; support interactive and switched two-way transmission, as

---

* Outside North America, the new digital hierarchy is called Synchronous Digital Hierarchy (SDH). SDH is nearly (but not completely) identical with SONET at the Electrical Carrier (EC) 3, 12, 24, 48, and 192 levels.

the telephone network does now; and provide global reach. Evolving broadband communications technologies, such as ATM, will play an important role in achieving these goals. These requirements must be supported not only by networks that can be considered as an overlay to the Internet, but by the Internet itself.

Apart from the Internet itself, a seamless high-speed network carrying voice, data, and video services will be used as a pipeline to bring an expanded universe of information and entertainment into the home and the workplace. But with the Internet, thousands of movies, mail-order catalogs, newspapers and magazines, educational courses, airline schedules, and other information databases will be available with a few clicks of a PC mouse or perhaps a TV remote control. Two-way video-conferencing may become integral to the family, to social life, and to business in the not-too-distant future. The information and communication infrastructure of the future, based on fiber optics, will provide the main conduit for global entertainment, commerce, information, and communication in the next century.

Consumers are a significant, if not primary, element in the evolutionary process. They will determine which services thrive, which services enhance lifestyles, and which afford greater financial opportunities. We might have a fair idea of what the technologies will look like, but it is the services they support and the content they carry that will ultimately determine a technology's future. The penetration and affordability of consumer equipment, a population with the necessary skills and training to use the services, a consumer base willing to adopt new means of interaction, and competitive service prices will also be influential in a technology's success.[2] For example, until recently you needed a $2000 PC to access the Internet. As of the fall of 1996, $300 devices to be used in conjunction with a TV set (called WebTV) were becoming available, opening up new opportunities.

The possibilities for the Internet seem almost endless. For example, voice connections via the Internet are now possible. This allows people to participate in telephone conversations anywhere in the world for the price of an Internet connection. Applications like these are what make the Internet so attractive to people. As more and more uses of the Internet become available, more and more users will be drawn to it. Competition among companies will make WWW pages more complex and will put further loads on the Internet.[3,4]

A ubiquitous system of broadband backbone networks will allow the United States to be competitive with other countries in terms of economic development and commerce: to create jobs; to ensure equity and quality in education and health care; to share limited resources; to reduce government costs and provide efficiencies; and to provide a platform for the delivery of Information Age services to consumers. Until recently, however, little visible progress has been made toward its realization. Telephone companies, newspaper publishers, cable-television operators, and other potential players have been involved in lengthy congressional and court battles. Meanwhile, the pioneers of the computer-mediated communication networks, collectively referred to as *cyberspace,* are not willing to wait. Employing whatever tools they can find, they are constantly pushing the techno-cultural envelope.* The Internet has become the de facto information superhighway.

Many expect a replacement of the existing broadcasting model of distributive (one-way) information services by a system in which consumers create and have access to information and exercise choice and control in their communications. This is called multicasting or point-casting. In the communications arena, people will be able to send or receive large amounts of information—video, audio, text, graphics, or data—anywhere at any time. But the major benefit will be the speed and ease of access to materials for production of publications. These examples are forerunners of new applications in media, travel, government, advertising, and general publishing, which have the potential to earn income either from the provision of information-content services or export of technology.†

8.2.2   Electronic commerce on the Internet

As the popularity of the Internet grows, so does the number of organizations that want to expand their visibility in this new global sales and communications channel. Most businesses start out by giving their employees electronic mail and by creating a home page on the World Wide Web. However, creating a strong marketing presence on the Web requires the thoughtful creation of an information architecture and a willingness to adapt to the electronic medium. The competitive landscape is changing so rapidly that reaching out to customers electronically is now becoming imperative in many industries. The ultimate benefit of commerce on the Internet will be its establishment as a new sales channel. Competing effectively, however, will require a degree of openness and accessibility to which many businesses might not be accustomed.[2]

Because the Internet has not been a traditional commercial marketplace, standard marketing and advertising techniques may not necessarily work. For example, you may be dealing with a global sales channel and customers who speak many different languages. The positive factor is that the Internet enables businesses to narrowly target potential customers with highly specific information in a manner that

---

* Internet source—Mitchell Kapor, 1995 Wired Ventures Ltd.

† Internet source—Broadband Services Expert Group, Australia.

would not be cost-effective within traditional channels. The information must be visually appealing and tailored to the on-line hyperlinked environment. Ultimately, the business must provide customers with the tangible benefits for using the Internet. Service must be better, transaction security must be higher, and costs should be lower, reflecting the more efficient delivery of goods and services.*

For customers to see the most value in the Internet, businesses need to integrate their Web presence with their core business applications. Many companies would like to have "click-here-to-purchase" buttons on their Web pages. This requires integration with order processing, inventory, billing, etc. In the banking and insurance industries, customers will be able to check the status of claims, obtain account balances, and so on—essentially the same kinds of transactions that some banks offer from PCs over dial-up connections today. The difference is that the Web browser becomes the standard interface for dealing with many companies, as well as for educational and recreational activities. Given such service availability, the number of possible users will push the requirement for a high-capacity backbone for the Internet.

Naturally, before money can be exchanged safely on-line, standards for security must be in place. This security must protect both the vendor and the customer. Multiparty security protocols will enable secure electronic transactions between business, consumers, and financial institutions. Credit card associations are in the process of establishing how they will handle Web transactions. When these standards are implemented, credit card transactions on the Web should become commonplace. Again, the number of potential users will ultimately drive the Internet to higher speeds.

8.2.3 Growth of the Internet

As discussed elsewhere, the Internet is seeing commercial use grow by 30 percent quarterly, and its backbone trunks are doubling in size each year. The growth rate of WWW traffic in 1994 was almost 2000 percent.[5-7] The Internet is also the primary e-mail mechanism for almost 20 percent of government agencies and 10 percent of the health industry. Increased use of WWW servers and audio and video applications has significantly increased the bandwidth needs of the Internet, as well as being at the root of the capacity problems. Popular WWW browsers such as Mosaic, Netscape, and Explorer have introduced millions of users to the convenience and power of downloading pictures, sound, and animation.

---

* Doug Wesolek, *NetNews-IBM,* issue 3, 1995, pp. 16–17.

There is also a growing residential market for the Internet. It is believed that revenues from electronic information services will eventually exceed revenues from entertainment video when both are delivered to the home through a broadband network. The time may soon come when (a subset of key) consumers will spend more on personal computers than on TVs. A total of about 40 percent of U.S. families and 50 percent of U.S. teenagers now own a PC.[5,6] State networks are also driving deployment with the construction of their networks, used primarily for telemedicine and distance learning.[8,9]

During the summer of 1994, overall Internet traffic jumped from 5 terabytes (TB) a month to 30 TB a month. Much of this traffic has been carried on 1.544-Mbps T1 backbone links. This growth of the Internet must be met with an upgrading of the underlying network of access and backbone facilities, or the Internet will no longer be able to support the users or their applications. Presently, the biggest bottleneck occurs not in the backbone, but in the access to the user. However, once those needs are met, the backbones must be able to support needs of all the users. Customers' complaints about network slowdowns prompted a number of networks to announce major upgrades of their Internet links. Major access providers must have DS-3 (45-Mbps) backbones or higher to avoid these network slowdowns.[7] There are currently problems obtaining the hardware to make the upgrades. MCI has had some difficulty finding switches to achieve their targeted switching capacity of OC-12 (622.08 Mbps) for the very high speed Backbone Network Service they are developing to link some National Science Foundation supercomputers.[7] However, as we enter the last few years of this decade, ATM switches capable of supporting these speeds are becoming widely available.

For the Internet to sustain its growth, these key issues must be resolved. There are already limitations on the data rates that can be achieved on the Internet. Observers advise: "Do not expect to get 500 Kbps over the Internet—10 or 20 percent of that is more typical."[5] The Internet is capable of those speeds but not to all users all the time. Because the Internet is global, there is no real off-peak time. The entire network must be upgraded to eliminate the bottlenecks that occur.[5]

Trials have been conducted in the recent past to measure consumer demand for services and also to test successes of different technology-access schemes. The amount of user demand for Internet services and revenue generated by these services will be a determining factor in how quickly the infrastructure can be upgraded. There is also a need for quality-of-service guarantees for new multimedia applications. Companies need service guarantees to be able to do business on the Internet. They also need guaranteed stability.[3,5]

If upgrading the Internet cannot keep pace with the demands of users, this may have the effect of retarding its future growth. The capacity problems and pricing constraints could prompt people to shy away from developing bandwidth-intensive applications involving interactive video and voice. It could also lead to a need to ration the capacity allowed by an individual user in order to avoid a total shutdown of the system.

The Internet applications are now primarily text-based, with limited graphics. Video and sound are just emerging. When a full multimedia Internet is a reality, the uses by the average person as well as the average business will expand. With the growth of on-line services and home PC sales, it is only a matter of time until the average person becomes a user of the Internet, especially if it can provide practical uses that go beyond cyberspace entertainment. As the Internet becomes more efficient, people will become more attracted to it, based on the amount of information they can obtain and the rate at which it is attainable. The introduction of a broadband infrastructure will allow for more complex, user-friendly applications, which will help avoid the loss of frustrated first-time users.

8.2.4 How to do it

In current parlance, *broadband* refers to an integrated, all-digital, interactive, high-speed network—typically operating at speeds higher than 1.544 Mbps. In practical terms, this type of network transports information at speeds of 45 Mbps (DS-3), 155 Mbps (OC-3), and higher.[*2] Such an integrated network can provide multiple services (e.g., from database access to on-demand interactive video).

One impediment to the quality of some services is the characteristics of the existing telephone network. Although many services can be transmitted over existing facilities, the data-rate constraints of these facilities (particularly in the access) limit the speed of transmission. There is, however, already a range of enhanced digital services available in most cities. Most metropolitan centers also have access to ISDN, which supports low-speed[†] digital services over telephone lines. Penetration of optic fiber is increasing significantly in the United States. Technology capabilities and costs are changing rapidly. Optical fiber costs continue to fall; new wireless services are being developed; computer memories are expanding; and digital processing techniques continue to reduce the data requirements of many services via compression. The direction is invariably toward broadband.

In recent years there has been a surge in interest in the information superhighway or National Information Infrastructure (NII). Despite

---

[*] Internet source—North Carolina Information Highway.

[†] Although the user can get more throughput over ISDN than over a traditional dial-up line, the speeds are still significantly lower than those obtainable with ATM.

extensive press to the contrary, the government's role will be limited to funding research, leading experiments with ultra-high-speed networks, helping promote standards, and protecting the public interest in areas such as privacy and freedom of speech. The private sector, not the government, will build and operate the NII. Telephone companies, cable-television operators, and the Internet itself, not the government, will be the principal carriers of traffic into the home.

For the Internet, there is the issue of increasing the speed internal to the Internet itself. Also, there is a need to provide higher and more efficient (aggregate) connectivity to the Internet's Point of Presence (POP). Finally there is the need to increase the speed from the home to the serving node (e.g., central office). (See Fig. 8.2.)

8.3 Network Architectures Supporting Broadband

The goal of this discussion is to sensitize the planner to issues related to the need for broadband communications over the Internet and to offer a set of choices for the access subnetwork (which is generally under the planner's control).

8.3.1 Approaches to broadband

In the discussion that follows, you may wish to differentiate between the physical connectivity service (e.g., ISDN, ADSL, HFC, or FTTC) and a value-added service such as ATM and frame relay (both of which can, theoretically, run over any physical medium). Note, however, that

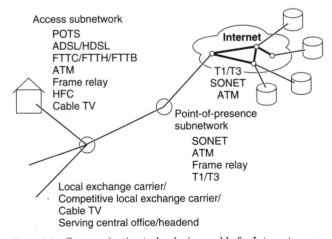

Figure 8.2 Communication technologies usable for Internet access.

not only do you need higher speed at the physical layer (e.g., ISDN, ADSL) and at the data link layer (e.g., frame relay, ATM), but also at the network layer. This is the idea behind new versions of IP. As discussed in Chap. 1, the IPng Working Group, a committee of the Internet Engineering Task Force, is developing a next-generation Internet routing protocol standard called IPv6. IPv6 has a 24-bit flow-label field in the header that can be used to accommodate interactive applications by aggregating packets that need a common quality of service. The flow ID will allow quality of service to be established for applications that need performance guarantees.[7] It will enable companies to receive service guarantees from their access providers.[10] Some, however, are unsure how widespread the adoption of the standard will be.[1] Furthermore, processing at network layer, that is faster routing, must be improved. Efforts such as Multiprotocol Over ATM (MPOA) and IP Switching are aimed at these concerns.

Compression capability is something that both businesses and consumers will need. Uncompressed material requires a lot of bandwidth, whether for still images or video. Tables 8.2[11] and 8.3[12] illustrate this point. Among the compression techniques in use or under development today are ADPCM and ACELP* (for voice), Joint Bi-level Image Expert Group (JBIG) (for images), JPEG (for images and video), MPEG (for video), and fractal (for images and video) compression. What is needed is greater compression in order to provide feature-length movies on demand and complex multimedia applications.

Adaptive Differential Pulse Code Modulation (ADPCM) looks at the differences between samples and scales them adaptively. Although this technique can be employed for any signal, its major interest is for compressed voice (over the Internet). ADPCM provides quality telephony at 32 Kbps, rather than requiring the traditional 64 Kbps. Note that there are other, vendor-proprietary and/or standardized methods that provide digital voice at 8 Kbps. JBIG is an international standard for compression developed by the Joint Bi-level Imaging Group under the auspices of ISO and ITU-T. Today, JBIG requires a hardware chip to achieve its impressive compression ratios of 200 to 1. Software-only versions are under development and will be used to compress documents and black-and-white image files before they are transmitted over networks and to reduce the massive storage requirements for image retention.

JPEG (Joint Photograph Experts Group) is a compression format that reduces an image's digital representation to smaller-size files, based on desired resolution (see, for example, Table 8.3). The image is divided into a series of blocks, which JPEG then processes and com-

---

* Algebraic Code Excited Linear Prediction provides relatively good voice at 8 Kbps or less, compared to 32 Kbps for ADPCM. ACELP is an ITU-T standard.

TABLE 8.2   Data Rate Associated with Business Imaging Systems

Resolution ->	200 dpi (ppi)	400 dpi (ppi)
Document type/compression		
Uncompressed A0 drawing, bi-tonal[†]	7.7 MB	31 MB
25:1 compressed A0 drawing, bi-tonal	0.3 MB	1.2 MB
Uncompressed A4 bi-tonal	0.5 MB (*)	2.0 MB (**)
10:1 compressed A4 bi-tonal	0.05 MB	0.2 MB
Uncompressed A4 256 tones	3.9 MB (***)	15.5 MB
(gray scale; 8 bits per pixel)		
Uncompressed A4 65,536 tones	7.8 MB (****)	31 MB
(gray scale; 16 bits per pixel)		
Uncompressed A4 4,294,967,296	15.5 MB (*****)	61.9 MB
color tones (12-bit per color, i.e.,		
32 bits per pixel)		
Computer monitor	1,000 × 1,000 pixels, 24 colors, uncompressed:	
	24 Mb (≈ 3 MB)	
Computer monitor (PACS)	1,280 × 1,024 pixels, 24 colors, uncompressed:	
	31 Mb (≈ 3.9 MB)	
Desktop Imaging System	2,048 × 2,048 pixels, 36 colors, uncompressed:	
for graphic arts	150 Mb (≈ 19 MB)	
Camcorder-quality digital camera	400,000 pixels, 24 colors, uncompressed:	
image	9.6 Mb (≈ 1.2 MB); compressed: 0.4 MB	
HDTV-quality digital camera image	1,500,000 pixels, 24 colors, uncompressed:	
	37.5 Mb (≈ 4.6 MB)	
High-quality digital camera image	4,000,000 pixels, 24 colors, uncompressed:	
	96 Mb (≈ 12 MB)	

[†] Common document sizes: A: 8.5 × 11 in.; A3: 297 × 420 mm; A4: 210 × 297 mm; A0: 1,189 × 841 mm; B: 11 × 17 in.
(*) 8.5 × 11 × 200 × 200 × 1/8 = 0.5 MB
(**) 8.5 × 11 × 400 × 400 × 1/8 = 2.0 MB
(***) 8.5 × 11 × 200 × 200 × 8/8 = 3.9 MB
(****) 8.5 × 11 × 200 × 200 × 16/8 = 7.8 MB
(*****) 8.5 × 11 × 200 × 200 × 32/8 = 15.5 MB
dpi = dots per inch
ppi = pixels per inch

presses, resulting in compression ratios of 10 to 1 or 20 to 1. JPEG supports both a lossy and a lossless compression scheme. Also, a number of PC-based videoconferencing systems that appeared in the mid-1990s used a version of JPEG, called Motion JPEG, to provide reasonable-quality video.

MPEG (Motion Pictures Experts Group) is a standard for compressing and storing video on compact discs. To achieve its ratio of 50 to 1 (or even 200 to 1), MPEG uses a compression scheme similar to JPEG. MPEG goes a step further and also eliminates any redundancies between frames. MPEG is actually two logical standards, MPEG-1 and MPEG-2, as shown:

Version	Speed	Device
MPEG-1	1.5 Mbps	PCs
MPEG-2	1.5–40 Mbps	Interactive TV

TABLE 8.3   Approximate Encoding Rates for Various De Jure/De Facto Standards

Standard	Approximate range of data rate	Compression (#)
JPEG (for video)	10(*) to 20(†) Mbps	7-27x
MPEG-1	1.2 to 2.0 Mbps (**)	100x
H.261	64 kbps to 2 Mbps	24x (***)
DVI	1.2 to 1.5 Mbps	160x
CD-I	1.2 to 1.5 Mbps	100x (***)
MPEG-2	3 to 10 Mbps	30-100x
CCIR 723	32 to 45 Mbps	3-5x
CCIR 601/D-1	140 to 270 Mbps	reference
U.S. commercial systems using "mild compression"	45 Mbps	3-5x
Vendor methods (e.g., Picturetel SG3)	0.1–1.5 Mbps	100x
Software compression (small windows)	2 Mbps (approximate)	6x

(#) Compared to broadcast quality
(†) 640 × 480, 24 bits color, 30 fps, 1:10 compression
(*) 640 × 480, 24 bit color, 15 fps, 1:10 compression; or, 640 × 480, 24 bit color, 30 fps, 1:20 compression
(**) Baseline standard; other rates are also possible
(***) Not same quality in terms of pixels and colors as reference

MPEG-2 is poised to launch the interactive TV market, including distance learning, because it provides a standard for set-top boxes and video-on-demand applications.

Fractal compression, an emerging technology, relies on mathematical modeling to "disintegrate" an image into repetitive shapes. Fractal compression requires only a small amount of information about each shape and can shrink the image file or video frame into a very small space, achieving ratios of up to 2500 to 1 for images and up to 100 to 1 for video playback at 30 frames per second.*

The rest of this section examines available Internet access/backbone technologies.

8.3.2   Integrated Digital Services Network (ISDN)

ISDN is a technology designed for the public switched telephone network that allows low-cost communication in data, voice, graphics, and video. It is designed to be used over the existing copper local loop that connects the telephone company's central office to the home. If offered nationwide and subject to affordable tariff rates, narrowband ISDN can support digital service to the home and office without requiring the significantly greater time or expense of infrastructure conversion to broadband (i.e., ATM).

---

* *LAN Times Guide to Multimedia Networking,* McGraw-Hill, New York, 1995, pp. 84–85.

ISDN's *basic rate interface* (BRI), the type that interests most consumers, gives two B channels, each with a data rate of 64 Kbps. The B channels are used for user information. In addition, a third channel, the D channel is used for call control running at 16 Kbps.

Another type, *primary rate interface* (PRI), offers 23 channels at 64 Kbps and a 64-Kbps D channel. *Currently,* for the individual and small business, BRI is what is being sought. For the wideband-type applications that need larger amounts of bandwidth, PRI will be needed.*,2

ISDN is not an information service, but a transmission medium for delivering and receiving information in a variety of forms. With the Plain Old Telephone Service (POTS), copper-pair wires reaching into the home can carry a single voice call or data at rates up to 28.8 Kbps. Compressions of 2 for 1 and 4 for 1 (apparent data-rate increase) are advertised by some modems, achieving 57.6 or 115.2 Kbps. With ISDN, bandwidth capacity is increased to 144 Kbps. Compression techniques (lossy or lossless, depending on the application) can push that figure even higher.

Problems that haunted ISDN in the past, such as a lack of standard hardware and software protocols and the corresponding gaps in interoperability, are being addressed through the national ISDN program, a set of early-1990s national standards. The development of these standards demonstrates that the Bell companies, long-distance carriers, and information providers can work together to provide the kind of ubiquitous, standards-based service that is critical to the overall success of ISDN. Skeptics remain, however. There is concern among advocates of broadband networks, coming from both technologists and policymakers, that ISDN is a diversion on the path to fiber. In reality, most of the money needed for ISDN has already been spent (estimated here to be in the range of $50 billion worldwide in the past 15 years) or committed to upgrades for digital switches in central offices. At issue is the availability and pricing of the service. ISDN is likely to find its place as a service for the "last mile."

The ISDN platform still uses existing telephone lines, but it supports a higher data rate than the standard telephone connection. This means that it can be implemented relatively cheaply, by installing processing equipment on the customer's premises. The higher data rate compared to POTS (specifically the 2B+D rate) is also sufficient for slow-scan or low-resolution video, such as interactive home-shopping services, video games between remote players, and videophones. By 1999 most metropolitan telephone exchanges will have been upgraded to support nar-

---

* James Bryce, "Using ISDN" QUE Corp., 1995, p. 15.

rowband digital services, but it will be at least 10 years before rural exchanges will be capable of supporting these services.

Market research firm Dataquest estimates that 448,050 ISDN lines were installed in the United States by the end of 1995, up from 247,050 from the previous year; this number is expected to reach 1 million by 1998.[13,14] ISDN has had a rocky road to the market. Just a couple of years ago, telecommuting was going to be ISDN's "knight in shining armor"; now telecommuting has lost its shimmer, and Web access is the latest, but probably not the last, shibboleth.* Many ISPs in metropolitan areas now offer ISDN access, but with the graphics-intensive Web pages, including VR-based pages, ISDN could, perhaps, be categorized (by some) as "too little too late."

Pacific Bell. Among the nation's local phone companies, Pacific Bell has the most ambitious goals for ISDN. The company has a goal of 1 million lines of ISDN by 1998. The only way to make that happen is to move direct channels to mass market.[13] To that end, Pacific Bell is looking at multiple sales channels, including retail stores, value-added resellers, and sales agents. Pacific Bell has priced its service aggressively at just $24.50 a month, and installation is free if a customer keeps the service for two years. By contrast, basic residential rates in California average $12 a month.

NYNEX. NYNEX has a toll-free order line, and it is working on standard ordering codes for customer equipment. But the sales push has barely begun. NYNEX is using trial ISDN service in the Boston area, tied to IBM's WaveRunner ISDN modem and Prodigy, to learn more about marketing the service. One of the big sales pitches is Internet access.[13,14]

BellSouth. BellSouth was among the first local phone companies to get a residential ISDN tariff, but it has yet to exploit the market. The company has toll-free ordering and support lines, and is participating in an ISDN trial in Nashville, Tennessee, along with Prodigy and IBM. The company is also supporting efforts to simplify service ordering codes. The company has turned to sale agencies that take full responsibility for selling ISDN service, installing the equipment, and handling applications.[13,14]

Ameritech. Ameritech recently began a market trial with ISDN service geared into the Internet in Champaign-Urbana, Illinois, home of the National Center for Supercomputing Applications and University of Illinois. The company is selling what is called the Ameritech Home &

---

* Some believe that in the future there will be more interest in telecommuting. (See Ref. 15.)

Business Professional Package, which includes Motorola's ISDN modem service and Ameritech's Call Manager software, which integrates with services such as Caller ID through a user's PC. The line is set up to work with the package and its Windows-based installation software. The company's goal is to trim the whole process, from ordering to servicing, down to five days. Service costs $22 per month plus the cost of a regular analog line, which now averages about $10 per month.[13,14]

SBC Communications. SBC Communications was still in the process of installing ISDN capabilities in its switches as of press time. SBC, formerly known as Southwestern Bell, offers a single ISDN tariff for business and residences with a service called DigitLine. The market probes include some advertising, showcasing of ISDN applications, and invitations to vendors. The company also sets up a toll-free number directing callers to ISDN service teams in their market areas.[13,14]

U S WEST. U S WEST is only now equipping switches in its 12 largest markets with ISDN software, allowing them to receive the service. The company has no residential tariffs in place. The business tariff is $69 a month, which includes 200 hours of use, after which the charge is 4¢ per minute.[13,14]

Bell Atlantic. In 1995 Bell Atlantic started a residential ISDN trial in Maryland. For business users, ISDN charges a one-time fee of $135 plus a $20 surcharge on the cost of a business line and a data surcharge of 2¢ per minute.[13,14]

8.3.3 ADSL

Asymmetrical digital subscriber line (ADSL) is a technology that allows for high-speed transfer of data streams over the existing copper plant. It supports between 1.5 and 6.2 Mbps, depending on the technology used. However, the higher rate is achievable only in one direction; hence the name *asymmetric*. An American National Standards Institute ADSL standards project initiated in 1992 released a first issue of the T1.143 standard for ADSL that specified downstream transmission of up to 6.2 Mbps and a return path of 224 Kbps over 12,000 feet of 24-gauge copper plant. It also cited a downstream rate of 1.5 Mbps being achievable over 18,000 feet. A 6.2-Mbps transmission rate allows the user to download files 200 times faster than a conventional modem using the same copper wire, and it does not affect normal telephone service. ADSL essentially allows the user to achieve T1 and greater speeds over low-cost unrepeated (existing) facilities.[1,3,16,17]

ADSL achieves its transmission performance over the existing copper loop through the use of advanced digital signal-processing techniques implemented in very large scale integration (VLSI) technology. A modulation technique known as *discrete multitone* (DMT) is specified in the standard. A pair of ADSL transceivers are used to perform digital logic and, if mass-produced, are estimated to cost approximately $500 per pair.[3,18] Manufacturers have developed complete ADSL chip sets that eliminate the need for the separate processing components originally required. This makes the processing equipment simpler and more economical.

A large percentage of telecommunications networks have high-capacity optical fiber going as far as the central office or even as part of the access subnetwork. By utilizing the existing copper plant for the remainder of the broadband network, the service provider avoids or delays investing in new network infrastructure, which can represent a considerable cost savings.

Much of the impetus behind a broadband connection to the home was to provide interactive entertainment as well as Internet access. Based on this fact, the 6.2 Mbps provided by ADSL was perceived to be insufficient to deliver the kinds of services and bandwidth offered by competing technologies. However, broadband service trials have shown that consumer interest in video on demand is lower, at this time, than previously believed. This has led to the repositioning of ADSL as an Internet access scheme. As for the commercial markets, the bandwidth demands are much greater than for residential applications, and the existing infrastructure does not play as large a role in the economic feasibility of broadband services as in residential markets.[16]

ADSL permits transmission of a single, compressed, high-quality video signal, at a rate of 1.5 Mbps (e.g., MPEG-1), in addition to an ordinary voice telephone conversation. ADSL offers a minimal investment in infrastructure, but is limited by the bandwidth constraints of the existing copper. This architecture (see Fig. 8.3) will offer only a temporary solution to the problem.

There is a vast public market that is seeking greater access to the services that require higher transmission speed in both the backbone and in the access subnetwork. ADSL is one of the technologies that is currently being addressed in order to reach that market. As an example, AT&T Paradyne has announced ADSL-based technology that supports 6 Mbps of bandwidth to a standard phone line. The same copper line now used for voice traffic could, in the near future, let telecommuters and small business users receive live television broadcasts (e.g., MPEG-based information), video images, and multimedia files from the Internet.* Telephone company plans have been scaled back in

---

* Stephen Loudermilk, *LAN Times,* vol. 12, issue 17, Sept. 11, 1995, p. 17.

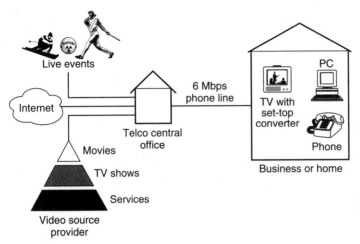

Figure 8.3 ADSL technology lets home and small-business users receive live broadcasts, movies, video services, and Internet files over a single phone line.

complexity and expense from the vision of fiber to the home. Companies have realized that the existing copper local loop can be used to deliver video through ADSL.

ADSL is not yet capable of providing a complete substitute for cable television, because it can send only one channel at a time and therefore cannot serve households where more than one television is in use simultaneously. ADSL's technical limitations are temporary, and within a year or two ADSL will be able to carry live news and sports and serve multiple televisions (e.g., carrying four simultaneous MPEG-1 channels with real-time MPEG-1 encoders).

8.3.4 HDSL

High-bit-rate digital subscriber line (HDSL) is a full-duplex, symmetrical technology that allows T1-like (1.544-Mbps) speeds over ordinary copper wire. This technology is similar to ADSL, except for the fact that it provides a symmetrical data flow with the downstream and upstream channels being equal.[*,17] Advances in HDSL signal-processing equipment have reduced the infrastructure required to implement the technology. New transceivers allow a single twisted pair to carry full T1 or E1 payload. The only drawback of the single-

---

* Some also use the term Symmetric Digital Subscriber Line (SDSL) to describe this technology.

pair configuration is that it will be limited to shorter distances than the dual-pair system.[1]

Due to the symmetry and full-duplex nature of HDSL, it will most likely be used for access by small businesses or home workers for applications such as telecommuting, data services, LAN interconnect, and frame relay rather than for entertainment. This will have limited use in residential markets, which are aimed more toward Internet access and entertainment and which tend to be asymmetrical.[8]

8.3.5 BDSL

Broadband digital subscriber line (BDSL*) was developed to overcome the bandwidth limits of ADSL by providing 25 Mbps over the existing copper plant, using a fiber-to-the-serving-area approach. Broadband signals are delivered over fiber to remote nodes for distribution to 100 or so homes. The remote nodes receive broadband signals from fiber feeders at rates of OC-12 (622.08 Mbps) or OC-24 (1.2 Gbps). These nodes are located within 3000 feet of the subscriber. The technology that is being developed for fiber-to-the-curb (FTTC) systems was adapted to provide a low-cost switching and feeder technology. Since the length of copper used was reduced by getting closer to the home, the signal-processing requirements have been considerably simplified. This reduction in signal processing reduces the amount of transistors per transceiver by 50 percent, even though the transmission rates are substantially increased. This reduces the cost of the technology that must be used at each of the nodes, which can serve several hundred subscribers.[1,3] This technology can be utilized to provide broadband services, including broadband Internet access, in Multiple Dwelling Units (MDUs), by placing the electronics in the basement or common space, and then using ordinary house wire in the raisers.

BDSL does not affect traditional telephony. These services continue to operate below 4 kHz on the copper plant using the current operations systems and powering methods. The 25-Mbps downstream digital stream is multiplexed above the 4-kHz analog POTS channel and carries cell- or packet-based video and data services. A 1.5-Mbps upstream information channel is also multiplexed on the line.[3]

BDSL provides the flexibility of delivering the POTS signal as a digital signal using a digital loop carrier system or utilizing the current analog form of the signal. Like ADSL, this provides a cost saving over other systems. This flexibility allows for the upgrading of the existing

---

* The terms ADSL and HDSL are well circulated and accepted. The terms BDSL and VDSL are relatively newer and not as widely accepted.

public network based on considerations such as making capital improvements to the outside plant.[3]

BDSL nodes have the capability of being upgraded as consumer demand increases. The nodes contain broadband shelves with each serving 32 subscribers. If you need to upgrade to more subscribers, you just add another shelf to the site. This is a significant advantage over FTTC, because it allows the network planner to upgrade the node with demand instead of putting an Optical Network Unit (ONU) on every street. By combining the existing copper plant, new optical-fiber feeders, and copper-wire transmission technology implemented with low-cost VLSI technology, BDSL can deploy broadband service for about $1000 per subscriber.[3]

8.3.6 VDSL

Very high bit rate digital subscriber line (VDSL) can be used in FTTC applications to provide a downstream link of 51.84 Mbps and up to 2 Mbps for a return channel over 200 meters or more of existing copper. This technology can also be used to implement an in-building multidrop wiring bus. This would allow all the devices in the home, such as set-top boxes and smart controllers, to communicate on an ATM bus. The ATM Forum has approved a 25.6-Mbps interface for low-speed ATM User-to-Network Interface (UNI) access.[1,19]

Note: End users would not call their serving carriers and ask for ADSL, HDSL, etc. These are *technologies* being considered by carriers to increase the bandwidth they can deliver to the user. Instead, the user could call the carrier and say, "I hear you have this new, inexpensive, 1.544-Mbps digital service [name probably based on local name-branding]. Please sign me up. . . ."

8.3.7 Wireless

Wireless applications have the advantage of allowing for rapid deployment of services to subscribers at a low cost. It also limits investment in customer-premise equipment (CPE) to those who have requested the service. However, this technology is not highly desirable for Internet access due to the lack of a return channel and/or low throughput.

8.3.8 HFC/cable modems

Hybrid fiber/coax (HFC) is another architecture that is being developed by cable television companies and telephone companies in an effort to increase their revenues by delivering multiple services to residential customers. An HFC network can carry telephony, but it will require a "cablephone" modem, which provides a normal telephone jack to the customer. In an HFC system, fiber is delivered to a neighborhood node serving several hundred homes. Coaxial cable is then run to the individual homes. Quadrature Amplitude Modulation (QAM) encoding is used to deliver the signal through the network. At the home, a modem decodes the signal for use by the consumer. The signal-processing logic for these modems has now been reduced to a single chip. Trials now being planned (or under way) will offer an asymmetrical 40-Mbps line to the home, which is only a fraction of coaxial cable's theoretical capacity of 750 MHz (1 GHz).[1,3,17,19,20]

The cable-TV network is primarily based on broadcast, unidirectional coaxial facilities, while the telephone carriers provide a switched, bidirectional, twisted-pair network. Retrofitting the existing cable-TV coaxial infrastructure for point-to-point, two-way digital service is not a trivial undertaking.[16,18]

Some trials of the HFC architecture were launched to look at the feasibility of HFC being the answer to a broadband network. Time Warner launched a trial using coaxial cable to deliver on-line services at 4 Mbps for $14.95 a month in Elmira, New York. They deliver various news and information services as well as e-mail. Internet access is offered at an additional $9.95 per month. The prices include the Zenith Electronics Corporation's HomeWorks modem and unlimited access. They plan to eventually offer an asymmetrical 40-Mbps line.[20]

PSI Cable in Cambridge, Massachusetts, has an HFC network trial in which a simple router and RF modem are installed at a customer's home, with available throughputs of 500 kbps and 4 Mbps. The router connects to a head-end router, which connects to the PSI Internet access network at the DS3 (45-Mbps) level. This service is offered for $125 per month. Greater throughputs are priced higher, but they are cost-effective for small- and medium-size businesses.[5]

8.3.9 FTTC

In an FTTC architecture, fiber is drawn to an ONU serving up to 30 homes. From the ONU, twisted-pair or coaxial cable is used to deliver a 50-Mbps downstream data flow with a 20-Mbps return path. FTTC is a technology that requires a significant investment in infrastructure. The carrier will need to run fiber down almost every street at a significant installation expense. Many believe that the advantages of the architecture seem to be good enough to offset this investment. Progress in optoelectronics is making FTTC a cost-effective option sooner than previously predicted.[17]

In the case of FTTC with coax, there is too much duplication of infrastructure: fiber for broadband communications, copper wire for power, and coaxial cable for cable TV. FTTC seems to be tending toward a twisted-pair solution that incorporates the reliability of power for telephony with the existing infrastructure.[18]

8.3.10 FTTH

Fiber to the home (FTTH) is the ultimate solution for a truly broadband end-to-end network. Electronic devices have limited bandwidth, while optical frequency carriers have almost unlimited bandwidth potential. This architecture will eliminate the restrictions placed on bandwidth by copper, but it has a problem powering the system. (New technologies are evolving to address this problem.[18,21]

An FTTH architecture has been labeled by some as overkill at this time. That may be the case today, but with the evolution of complex communications and applications, there will come a time when the bandwidth offered by this architecture could be utilized.

8.3.11 FTTB

Fiber to the building (FTTB) is more economically feasible than FTTH due to the current bandwidth needs of medium- to large-size businesses. It is also easier to justify fiber to the building in the case of businesses. Traditional carriers are under competition from alternate access providers (such as Teleport Communications Group) and long-distance companies that can simply run a line directly from their POP to the business.[19]

8.3.12 Comparison of the various architectures

BDSL and HFC seem to be viable solutions for the short term. As fiber technology makes its way into the infrastructure, there will be a migration to the FTTC solution and possibly an FTTH solution at some point. If the signal-processing and hardware costs of BDSL and HFC prove to be too great to produce revenue, and if advances in FTTC technologies continue, FTTC may become the most economical solution to implement.[22]

8.4   Broadband Carrier Services for Intranets and for the Internet

8.4.1 Frame relay and SMDS

Frame relay and switched multimegabit data service (SMDS) meet the requirements for multimedia application only in a borderline mode.

They are both oriented to data traffic and could not support voice and video applications effectively.[23] However, a service such as frame relay may be a reasonable Internet access vehicle for a number of years.

8.4.2 ATM

ATM is a standards-based network technology designed for high-speed transmission of sound, images, and video over a single network. This networking technology is being widely deployed on public WANs, LANs, and, in some measure, at the desktop. Speeds today include 25, 45, 155, and 622 Mbps. ATM includes a switching mechanism that provides a means of switching high-capacity channels that have time-delivery constraints, such as video and voice signals, as well as supporting more bursty information flows with widely variable bit rates.[24] ATM was introduced in Chap. 1. Migration to broadband-based services is really being driven by the business sector. Today's users need more bandwidth and isochronous (continuous bit rate) services over a packet-switched infrastructure in order to support new time-sensitive multimedia and videoconferencing applications. ATM is the solution because of its high speed, quality of service, connection on demand, scalability in deployment, and traffic-management features. It is applicable to both the Internet access and Internet backbone component; also, it can be utilized in corporate intranets.

ATM combines support of high bit rates and simplicity of circuit switching with the flexibility of packet switching. With switched virtual circuit service, users will be charged by the amount of bandwidth they use, and the length of time they use it instead of paying for a dedicated line that may not be fully utilized.[21,24]

ATM supports a number of service classes. The classes determine how the information will be converted into ATM format and how the cells will be treated in the network. Class A is for constant-bit-rate (CBR) services such as voice and video. Class B includes variable bit rate (VBR). Class C deals with connection-oriented services, and Class D with connectionless services.[21] Class X is a pure (native) cell relay service that requires no adaptation. In reality, only Class A (circuit emulation) and Class X (native cell relay and/or frame relay and LAN emulation support) have emerged commercially (even there, the support of circuit emulation is limited). Class D was slated to be used to support SMDS internetworking, but the commercial viability of this service is bleak. ATM utilizes a transfer mechanism that is independent of the type of service. However, provisions must be made to deliver the agreed-upon (serviced-based) grade of service. Another way of looking at ATM services is simply to focus on the kind of cell-transport contract that is supported: CBR, VBR, unspecified bit rate (UBR), and available bit rate (ABR). Refer to Refs. 25 and 26 for more extensive treatment.

ATM uses the cell as its basic unit throughout the network. An ATM cell is a protocol data unit with a fixed length, a header that contains routing information to be used by the network switches, and an information field. The ATM standard specifies that all data be encapsulated within a 48-byte section; each cell also includes a 5-byte header section containing virtual circuit routing information. These fixed-length cells of 53 bytes require less processing overhead to switch them, so they can be routed at much higher speeds. Due to the fixed format of the two cell fields, switching can be done in hardware, effectively reducing the intraswitching processing time. The network uses only the header information, regardless of the payload, except in case of service interworking (e.g., frame relay-to-ATM network interworking).

ATM uses virtual channels that have a prespecified rate, based on either administrative-based provisioning (specifically for permanent virtual connections), or on a per-call signaling basis (specifically for switched virtual connections). Both a maximum rate (called *peak cell rate,* or PCR) is specified (this bit rate is less than or equal to the physical bit rate of the user-to-network interface), and an average rate (called *sustainable cell rate,* or SCR). In effect, this mechanism supports *bandwidth on demand.* This much-abused term simply means that the user can send cells (at the access channel speed) at a time-averaged rate of SCR, but can occasionally "burst" up to a time-averaged rate of PCR. (Note that in both cases the speed of cell injection is always the same, but the average over the time horizon in question is different, as described.)

Cells are identified as belonging to a virtual channel by information in the header. This information can change as it flows from switch to switch because this information is only a relative connection pointer. However, ATM is connection-oriented, which means that a connection must be set up before information is transferred. The switch analyzes the header information and switches the cell from the incoming multiplexed stream to the outgoing multiplexed stream. The switch also maintains the integrity of the cell sequence.[24]

Independent of transmission speed, ATM is also unconstrained by the physical media of the network. It can operate over twisted-pair coaxial and fiber and also by means of wireless technologies. Public carriers offering ATM-based services include Teleport Communications Group, AT&T, Sprint, MCI, BellSouth, Pacific Bell, Ameritech, and Wiltel.

ATM provides for an integrated, service-independent network that can transport the services of today as well as the services of the future without requiring a new infrastructure. Organizations are now planning to use ATM for their enterprise networks. Service providers offering various services are connected to the access subnetwork (to which users connect); a core ATM network is used for citywide or regionwide aggregation. In ATM, just like in ISDN and frame relay, bidirectional logical channels are used for user-to-network signaling and control.

In the Internet application, ATM can be used as a customer-visible access technology, or as a backbone NSP technology to interconnect the provider's routers. The computer systems and the Web servers can be equipped with ATM interfaces compatible with those available on ATM switches. The belief is that the backbone network of the Internet should ultimately be ATM-based. If the access network is also ATM-based, the resulting end-to-end network can support high-speed communications. ATM is currently available at 45-Mbps to OC-3 speeds. In the future, ATM is expected to run at OC-12 (0.6 Gbps), or even higher speeds.

Various high-speed user services can use ATM for hardware-level, high-speed switching. This enables ATM to be a switching technology for multiprotocol applications. An ATM interface adapter card can provide multiprotocol access by converting traffic coming from different end systems into ATM format.[21]

Interworking units (IWUs) could be used to link a non-ATM-access networks to the core ATM network. The IWU terminates the ATM virtual channel by providing an appropriate protocol peer. An example is frame-relay-to-ATM or Ethernet-to-ATM interworking. The processing required by the IWU compared to the hardware-based cell routing will affect the throughput of the network.[6]

The user-to-network interface can be implemented according to the needs of the user and the primary function of the user's network. Interfaces can be developed for physical interfaces of different rates and formats.[6]

There is also a need for standards to specify the interface between ATM and the customer-premise equipment (CPE), as well as the residential broadband access network. Standards are also needed for the internal home bus of the future where PCs and set-top boxes can communicate.[19] ATM must have different-speed interfaces for access lines slower than SONET rates and must also overcome the problems of technology costs and interoperability problems among ATM products.[21]

The business created by broadband/ATM networking by the end of the decade could be approximately $3 trillion. David Dorman, chairman and CEO of Pacific Bell, predicted the information superhighway "media frenzy" will only intensify in the years ahead. A ubiquitous, nationwide, broadband network, he said, will cost upward of $250 billion but will create $3 trillion ($3000 billion) in commerce by the end of the decade. Dorman predicted that telecommuting would become the first commercial hit of broadband networks, although others disagree. Companies manufacturing and designing ATM systems are trying to make the transition to higher-speed networks as painless as possible. In an enterprise context, the corporate information data warehouses are probably the best locations to upgrade. This is where a major portion of network traffic occurs as users access the warehouse seeking information. If the throughput is increased, then productivity is increased.

8.4.2.1 ATM drivers. There are a number of attributes of ATM technology that are important in analyzing ATM adoption in the market. ATM is a statistical multiplexing technology designed for broadband applications and therefore needs relatively large amounts of aggregate bandwidth (i.e., ATM users) to be effective. It is generally agreed that, for this reason, there will be virtually no use of ATM *below* T1/E1 rates (1.5/2.0 Mbps) and higher rates are really required for ATM to be effective. There may be some deployment at T1/E1, but it will be limited. ATM provides a technology that for the first time applies equally to both LAN and WAN environments. It promises to eliminate the protocol translation at the LAN/WAN boundary that exists today, although there are significant problems to be solved before this vision is realized.

Economic. In studying the economics of ATM in the WAN there are two cases to consider: (1) ATM over private line services, such as between ATM-based user enterprise switches and (2) the use of carrier ATM services, either between ATM enterprise switches or between conventional bandwidth managers and routers.

The use of ATM over conventional lines has some problems. The benefits of statistical multiplexing with ATM can only be achieved when there is enough aggregate traffic. It is doubtful that there will ever be any economic benefits at T1/E1 rates and below (this is partially due to the relatively high overhead of ATM). The limited use of DS3 lines in enterprise networks at the relatively economical rates prevailing in the United States is an indicator that few enterprises will be able to take advantage of ATM for its economic benefit in a DS3 private-line scenario. Given the aggressive public tariff strategies to be adopted by carriers with regard to ATM services, there will be little use of ATM over private-line facilities. The utilization of a carrier service means that the statistical multiplexing works in favor of the user, resulting in lower transmission costs. Additionally, the user is outsourcing the "risk" associated with the technology to an outside party.[27]

Carriers can clearly encourage users to utilize ATM services by pricing them more attractively than frame relay or private line. Given the competition for enterprise users in the United States, it seems likely that carriers will adopt this strategy. This would drive the relatively rapid adoption of ATM in the same way that frame relay is being driven by aggressive carrier pricing.

Application. A key point to note is that ATM is a multiservice technology. For voice-only or data-only applications between two single points, there are unquestionably better solutions, such as TDM and frame relay. Multipoint applications immediately favor ATM (and/or a switched service). It is likely that in the next few years all Internet backbone networks will migrate to OC-12 ATM.

Technology. Over time, ATM switching will likely become more cost-effective than time-division multiplexing systems (currently the mainstay of WANs). This is likely to occur toward the end of the decade. Once the ATM infrastructure is in place, applications will follow. Perhaps a large portion of the *initial* ATM usage will be by way of adaptation of legacy environments.*

8.4.3 Cable TV

When regulations restricting competition are relaxed, new service options will become available. As the public policy continues to enable more and more competition, the regulatory barriers that have kept cable and telephone companies out of each other's base businesses are surely going to fall.

During the next few years, distributive broadband cable networks will continue to be installed and/or upgraded in major metropolitan areas of the United States. These networks will be based on HFC technology. It is likely that a new network would have one cable per household carrying both subscription television services and telephone traffic.

The digital technology for these systems is still relatively undeveloped. They are expected to begin with analog video, limiting the number of channels to around 60. This system operates in much the same way as existing broadcast services: all the channels are transmitted down every cable. The system is relatively simple because services do not need to be "switched" at the local exchange to be sent to each customer. The transition to digital transmission will increase the number of channels available because of the compression technology, discussed earlier. The timing of the transition will depend on demand for the services and future technology developments affecting the cost of digital video servers and consumer equipment. In a multichannel environment many "niche" services might also be available.

---

* David Owen, ATM Adoption in the WAN, NET 1995, pp. 10–12.

The next significant step will be the transition to digital-interactive or video-on-demand services. This enables you to access any program you want to watch, any time—with the video controls of Pause, Fast-forward, and Rewind. However, only those programs digitized and stored in video servers connected to the network will be available. And, currently, the cost and time involved in converting old program material to digital is considerable. As noted, high-quality real-time compression is becoming available, and its cost is expected to decrease considerably over time.

Although decreasing rapidly, the cost of memory space is also a factor. Video on demand is a broadcast system. Each time a program is ordered, the video server will locate the program in its memory banks and send it through the switched network of exchanges to the household requesting it. If there are few video servers for programs that need to be transmitted between cities, heavy demands will be placed on the communications network. The costs of digital video servers, of broadband switching, and of transmission will have to fall substantially if a video-on-demand service is to be widely available within the next decade. The cost of computer memory and transmission is falling, and broadband switches are still being developed. Substantial restructuring of tariffs will also be needed if a video-on-demand service is to compete with video rentals.

Once an interactive digital network is in place, it will be possible to combine the separate broadband and telephone services of the network on a single cable. Bandwidth or data-rate limitations of copper-wire pairs used for telephone services will be overcome. The final step in developing an interactive broadband network—the capacity to send high-speed data both from and to each "telephone" connection—requires cable technology that can support high-bandwidth two-way services. Optical fiber offers this capability, but the coaxial cable technology currently being used in the broadband networks has limited return-path capability. (See Fig. 8.4.)

In the recent past, both TCI and Time Warner Cable, the two largest cable operators, have announced major infrastructure upgrades. TCI plans to increase the channel capacity in its systems from 50 to 500 channels through the use of digital compression. Time Warner developed a full-service network in Orlando, Florida, that offered cable television, video on demand, and fully interactive capabilities. Bell Atlantic also began testing an interactive, switched, broadband network for delivering cable television, telephone, and other services over the same wire. At the other extreme, Southwestern Bell, in the first transaction of its kind, purchased two major cable-television systems in Virginia.

Both cable and telephone companies want to offer video-on-demand services to compete with video rental stores (a $12 billion market).

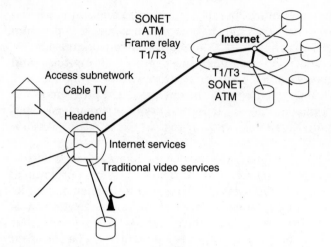

Figure 8.4   Cable-TV access to the Internet.

Besides providing video on demand, cable companies want to compete for a share of local telephone business (an $80 billion market) by offering a new generation of cordless phones that can enable communication with a cable set-top converter. Conversely, telephone companies want a share of the market that provides basic cable television service. And everyone is hoping major new markets for interactive shop-at-home services will open up.*

In the meantime, while waiting for the digital video market to develop, the cable TV companies are offering Ethernet-based 10-Mbps Internet access services over their cable infrastructure.

For a comprehensive treatment of video-on-demand technology, markets, and opportunities, see Ref. 28.

8.4.4 Economics: approaches and direction

Pricing of *access* will most likely be the biggest factor in the expansion and development of the Internet. Companies must balance their pricing with a look toward growth and building of infrastructure to support it. The faster a company can find a solution that will generate returns, the sooner it can upgrade its systems. Whoever strikes the best mix between the two will be the most successful.[29]

If carriers can effectively communicate what they have to offer to businesses and consumers and can convince them that Internet access is something they need, they will effectively generate revenue to reinvest

---

* Internet source—Mitchell Kapor, 1995 Wired Ventures LTD.

in their networks and offer more services. By effectively communicating the Internet's advantages, they can ensure its growth and their own profitability as an ISP. But up to this point most IXCs and local exchange carriers (LECs) have in general not done a good job of advertising some of their other services.[29]

Internet access offered by the local telephone companies has been hampered by existing regulatory constraints. The Modified Final Judgment ruling issued as part of AT&T's 1984 divestiture prevents Bell Operating Companies (BOCs) from carrying traffic across local access transport area (LATA) boundaries, although this is expected to change soon, with the Communications Act of 1996. The traditional restrictions have prevented most BOCs from playing a significant role as an ISP.

Alternate access providers, such as TCG, are well positioned to provide access to the Internet. One approach is to be a pure bandwidth provider using dial-up, ISDN access, dedicated access (e.g., fractional DS1, DS1, DS3, or OC-3), frame relay, or ATM. The service could be packaged with ISPs (e.g., PSI). As another alternative, providers could offer trunking and backbone capacity to ISPs. Dial-up can serve single-user accounts for e-mail, FTP, and Web access. High-speed dedicated access is targeted to business users. To get into the business, these providers have establish servers, such as domain name servers, FTP servers, e-mail gateways, and Web servers. Also, they can lease space to content providers. Furthermore, they could themselves be information service providers (own and manage servers and information). Figure 8.5 exemplifies the technology required to support these and related access services. As an example, TCG offers high-quality, low-overbooking access to the Internet at 1.544 and 10 Mbps now, and 45 and 155 Mbps in the near future.

Elimination of government subsidies for the NSF backbone has had an impact on pricing structures for Internet usage. When the subsidies were in place, flat-rate pricing developed as the norm. With the elimination of subsidies, money will need to be recovered from the consumer. Just how much is unclear. The biggest impact will be seen in the carrier-to-carrier pricing. This could also be passed down to customers. Telephone companies will be pushing for usage-sensitive pricing. This could cause strong companies to refuse interconnection with these companies. Because of this ". . . many Internet experts share a concern that pricing issues could lead to isolated networks."[29]

As the Internet access business gets more competitive, small upstart companies have the option of either being bought out or folding. The market is seeing a consolidation of the Internet access providers into major players. If providers stick with the standard flat-rate access fees that exist today, they will need to have an extensive client base in order to stay in business and offer quality service. If they implement IPng in

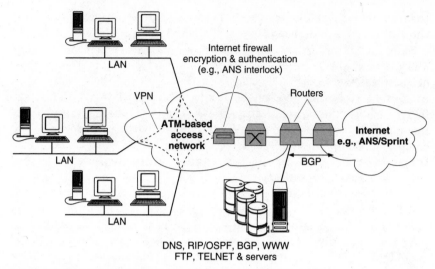

Figure 8.5   Example of alternate access providers' Internet service.

their systems, they will be able to offer special service guarantees needed by real-time applications and can charge premium prices for the service.[29]

8.5   Example of Broadband-Based Application: WebTV

This section provides a short discussion of an interesting cross-pollination of Internet and broadband technology, called *WebTV* by some and *intercasting* by others. This concept was just appearing at press time; hence, only basic capabilities are discussed. Although WebTV is not exactly a broadband service as discussed in the early part of the chapter, it "mingles" with broadband, and benefits from broadband (as will be discussed shortly). Furthermore, WebTV illustrates the fusion or convergence of technologies, eliminating previous lines of demarcation.

Intercasting is a technology developed by Intel that intertwines WWW pages with TV broadcasts. With it, video producers can back up their real-time broadcasts with all the resources of the Internet.[30] For example, a sports fan could call up batting averages to a window in the screen of a baseball game; news programs could provide background analysis for those who want to go beyond a two- to three-minute story; advertisers could offer viewers the opportunity to purchase their product or obtain more information about it. It can be considered a new media; however, it is expected to complement rather than supplant existing media. It is being positioned as a medium that can "combine the digital power of the PC, the global interactivity of the Internet, and the rich programming of television."[31]

Station KGW (Portland, Oregon) ran a successful demonstration in 1995. PC manufacturers such as Gateway, Hewlett-Packard, and others are planning to introduce support equipment. In fact, WebTV decoders could already be purchased from several manufacturers at press time, for as little as $300. Table 8.4 depicts kickoff milestones in 1995–1996, including the formation of the Intercast Industry Group. The group is composed of PC manufacturers, broadcast, and cable TV industry representatives. Proponents hope that intercasting will take off as soon as the PCs support the decoding function.

Intercasting will probably not reorder the world to the point where people will be reading newspapers on TV screens or watching real-time TV on the PC. However, intercasting, that is, the Internet media added to the TV, is expected to enrich print and broadcast with its unique capabilities.

TABLE 8.4   Intercast Technology (from press releases by the Intercast Industry Group)

2/8/96	Continental Cablevision, Inc., General Instrument Corporation, TCI Technology Ventures, and Time Warner Cable Programming to join the Intercast Industry Group.
10/23/95	Leaders in PC, broadcast, and cable industries announce formation of Industry Group to promote new digital medium for the home PC.
10/23/95	America Online, Inc., has licensed its award-winning World Wide Web browser for use with Intercast.
10/23/95	Packard Bell will offer Intercast-enabled PCs in mid-1996.
10/23/95	QVC to support the Intercast medium.
10/23/95	Gateway 2000 to support the Intercast medium.
10/23/95	CNN Interactive to support the Intercast medium.
10/23/95	NBC to support the Intercast medium.
10/23/95	Starting in 1996, WGBH will produce programs like *NOVA, This Old House,* and *Frontline* with new Intercast content.
10/23/95	Viacom, Inc., to support the Intercast medium.
10/23/95	EN Technology to support the Intercast medium.
10/23/95	Intel currently testing prototype Intercast systems with home PC users.
10/23/95	Intercast TV window will be embedded in Netscape Navigator 2.0 and appear as an additional capability.
10/23/95	Asymetrix to support the Intercast medium.
10/23/95	Comcast Corporation to support the Intercast medium.
10/96	Several products available in stores.

Television signals contain pauses, called *vertical blanking intervals* (VBI),[32] to allow for the electron beam that creates the picture in the cathode ray tube (CRT) to move from the bottom of the CRT to the top of the CRT. These "lines" already contain information—for example, captioning; in Europe these lines are used for teletext information. Intercast takes up about half of the remaining capacity (96 Kbps) to broadcast Web pages. Note that this is about three times the speed of a high-end modem. The Web pages are stored on a hard disk on the Intercast PC/TV and are displayed in a window on the screen. The only new component needed to make this work is an intercast chip (estimated to cost $50[30]) to decode the broadcast Web pages. However, the VBI information is *one-way only:* it is a *receive* mechanism.

The received Web pages would typically contain background information about the broadcast. (See Fig. 8.6.) If the PC is further connected to the Internet (via a dial-up line), the pages can then add an interactive character to the broadcast. This can be accomplished by following the links from the intercast Web page *received* in the VBI. Proponents see this as instant interactive TV, using infrastructure and technology that already exists. Because Web pages can connect to computer programs or people (e.g., via e-mail or low-end video-conferencing), the only limit on the interactivity is the bandwidth of the link from the PC/TV to the Internet. Although the dial-up speed is now only around 28.8 Kbps, this chapter discussed a number of ways to increase that speed in the future using ADSL and other technologies, such as ATM. Furthermore, if the signal is received via cable, there now are services providing Ethernet-level speeds right over the same media using cable modems (e.g., a U.S. service called @Home).

It appears that this service will initially be targeted at residential customers. However, it is possible that business applications may evolve in the near future. For example, financial-news TV/cable networks could start to embed pages that contain additional analytical information (tables, reports, analyses, etc.) as part of their programming. Another example could be distance-learning applications over broadcast TV (see Ref. 9 for a comprehensive discussion), where Web pages can be used by specific (corporate) learners based on their specific needs or interests.

The following material, found at http://www.intercast.org, provides additional details on this concept.

8.5.1   General questions on intercasting

1. What was announced on October 1995?

ANSWER: On October 23, 1995, it was announced the planned formation of an industry group to promote a new digital medium for the PC, called *Intercast,*

1. **Regular Television Programming** — The Intercast medium incorporates the same cable and broadcast programs you're used to watching now.

2. **Real-Time Information** — With Intercast technology, programs can now easily carry continuously running text such as stock prices.

3. **Web (HTML-formatted) Pages** — Imagine the wealth of information you can have access to when television programs are accompanied by Web pages filled with text and colorful graphics. The Intercast medium includes the ability to broadcast Web pages, as well as hyperlinks in these pages to related Internet sites. Your favorite programs can now be your guide to the World Wide Web.

4. **Television Station** — All three components of the Intercast medium (your regular television program, accompanying Web page, and real-time information) are combined into a single signal here.

5. **Transmission Path** — The Intercast medium is transmitted just like your regular television program. It is sent via transmission tower, cable or satellite. It is received at the home through either a regular antenna, cable connection or C-band satellite dish.

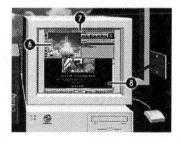

6. **Program Window** — Your favorite television programs appear on your computer's screen in a sizable window. Watch in a quarter-screen window when you want to see the accompanying Web page, or go full-screen when all you want to see is your show. Picture quality has higher resolution than standard color television screens.

7. **Real-Time Stock Ticker** — Stock prices continuously run here at the top of your screen (15-minute delay).

8. **Web Page** — Your PC breaks down the television signal, extracting the Web page information from your signal. The Web page is viewed right alongside your television window.

Figure 8.6 WebTV operation. (*Courtesy of Intercast Technology.*)

which combines the digital power of the PC, the global interactivity of the Internet, and the rich programming of television.

2. What is in the Intercast Industry Group (IIG) and what is their charter?

ANSWER: America Online, Asymetrix, Comcast, En Technology, Gateway 2000, Intel Corporation, NBC, Netscape Communications Corporation, Packard Bell, Turner Broadcasting's CNN Interactive, QVC, Viacom, and WGBH Educational Foundation have agreed to be the founding members of IIG. The proposed charter of the group is to develop and promote the intercast medium. They share the common goal of developing technology, PC platforms, software applications, and content for broad market deployment beginning in midyear 1996. Their goal is to create an industry-accepted, open medium that will spawn industrywide implementations.

3. What will a home PC user be able to do differently when PCs using intercast technology are available?

ANSWER: Home PC users will be able to receive and interact with unique content created around existing TV programming. The intercast medium links the Internet and television on your PC. It combines two mediums already popular with end users—the Internet and television—and enhances both by adding interactive digital information to television and full-motion video and a familiar context to the Internet. For home PC users who value immediate access to Internet information, the intercast medium provides a fun and easy way to get more from what they watch. Examples of this new content include in-depth stories on a news topic being broadcast, concert schedules for the artist whose video is playing, and continuous sports statistics for the football game you are watching.

4. What exactly is intercast technology? Who is developing it?

ANSWER: Intel is developing intercast technology. Intercast technology is a series of protocols and data formats that allow the transmission of data along with a television broadcast, and reception of that data by PCs equipped to do so.

5. How does my PC get this intercast content? Who is going to sell Intercast-enabled PCs, and when?

ANSWER: Intercast content is received in the same way you now receive TV—whether it is through a conventional TV antenna, cable, or C-band satellite dish. The methods now used by your television set to receive analog transmissions can also be used by your intercast technology–enabled PC. The PC manufacturers named in the press release intend to build PC platforms that incorporate the intercast technology.

6. Has intercast technology been tested in the "real world"?

ANSWER: Working-prototype systems are currently being tested in Portland, Oregon, metro-area households. In addition, on October 10, 1995, KGW, a Portland NBC affiliate, successfully completed the first live transmission of broadcast video and Web pages to an intercast-enabled PC. Nationwide testing will begin in February.

7. Will the intercast medium be available outside of the United States? What are the plans for implementing intercast on the PAL broadcast standard?

ANSWER: Initially, intercast technology will be developed and deployed in the United States and is based on the NTSC broadcast standard. PAL is expected to be supported by the end of 1996. Differing TV standards and government regulations in various countries will have to be addressed before the intercast medium can be broadly deployed outside of the United States. This will be one of the issues the Intercast Industry Group plans to address.

8. How do I join the Intercast Industry Group? Is the IIG an open industry effort? How can other companies get involved?

ANSWER: All public information about the Intercast Industry Group (IIG) is available on its Web site. The initial IIG members will be companies that have joined together to take a leadership position in defining and developing the intercast medium. The goal is for the intercast medium to become an open, generally accepted, industry approach supported by all PC manufacturers and broadcast companies. If your company is interested in joining, please write to: The Intercast Industry Group, PO Box 10266 Portland, OR 97210. You'll be put on the mailing list and you will be notified when further information becomes available.

9.   How will the IIG promote the intercast medium and ensure its success?

ANSWER: The member companies will develop product and content that supports the intercast medium. The IIG plans to build awareness of the link between intercast content and intercast technology through press and marketing campaigns. The IIG hopes to ensure its success by broadening the array of products and services that can take advantage of this new medium.

10.   Who else is developing a capability like this?

ANSWER: There are no solutions in the marketplace with the same capabilities of the intercast medium. There are products that broadcast data to PCs, and products that send simple program information to TVs. However, this is the first announced technology aimed at the integration of the Internet and television on a PC.

11.   How is this different from interactive TV?

ANSWER: The intercast medium takes advantage of the digital power of the PC to merge the Internet and television and provide an interactive experience on the existing communications infrastructure. The interactive TV model is based on video servers that would send programming over a two-way broadband communications network to a set-top box connected to a TV. The intercast medium is not meant to displace TV or to compete with interactive TV. Depending on the program and individual preferences, some content will be better-suited to the Intercast medium, and some will be better-suited to the interactive TV model.

12.   How is this different from the Web terminal product recently announced? Isn't this just Web pages on your TV?

ANSWER: The fundamental difference between the intercast medium and other Web terminal or WebTV products is the unique capabilities made possible by the digital power of a high-performance PC. With the intercast medium, the user—not a video server—controls the interactive experience. The hard disk of a high-performance PC can store hundreds or even thousands of broadcast Web pages, making this information available at any time for the user to manipulate. The high-resolution graphics of a PC are unmatched by conventional TV monitors. Pentium™ processor–based PCs enable a level of integration of the Internet and television impossible on a conventional TV set.

13. What is the difference between intercast technology and cable modem technology? .

ANSWER: The two technologies are different but complementary. The intercast medium will be the way in which you receive television programs and associated data on the PC. This information is received in the same way that you receive television today—whether that is by antenna, cable, or C-band satellite dish. The Intel CablePort Adapter is a cable modem that is part of an end-to-end high-speed data communication system for Hybrid Fiber Coax Cable systems. It will facilitate very fast access to the Internet from a home PC. A cable modem could be used as a back channel to speed the Internet access you may choose to initiate using the hyperlinks contained in the intercast content.

14. What type of video input will intercast technology–enabled PCs accept?

ANSWER: The fundamental difference between the intercast system and television is the unique capabilities made possible by the digital power of a high-performance PC. Simply put, at this time, this convergence of the Internet and TV is only possible on a PC. The hard disk of a high-performance PC can store hundreds or even thousands of broadcast Web pages, making this information available at any time for the user to manipulate. The high-resolution graphics of a PC are unmatched by conventional TV monitors. Pentium processor–based PCs enable a level of integration of the Internet and television impossible on a conventional TV set.

8.5.2 Questions about hardware, software, and intercast technology features and availability

15. Will intercast content be accessible by my existing PC platform via an add-in card or other technology upgrade?

ANSWER: In order to receive the full benefits of the intercast medium, the user will need to purchase an intercast technology–enabled high-performance PC. These PCs take advantage of the speed of the PCI bus, which results in cost-effective video delivery and display. However, third-party hardware vendors are expected to provide solutions for the existing PC-installed base.

16. What kind of hardware is really necessary to make the intercast system work on the typical new home computers that are being sold today?

ANSWER: Intercast technology will be bundled with new multimedia PCs. The following configuration is typical of new multimedia PC: 100-MHz Pentium/E processor, PCI bus system board very fast graphics adapter (similar to ATI mach 64 with 1 MB) 8-MB RAM, 28,800-bps modem, CD-ROM Soundblaster™ or equivalent 800-MB hard drive.

17. What type of video input will intercast technology–enabled PCs accept?

ANSWER: High-performance PCs enabled with intercast technology also become video-capable platforms for a wide range of applications. Video input from a camcorder could be turned into a .AVI file, or video from a camcorder could be compressed for a video phone application. Intercast content from broadcasters cannot be recorded on most home VCRs, however, as most of the high-speed associated data is lost in the recording process on consumer-grade VCRs. Of course, you can use your PC to capture and cache Web pages, and your VCR to record video.

18. With which operating systems will the intercast medium work?

ANSWER: Intercast technology is a transport standard for digital data associated with TV signals. As such, it can be adapted to many different operating systems. Intercast technology is based on open industry standards, many of which are based on Internet protocols that were pioneered on UNIX systems. The first implementation is expected to be on Windows 95.

19. Will this work on my Mac?

ANSWER: Yes, technically intercast medium will work on an Apple Macintosh™ computer. Intercast technology will be available to all PC manufacturers. Apple is in the best position to tell you their plans regarding support of intercast technology.

20. Do I have to use a different browser for intercast content than regular Web content?

ANSWER: No. The intercast Web browser can be used like any other Web browser for accessing sites on the World Wide Web. Eventually, intercast technology–compatible browsers will probably also be available from a number of vendors. The intercast Web browser can also receive Web pages broadcast to your hard disk using intercast technology. These broadcast Web pages will be cached and retrieved from your hard drive. When you follow a link from a broadcast Web page out of the cache to the Web, the browser will connect you to your regular Internet service provider. At that point, it functions as any other Web browser.

21. Do I need a modem to receive intercast content?

ANSWER: No, a modem back channel is not required to receive broadcast Web pages. Intercast uses one-way broadcast communications to receive the TV programming and related Web pages. Embedded in these broadcast Web pages are hyperlinks to additional Web pages. Some of these hyperlinks send the user to broadcast Web pages previously stored on the user's hard disk, while others connect the user to related sites on the actual World Wide Web. Users with direct Internet connections can use the hyperlinks to seamlessly connect to actual sites on the Web.

22. Do I need ISDN?

ANSWER: No, ISDN service is not required. The main path for broadcast data is the television signal. A standard PC modem (28,000 bps recommended) is used for back-channel transactions.

23. How do I request a specific page?

ANSWER: Intercast technology uses one-way broadcast communications to broadcast TV programming and related web pages. Embedded in these broadcast Web pages are hyperlinks to additional Web pages, some of which have already been broadcast and stored on the user's local hard disk, and some of which are on the actual World Wide Web. To request a page that has been broadcast to the user's hard disk, the user simply clicks on that page's title, which is displayed in the Media Library section of the viewing screen. To request a page located on the World Wide Web, a user clicks on a hyperlink, if provided, or types in the URL address of the Web site.

24. How do you request a specific page? Are you on-line while watching TV? Do requests go out over the Internet and responses over TV signals?

ANSWER: To request a Web page that has not been broadcast to a user's hard drive via the intercast medium, the user will need to go on-line with an Internet service provider via a modem *back channel*. For example, a television advertiser may send down three "pages" of information related to its ad, along with the television commercial. The intercast technology user can browse these three pages at leisure. The advertiser may also embed within these pages a hyperlink to the advertiser's Web site on the Internet. By clicking on this hyperlink, the user will be connected to the advertiser's Web site via the modem back channel. To go to a site on the Internet for which a link is not provided in the broadcast Web page, a user will need to type in the URL and use the intercast browser just as he or she would use any other Web browser.

25. If you are using the VBI as a "shared pipe" among many users, then does the interactivity come from downloaded content that the user subsequently browses?

ANSWER: Each broadcaster will broadcast Web pages with content about its particular programming. The user receiving these broadcast pages on an Intercast technology–equipped PC will be able to interact with these pages or store them for later use on his or her PC. When transactions occur between the user and the advertiser or broadcaster (e.g., purchasing an item or participating in a viewer poll), a telephone modem back channel is necessary.

26. Closed captioning is also broadcast in the VBI. Does this mean I will not be able to see the closed captioning if I am receiving Intercast content?

ANSWER: No. There are many lines in the VBI. Closed captioning is broadcast on a different line than intercast content. You will be able to view both closed captioning and intercast content on your PC while you watch TV.

27. When will PCs be available with intercast technology? Who is going to be shipping them? How will I know if they are intercast technology–ready?

ANSWER: The PC manufacturers named previously intend to build PC platforms that incorporate the intercast technology beginning in 1997. We expect other PC manufacturers to incorporate the technology in the future.

PC manufacturers will use the intercast symbol on external PC packaging and in the retail environment to denote those systems which are intercast technology–enabled, allowing the user to easily recognize systems with this capability.

28. Who is planning to produce this new medium? When can I expect to see it?

ANSWER: The content providers announced today are already working on the first pilot programs for the intercast medium. Intercast content is inserted into the existing television signal by a PC-based authoring system designed by Intel. Television producers will be integrating the new Web-formatted content into their shows beginning in mid-1996.

29. Will home users have to pay a premium to be able to access the intercast broadcast data for a particular television program?

ANSWER: Intercast content is expected to be delivered along with the regular television signal, similar to today's economic model for TV. Some content will be free or advertiser-subsidized; some will be included as part of basic cable services; and some will be offered as a premium service.

30. What is going on with vertical applications?

ANSWER: Intel will publish an applications programming interface (API) for intercast technology that independent software vendors can develop by mid-1996. It is the software vendors who will develop vertical applications for this medium.

31. I have heard that some cable operators already use the VBI for other services. Will I still receive intercast content?

ANSWER: Currently, certain local cable operators strip VBI data sent by national networks and use the space for their own purposes. In this case, users of intercast technology–equipped PCs may not be able to receive intercast content. The Intercast Industry Group plans to address these issues. However, users may also need to call their local cable provider to alert them to the problem.

References

1. Hennigan, Peter, "Broadband Communications in Web/Internet Context," Stevens Institute of Technology, class project, fall 1995.
2. Burns, Mark, "Broadband and the Internet," class project, Stevens Institute of Technology, fall 1995.
3. Olshansky, R., "Broadband Digital Subscriber Line: A Full Service Network for the Copper Plant," *Telephony,* June 12, 1995, pp. 52–60.
4. "Apple Looks to Exploit Internet for Conferencing," *Multichannel News,* June 12, 1995, p. 25A.
5. McQuillan, J., "Reinventing the Internet for Broadband?," *Business Communications Review,* March 1995, pp. 12–14.
6. Sharpe, R., and H. Lalani, "Taking ATM Home," *Telephony,* August 21, 1995, pp. 38–42.

7. Hudgins-Bonafield, C., "How Will the Internet Grow?," *Network Computing,* March 1, 1995, p. 80.
8. Wires, G., "Broadband Deployment: A Salad Bar of Services for the Masses," *Telephony,* May 23, 1994, pp. 35–40.
9. Minoli, D., *Distance Learning Technologies,* Artech House, Norwood, Mass., 1996.
10. Wilson, L., "Overpopulation in Cyberspace," *Communications Week,* August 21, 1995, p. 3.
11. Minoli, D., *Imaging in Corporate Environments,* McGraw-Hill, New York, 1994.
12. Minoli, D., and B. Keinath, *Distributed Multimedia Through Broadband Communication Services,* Artech House, Norwood, Mass., 1994.
13. Blackenhorn, D., "ISDN Gets Big Push from Telcos," *Interactive Age,* July 31, 1995.
14. Bowling, B., "Online Services: Technology, Applications, and Vendors," class project, Stevens Institute of Technology, fall/winter 1995–96.
15. Eldib, O., and D. Minoli, *Telecommuting,* Artech House, Norwood, Mass., 1995.
16. Baines, R., "Getting Information to Everyone's Home," *Electronic Engineering Times,* October 2, 1995, p. 48.
17. Wirbel, L., "Digital Standards Promise Expansion," *Electronic Engineering Times,* October 2, 1995, p. 43.
18. Mankikar, M., " 'Highway' Power Needs," *Electronic Engineering Times,* May 8, 1995, p. 82.
19. Joshi, B., "Residential Broadband Access Networks and Technologies," *TELECOMMUNICATIONS International Edition,* July 1995, pp. S33–S40.
20. Dawson, F., and R. Katz, "Time Warner Does Online Homework in Elmira," *Multichannel News,* July 24, 1995, p. 4.
21. Nigam, S., "ATM and ISDN: The Odd Couple," *Telephony,* September 4, 1995, pp. 26–30.
22. Wirbel, L., "Renaissance for SDV?," *Electronic Engineering Times,* September 18, 1995, p. 94.
23. Nolle, T., and M. Raymond, "Broadband in Enterprise Network," *Datapro Communications Analyst,* July 1995.
24. Delisle, D., and L. Pelamourgues, "B-ISDN and How It Works," *IEEE SPECTRUM,* August 1991, pp. 39–42.
25. Minoli, D., and M. Vitella, *ATM and Cell Relay in Corporate Environments,* McGraw-Hill, New York, 1994.
26. Minoli, D., and A. Alles, *LAN, LAN Emulation, and ATM,* Artech House, Norwood, Mass., 1997.
27. Minoli, D., "Introducing New Technologies," *WSTA Ticker,* November/December 1995, pp. 10 ff.
28. Minoli, D., *Video Dialtone Technology: Digital Video over ADSL, HFC, FTTC, and ATM,* McGraw-Hill, New York, 1995.
29. Heckart, C., "Serving Up Broadband Services," *Telephony,* April 17, 1995, pp. 38–44.
30. Browning, J., "Television Arrives on the Internet," *Scientific American,* May 1996, p. 28.
31. Intercast Industry Group press release, October 23, 1995.
32. Minoli, D., *Telecommunications Technology Handbook,* Artech House, Norwood, Mass., 1991.

Virtual Reality Applications on the Internet and Intranets

Virtual reality* (VR) is a set of hardware/software-based applications now entering mainstream commercial application. Applications are appearing both on the Internet and in intranets. The technology is particularly well suited to applications that simulate the experience of actually "being at" the remote site, such as enhanced videoconferences, industrial and architectural walkthroughs, interactive travelogues of distant cities, house-hunting, product modeling, marketing, and training. Major commercial on-line service providers are either readying virtual reality on-line offerings, or are planning to do so.

Fortune 500 companies are finding savings, competitive advantages, or greater customer satisfaction—or all three—from virtual reality business applications. The most promising uses are in training and in design. Motorola and Nortel have applied the technology to train their staff and/or clients, and have documented significant savings compared to other methods of achieving the same goal.

There are now over 300 companies selling approximately $255 million worth of virtual reality products and services. The VR market is expected to reach $6 billion in 1999[1] according to aggressive estimates, and $1 billion according to more conservative estimates[2] (the lower figure is the safer one to use). Although about half of the 2000 market will go for home- and site-based entertainment, virtual reality products will be used by all facets of society, including commercial/industrial, the government, the military, and university and secondary schools. Just the instructional and development market for virtual reality is expected to grow from $1

* This work was supported by IMEDIA, Morristown, NJ (Imedia1@1X.NETCOM. COM). Jo-Anne Dressendofer is thanked for her support.

million in 1995 to $355 million by 2000, resulting in an annual average growth rate (AAGR) of 31 percent. This figure includes virtual reality technology that will be present in technical/engineering colleges and universities, and the "developmental" virtual reality expenditures on advanced (but not yet commercialized) applications, along with pure science and research systems not included in the other categories.

Given this potential and given the corporate interest, this chapter provides a self-contained discussion of the topic, from the perspective of the operative question: "Is virtual reality the evolving killer-app for the Internet?"

9.1   Virtual Reality Technology: A Synopsis

Over the past five years there has been increased commercial interest in VR. Some think that VR will have as great an impact on society as television. At this juncture, however, VR is still an evolving technology in the early stages of development. The term *virtual reality* was coined by Jaron Lanier, the founder of the first commercial VR company (VPL Incorporated), in 1989.[3]

VR covers a range of definitions. A definition advanced by Sheman and Judkins, termed the "five *i*'s of VR," applies to the characteristics it possesses. The "five *i*'s" are *i*ntensive, *i*nteractive, *i*mmersive, *i*llustrative, and *i*ntuitive.

Intensive.   In a VR setting, the user should be concentrating on multiple, vital information, to which the user will respond.

Interactive.   In a VR setting, the user and the computer act reciprocally over an appropriate interface.

Immersive.   VR should deeply involve or absorb the user.

Illustrative.   VR should offer information in a clear, descriptive, and illuminating way.

Intuitive.   Information (virtual or otherwise) should be easily perceived.

Some see VR as the fusion of three other technologies—telephone, television, and video game—to arrive at a technology that is better than the linear sum of the three. In VR, there is strong emphasis on communicating with *virtual worlds* (VW) via a more intuitive and more sense-inclusive human-computer interface (HCI) than would otherwise be possible. The goal is to make the technology accessible to non-computer-language-literate users. Until the present, the input/output to a computerized system has been restricted to a fairly unintuitive textual user interface (TUI) or to an improved, but still limited, mouse-based GUI. With VR, the interface is the human's hands, legs, eyes, or body; a mouse can also be used.

In a VR environment, what happens in the virtual world depends on the user. The user's inclusion in the virtual world and the ability to influence what happens in it are key advancements of VR compared with earlier technologies. VR facilitates spatial navigation, a method of using graphical symbols to shop on-line and to travel through cyberspace.[4]

It is possible to trace VR concepts back 70 years, to work in vehicle simulation (in the late 1920s), teleoperation (in the 1940s), three-sided screens in "cinerama" (mid-1950s), and head-mounted CCTV-based teleoperation work at Philco and Argonne National Laboratory. Flight simulations conducted by NASA in the mid-1960s started to give shape to VR as we know it today. Computer-generated synthetic displays for virtual environments started to appear in late 1960. Work continued in the 1970s, when the term *artificial reality* was coined. In 1989, the term *VR* was coined to refer to all virtual environments (e.g., virtual cockpits, virtual environments, and virtual workstations). More work continued into the 1990s, with added emphasis on technology and applications. As early as 1990, you could purchase $90 gloves (e.g., Mattel's Power Glove), although these had no tactile feedback. High-end systems used by organizations such as NASA cost millions of dollars.

An application often talked about is the use of VR in architecture. Proponents prognosticate that eventually every aspect of product design, manufacturing, and testing will be done using VR equipment and workstations. Almost anyone with a training or visualization problem should check it out.[1] However, for many applications, VR development for practical use has been hampered until recently by lack of money and available technology. Progress continues to be made. Today's low-end VR software costs less than you might suspect and runs on a standard desktop PC.

9.1.1 Baseline hardware to support VR

Several technologies have converged to bring 3-D visualization and VR interfaces into mainstream commercial use: faster PCs, improved digital-compression techniques, better video-capture boards, high-resolution bit-mapped displays, and live data feeds (e.g., stock market feeds). There are software development tools for building VR applications (e.g., World ToolKit from Sense8). Until very recently, VR application required specialized platform and programming skills. Tools now appearing bring the technology to Windows-based PCs and other workstations.

The following hardware is needed to support VR applications:

1. *Powerful computer platform* (workstation/PC).

2. *Visual displays* supporting stereoscopic vision (three-dimensional environments). Initially these displays are incorporated in either

headgear or in multiple curved or angled screens (not a single flat screen). Later on, retinal imaging may replace other external hardware. Eye-tracking devices may also be utilized, but it is important to reduce the lag time between eye movement and what the user sees on the visual display more than is achievable at this time.* There are three basic types of high-end visual systems: (1) head-mounted display; (2) an apparatus resembling binoculars atop an articulated arm; and (3) projection-based VR, wherein images are projected on the walls and floor of a room called Cave Automatic Virtual Environment (CAVE).

3. *Tactile recognition and feedback devices* (e.g., data gloves and data suits). On the input-interaction side, cameras may eventually be able to track sensors on the hand/body and not require a traditional data glove.

4. *Hearing devices,* typically incorporated in the headgear.

Advances in computing power (processors, memory, etc.) will improve VR realism and reduce cost. However, other improvements are needed. Technical advances are required in sensory-perception interfaces, automated input, computer-base platform, and 3-D graphic displays. Photorealism is required to make VR useful and believable to the user. Displays should be shown in three dimensions using stereoscopic vision. Stereoscopic vision requires quite a bit of computing power, since twice as much information needs to be processed than in monoscopic vision. The frame rate must be adequate, and the size/perspective of objects in the VR world must change as appropriate. Typical tools now consist of a helmet containing visual screens and a steerable treadmill operated by the user to control speed and direction. Other realizations of VR are strictly desktop PCs with a way to navigate 2-D renditions of 3-D environments.

Table 9.1 depicts some key VR suppliers (hardware and/or software). About 50 independent software vendors (ISV) are now at work on VR projects, including large companies such as IBM, Digital Equipment Corporation, Silicon Graphics, Sony, and AutoDesk. In addition, most of the major commercial on-line service providers are either readying VR on-line offerings or are planning to do so. VR is particularly well suited to applications that simulate the experience of actually being at the remote site, such as interactive travelogues of distant cities, or house-hunting. It can also help facilitate computer access among people who do not speak English.[5]

---

* Using this technology, the VR system can produce higher resolution for the images within the range (cone) of vision than for those currently outside this area.

TABLE 9.1   Key VR Suppliers

Company	Key VR product
3Dlabs	Graphical chips for PCs
Ascension Technology Corp.	3-D tracking
AutoDesk	VR software
Creative Labs	3-D Blaster for PCs
Crystal River Engineering	3-D sound
Division Ltd.	VR software/hardware
ERG Engineering Inc.	VR for education & museums
IBM TJ Watson Research	3-D graphics accelerator
Intergraph	GLZ boards for PCs
Sense8	WorldToolKit
Silicon Graphics, Inc.	Workstations
SRI	Contract VR research
StereoGraphics	Stereo displays
Virtual i-O	HMD manufacturer
Virtual Technologies	VR gloves
Virtuality	VR entertainment

9.1.2   Software and tools

VR applications are required to deliver the VR experience to the user. This discussion focuses on software tools to be used to develop these applications.

Computer software capabilities are required to create and manipulate virtual environments. There is a need to have nontechnical designers utilize the software. There must be capabilities to quickly create geometry, surface finishes, and lighting in a window-based menu/palette-driven manner. For other applications, motion, timing, synchronization, sounds, and other features are important. Interoperability of software is another requirement. Some existing tools used in 2-D/3-D graphics, such as pull-down menus, drawing, painting, light modeling, and material-modeling tools can be extended to support VR.

Most of the development work in building a VR application involves the graphical description of the 3-D world (the database) and writing the behavior for the objects. The former involves manipulating prebuilt objects from libraries of common visual displays (buildings, cars, airplanes, etc.), or adding your own graphical items from a CD clip or graphical modeling tool.

At this time, these tools draw from a variety of techniques and approaches that have evolved over the years. User interfaces proposed/used include 3-D pull-down menus and CAD techniques such as snap, move, and rotate. For example, a system by Strayling called PhotoVR combines a VR authoring system with AutoDesk's AutoCAD, AutoShade, and 3-D Studio Products.

VR technology is also being added to Web browsers. Section 9.1.2.2 describes languages being developed to reduce the size of files that have to be sent over the Internet to support 3-D.

9.1.2.1 Graphics subsystems. The graphics subsystem (GS) is the part of a VR system's reality engine that handles image generation.[6] The GS supports rendering and animation. Rendering and animation are the basis for almost all visual displays in a VR system. In most VR and telepresence environments, the system has some three-or-more-dimensional models of the application domain, whether it is an artificial world, the inside of a body, the stock market, or molecular modeling. *Rendering* is the process of producing a representation of this world that can be displayed using whichever two-dimensional output devices are available. *Animation* is the process of repeatedly drawing slightly different views of the world to represent changes that occur, either under the control of the system or through actions taken by the user. Rendering algorithms and animation quality are intricately linked, since the more efficient the rendering algorithms are, the higher the animation frame rate can be.

Animation means, literally, "bringing to life." Rather than a static picture of a scene, animation allows a system to change, whether that change is caused by the passage of time or by actions taken by agents in the scene. This capability makes animation critical to VR—without it, we would simply be looking at three-dimensional photographs. Animation is key to the interaction capabilities of virtual environments. Animation does not imply that objects in the scene are moving; it could be that the viewpoint of the user is changing, as in an architectural walkthrough application. Colors of objects in the scene can change in relation to changes in properties of those objects; for example, heavily traded stocks could become brighter in a financial analysis application. Animation also must handle objects that move: people working in a cooperative environment; agents controlled by the system; bouncing balls in a virtual physics laboratory; walls, doors, and windows in an architectural-design application.

The well-developed field of computer graphics has produced many algorithms for rendering three-dimensional objects onto two-dimensional displays. There are many complications involved in this process, including (but not limited to) drawing polygons, filling polygons, shading, shadowing, displaying patterns, changing line and pen styles, and clipping and visible-surface determination. In general, objects are represented using polygons because they are relatively simple to draw and, by using a sufficient number of polygons, most shapes can be closely approximated.[6] Patterns are important because they can be used to reduce the number of polygons necessary to adequately represent real-world objects. Since rendering time is generally proportional to the number of polygons to be drawn, reducing the number of polygons to be drawn allows increased animation quality through higher frame rates.

Clipping and visible-surface determination are among the most important stages of rendering. Clipping determines which objects in the three-dimensional world show through the viewport. Visible-surface determination is the process of determining which parts of the visible objects are visible from a particular viewpoint. Conceptually, it is not very difficult; unfortunately, unless the hardware being used has built-in support for visible-surface determination, the algorithms take a lot of computation (there is a lot of active research in the area of improved visible-surface determination algorithms).

The GS receives graphics commands from the VR engine's CPU, builds the image specified by the commands, and outputs the resulting image to display hardware. Separation of graphics processing from the CPU has the advantage of allowing hardware specialized for graphics to work in parallel with the CPU. However, because effort is expended in the communication, the bus between the CPU and the GS must have the bandwidth to make the advantage worthwhile. (Thus, when selecting or designing a GS it is important to be aware of the capabilities of the bus interface.) Once graphics commands are read from the GS to CPU bus, a GS performs four basic functions: geometric processing, scan conversion, raster management, and display generation. During geometric processing, input vector and polygonal data is received in 3-D-world space coordinates. During display generation the digital frame buffer is scanned and converted to video signals. Digital-to-analog converters combined with other circuitry support the generation of the video signals.

GSs range in capabilities and price. There are high-end million-dollar subsystems that are included with highly specialized systems (e.g., flight simulators). For VR, GSs that are part of a general development platform are usually more suitable. For GSs of this type, the Silicon Graphics Reality Engine 2 and the Evans and Sutherland Freedom Series 3000 sit at the high end. In the midrange, Silicon Graphics' Elan GS and Evans and Sutherland's Freedom 1000 are representative offerings. Silicon Graphics' Indy and Intel's ActionMedia are low-end examples.[6] In addition to price, the most useful metric is the number of shaded, textured, antialiased polygons that can be drawn in a second. When combined with the desired frame rate of the application, this metric defines the maximum complexity of a scene in the virtual environment. Typically, vendors quote figures obtained when using optimal input data (e.g., triangular meshes of 25 vertices). An application will usually be unable to provide optimal input data and will therefore achieve significantly poorer performance—sometimes by as much as 50 percent. The Reality Engine 2 and Freedom 3300 systems can produce over 200,000 textured, shaded, antialiased polygons per second and around 600,000 shaded (not textured) polygons per second for around $80,000. SGI's Elan and the Freedom 1100 can output about 80,000 textured polygons per second and 200,000 shaded polygons per second for around $25,000. At the lower end, an Indy GS can produce 24,000 shaded polygons for around $5000. Intel's ActionMedia GS outputs 3000 shaded polygons per second for about $3000.

Another important consideration is the graphics language available to application developers. Each GS now seems to recognize its own proprietary set of commands requiring translation or redevelopment of software when switching platforms. An emerging graphics programming language interface standard in the PC and workstation arena is OpenGL. OpenGL is based on Silicon Graphics' Iris GL (graphics library) and has been endorsed by many leading PC and workstation vendors (e.g., Sense8's WorldToolKit uses OpenGL).

9.1.2.2 Language support. Generic application languages are important to develop VR environments and applications. VRML, discussed in Chap. 4, is considered by some the next step in presenting graphical embellishments to the World Wide Web sites. VRML works much like HTML, except it works in 3-D. It is a language for describing multiuser interactive simulations, or virtual worlds networked via the global Internet and hyperlinked with the World Wide Web.[7] On a VRML site, you "walk" around a three-dimensional world that contains different objects and places. As the users walk through the site, they can interact with the objects and even communicate with them. For instance, a VRML site might look just like a museum, and the user could walk the hallways looking at different paintings or sculptures. "Touching" one of the pieces of the art might take the user to another VRML site, or even to a regular HTML site with information about the artist, much the same way that HTML hyperlinks work. VRML allows application developers to describe the physical attributes (size, shape, shading, etc.) of 3-D objects, but it cannot be used to describe their behavior. For that, a scripting language is necessary. VRML is still new and under development.[5]

VWs in the World Wide Web can be navigated, but the user cannot interact with anything. By linking Java, virtual world developers will be able to create objects with which viewers can interact by picking up the objects, rotating them, moving them elsewhere, and eventually altering them. There is, reportedly, a huge pent-up demand for 3-D on the Web.[8]

VRML is a demanding application. Quite a bit of computer power and bandwidth is needed. On the plus side, VRML works well and offers vivid, accurate scenes. VRML 1.0 does not allow for multiple avatars in shared spaces: it is a one-camera view of inanimate objects. VRML will continue to evolve quickly. VRML+, an initiative from World Incorporated, with IBM backing, is expected to add behaviors to objects, which would create multiuser capabilities. Also, there is discussion of developing VRML 2.0.

The term Virtual Reality Modeling Language was coined in late 1993 by Mark Pesce and Tony Parisi. Soon thereafter, the group (headed by Pesce and Brian Behlendorf, of *Wired* magazine) began work on a VRML specification immediately following the conference.[9] The list members proposed several candidates. There are five competing proposals currently under consideration by the VRML Architecture Group, including approaches offered by Microsoft, Apple, and Sun Microsystems.[10]

The VRML Architecture Group, developers of VRML, have designated Sun Microsystems' Java as the reference scripting/animation language for writing VRML applications. Java will be the reference language for VRML, not the standard language. It is the group's intention that VRML be completely open. To that end, VRML will support such other languages as Perl, C++, OLE SafeTCL, and Python. At this point, however, Java is particularly suitable for animating VRML objects and will be more widely accessible sooner, with the introduction of Netscape Communications' Navigator 2.0 browser.[8]

In the two years since VRML was invented, it has attracted considerable attention and has spanned many start-ups. Many companies are working on browsers.

9.1.3   Current limitations of VR technology

Field use of the VR viewing technology can be difficult, disorienting, and nausogenic.* Displays used in VR do not come close to TV quality (they are said to make the user "legally blind"). But proponents indicate that the current limitations are beside the point: it is the potential of the medium that is worth consideration. In addition, looking back two to three years, it can be seen that the quality has improved significantly over this period. A number of related approaches are also being explored. For example, techniques based on cognitive principles are being investigated (this implies the use of symbols to trigger photo-

---

* This is treated in more detail later.

realism). In other approaches, the brain is allowed to fill in the gaps (this is based on techniques developed for 3-D computer graphics animation). The development of "believable" computer-generated images is vital to the success of VR in many applications (medicine, architecture, telepresence, etc.). This relates to the five i's discussed earlier.

Computer-generated models of simple environments (for example, architectural models) are based on accurate information relating to scale, measurements, and relative positioning of objects. This leads to a reasonable degree of believability. Software applications are good at simulating the effects of light on objects and textual properties of materials. However, other aspects need refinements (e.g., showing light reflections off buildings when there are many objects in the virtual world, as in an urban setting, and introducing the more distant environment in a more feature-rich manner).[6]

In terms of visual devices aimed at supporting total immersion in VR, progress is needed in these areas:

- Development of eye-tracking technology to reduce the amount of visual information that has to be supported at any point in time. (Note that this refers to a self-VR experience rather that to a group-VR experience".)

- Support of adequate frame-refresh rates to ensure "believability."

- Support of a 270° field of view.

- Introduction of ergonomically based, technically advanced optics/display hardware and software, including "retinal displays."

- Sounds spanning the virtual environments, giving the user a sense of where the sounds are coming from in the VR space. Sound spaces with good position and orientation tracking must be supported. This includes echoes, Doppler effect, impact sounds when collisions occur, sound waves and effects, and satisfying the psychology of hearing.

Another area where active research is under way relates to input mechanisms, and especially to the development of intuitive mechanisms. Voice and gestures would be ideal methods, but these are technically difficult to implement. Voice recognition is difficult, particularly in noisy environments and/or as the voice of the speaker changes due to emotions, colds, or just time spans. Gestures have been implemented using "VR gloves," but so far this approach is not as intuitive as hoped. One promising method uses radio tracking of body parts with radio transmitters called "body jewelry"; these devices do the same job as the Data Suit but without the cumbersome gear.

Tactile devices are used to make the total immersion in a VR environment more believable by recognizing that materials have weight, resistance, texture, etc. This entails supporting modeling of the tactile texture by the VR system, including density, malleability, heat absorption/reflectivity, and smoothness/roughness. This involves not only the mechanics of developing noncumbersome, technically correct, and realistic tactile devices, but also the physiology of touch, the nature of materials, and physics.

VR environments must provide a high degree of changeability. For example, a virtual workspace should have furniture that is easily rearranged and should have a choice of view through the window. VR may become the place to do things that cannot be done in architect-designed buildings. Additionally, spaces based on non-Euclidean geometry can be built. Virtual money could be used in virtual environments, as an abstraction of current "plastic/bank server/electronic" money.

Finally, applications must be easily developable, and the hardware platform on which they ride must be fairly inexpensive.

The following is a list of reasons, based on surveys, for slow penetration this far.[11]

1. The experience may not be compelling.

2. The price point is too high.

3. There is not enough software support.

4. Distribution is poor.

5. Quality and reliability are lacking.

In developing business and training applications, these factors have to be taken into account.

9.1.4 Networking

Currently there are a number of VR sites on the Internet. However, to get the full benefits of VR, you need to employ broadband networks. For example, Argonne National Laboratory is testing wide area ATM to connect leading supercomputer sites with VR CAVEs.[12] The linkup supports interactive simulations in CAVEs, proving that geographically dispersed research and development staff can effectively collaborate on projects. The network is open to those groups that submit projects to the NII Testbed to demonstrate large-scale simulations, interactive CAVE/virtual reality applications, or large-screen stereoscopic applications.* OC-3 (155-Mbps) ATM links will be utilized. This is increasingly the trend. Many applications in the future will require this kind of bandwidth.

---

* For more information contact Tim Kuhfuss at kuhfuss@anl.gov.

9.2   Evolving Virtual Reality Applications

9.2.1   Market status

According to The Perth Institute (Hawley, Pennsylvania), the VR market will grow from more than $100 million in 1994 to about $6 billion by 1999.[1] Business applications will be a sizable fraction of that total. Companies such as Silicon Graphics and Hewlett-Packard are expected to be big beneficiaries. A more conservative $1 billion forecast has been advanced by other analysts.

There has been a large amount of media hyperbole about the technology. Fortunately, VR is a lot closer to reality now than just a while ago, but widespread introduction is not going to happen overnight. Researchers expect that it will be 5 to 10 years before the technology actually does what the press currently claims it can.* Cost remains a factor, but prices are dropping. Computing power is getting cheap. You can buy a VR workstation, software, and peripherals for as little as $75,000 (high-end systems sell for $1 million or more). For some applications these prices may well be justified: for example, if a company needs to redesign the floor space every 12 months or so, then the investment in a VR-based layout tool may well be worthwhile. Low-end VR software also runs on high-performance PCs.

In spite of the limitations, VR has already been commercially successful for computer games and arcades. The main market for VR has so far been in the area of entertainment; however, new applications are evolving. For example, in Japan, people can shop for new kitchens. Applications to architectural designs are being developed.[3] For rapid prototyping, VR is well suited. Training applications are appearing. Military simulations also continue to be a sizable market.

The outlook for VR business applications has changed dramatically since 1994. Observers believe that "the hype peaked in 1994. . . . Now VR companies are making money . . . early adopters are saving money."[1] Several "bleeding-edge" users are finding savings, competitive advantages, or greater customer satisfaction—or all three—from VR business applications. The most promising uses are in training and in the design of everything from big manufactured items to entire factories.[1] As an example, the Detroit Virtual Reality Center, developed by EDS, has more than 50 business partners codeveloping various VR commercial applications.

VR software is getting easier to use and to program. A new generation of 3-D object-oriented GUIs is replacing C and C++. These kinds of languages let the user define the models according to the job, then

---

* Some say that VR is today where PCs were 15 years ago.[1]

assign motion, weight, and other properties. Some of these languages were discussed earlier.

There is now commercial interest in VR in the field of design. Simulation software for manufacturers, companies involved in design, and architects have already put VR to use. VR business applications provide companies with the opportunity to save money, develop competitive advantages, and improve customer service. The technology is mostly used for training purposes and design projects, including buildings, automobiles, and products. Continuing improvements in hardware and software are bringing the cost of the technology down to affordable levels. Many companies, including McDonnell Douglass Aerospace, General Motors, and Bechtel Corporation, are using the technology in many aspects of business such as engineering and product design.[1,13]

However, as noted, there are deployment limitations based on performance and price. For a number of applications, developers may be disappointed about the features actually available. For other applications, the features may be rudimentarily adequate. Application of VR to specific applications has not yet been as successful as hoped. It may be that developers underestimate the challenges to be faced to get the technology to a workable level. Even well-funded projects may lead to limited results. For example, NASA funded a project, with partial success, to use telepresence in harsh environments such as Antarctica.

There have been documented applications in the following fields:

- Banking, financial trading, investments
- Art, science
- Engineering
- Games, amusement, entertainment
- Building
- Marketing (including shopping)
- Military
- Education
- Shopping[14]

There is a growing community of integrators that can assist users in deploying the technology.

VR has been identified as one of the 10 most promising technologies currently under development.[2] There are now over 300 companies selling approximately $255 million worth of VR products and services. By 2000, the VR industry will be posting annual sales of over $1 billion and reaching an AAGR of 33 percent. Although about half of the 2000 market will go for home- and site-based entertainment, VR products will be used by all facets of society, including commercial/industrial, the government, the military, and university and secondary schools.

As noted previously, a market report conservatively projected the VR market as follows[2]:

VR market (in $ millions)	1994	1995	2000	1995–2000 AAGR%
Instructional & development	70	95	355	31
Design & development	25	30	150	40
Entertainment	60	110	500	35
Medical	10	20	50	20
Total	165	255	1,055	33

The table shows that the instructional and development market for VR is expected to grow from $1 million in 1995 to $355 million by 2000, resulting in an AAGR of 31 percent. This figure includes VR technology that will be present in technical/engineering colleges and universities and the "developmental" VR expenditures on advanced (but not yet commercialized) applications, along with pure science and research systems not included in the other categories.

Applications of the design and development VR market are in engineering, architecture, and chemical design and development. This market will grow from a 1995 market value of $30 million to $150 million by 2000, reaching an AAGR of 40 percent.

Entertainment uses account for the largest VR market value, and these are expected to continue growing at a rate of 35 percent AAGR to the year 2000. Mass-produced, single-user, entertainment VR systems will be the driving force behind this market growth, from a 1995 value of $110 million to $500 million by 2000.

The medical treatment VR market will also sustain growth. The 1995 market value of $20 million is projected to reach $50 million by 2000, reaching a 20 percent AAGR.

9.2.2 Examples of applications

Some apply Fubini's law to VR technology, which describes a four-step evolution:

1. People initially use the technology to do what they do now, but faster.
2. They gradually begin to use technology to do new things.
3. New things change lifestyles and work styles.
4. New lifestyles and work styles change society . . . and eventually change technology, introducing new technology, at which point the cycle starts over.

Initially, VR can be seen as a natural progression of 3-D computer-generated models. Applications in development and design, for example, could include a more complete analysis of the design due to viewing it from any angle, as well as the communication of designs to clients using 3-D walkthroughs, which might have voice commands, sounds, and touch. As a future application, clients may walk to an empty building site and put on a pair of glasses that lets them see their proposed designs, as well as the site, and move things around to meet their architectural expectations. Automotive companies in Detroit, for example can access real-time feedback from design consultants in Europe. By linking geographically dispersed CAVEs, designers can simultaneously view a virtual life-size car model and interactively move or restyle body parts so participants at other sites get a firsthand look at proposed alterations.[12]

Early adopters include McDonnell Douglass Aerospace, which is conducting VR design analysis in early product development. General Motors is applying VR in the design of 1997 and 1998 models, as discussed in the previous paragraph. Ford Motor and Chrysler are also using VR methods. Bechtel is trying VR in many phases of architecture and engineering.[15] Electrolux, a Belgian appliances maker, used a VR showroom in 1995 to test-market new appliances. The Port of Rottterdam is training harbor pilots with a VR simulator. Motorola has tested a $0.5 million portable VR training center that could replace a $5 million training facility. Gulfstream Corporation uses VR to let clients choose comforts for corporate jets.[1,13]

Some specific examples of applications follow (these are often called "VR Demonstration Prototypes").[3]

- VR has been used as a marketing and presentation tool by furniture companies in Europe, Japan, and the United States. The VPL Incorporated VR system (introduced in 1989) was used commercially in Matsushita's Shinjuku store to sell kitchens.

- At the University of North Carolina, VR technology has been used for the architectural design/walkthrough of an addition to a church.

- At the University of North Carolina, VR technology has been used to design the University's new computer science building (Sitterson Hall).

- Architectural prototypes at the ACG Centre, although still expensive, are nonetheless proofs of concept.

- Intel and Sense8 cosponsored "Designing a Virtual Home," a two-day demonstration of a prototype architectural application. This two-person "VR station" represented the architect working with the client. It included helmets, a joystick, and a pointing wand used to move surfaces and to change their appearance.

- Work is under way to make virtual explorations of long-lost monuments and buildings.

- EDS has opened the Detroit Virtual Reality Center to generate demand for virtual reality solutions.[1] About 2600 businesspeople from more than 350 companies have seen the demos as of late 1995. The company believes that the opening of the center signifies a transition from primarily entertainment and government use to a broader VR use. The company has a VR theater and a VR CAVE. It develops applications, lets clients use the facilities, consults with companies that want to set up their own operations, and works with partners to improve hardware and software.

- Albert Kahn is an architectural firm that does $600 million a year in construction design for factories, hospitals, auto makers, R&D centers, and public institutions. The company has used VR for initial design work. They want to give the customer a sense and feel of different options.

- GM R&D Center uses VR for model design. CAD data is fed into VR programs using homegrown software packages and a VR CAVE.[16] The CAVE is a barren room with a car seat in the middle. The walls of the CAVE are screens that, with the help of shutter glasses flickering on and off every $\frac{1}{60}$ of a second, provide the illusion of a 3-D environment. The company uses it to market-test new designs without having to spend time and money building prototypes out of wood.[17,18]

- Newbridge showcased VR, multimedia, and other broadband applications at Interop 1996.[19]

- Nortel joined Superscape to train telephone attendants using VR methods.[20]

- Three-dimensional VR tours use real 360° photography to show travel destinations.

- VR videoconferencing.[21]

- The Berlin Multi-media Arts and Communications Center also has used the VPL Incorporated VR system.

- Computer graphics have been developed using VR techniques by the Advanced Computer Graphics Center, Royal Melbourne Institute of Technology (Australia).

VR is being utilized in the field of architecture as the natural evolution from CAD. The process of design in architecture is usually consultative, and a "virtuconference" between the architect, consultants, and clients is a desirable way to undertake these and related tasks. Earlier we listed the Intel Sense8 prototype. Potential future applications of VR, not only in architecture but also in other areas, include the following:

- *Marketing tool.* Interactive adaptive displays demonstrate the use of different roofs, finishes, landscaping, etc. Also included are inside walkthroughs. This application can also be put to work in many other settings.

- *Communications tool.* To cross distance and language barriers between the architect/marketer and the client. This application can also be put to work in many other settings.

- *Education tool.* To train the architect/professional or walk through a repository database of designs. This application can also be put to work in many other settings.

- *Evaluation modeling tool.* For example, to study effects of lighting (of electrical systems and/or natural lighting) or other factors. This application can also be put to work in many other settings.

- *Modeling/design tool.* To analyze spaces by "getting inside them." Also to incorporate data during schematic design stages, then look at different solutions. Also VR can be used for macroscale urban design planning.*

One consequence of VR on the physical environment will be the reduced need for buildings due to more tele/virtucommuting. Virtu-commuting will bring the workspace to the user. Already, a large amount of banking is carried out over telecommunication links. Admin-istrative and consultation work, sales, and writing/publishing are examples of applications where tele/virtucommuting will play an increasingly important role. Design and architecture are also suited to this VR application.

Service-oriented buildings, such as shops, will be reduced in size, since these services have the potential to be carried out at home using VR links (this has been called virtual shopping). Entertainment in vir-tual theaters is a possibility. Medical diagnosis is another possibility. Travel agencies and virtual vacations will be other applications.

---

* There has been work in VR to support urban design. Such design necessitates an understanding of how to best use spaces in urban settings by taking into account the impact of traffic of people, cars, and trucks. Applications to the London Underground, Cross Rail, and the city of Berlin have been documented. In this application, VR aims at convincing the appropriate client (regulating body, lobbying groups, the public, the politi-cians, the bankers, etc.) that the proposed urban guidelines can be implemented in a suc-cessful, practical, functional, and pleasing manner. VR also aims at convincing the urban designers that models and simulations are realistic and accurate, and that VR can be used as a powerful and useful tool in urban design.

Widespread use of VR for applications such as groupware, travelogues, and product ads is only about one year away, according to industry observers.

9.2.3 Application aspects

This section describes other applications of VR. Many of these same applications can be extended to any field, including marketing and corporate training.[6]

9.2.3.1 Science. Scientists collect large quantities of data to analyze in order to come up with some hypotheses. Since we live in a three-dimensional world, much of the information comes from events that are inherently three-dimensional. VR technologies give scientists new ways of data visualization. Mathematicians can see three-dimensional equations. Biologists can build 3-D models of genes. VR also helps researchers to create interactive simulations of scientific phenomena.

Virtual physics laboratory. A virtual physics laboratory is a virtual laboratory in which the users can conduct simple experiments that cannot be done in a real world. It was developed at the University of Houston-Downtown. A user wearing headgear and a control glove has a panoramic view of the virtual laboratory. There is a table, a pendulum, some balls, and a few odd devices that govern the actions in the laboratory. Users see an image of their hand that duplicates the motion of the real thing. Certain gestures of the control glove mean specific actions. Pointing the index finger, for example, sends the virtual physicist flying across the room. Parameters in the room such as gravity, friction, and drag can be controlled by users. The effects of the changes in the variables appear in the movements of the pendulum and the bouncing balls. Here, a ball can bounce as it would on Jupiter. The main goal of this virtual reality system is to demonstrate to students proper concepts about physical laws in order to avoid misconceptions. In this artificial environment, it is easy to see the effects of gravity without any interference of friction, which almost always plays a role in the motion of objects.

Biology. Virtual reality helps us to manipulate 3-D structure models. The GROPE-III system, developed at the University of North Carolina, is a molecular docking tool for chemists. Detecting allowable and forbidden docking sites between a drug and a protein or nucleic acid is crucial in designing effective drugs. Because both drugs and nucleic acid molecules are complex 3-D structures, locating effective docking sites is a complex task. Wearing polarized eyeglasses, the chemists view a stereoscopic image of the molecules. They can then use a special control device, the ARM, to grab one of the molecules and attempt to dock it with the other. The chemists can even feel the force field surrounding the molecules.

9.2.3.2 Medicine. Medicine has become a computer-integrated high-technology industry. VR and telepresence may have much to offer with its human-computer interfaces, 3-D visualization, and modeling tools.

Information visualization. Medical professionals have access to a volume of information and data formats, including magnetic resonance imaging (MRI), computerized axial tomography (CAT), electroencephalogram (EEG), ultrasound, and X rays. VR's graphics and output peripherals allow users to view large amounts of information by navigating through 3-D models. For example, radiation planning can be aided by adjusting virtual laser beams on a virtual body and seeing how well they will converge on a tumor. See-through displays could also be used to view real-time information such as patients' vital signs during surgery.

Motion analysis. The advanced input sensors of VR can be used for motion analysis, rehabilitation, and physical therapy. Motion analysis can help train athletes to prevent injuries and improve performance. For example, the Boston Red Sox used a data glove to analyze the pitcher's windup and pitch. In rehabilitation and physical therapy, full body suits may pinpoint motor-control problems. In other applications, virtual environments could be adjusted to the level of the user. For example, it may be easier to learn how to juggle if you started in an environment with reduced gravity.

Advanced 3-D medical modeling. These tools can be used to develop useful models of the human body and design artificial organs. Medical professionals can use VR to study the body by navigating in and around it. For example, a 3-D model of leg motion could be used to observe muscle dynamics while peering inside at the joints. Young surgeons can practice operations on VR cadavers and experienced surgeons could learn new techniques. As previously discussed, at the University of North Carolina, molecular models help biochemists visualize how well drugs will work by allowing them to maneuver molecules in space and actually feel the resistances between them.

Telepresence. Telepresence techniques could allow surgeons to conduct robotic surgery from anywhere in the world, offering increased accessibility to specialists. Prototypes have been tested that let the surgeons experience all the sensory feedback and motor control that they would in person. Telepresence could also be used to protect the medical professionals from potentially harmful situations such as AIDS exposure and battlefields.

9.2.4 Technology concerns

In spite of the potential, there are documented concerns about health effects of VR. NASA has shown that up to 90 percent of people tested show some kind of simulator sickness. Symptoms include motion sickness, cold sweats, nausea, salivating, turning pale, and vomiting. Also headaches, fatigue, and flashbacks can be experienced.[22,23] These symptoms arise from sensory conflict between what you see and what you think you see.

Dramatic disorientation may occur when using VR gear. At the University of North Carolina, some who used headsets designed to show doctors how organs and muscles were likely to appear inside the body were disoriented after such usage. "When she took off the headset and went to drink from a can of soda, she found she was pouring the soda into her eyes. . . . You can see that this has distressing implications in a system intended to be used in an operating room."[22]

In 1993 Sega Enterprises announced its $200 VR game based on Genesis. Then Sega got the results of a study they had commissioned from SRI. Soon thereafter the project was shelved. Some users who had used the prototype suffered jarring symptoms, from nausea to sore eyes. The U.S. military grounds pilots who experience "simulator sickness." Sega's retreat "sent a chill through the young VR industry."[23] There is concern about possible lawsuits.

Industry analysts say that cybersickness may create roadblocks to greater use of the technology.[22] Nonetheless, by the year 2000 a third of all video games are expected to be using such technology. Reducing lag time may diminish the effects in a number of applications.

Private companies are trying to head off potential complaints in a number of ways. In developing the VR goggles, Virtual i-O deliberately leaves clear viewing spaces around and under the image projected in front of the eyes.

9.3 Opportunities for Corporate Education/Training

This section describes applications of VR in business design, visualization, task integration, and in corporate and business training.[6] In fact, business applications have been discussed throughout this report, and the reader is encouraged to refer to the rest of the document for a more complete view.

Training: design. VR is proving beneficial to the process of design because of its value in communication and visualization. In addition, it will allow the designer to come up with trial runs; it is easier to recognize potential difficulties, errors, or problems when moving inside a design than when looking at a 2-D rendition. Because of the intuitive and interactive HCI, VR tools will be easier to use than CAD. Proponents believe that a VR system will act as a catalyst, stimulating creative thought and new end results.

Training: visualization. VR is an ideal tool for visualization. This will help architects, designers, decision makers, and so on. Today, 3-D computer-modeled animations allow visualization on a 2-D screen. When viewed at the appropriate perspective, a 2-D space gives a relatively good rendition of 3-D objects. In turn, when viewed at the appropriate perspective, a 3-D space gives a relatively good rendition of 4-D objects—many complex problems have four or more dimensions. Looking at 3-D animations on a 2-D screen gives the design some reality; however, there are limits to the believability; VR addresses these limitations and provides a quantum improvement.

Training: task integration. Task integration is common to many applications, including architecture and design. VR also addresses these requirements. For example, you may want to integrate a VR walk-through, drawings, specifications, estimates, and construction plans. Or you may want to integrate a presentation, product development, marketing, advertisement, and training to ensure a life-cycle-long synthesis. This is accomplished by linking the various computer subsystems that support the aspects to be integrated.

Training: real-time simulators. In a typical VR system, the user is immersed in a simulated world that exists only as an abstraction that comes to life by means of sensory stimulation. The user's actions in that virtual world are, for the most part, innocuous with respect to the real world. On the other hand, VR lends itself to applications where the artificial environment perceived by the user is a simulacrum of some real environment. To maintain the similitude of these two, it is necessary to map changes from one environment to the other. Changes in the real world are detected by sensors, which feed the reality engine, which in turn modifies the world as seen by the user. In the same manner, user actions that cause some modification of the virtual world also trigger actuators that will effect the change in the real world. One example is Tom Furness' "Super-Cockpit" project. The virtual world in this case is an artificial environment containing objects such as the landscape over which the airplane is flying, controls, and instruments. As the plane travels, the real-world landscape changes and so must the mock-up landscape in the pilot's artificial world. If the pilot decides to turn left at some point, the instruments in the virtual cockpit must reflect the change in course, and the airplane itself must be steered to the new direction. The development of interactive simulators that feature VR systems has shifted from being a military initiative to becoming an entertainment-driven technology trend. This is reflected in Martin Marietta's collaboration with Sega Corporation and the percentage of entertainment business done by firms such as Greystone Technologies and Thomson Training and Simulation. Until the present, work on such systems was concentrated on head-mounted displays for flight simulators and military training systems.

General training. Through virtual exploration of buildings, hostile sites, other countries, unbuilt buildings, or long-lost buildings, multidimensional data display and analysis education can be supported. A virtual design studio might include a virtual site that students could visit as often as they wanted on their way to realizing a design or some other project. The final result could be a VR presentation. Many applications are conceivable, including uses for business. VR is a powerful tool for education or, more generally, analysis, since people comprehend images much faster than they grasp lines of text or columns of numbers. Participation is critical to learning, and VR offers multisensory immersive environments that engage students and allow them to visualize information.

Training and simulation. VR simulators are useful for training that would otherwise be too expensive or too dangerous. Different training scenarios can be constructed and simply altered for variety. The U.S. Navy uses flight simulators to help train pilots for general navigation as well as special assignments. Battlefield simulations have been developed using real data from Desert Storm. These types of simulations can be used for training as well as planning. Distributed simulations allow users in remote locations to participate in the same environment. Training tools can also be used for common citizens. For example, virtual cars could be used for drivers' education classes, reducing the expense of cars and insurance and perhaps minimizing costly accidents by inexperienced drivers.

Classroom activities. VR offers tools for increased student participation. Classroom activities can use VR tools for hands-on learning, group projects and discussions, field trips, and concept visualization. Traditional teaching involves text, oral, and screen-based presentations, which do not use a human's full capacity to learn. VR allows natural interaction with information. Instead of reading about foreign places or watching a videotaped program, students can explore worlds of foreign countries, ancient times, or the human body. A current VR program for seventh graders lets students act as parts of algebra equations. VR offers a learning experience that many children and adults find interesting, thus giving motivation to learn.

Virtual classroom.   Telepresence offers remote learning with virtual classrooms. Students are not limited to classes that are taught at their school, in their town, or even in their nation. For business users, presentations are not limited to their company only; workers (especially knowledge workers) can be made aware of what other companies, labs, consortia, forums, and industry/standards groups are doing. Teleconferencing has allowed persons at different sites to form a virtual classroom with active class discussions. Telepresence has also allowed remote students to work together on group projects which may be an important part of class participation and learning.

Abstract representation and visualization.   VR provides the tools to visualize and manipulate abstract information, thus making it easier to understand. NASA has developed a virtual wind tunnel that allows the participant to use hand gestures to navigate around the virtual aircraft and view the airflows. Eastman Kodak engineers gained new insights using a 3-D model showing the interactions of heat, temperature, and pressure. Virtual environments can allow participants to experiment with physics concepts such as a virtual physics lab that allows students to control gravity, friction, and time.

Information retrieval.   Tools such as the GopherVR Organized Directories of Titles (GODOT) are VR servers for retrieving and displaying bibliographical information in 3-D from UNIX servers running a GopherVR browser. GODOT extracts an author's canon from on-line library catalogs and organizes the information in VR. Included are the author's books, books the author has contributed to, books about the author, books by the author's friends, and video clips, all displayed in 3-D navigable scenes showing the length and breadth of the author.[24]

Organizations find that trainees retain more material when the teaching environment is in VR and not in a traditional classroom.[25] Among those pioneering the effort are Motorola and Nortel, which have traditionally invested heavily in classrooms and training centers. The companies have recently begun migrating to desktop VR software that simulates hands-on work experience. For instance, the computer screen might show a 3-D schematic of a control station, pieces of equipment, or overview a manufacturing line. Students can interact with the virtual objects while learning the same sounds they would hear on real equipment.

Motorola and Nortel found that their low-end VR training software not only is cheaper and easier to deploy for geographically dispersed students, but in general also yields better results.[25] Another advantage is the capability to portray working scenarios that may not currently exist or to simulate critical experiences without real-life risks. VR training can reduce the cost of travel, instructors' fees, and maintaining large training centers.

Motorola tested VR in 1994 before implementing a pilot program. The test compared a sample of people trained with VR to those trained in the classroom. The results showed VR students outperformed the others once they were placed on the job. Observers say that there is excitement about these training prospects, since people are able to jump in and start working right away. Nortel is reportedly finding an average savings to customers of $3800 per student per course (figures provided by Superscape Incorporated).

Specifically, Nortel has developed, using the Superscape software, training software for telephone console attendants. The new Meridian 1 Attendant Console Simulator empowers even those who have low familiarity with consoles and computers to master a complicated multiple-button system in just a few hours. This fast, convenient, and relatively inexpensive PC-based approach to training is well suited for call-intensive sites that use attendant consoles, such as hotels, motels, hospitals, and government offices. Advantages of VR have already been proven, according to Nortel.[26]

Training that involves the actual handling and use of machinery is an effective way for industrial manufacturing workers to learn more about their jobs. However, hands-on training is costly because it requires a fully equipped laboratory that has to have all the machinery found in a real factory floor. If no such laboratory exists, a production line has to be shut down so that it can serve as a training facility. To find a more cost-effective training approach, Motorola's training organization is currently testing the use of VR in simulating the assembly-line setting so that training can be performed at any Motorola site.[27]

VR training software generally does not require special graphics boards or accelerator cards. VR applications can run on all sorts of desktops or notebook PCs. A number of Fortune 500 companies now use these tools. A customized VR training tool can be designed, produced, and implemented within four to six months—less if the customers know from the outset what they want and/or need. However, the high cost of VR still makes it a big-ticket item: a customized VR application costs anywhere from $10,000 to $100,000.

9.4 Opportunities for Marketing and Business Applications

Marketing. Proponents see significant opportunities for VR in marketing. Marketing is an area that has already benefited from VR technology. In London, real estate agents are using computer graphics, called *desktop VR,* to walk their clients through high-end real estate listings. The walkthroughs are not predetermined, and so are better than still photos or even videotape. This application highlights the convenience of showing real estate to clients who are at a distance. Another example of using VR technology in marketing is an exclusive U.S. furniture manufacturer who designs chairs with the client, using a similar walkthrough system to help customers make decisions. Prestige and personalized service are the highlights.

VR will allow marketers that currently rely on video presentations to add another dimension to product viewing, while data-mining programs would seek out correlations between large amounts of data to identify patterns.[28] Shopping simulations have been described in the literature as a way to better market products.[29] Banking applications are also on the horizon.[30] Recently, MBA students at Harvard Business School were taught to develop VR-based businesses.[31]

New interactive installations are being assembled in shopping malls in an attempt to expand consumers' interest in multimedia and VR technology. At Tempus, in the Mall of America in Minneapolis, shoppers can browse through an interactive corridor that turns into a whitewater river adventure, including motion simulation.[32]

VR helped the city of San Diego compete as a prime venue for the 1996 Republican National Convention. The city's data processing arm developed a 3-D model of the convention center that was used as a VR walkthrough.[33]

Business communication.   Business communication is just another form of marketing. VR enables the use of a 3-D paradigm of communication. This is beneficial in fields such as architecture, design, modeling, engineering, training (e.g., cockpit), medicine, and even representation of complex business data. One of the aims of VR is to have interactive environments in which humans can interact with one another; these environments are known as VWs. To make education and training more effective, you may need to employ VW concepts. This requires understanding the psychological effects of computer-generated space on people inside them. VWs should be made pleasant places to live. Some are using VR for advertising. VR seems to work best for packaged goods as opposed to computer products, which call for a substantial amount of informational content. Elements of VR are already starting to appear in some food ads.[5]

Business applications.   Businesses can reduce their costs, increase their decision-making capabilities, and become more directly involved with communicating data with others. VR offers improvements and inexpensive alternatives to present systems that are being used in the industry. Just some of the areas in which VR is having an effect are in spreadsheets, the stock market, information management, virtual designs, and virtual prototyping. Businesses can customize the way they represent and communicate real and abstract data in order to allow employees to utilize their human talent to their maximum potential. Proponents describe applications that can be made to simulation chambers that senior executives can use to formulate long-term corporate strategic plans.[34] For example, the technology can be used for "virtual downsizing": the modeling can help convince CEOs that the proposed organizational actions do not disrupt the company.

Finances. Companies and industries have traditionally made it a high priority to manage their finances. Spreadsheets are a tool that allow business people to simulate the behavior of their markets, products, and competitive companies. They can model and monitor the accumulation, distribution, and investments of their properties. The creation of a large-scale *virtual* spreadsheet, where information encompassing many variables can be interactively modified and examined, might be the justification for many businesses to purchase a VR system. The company users would have the ability to "experience" several days or weeks of a company's activities in just a matter of minutes. Bradford Smith, director of research for the Institute for Nonprofit Organization Management, has been working on such a system that would graphically represent how various tasks and activities contributed to the creation of wealth.

Stock market. The stock market deals in vast amounts of abstract data. Money managers are constantly looking for more effective ways to condense and streamline the way abstract information reaches them. VR offers the ability to creatively express the many variables of this information in real time. Planners can then organize the information in ways such that relationships between variables can be visualized in 3-D. Paul Marshall, president of Maxus Systems International got involved in 3-D representation of information by developing surface maps for his business. He has created a virtual system using Sense8's WorldToolKit to monitor many different variables, such as the attributes of stocks, abnormal volumes or occurrences, and fundamental inefficiencies. In the system, he can interactively choose certain industries and compare them across certain markets of choice. The viewer of the system can "fly" down into the specified subregions and move among the stocks and bonds that rise and fall. Depending on market conditions, the polygons of the stock will change their shape, position, behavior, and color.

Business prototyping. Virtual prototyping may be thought of as creating "soft designs." These virtual designs can save money and time in the development of new products. Using a CAD system for a design has the advantage of saving money, but the engineer or user cannot actually experience the product as in the real world; VR brings CAD designs one step closer to this ability. There are many advantages to creating virtual designs and prototyping those designs for the users. A major advantage is that many ideas and possibilities can be tried in a short period of time. Large changes that could be costly may take only a few minutes for a user to evaluate. The immediate effects that can be seen can allow a design to have shorter overall development stages. Not only can money be saved by doing immediate changes, but virtual simulation of a production and manufacturing process may reveal problems early in its design phase. Caterpillar Incorporated uses VR in its prototype designs. Typically, Caterpillar will have a small number of actual products that are run on the manufacturing line. Therefore, money cannot be invested on generations of iron prototypes, since each may cost millions to make. When evaluating the virtual prototype, safety and efficiency are important aspects, since the operators may control large hydraulic shovels or release large crushing devices on their surroundings. Although their visibility of the outside environment does not have the high detail of the real world, they do use real-time simulation.

Besides flight simulators, Boeing used VR to design its new 777 aircraft. This is its first aircraft to be designed without the use of a full-scale physical mock-up. With the system, Boeing can view passenger compartment interiors and some of the engine hydraulics. The ability to visualize a part installed among other parts enables B to determine if the part can be easily maneuvered during maintenance.

9.5 Internet's Next Killer-App

Proponents see Internet-based VR applications, such as those described here, as the next killer-app. Time will tell if these proponents are right.

References

1. Bills, R., "Reality At Last," *PC Week,* November 13, 1995.
2. *The Virtual Reality Business,* Business Communications Co. Inc., 1995.
3. McMillan, K., "Virtual Reality: Architecture and the Broader Community," May 1994.
4. Haight, T., "The Limits of VR," *Network Computing,* March 1, 1996.
5. *Newsbyte,* Nov. 3, 1995.
6. Discussion based on material freely available on the Internet at various Web sites.
7. Vacca, J., "A Whole New World: VRML Opens the Door to 3-D Environments," Feb. 26, 1996.
8. Santo, B., "Java Chosen for VRML," *Electronic Engineering Times,* Nov. 13, 1995.
9. Santo, B., "Upstart VRML Group See Big-Time Support," *Electronic Engineering Times,* Feb. 19, 1996.
10. Karpinski, R., *Comm. Week,* Feb. 19, 1996, p. 1.
11. SIMBA Information Inc., "Multimedia Business Report," Dec. 15, 1995.
12. Bruno, C., "User Testing Virual Reality ATM Networking," *Network World,* Feb. 27, 1995.
13. Studt, T., "Real Hardware Moves Virtual Reality into the Workplace," *R&D Magazine,* August 1995.

14. Cohen, S., and M. Gadd, "Virtual Reality Shopping Simulation for the Modern Marketer," *Marketing and Research Today,* February 1996.
15. Mohoney, D., "Virtual Reality in the Real World," *Computer Graphics World,* Jan. 1996.
16. "Virtual Reality," *The Economist,* May 27, 1995.
17. Kobe, G., "Virtual Interiors," *Automotive Industries,* May 1995.
18. White, T., "Designers: Reality Isn't Enough," *Automotive News,* Sept. 18, 1995.
19. PR newswire, March 1996.
20. Business wire, March 25, 1996.
21. America's Network, March 1, 1996.
22. *Technology Review,* "Cybersickness—The Side Effects of Virtual Reality," July 1995.
23. "Seasick in Cyberspace," *Business Week,* July 10, 1995.
24. Johnson, R., "No More Waiting: Godot Serves up Library," *Electronic Engineering Times,* Jan. 8, 1996.
25. Kaneshige, T., "Virtual Reality-based Lessons," *LAN Times,* Jan. 8, 1996.
26. Business wire, "Nortel Joins Superscape to Train," March 25, 1996.
27. Adams, N., "Lessons from the Virtual World," *Training,* June 1995.
28. Fenn, J., and P. Hodgdon, "How Emerging Technologies Will Affect Direct Marketing," *Direct Marketing,* August 1995.
29. Cohen, S., "Virtual Reality Shopping Simulation for the Modern Marketer," *Marketing and Research Today,* February 1996.
30. MacRae, D., "Virtual Reality for Banks May Be Closer than You Think," *American Banker,* Jan. 8, 1996.
31. Rupley, S., "MBAs Tackle Web Commerce," April 9, 1996.
32. Cleland, K., "Playgrounds Take a High-Tech Turn," *Advertising Age,* April 24, 1995.
33. Roller, M., "Virtual Reality Exists," *Marketing News,* Jan. 15, 1996.
34. Queenan, J., "Getting Virtually Real," *Chief Executive,* November 1995.

Company Information for Key Browsers

Browsers Discussed in Chapter 5

Netscape Communications Corp.
  (Netscape Navigator)
800-638-7483
email: info@netscape.com
http://www.netscape.com

Spry Inc. (Air Mosaic)
800-777-9638
email: info26@spry.com
http://www.compuserve.com

NetManage Inc. (WebSurfer)
408-937-7171
http://www.netmanage.com

Silicon Graphics Computer Systems
  (WebSpace)
415-960-1980
http://www.webspace.sgi.com

Sun Microsystems (HotJava)
email: Java@Java.sun.com
http://Java.sun.com

Other Web Browsers

The Legal Information Institute
  (Cello)
607-255-6536
http://www.law.cornell.com

The Wollongong Group
  (Emissary)
800-872-8649
email: sales@twg.com
http://www.twg.com

Spyglass, Inc. (Enhanced Mosaic)
708-505-1010
http://www.spyglass.com

Quadralay Corp. (WebWorks)
512-305-0240
email:info@quadralay.com
http://www.quadralay.com

IBM (Internet Connection
  for Windows)
800-IBM-3333
http://www.raleigh.ibm.com.

Trade Wave Corp. (WinWeb)
512-433-5300
email: info@tradeware.com
http://www.einet.net/EINET/WinWeb

NaviSoft (InternetWorks)
800-453-7873

Center for Supercomputing
  Applications (NCSA Mosaic)
217-244-3473
http://www.ncsa.uiuc.edu

Netcom On-line Communications
  Services (NetCruiser)
800-353-6600
http://www.netcom.com.

Frontier Technologies Corp. (Super-
  Highway Access for Windows)
800-929-3054
http://www.frontiertech.com

Quarterdeck Corp. (Quarterdeck
  Mosaic)
http://www.qdeck.com

University of Kansas (Lynx)
http://kuhttp.cc.ukans.edu

Microsoft Corp. (Internet Explorer)
http://www.windows.microsoft.com.

Glossary

Archie   A system for locating files that are available on FTP servers.

attribute   A characteristic quality of an element other than type or content.

browser   A tool used to read electronic hypertext, hypermedia, and other files.

browsing   Moving from one Web page to another, regardless of whether those pages are stored on a single computer or scattered on servers around the world.

client   An application program that establishes connections for the purpose of sending requests.

Common Gateway Interface (CGI)   The protocol for processing user-supplied information through server scripts and applications, including SQL queries.

connection   A transport layer (virtual) circuit established between two application programs for the purpose of communication.

cruising   See **browsing.**

daemon   A background UNIX process, usually for handling low-level operating system tasks.

DNS (Domain Name Service)   A method for translating strings of word segments denoting usernames and networks/subnetworks into Internet addressing information. For example, DNS would resolve a computer name such as minolid.tcg.com to the machine's actual numerical IP address, which is in the format xxx.xxx.xxx.xxx. This allows humans to refer to the more common, easy-to-remember domain names when interacting with a remote computer. Specified in RFC-1034, 1987. DNS is supported by network-resident servers, also known as domain name servers or DNS servers.

document (HTML)   An HTML instance.

domain   A group of end systems on a network that share something in common, such as the function they serve, the organization type they belong to, or their location. Top-level domains include .com for commercial organizations, .edu for educational institutions, .gov for government organizations, or others specifying foreign countries.

element (HTML)   A component of the hierarchical structure defined by the document type definition. It is identified in a document instance by descriptive markup, usually a start tag and an end tag.

finger   A software tool used to determine whether another user is logged on the Internet. It can also be used to find out a user's e-mail address.

freeware   Software given free of charge.

FTP (File Transfer Protocol)   A service to transfer computer files from one computer to another over a network. Provides a low-overhead means of transferring files from one system to another on a TCP/IP network. The user-id and password is often the user-id "ANONYMOUS" and the password in almost all FTP sites is commonly the user's own e-mail address. This is done to allow the FTP sites to gather some data about usage and to fostering more usage. Some FTP sites contain proprietary data and require additional user-id and true passwords.

get, post   Two methods of submitting information from a browser to a server. GET uses only environmental variables. POST sends contents of forms via standard input.

Gopher   A search tool that presents information in a hierarchical menu system similar to a table of contents. It is a distributed information service developed at the University of Minnesota.

host   Any computer directly connected to the network and not the same as a server.

HyperText Markup Language (HTML)   A language that developers, home page originators, and server builders use to specify the appearance and formatting of a document, including special tags for input, tables, and indexing.

HyperText Transfer Protocol (HTTP)   The transport protocol used to transmit hypertext documents around the Internet. A generic, stateless, object-oriented protocol that may be used for many similar tasks by extending the commands, or "methods," used. For example, you might use HTTP for name servers and distributed object-oriented systems. With HTTP, the negotiation of data representation allows systems to be built independently of the development of new representations. For more information see http://www.w3.org/hypertext/WWW/Protocols/Overview.html.

Internet backbone   A high-speed network—the NSFnet, for example—that connects smaller, independent networks.

Internet   An international fabric of interconnected government, education, and business computer networks—in effect, a network of networks. A person at a computer terminal or personal computer with the proper software communicates across the Internet by placing data in an IP packet and "addressing" the packet to a particular destination on the Internet. TCP guarantees end-to-end integrity. Communications software on the intervening networks between the source and destination networks "reads" the addresses on packets moving through the Internet and forwards the packets toward their destinations. From a thousand or so networks in the mid-1980s, the Internet has grown to an estimated 1 million connected networks (by 1997) with about 100 million people having access to it (by 1997). The majority of these Internet users live in the United States and Europe, but the Internet is expanding as telecommunications lines are improved in other countries.

intranets   Corporate networks that use the same networking/transport protocols and locally based Web servers to provide access to vast amounts of corporate information in a cohesive fashion. Documents must be stored in HTML and clients need Web browser software.

IP   A de facto standard that describes how protocol data units are transported across the Internet and recognized as an incoming message.

IP address   On a TCP/IP network, an assigned number that uniquely identifies each system. The network and the computer itself are both represented in the sequence of numbers.

IRC (Internet Relay Chat)   A software tool that makes it possible to hold real-time keyboard conversations on-line, often with many people reading, and perhaps contributing, simultaneously.

Lynx   A text-based browser.

markup   Text added to the data of a document to convey information about it. There are four different kinds of markup: descriptive markup (tags), references, markup declarations, and processing instructions.

MIME   Multipurpose Internet Mail Extensions as defined in "Mechanisms for Specifying and Describing the Format of Internet Message Bodies," September 9, 1993. (pages=81) (format=.txt, .ps) (obsolete RFC 1341) (updated by RFC 1590). A way to attach files to e-mail and define the document type using extensions.

Mosaic   A freeware World Wide Web browser that uses a graphical user interface to access and view on-line hypertext documents with embedded graphics and, occasionally, sound and animation.

newsgroup   A bulletin-board-like forum or conference area where you can post messages on a specified topic.

PING (Packet Internet Gopher)   A TCP/IP utility that sends packets of information to a computer on a network and can be used to determine whether a computer is connected to the Internet.

proxy server   A type of firewall, proxy servers provide extra security by replacing calls to unsecure systems' subroutines.

rendering   Formatting and presenting information to human readers.

representation (HTML)   The encoding of information for interchange. For example, HTML is a representation of hypertext.

router   A hardware/software entity that directs messages between LANs over a backbone (campus or WAN).

Secure HTTP (S-HTTP)   A method of data encryption used in some security schemes.

Secure Sockets Layer (SSL)   A security protocol for the Internet.

sendmail   The most commonly used message transfer agent for UNIX systems.

server   An application program that accepts connections in order to service requests by sending back responses.

SGML   Standard Generalized Markup Language as defined in ISO 8879: 1986, "Information Processing Text and Office Systems."

shareware   Software for which the developer asks for a registration fee.

Simple Mail Transfer Protocol (SMTP)   The protocol in a TCP/IP network that describes how e-mail moves between hosts and users.

SLIP/PPP   Serial Line Internet Protocol and Point-to-Point Protocol, allows computers to communicate over a serial link, such as a telephone line. PPP also provides error detection and compression.

surfing   See **browsing.**

tag   Descriptive markup. There are two kinds of tags; start-tags and end-tags.

TCP/IP   Transmission Control Protocol and Internet Protocol, a key set of networking protocols.

TELNET   A service that allows a user to log on to a remote computer.

Uniform Resource Locator (URL)   The Web address of a particular document or database.

USENET   A public network made up of thousands of newsgroups and organized by topic.

uucp   Originally a UNIX program that permits file transfer between two UNIX-based PCs.

virtual reality (VR)   a set of hardware/software-based applications now entering mainstream commercial application. Applications are appearing both on the Internet and in intranets. Technology is particularly well suited to applications that simulate the experience of actually being at the remote site, such as enhanced videoconferences, industrial and architectural walkthroughs, interactive travelogues of distant cities, house-hunting, product modeling, marketing, and training.

WAIS   Wide Area Information Server, a system that searches for a subject located on several databases over the world.

WHOIS   A TCP/IP utility that lets the user query compatible servers for detailed information about other Internet users.

Winsock connection   An application programming interface designed to let Windows applications run over a TCP/IP.

W3   The World Wide Web, a global information initiative. For bootstrap information, telnet www.w3.org or find documents at ftp://www.w3.org/pub/www/doc. (See also **WWW.**)

WWW   World Wide Web, a(n emerging) standard format on the Internet used to easily access and display documents. The format supports pictures and hypertext links to other documents, thus forming, figuratively speaking, a web. (See also **W3.**)

Index

ABOUT THE AUTHOR

Daniel Minoli is Director of Engineering and Development, Broadband Services and Internet, with the Teleport Communications Group, a national leader in local access communications and Internet services. A former developer of broadband technology and services with Bellcore, he teaches at Stevens Institute of Technology and New York University's Information Technology Institute. Mr. Minoli has written over 20 broadband books on communications technology and information systems, including *Video Dialtone Technology* and *Telecommunications Technology Handbook*.